D1666009

Innovation and Institutional Embeddedness of Multinational Companies

NEW HORIZONS IN INTERNATIONAL BUSINESS

Series Editor: Peter J. Buckley
Centre for International Business,
University of Leeds (CIBUL), UK

The New Horizons in International Business series has established itself as the world's leading forum for the presentation of new ideas in international business research. It offers pre-eminent contributions in the areas of multinational enterprise – including foreign direct investment, business strategy and corporate alliances, global competitive strategies, and entrepreneurship. In short, this series constitutes essential reading for academics, business strategists and policy makers alike.

Titles in the series include:

Innovation and Institutional Embeddedness of Multinational Companies

Edited by

Martin Heidenreich

Carl von Ossietzky University of Oldenburg, Germany

NEW HORIZONS IN INTERNATIONAL BUSINESS

Edward Elgar

Cheltenham, UK • Northampton, MA, USA

© Martin Heidenreich 2012

All rights reserved. No part of this publication may be reproduced, stored in a retrieval system or transmitted in any form or by any means, electronic, mechanical or photocopying, recording, or otherwise without the prior permission of the publisher.

Published by
Edward Elgar Publishing Limited
The Lypiatts
15 Lansdown Road
Cheltenham
Glos GL50 2JA
UK

Edward Elgar Publishing, Inc.
William Pratt House
9 Dewey Court
Northampton
Massachusetts 01060
USA

A catalogue record for this book
is available from the British Library

Library of Congress Control Number: 2011939353

ISBN 978 0 85793 432 1

Typeset by Servis Filmsetting Ltd, Stockport, Cheshire
Printed and bound by MPG Books Group, UK

Contents

Boxes

Figures

Tables

Contributors

Petra Ahrweiler, Professor of Technology and Innovation Management, UCD Innovation Research Unit, Michael Smurfit School of Business, University College Dublin, Ireland.

Björn T. Asheim, Professor and Chair of Economic Geography, and Deputy Director of CIRCLE (Centre for Innovation, Research and Competence in the Learning Economy), Lund University, Sweden; and Professor II at University of Agder, Norway.

Elisabeth Baier, scientific researcher in the Competence Center 'Policy and Regions' at the Fraunhofer Institute for Systems and Innovation Research (ISI) in Karlsruhe, Germany.

Christoph Barmeyer, Professor of Intercultural Communication, University of Passau, Germany.

Philip Cooke, Research Professor of Regional Development and Director of the Centre for Advanced Studies, Cardiff University, UK. Adjunct Professor, School of Development Studies, University of Aalborg, Denmark.

Javier Revilla Diez, Professor and Chair, Institute of Economic and Cultural Geography, Leibniz University of Hanover, Germany.

Bernd Ebersberger, Professor of Innovation Management and Economics, Management Center Innsbruck, Austria.

Nigel Gilbert, Professor of Sociology and Director of the Centre for Research in Social Simulation, University of Surrey, UK.

José Guimón, Assistant Professor, Department of Economic Structure and Development Economics, Universidad Autónoma de Madrid, Spain.

Bob Hancké, Reader in European Political Economy, London School of Economics and Political Science, UK.

Martin Heidenreich, Professor of Sociology and Jean-Monnet Chair of European Studies in Social Sciences, University of Oldenburg, Germany.

Sverre J. Herstad, Senior Researcher at the Nordic Institute for Studies in Innovation, Research and Education, Oslo, Norway.

Simona Iammarino, Reader, Department of Geography and Environment, London School of Economics and Political Sciences, and SPRU, University of Sussex, UK.

Benjamin Klement, Researcher, Department of Geography, Philipps University of Marburg, Germany.

Knut Koschatzky, Head of the Competence Center 'Policy and Regions' at the Fraunhofer Institute for Systems and Innovation Research (ISI) in Karlsruhe, Germany, and Professor of Economic Geography at Leibniz University of Hanover, Germany.

Jan-Philipp Kramer, Research Associate, Institute of Economic and Cultural Geography, Leibniz University of Hanover, Germany.

Katharina Krüth, doctoral student of European Studies, University of Passau, Germany.

Elisabetta Marinelli, Research Associate, Department of Geography and Environment, London School of Economics and Political Sciences, UK and Institute for Prospective Technological Studies, European Commission – DG JRC.

Jannika Mattes, Assistant Professor for the Sociology of European Societies, University of Oldenburg, Germany.

Rajneesh Narula, Professor of International Business Regulation and Director of the John H. Dunning Centre for International Business, Reading University, UK.

Andreas Pyka, Professor of Economics, Chair of Innovation Economics, Faculty of Economics and Business Administration, University of Hohenheim, Germany.

Dieter Rehfeld, Head of the Department Innovation, Space & Culture, Institute for Work and Technology, University of Applied Science Gelsenkirchen, Germany.

Michel Schilperoord, UCD Innovation Research Unit, Michael Smurfit School of Business, University College Dublin, Ireland.

Örjan Sölvell, Professor of International Business and Deputy President of the Stockholm School of Economics.

Simone Strambach, Professor of Geography of Services, Communication and Innovation, Department of Geography, Philipps University of Marburg, Germany.

Abbreviations and variables

AA	advanced aggregator
ABB	Asea Brown Boveri
ABM	agent-based modelling
ANR	Agence Nationale de la Recherche; French National Research Agency
APP	sector-level appropriability conditions, measured as share of innovating companies in a sector indicating that competitors provide important information input to innovation
BIO	(Uppsala) Biotechnology Initiative
CEE	Central and Eastern European countries
CEO	chief executive officer
CIS4	Fourth Community Innovation Survey (Norway)
CMEs	coordinated market economies (cf. Hall and Soskice, 2001)
CNRS	Centre National de la Recherche Scientifique; French National Centre for Scientific Research
CRIT	Centre for Research, Innovation and Technology
CURE	corporate culture and regional embeddedness (a European joint project funded by the European Commission in the 6th framework programme)
D_SYN	dummy variable indicating synthetic (=1) or analytic (=0) knowledge bases
DGEO_EU	variable capturing the number of different collaboration partners used in other (non-Nordic) European countries
DGEO_ND	variable capturing the number of different collaboration partners used in other Nordic (Norway excluded) countries
DGEO_NO	variable capturing the number of different collaboration partners used in Norway
DGEO_SCI	variable capturing the geographical diversity (number of world regions) of science system collaboration

DGEO_US	variable capturing the number of different collaboration partners used in the USA
DGEO_VER	variable capturing the geographical diversity (number of world regions) of customer and supplier collaboration
EPO	European Patent Office
ERIS	entrepreneurial regional innovation system
EU	European Union
EXPSHR	export share
FDI	foreign direct investment
GDP	gross domestic product
GE	General Electric
GM	General Motors
GMO	genetically modified organism
GOVERD	governmental expenditures on R&D
GPN	global production networks
GVC	global value chains
HAMNO	dummy indicating that no factors hampering innovation activities are stated
HERD	higher education expenditures on R&D
HQ	headquarters
HR	human resources
ICC	international chamber of commerce
ICT	information and communications technology
IDA Ireland	Industrial Development Agency Ireland
INTMARKT	share of sales on foreign markets
IRIS	institutional regional innovation system
ISC	integrated supply chain
IT	information technology
KIBS	knowledge-intensive business services
LCCGs	local collective competition goods
LEMP	size control, log of number of employees
LMEs	liberal market economies (cf. Hall and Soskice, 2001)
M&A	mergers and acquisitions
MHC	multi-home-based corporation
MLP	multi-level perspective
MNC(s)	multinational corporation(s) company(ies)
MNE(s)	multinational enterprise(s)
NIH	'not-invented-here' syndrome
NIS	national innovation system(s)
NMS	new member states of the EU (acceded in 2004 and 2007)

NUTS	nomenclature des unités territoriales statistiques; the nomenclature of territorial units for statistics
ODIP	organizational decomposition of innovation processes
OEM	original equipment manufacturer
OL	organizational learning
OLS	ordinary least squares estimation
ORG_DM	dummy indicating affiliation with a domestic (Norwegian) multinational corporate group
ORG_FO	dummy indicating affiliation with a foreign corporate group
ORG_FO_EU	dummy indicating affiliation with a European (Nordic countries excluded) corporate group
ORG_FO_ND	dummy indicating affiliation with a Nordic (Norway excluded) corporate group
ORG_FO_OT	dummy indicating affiliation with a corporate group based in other countries
ORG_FO_US	dummy indicating affiliation with a US corporate group
PARC	Palo Alto Research Center
PHARE	Poland and Hungary: Aid for Restructuring of the Economies: a pre-accession instrument financed by the EU to assist the applicant countries of Central and Eastern Europe in their preparations for joining the EU
PROPAT	patenting propensity
R&D	research and development
REC	renewable energy corporation
RIS	regional innovation system(s)
RUV	relative unit values
S_EU	variable indicating the existence of a collaborative relationship with a parent group unit in another (non-Nordic) European country
S_ND	variable indicating the existence of a collaborative relationship with a parent group unit in another Nordic country
S_NO	variable indicating the existence of a collaborative relationship with a parent group unit in Norway
S_US	variable indicating the existence of a collaborative relationship with a parent group unit in the USA
SE	science excellence
SEE	South-Eastern Europe
SFI	Science Foundation Ireland
SFIN	Skåne Food Innovation Network

SKIN   Simulating Knowledge Dynamics in Innovation
            Networks
SPL   Système productif local; productive local system
SSP   social systems of production (approach)
SUV   sports utility vehicle
TNC   transnational corporation
TPA   The Packaging Arena
UK   United Kingdom
V4   Visegrád 4 countries (Czech Republic, Poland,
            Hungary and Slovakia)
VoC   varieties of capitalism (approach)

Acknowledgements

This book originated during a conference held at the University of Oldenburg in February 2010, with financial support from the Volkswagen Foundation, the German Research Foundation and the Jean Monnet programme of the European Union. From that conference, the editor selected the most promising papers and then recruited additional contributions from other authors in order to secure broad coverage of countries, issues and theoretical approaches. All of the chapters have been extensively revised in response to comments from the editor and the other contributors. The result, I believe, is much more than a conventional conference volume, although it is deliberately designed as a conversation among authors with distinct but intersecting perspectives rather than as the product of a unified research project based on a common theoretical framework.

As the editor, I am grateful to Edward Elgar for agreeing to publish this volume and to Jannika Mattes for providing me with valuable suggestions for improving its quality and coherence. I would also like to acknowledge the helpful contributions to the project made by the other participants in the Oldenburg conference. My final thanks go to Dorinda Valle del Campo, Isolde Heyen and Natalie Chandler for all their help with organizational matters.

1. Introduction: the debate on corporate embeddedness

Martin Heidenreich

Some time ago, my students and I visited the divisional headquarters (HQ) of a multinational company (MNC) to find out how it organized its innovation processes. One of the company's representatives explained that it operates in most countries of the world, that two-thirds of its staff are employed abroad and that its research facilities are spread all over the world. He emphasized the strength of these foreign research and development (R&D) sites, the high technological competences of its employees, and the public support for and generally positive attitude to innovation in many foreign countries. In a publication, the company stressed the necessity 'to think and act internationally' because 'the significance of national economies is declining'. We were deeply impressed because obviously the company was able to make full use of the advantages of a global economy without any problems. However, the representative then explained how the innovation process was organized for one of the most successful product lines of his division and this proved to be much less internationally structured than anticipated. Most of the R&D for that product line still took place about ten miles away from the divisional HQ – close to its central production site and close to many important internal and external suppliers. Only in the last decade was a Chinese R&D unit set up for a product designated especially for the Chinese market and which took into account the specific budget constraints and requirements of developing countries. Even though the technological core competences of the division were still concentrated close to its HQ, six years after its foundation the foreign R&D site had developed sufficient competences to assume a leading role in the development of a new product (although crucial decisions were still taken in the home country of the MNC). This R&D site also appeared to be much less globally organized than anticipated, as its major advantage was its local embeddedness in a publicly supported high-tech cluster also accommodating public R&D facilities, production, training, regulatory agencies, important pilot clients and the R&D facilities of two of its globally most important competitors.

1

This example shows that MNCs are crucial actors in a global knowledge-based economy. They are able to 'transfer' knowledge across national borders without sacrificing the advantages of inner-organizational coordination (Dunning and Lundan, 2008). However, our example also illustrates that these companies are not territorially disembedded, footloose organizations that are only able to transfer knowledge across borders. They are also important arenas for the creation of knowledge, especially by combining the advantages of inner-organizationally coordinated cross-border production and innovation strategies with the advantages of local proximity and the use of specific regional and national factors (Bartlett and Ghoshal, 1989; Sölvell and Birkinshaw, 2007). The R&D units of the company we visited were regionally embedded in both its home country and its host country. These external contexts were important bases for the global innovativeness and competiveness of the company. Therefore our example (and other, more systematic evidence on the 'non-globalization' of innovation; cf. Patel and Pavitt, 1991 and Heidenreich et al., 2010) questions the assumption that MNCs are footloose companies operating in a globally interlinked economy (Ohmae, 1990). On the contrary, instead of being footloose, they more resemble a millipede whose subsidiaries represent multiple feet in different regional and national arenas.

A major advantage of the regional and national embeddedness of MNCs is that they may facilitate learning processes with companies in the proximity (customers, competitors, suppliers and service providers). In addition to inner-organizational forms of learning and knowledge exchange between HQ and subsidiaries, MNCs can thus rely on external competences. These external learning processes are supported by institutions that shape the cooperation between heterogeneous actors and that provide collective competition goods, for example qualified employees, basic research, advanced technological competences, consensual relations with employees or network brokers (Meyer et al., 2011). This institutional environment also shapes the technological competences and market positions of subsidiaries (Andersson et al., 2002, 2007). At the core of corporate innovation strategies is thus the ability of internationally distributed organizations to combine two different forms of learning: first, organizational learning within and beyond national boundaries; second, institutionally stabilized learning with external partners, usually within the same national or even regional context. MNCs thus translate the relationship between globalization and regionalization that is characteristic of a globalized economy (Giddens, 1990; Held et al., 1999) into an organizational challenge: the challenge of combining inner-organizational and institutionally embedded learning with external partners (Phene and Almeida, 2008; Heidenreich et al., 2012).

The question is how MNCs can combine the advantages of internationally distributed innovation processes with nationally and regionally embedded competences and know-how. How can the observed internationalization of companies be reconciled with the crucial role of different domestic locations and competences? To answer this question, in the following we shall briefly review four different academic debates. First, we shall review selected aspects of the debate on embeddedness in order to avoid the traps of over- or underestimating the determining role of societal environments on companies (section 1.1). Second, the debate on national systems of production and innovation conceptualizes the context of organizations as (mostly formal) institutions that contribute to the solution of the uncertainties of innovation processes and the coordination problems faced by companies in relation to their stakeholders (section 1.2). Third, in addition to institutions, regional studies highlight two other aspects of corporate embeddedness: the role of inter-organizational networks and the role of informal rules that are often the result of the social, organizational and cognitive proximity of regional actors (section 1.3). Fourth, similar to regional studies, international business studies also highlight the essential role of business networks in the embeddedness of MNCs and their subsidiaries. They additionally stress the role of institutions and (mostly national) political decisions (section 1.4). On the basis of these approaches we are able to propose an understanding of corporate embeddedness that takes into account crucial results of these four, largely unrelated, debates (section 1.5). Finally, we shall present the contributions in this volume that highlight three different dimensions of this embeddedness: the dilemmatic nature, the essential role of 'knowledge infrastructures', that is, organizational and institutional conditions essential for corporate innovation processes, and the cultural and political environment of MNCs (section 1.6).

1.1 STRUCTURAL AND RELATIONAL CONCEPTS OF EMBEDDEDNESS

A starting point for the debate on the societal context of organizations is that institutions, that is, 'the humanly devised constraints that structure political, economic and social interaction' (North, 1991: 97), shape the behaviour and the strategies of economic actors. Faced with the uncertainties of economic life and the manifold coordination problems associated with innovation processes, companies tend to turn to established rules, practices and social norms for guidance and orientation. The concept of institutions is very broad and comprises formal institutions, for example legal ones, and informal institutions, which are often designated as cultures and traditions of a specific community.

In neo-institutional approaches their role is often analysed as a sort of inescapable isomorphic pressure to which a company has to defer in order to gain legitimacy. Such institutional determinism can be avoided by the embeddedness concept that was initially proposed by Karl Polanyi in the 1940s. He proposed the concept of embeddedness in order to distinguish traditional, institutionally embedded societies from modern, disembedded market societies. He summarizes his discussion of the social conditions for the emergence of a relatively autonomous economic sphere in the nineteenth century as follows: 'Instead of economy being embedded in social relations, social relations are embedded in the economic system' (Polanyi, 1944: 57). His macrosociological or structural notion of embeddedness has become an essential cornerstone of economic sociology in criticizing the neoclassical assumptions of atomistic, self-interested economic actors (Krippner and Alvarez, 2007). In contrast to Polanyi, Granovetter (1985: 504) proposed a less structural and more relational understanding of embeddedness. He uses this concept to highlight the social dimensions of economic action and assumes that economic 'behavior is closely embedded in networks of interpersonal relations'. In contrast to an 'oversocialized approach of generalized morality' and an 'undersocialized one of impersonal, institutional arrangements', he proposes a dynamic, process- and experience-based approach to trust and order that focuses both on pre-existing structures (or 'networks') and on the direct experiences of competent, knowledgeable social actors: 'Better than the statement that someone is socially known to be reliable is information from a trusted informant that he has dealt with that individual and found him so. Even better is information from one's own past dealings with that person' (Granovetter, 1985: 490).

Beckert (2003: 769) combines the structural and the relational notions of embeddedness in the following definition: 'Embeddedness refers to the social, cultural, political, and cognitive structuration of decisions in economic contexts. It points to the indissoluble connection of the actor with his or her social surrounding.' This definition, which we adopt in this chapter, reflects the crucial insight of the structuration theory by focusing on the important role of individual or collective actors (e.g. companies) in the reproduction of social structures (Giddens, 1990). Embeddedness therefore is not merely an external or contextual determinant of organizational strategies; it is also the result of organizational strategies: MNCs also shape strategically their institutional environment (cf. Hancké, Chapter 12 in this volume; Cantwell et al., 2010).

In a dynamic perspective, the mutual shaping of companies and their societal environments can also be analysed as 'co-evolution' (Nelson,

1994). The concept of co-evolution offers a conceptual framework for analysing the recursive reproduction of entrepreneurial strategies and their institutional environment in a more dynamic way than concepts that focus only on isomorphic pressures, the search for organizational legitimacy or path dependencies.

A major insight provided by the debate on embeddedness is that an MNC is not only linked to its multiple environments by personal relations, networks and non-economic motives as a 'Granovetterian' interpretation of the conception of embeddedness would suggest, but by social institutions that are a crucial factor in corporate embeddedness. These institutions systematically shape the perception of organizational challenges, of the best or most appropriate organizational strategies and the available resources. They are dynamically reproduced by skilled social actors (Fligstein, 2001), for example MNCs. In this volume Heidenreich and Mattes (Chapter 2) as well as Rehfeld (Chapter 10) show that corporate embeddedness is not a quasi-natural, taken-for-granted phenomenon but often an explicit, strategic choice.

1.2   EMBEDDEDNESS VIA NATIONAL INSTITUTIONS

National institutions are especially important for the embeddedness of companies in their societal context. In the following we shall discuss four approaches that focus on national institutions and their role in entrepreneurial structures and strategies. In this way we want to show how the role of institutions is conceptualized in the coordination of economic action and the choice of organizational innovation strategies. These four approaches are the 'social systems of production approach' (Hollingsworth and Boyer, 1997), the 'varieties of capitalism approach' (Hall and Soskice, 2001), the 'business systems approach' (Whitley, 1999) and the 'national systems of innovation approach' (Lundvall, 1992; Edquist, 2005).

The starting point of the 'social systems of production approach' (SSP) is that the emergence and stability of national production models, for example the diversified quality production in Germany (Streeck, 1991), lean production in Japan (Womack et al., 1990), modular production networks in the USA (Sturgeon, 2002) or flexible specialization in Italy (Zeitlin, 2008), depend on specific institutional configurations that provide the habits, the taken-for-granted accounts, the rules and the resources required for the stabilization of the country-specific product, management and organizational models. Diversified quality production for example requires a public system of vocational training and strong trade unions in order to provide skilled workers. Otherwise hire-and-fire policies and labour poaching would undermine the stability of internal labour markets, which form the basis for high-quality products as the 'societal effects' approach already demonstrated in the 1980s (Maurice et al., 1986). The SSP approach assumes that national institutions are essential for the co-ordination of economic activities between companies and their employees, their shareholders, their banks, their customers and suppliers, schools, politics and the broader public: '[T]he choices of coordinating mechanisms . . . are constrained by the social context within which they are embed-ded' (Hollingsworth and Boyer, 1997: 11). A social system of production is characterized by 'institutional complementarities' between its different components[1] – an assumption that also explains the strong and stable concentration of MNCs in the core European regions (cf. Koschatzky and Baier, Chapter 9 in this volume).

This assumption is also fundamental for the 'varieties of capitalism approach' (Hall and Soskice, 2001; Hancké et al., 2007). In contrast to the SSP, however, which allows for multiple and heterogeneous national pro-duction models, the varieties of capitalism approach (VoC) distinguishes only two basic models: coordinated and liberal market economies. These types are characterized by either a high or a low degree of coordination between the actors at the core of the different institutions (e.g. between employers and employees in the industrial relations system; Hall and Gingerich, 2009). Similar to the SSP approach, these two types of market economies are interpreted as complex configurations of different, mutu-ally reinforcing institutions (especially the education and training system, the industrial relations system, the patterns of corporate governance and intercompany relations). The coordinated type of market economies is characterized by institutionally embedded forms of production (e.g. in Germany and Japan), while the liberal type is described as a disembedded economy with only very weak and arm's-length forms of coordination between companies and their societal environments (for example in the USA). The VoC approach places the firm and its ways of dealing with major coordination problems at the centre of its interest. It insists on the fact that 'institutions cannot be taken for granted but must be reinforced by the active endeavors of the participants' (Hall and Soskice, 2001: 17) Hancké (Chapter 12 in this volume), for example, shows that MNCs play a decisive role in shaping their institutional environment when their sub-sidiaries contribute to stronger collaboration between major companies in a region as a prerequisite for an industry-wide training system.

Whitley (1999: 34) defines national business systems as 'systems of economic coordination and control'. National business systems vary especially in three dimensions: in the governance dimension (i.e. the relationships between owners and controllers of economic resources); in the collaborative dimension (i.e. the coordination within production chains and industrial sectors and between competitors); and in the employment dimension, which refers to the relationship between employers and employees and the delegation of authority to employees. Different institutional contexts are distinguished according to the following institutional dimensions: dominant, risk-sharing state; strong intermediary associations; strong market regulation; capital market financial system or credit-based financial system; strong collaborative public training system; strong unions; centralized bargaining; low trust in formal institutions; paternalist authority relations; communal formal authority (cf. Whitley, 2002). In contrast to the aforementioned approaches, Whitley also takes into account informal, cultural dimensions of labour and management. In this volume, Barmeyer and Krüth (Chapter 11) as well as Rehfeld (Chapter 10) demonstrate that these informal institutions are an important element of the organizational environment. They shape the possibilities of public network policies (e.g. the French cluster policy focusing on *pôles de compétitivité*) and they also shape corporate globalization strategies.

In contrast to the previously discussed concepts, 'systems of innovation approaches' focus on the ability of a country, region or industrial sector to generate and recombine scientific and technical knowledge and to create new products or processes on this basis. Essential factors here are national, regional or sectoral institutions that reduce the uncertainties linked to innovations and facilitate the recombination of knowledge. A system of innovations has therefore been defined as a 'set of distinct institutions which jointly and individually contribute to the development and diffusion of new technologies . . . it is a system of interconnected institutions to create, store and transfer the knowledge, skills and artefacts which define new technologies' (Metcalfe, 1995: 462–3). Lundvall (1992) focuses on the crucial role of socially embedded interactive learning processes between heterogeneous actors and distinguishes between narrowly and broadly defined concepts of national innovation systems. While the former embraces only R&D organizations and institutions, a broader definition of national innovation systems 'includes all parts and aspects of the economic structure and the institutional set-up affecting learning as well as searching and exploring – the production system, the marketing system and the system of finance'. Despite the remaining methodological weaknesses of the systems of innovation approaches (Edquist, 2005), they stress the role of institutions in organizational learning processes. However, it remains unclear how these institutions exactly shape innovation processes within companies and which institutions really 'influence the development, diffusion, and use of innovations' (Edquist, 2005: 200).

One conclusion that can be drawn from this discussion of these four approaches focusing on the national embeddedness of companies is that these institutions contribute to reducing uncertainties and solving organizational coordination problems. Institutions shape the relationships between companies, their own employees, employer associations, unions, schools, capital owners, competitors, suppliers and customers. In addition they provide crucial resources such as skilled employees and innovative competences. In this way they contribute towards solving collective-goods problems because private investments in R&D or in the education and training of employees are in general not sufficient (due to free-rider problems).

A limitation of these approaches, especially for the debate on embedded MNCs, is that companies are conceived as rule takers that play according to the national rules of the game and do not function as rule makers. Their active involvement in the definition of these rules as well as the choice and the tensions between different national sets of rules are ignored. It is also assumed that companies are bound to only one set of rules: the rules of the respective national system. Both the possibility of transferring these rules to other national environments through the internationalization strategies of domestic MNCs (e.g. to Eastern European countries; cf. Narula and Guimón as well as Hancké, Chapters 12 and 13 in this volume) and the question of how international organizations deal with multiple institutional environments are ignored (cf. Kostova et al., 2008; Meyer et al., 2011). The debate on corporate embeddedness thus has to begin with national institutions and should take into account their functions (coordination, reduction of uncertainty, provision of resources and facilitation of interactive learning) as well as their relative stability and the institutional complementarities between them. However, the debate does not stop there.

1.3   EMBEDDEDNESS IN REGIONAL NETWORKS AND INSTITUTIONS

Not only nations but also regions are important environments for MNCs (Cooke et al., 2011; Iammarino et al., Chapter 7 in this volume). Similar to the national institutions, regional institutions also contribute to the private or public provision of products, services and qualifications (Le Galès and Voelzkow, 2001) and facilitate and stabilize cooperation, mutual exchange of knowledge and trust relationships, which might lead also to lock-in effects (Grabher, 1993). However, the advantages of regional economies are not only based on institutions but also on regional clusters and networks. These networks are a prerequisite for inter-organizational learning due to the spatial and social proximity of regionally concentrated companies; they facilitate the exchange of implicit, experience-based, uncodified knowledge and the recombination of previous knowledge (Boschma, 2005 and Asheim et al., Chapter 4 in this volume).

In early studies the advantages of regional proximity were analysed as a result of transaction cost advantages (Krugman, 1991). Other studies explain regional advantages by the possibility to exploit the experience, knowledge and skills of proximate companies. Taking the example of the textile industry in Lancashire in the nineteenth century, Marshall (1982: 225) described these learning and network effects: 'The mysteries of the trade become no mystery, but are as it were in the air'. Porter (1998) systematizes this intuition by explaining the competitive advantages of regionally concentrated clusters through their proximity to competitors and challenging clients, efficient regional suppliers and service providers and the availability of a qualified workforce. In this perspective regional advantages are not only the result of transaction cost savings but are also the result of mutual learning facilitated by geographic proximity, that is, by network effects (cf. also Cooke, Chapter 5 in this volume).

As early as the 1980s Piore and Sabel (1984) drew attention to the institutional bases of regional learning and innovation, which in the case of the Central Italian industrial districts they mostly conceive as stable communities and personal, direct, trust-based interactions. Storper (1997) proposes a less Granovetterian concept of regional embeddedness. He analyses regional economic relations as conversation and coordination, pointing to the crucial role of 'untraded interdependencies', that is, non-market relations, conventions, informal rules and habits that coordinate an economy faced with uncertainty. Regions are 'worlds of production' characterized by 'taken-for-granted mutually coherent expectations, routines, and practices, which are sometimes manifested as formal institutions and rules, but often not' (Storper, 1997: 38). These regional institutional orders shape the 'action capacities' of economic agents and the economic identities of territories and regions.

In comparison with the 'relational perspective' of Storper and similar (but largely independently) to the concept of national innovation systems (Edquist, 2005), the concept of 'regional innovation systems' (RIS) more strongly emphasizes the role of formal regional institutions (Cooke et al., 2004): an RIS consists of

> firms in the main industrial cluster in a region including their support industries. Secondly, an institutional infrastructure must be present, i.e., research and higher education institutes, technology transfer agencies, vocational training organisations, business associations, finance institutions etc., which hold important competence to support regional innovation. (Asheim and Isaksen, 2002: 83)

This definition stresses the fact that regional innovation systems are not only integrated through production and value chains (e.g. by supplier and buyer networks) but also by (formal) institutions and (informal) communities. The potential strengths of these systems consist in the capability to provide collective resources (cf. also Iammarino et al. in Chapter 7 for the regional embeddedness of MNCs especially in Germany and the UK). Examples of these regional collective goods are access to specialized technological knowledge, information about new markets, the vocational training of qualified and motivated manpower adapted to the needs of regional industry and also the stabilization of regional networks and patterns of cooperation between regional companies, schools, universities, technology transfer, R&D facilities and political and administrative actors: 'Provision of such goods must be ensured by social or political arrangements, that is by forms of local governance' (Le Galès and Voelzkow, 2001: 1).

In conclusion, the regional embeddedness of companies is also based on institutions that may stabilize inter-organizational networks and contribute to the provision of 'local collective competition goods'. In contrast to the national level, these institutions are often closer to the specific companies, sectors and networks in the region, thus increasing the possibility of providing goods and services targeted to the specific needs of local companies. In addition, the territorial, social and often also technical proximity of regionally concentrated companies facilitates networks between suppliers, customers and competitors and the inter-organizational collaboration of heterogeneous actors, the exchange of personal information and contacts, and the specialization of companies at different phases of the same value chain. Often these regional institutions are more informal than the national ones; therefore they are designated as regional communities, milieus or cultures. These network-based, institutional and cultural dimensions of regional embeddedness may contribute to the regional agglomeration of companies (for the agglomeration of corporate HQ in Europe and the corresponding knowledge spillovers cf. Ahrweiler et al. and Koschatzky and Baier, Chapters 6 and 9 of this volume).

1.4   THE EMBEDDEDNESS OF MULTINATIONAL COMPANIES

The national and regional embeddedness of MNCs is an increasingly important topic in various streams of international business research (Heidenreich et al., 2012) because MNCs have to disembed their capabilities from their original context in order to transfer them to foreign subsidiaries (cf. Strambach and Klement, Chapter 8 in this volume). They can also use locally embedded competences in the corporate network. In the debate on the embeddedness of MNCs, the role of the societal context has been conceptualized in international business studies in basically three different ways: as the result of political decisions; as inter-organizational networks; or as institutions.

First, in transaction cost and internalization approaches, the context of MNCs is characterized by mainly politically induced market imperfections (Buckley and Casson, 1976). In the eclectic paradigm of international production, locational advantages of corporate sites are conceived as the result of immobile factors and non-transferable characteristics of national economies (cf. Dunning 1988, 1998). Examples of locational advantages are production factors such as labour, tariff and other trade barriers that induce companies to engage in foreign production. A foreign locality thus is basically analysed as a bundle of static and immobile assets that can be exploited by subsidiaries present in this country. In more recent versions of this paradigm, the focus has shifted to national institutions and cultural factors as belief systems and social capital, which are deemed to be crucial for the attractiveness of a country. However, also in this case locational advantages are conceived as the result of external, mostly political decisions (Dunning and Lundan, 2008: 138–9). The embeddedness of MNCs implied in classical approaches to international business is therefore conceptualized in a Polanyian way. National policies and market regulations, but also the inertia and territorial rootedness of social relations, constrain and shape the dynamics of market processes and corporate actors.

A second stream in international business studies analyses the MNC as a differentiated network of relatively autonomous subsidiaries with varying resources and capabilities (Ghoshal and Bartlett, 1990). This approach operationalizes the embeddedness of corporate subsidiaries and HQ through the relationship of these units to their suppliers, customers and competitors. The external networks in which the company is embedded shape the structures and strategies of the organization, especially 'the configuration of its organizational resources and the nature of interunit exchange relations that lead to such a configuration' (Ghoshal and Bartlett, 1990: 604).

On the basis of the network approach proposed by Ghoshal and Bartlett, a group of Swedish researchers have carefully analysed the role of these business networks in the technological competence of subsidiaries, their importance and their bargaining position within the MNC (Andersson et al., 2002, 2007; Forsgren et al., 2005; Holm et al., 2003 and Sölvell, Chapter 3 of this volume). They propose a concept of the embedded MNC for companies 'whose subsidiaries operate in business networks that, to a notable extent, are characterized by a high level of embeddedness among the relationship actors' (Forsgren et al., 2005: 97). Andersson et al. (2002) show that the business embeddedness of subsidiaries (i.e. the relations with customers and suppliers) and their technical embeddedness (i.e. the collaborative development of new products and processes, mostly with customers and suppliers) influence the performance of the subsidiary and its importance for the technological competence of the whole company: 'a high level of external embeddedness is positively related to the subsidiary's ability to provide expertise to the MNC', which in turn depends on the external embeddedness of the subsidiary (Andersson et al., 2007: 816). This research stream also develops the conceptual tools for analysing the systematic differences between the external embeddedness of subsidiaries in business networks and their internal embeddedness in the corporate context (Yamin and Andersson, 2011). Until now, however, regional, national or other proximities between the subsidiaries and their external partners have not been taken into account. The attention is exclusively focused on the role of external networks in the technological competences of MNCs and the relative influence of subsidiaries within the corporate network (Bouquet and Birkinshaw, 2008). The embeddedness argument implied in these network approaches to the MNC is therefore of a Granovetterian type: business relationships develop from arm's-length relationships to relatively stable, trust-based relations dependent on mutual adaptation and technological learning.

The institution-based view in international business studies has moved beyond these 'rationalist and functionalist concerns of efficiency and performance' (Clark and Geppert, 2011: 396). The basic assumption of this perspective is that formal and informal institutional rules shape organizational and individual behaviour (Peng and Khoury, 2008). The institutional embeddedness of a subsidiary in a particular business system influences the strategies of local subsidiaries (Geppert and Williams, 2006: 64). MNCs have to face not only pressures for efficiency, but also demands for national or regional legitimacy (cf. Westney and Zaheer, 2008: 356). However, MNCs do not operate in a homogeneous societal field characterized by unequivocal patterns of legitimacy and strong isomorphic pressures; they are embedded in heterogeneous national and regional business systems and cultures (cf. Sölvell, Chapter 3 of this volume). Especially the conditions in the country in which the headquarters are situated shape the configuration and control mechanisms as well as the globalization and innovation strategies of the whole company (cf. Geppert et al., 2003 for this home-country effect). Furthermore, the local transposition and adaptation of global corporate strategies is not only shaped by the strategic importance of the subsidiary in the corporate context, but also by its embeddedness in its institutional context and the legitimacy of the corporate strategy in the context of the host country: 'National business systems . . . provide local managers with different power resources, which support some strategies and politics while at the same time discouraging others' (Geppert and Williams, 2006: 54). MNCs are therefore confronted with conflicting isomorphic pressures and conflicting demands for legitimacy in their various national contexts (cf. Westney and Zaheer, 2008; Kostova et al., 2008; Meyer et al., 2011). In the globalization–localization framework of Bartlett and Ghoshal (1989) the conflicting aims of global integration and local adaptation give rise to a dilemma of institutionally embedded MNCs: '[T]he greater the degree of social embeddedness of the local subsidiary in a highly integrated business system, the more problematic the implementation of global practices' (Geppert and Williams, 2006: 63). Subsidiaries therefore should not only be externally embedded in heterogeneous national contexts, but also integrated in the corporate network in order to facilitate the corporate integration of heterogeneous capabilities (Meyer et al., 2011).[2]

In conclusion, for the analysis of MNCs and their subsidiaries, understanding their external context plays a major role because an MNC is by definition a cross-border organization embedded in different national contexts. In addition, the external context is a major or even the most important source of innovativeness. In different streams of the international business literature these national contexts are conceived in different ways. Studies highlight either the political embeddedness, the embeddedness in inter-organizational networks or the institutional embeddedness of MNCs: (1) in transaction cost and internalization approaches the context of MNCs is analysed as the result of (mostly) political regulations of economic processes (Buckley and Casson, 1976; Dunning, 1988); (2) in approaches that conceive MNCs as differentiated networks (Ghoshal and Bartlett, 1990) corporate environments are in general conceptualized as 'business networks' (Andersson et al., 2007; Forsgren et al., 2005), and these approaches focus on the patterns of exchange and cooperation between companies and their suppliers, customers and sometimes also competitors; (3) institutional approaches focus on the influence of (mostly) national business systems and the corresponding norms, values and rationalities. Formal and informal rules in different national environments shape the interpretations, strategies and norms that regulate the behaviour of individuals and collective actors (Geppert and Williams, 2006; Peng and Khoury, 2008). The environments of MNCs are thus characterized by (politically induced) market imperfections, networks and institutions.

These three forms of embeddedness reflect different facets of the dilemma between globalization and localization that are constitutive for MNCs (cf. Sölvell, Chapter 3 in this volume). MNCs are confronted with the contradictory challenges of territorially unbound economic logics and challenges and politically regulated national markets. They have to decide how to combine global marketing and procurement strategies with the advantages of specific business networks (Mattes, 2010). They are also confronted with the contradictory and conflictual demands of company-wide control and coordination mechanisms (which are often shaped by the home-country context of the corporation) and the interests and coordination patterns of locally embedded subsidiaries.

1.5   THE EMBEDDEDNESS OF MNCs: TOWARDS AN INTEGRATED PERSPECTIVE

We began with the observation that the competitive advantage of MNCs under worldwide competition also depends on the cross-border utilization of regional and national capabilities. Not only the organizational coordination of internationally distributed innovation processes but also the capability of a company to tap into regional and national contexts is crucial for the innovativeness of a company. While the internationalization of a company facilitates cross-border processes of learning, its regional and national embeddedness fosters the exploitation of sticky, tacit knowledge (cf. Bathelt et al., 2004 for the role of local buzz and global pipelines in interactive learning). This introductory chapter has discussed the possibilities and challenges of exploiting territorially embedded competences and of combining them with inner-organizational learning processes in MNCs from four different angles.

First, a major assumption of the embeddedness concept is that companies orientate themselves towards established practices, routines, taken-for-granted accounts and formal rules of their societal context in order to reduce the uncertainties that emerge from instable and unpredictable organizational environments and to solve the coordination problems arising between heterogeneous actors. The two 'founding fathers' of the embeddedness debate have proposed two complementary, either structural or relational, conceptualizations. The Polanyian and the Granovetterian versions of the embeddedness concept can be used for specifying the duality of national and regional institutions and corporate actors in a dynamic and recursive way. An initial insight of the previously summarized debates is thus that the relationships between companies and their environment cannot be reduced to a unilateral determination or to isomorphic pressures. Companies use specific assets of their environment and choose to adapt or not to adapt to specific institutional constraints and opportunities, just as institutions take into account economic and organizational challenges. Companies and institutions therefore adapt to each other and affect each other's evolution ('co-evolution').

Second, we briefly summarized the debates on the (mostly formal) national institutions that shape corporate strategies and structures. Of particular importance are the relations of companies with their employees, customers, clients, owners and banks and their relation to schools, training facilities, universities and research institutes. The concept of 'institutional complementarities' refers to the fact that the institutional patterns in these fields are not isolated but are closely related and that the (mostly national) patterns of economic governance, labour relations, social and innovation policies, education and training are mutually interdependent and stabilize each other. This concept runs the risk of underestimating the tensions between different institutional logics, the conflicts between different actors, supranational learning processes and incremental change, but it rightly stresses the relative coherence, the relative closure and also the relative stability, especially of national institutional orders.

Another insight of this debate is that institutions contribute towards solving organizational coordination problems with economic and non-economic actors; they facilitate interactive learning and provide collective goods and resources.

Third, we referred to debates on the regional embeddedness of economic processes and especially of MNCs. We highlighted the role of (formal as well as informal, i.e. cultural) regional institutions and of inter-organizational networks in the provision of resources and the ways in which companies deal with uncertainties and coordination problems. Basically this is also true at the national level. Regional institutions, however, are often more focused on the specificities of regional companies and therefore can provide products, services and qualifications targeted more directly at the specific requirements of the local industry. In addition, the organizational, institutional and cognitive proximity of regionally agglomerated companies and actors facilitate interactive learning (Mattes, 2011). Therefore the regional level is especially important for the innovativeness of subsidiaries (cf. the contributions of Heidenreich and Mattes, Asheim et al., Cooke, Iammarino et al., Koschatzky and Baier, and Barmeyer and Krüth, Chapter 11 in this volume).

Finally, we identified three dimensions of corporate embeddedness: market failures due to political decisions and immobile production factors; business networks; and institutions. MNCs and their HQ are thus socially embedded as the result of political decisions and restrictions, by business networks with their suppliers, customers and competitors, and by formal and informal institutions. However, these forms of embeddedness potentially contradict a corporate strategy aimed at the global integration of subsidiaries from different countries and thus has to disregard national and regional particularities. Therefore the general dilemma between

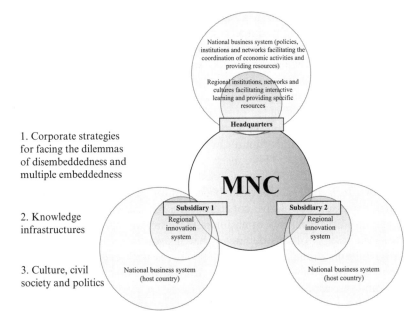

1. Corporate strategies
for facing the dilemmas
of disembeddedness and
multiple embeddedness

2. Knowledge
infrastructures

3. Culture, civil
society and politics

Figure 1.1   Multinational companies and the dilemma between multiple
embeddedness and disembeddedness

globalization and localization that is characteristic for MNCs is also
transformed into a dilemma between embeddedness and disembeddedness
and the respective advantages and risks. Therefore it can be assumed that
MNCs use selectively and strategically the advantages of embedded and
disembedded production and innovation strategies. In addition, MNCs
are not only embedded in a single national or regional context, but have
to take into account the institutional contexts in different home and host
countries ('multiple embeddedness').

The basic insights of this discussion can be condensed as follows.
Corporate embeddedness has to take into account the co-evolution of
institutions and organizations, the role of institutional complementarities especially at the national level, the contribution of institutions to the
solution of coordination problems, the political, institutional, cultural
and network-based embeddedness of MNCs and their subsidiaries at the
national and the regional level, multiple embeddedness and the dilemma
between embeddedness and disembeddedness. These six insights are summarized in part in Figure 1.1, illustrating the co-evolution of multiply
embedded MNCs and their national and regional contexts (policies, institutions, cultures and networks) as well as the related dilemmas.

Figure 1.1 also serves as a general framework for the three topics discussed by the following contributions in this volume: (1) the varieties of corporate strategies facing the dilemmas of embeddedness and disembeddedness; (2) the role of national and regional knowledge infrastructures in corporate embeddedness; and (3) the role of culture, business associations and politics in the embeddedness of multinationals.

1.6 OVERVIEW OF CONTRIBUTIONS TO THIS VOLUME

The structure of this volume reflects the aim of integrating contributions mostly from regional studies and international business studies on the strategies and varieties of corporate embeddedness. In these contributions three of the most important topics as previously mentioned are discussed in detail: (1) the dilemma of globalization and localization and the corresponding types of knowledge and corporate embeddedness; (2) the essential role of the national and regional knowledge infrastructure (companies, inter-organizational networks, knowledge-based services, regional scientists and R&D institutions) in embedded learning and innovation processes; and (3) the cultural and political construction of corporate embeddedness.

The innovativeness of MNCs is based both on the complementary use of international but inner-organizational networks between headquarters and subsidiaries as well as on the advantages of external, for example regional, linkages. Internal and external networks and learning processes, however, are fundamentally different. In their chapter, Martin Heidenreich and Jannika Mattes analyse the different dimensions, the challenges and the risks of regional embeddedness on the basis of international business and regional studies. The authors theorize that regional institutions can bridge the gap between inner-organizational and regional logics and networks by informal norms and rules based on proximity, by formal institutions stabilizing regional patterns of interaction and cooperation, and by the provision of resources for knowledge generation and diffusion that contribute to the emergence and stabilization of regional networks. However, strong forms of regional embedding are not always the best option for the involved companies. Also, for regional industrial policies, a specific focus on MNCs may be risky. On the basis of four regional and organizational case studies, the authors derive four different types of regional embeddedness as the combined result of corporate and regional strategies, showing that each constellation brings its own chances and challenges. In any case, regional embeddedness remains a highly challenging strategic option for subsidiaries as well as for other regional actors.

The chapter by Örjan Sölvell on multi-home-based corporations effectively links the debates on clusters and MNCs by analysing the choice between globalization and localization strategies as the dilemma between 'insiderization' and 'outsiderization'. While insiders in a cluster can tap locally bound capabilities and gain access to local networks but require a certain autonomy within the corporate network, outsiders can benefit from the advantages of global coordination and can exploit globally available capabilities, technologies and opportunities: 'Global markets are central for MNCs' cost position, while insider positions in clusters are central for their innovation processes'. Multi-domestic and transnational corporations exploit either the insider or the outsider advantages. By co-locating divisional HQ, R&D and design functions in multiple home bases, the multi-home-based corporation (MHC) attempts to mitigate 'the dilemma of increased insiderization in host clusters, leading to increased outsiderization of subsidiary units within the overall MNC'.

Bjørn T. Asheim, Bernd Ebersberger and Sverre J. Herstad analyse in their contribution how the specific type of organizational knowledge affects embeddedness in national and international innovation networks. They distinguish between analytical (scientific, deductive) and synthetic (experience-based, inductive) knowledge and, on the basis of the Norwegian community innovation survey (2005), test whether a synthetic knowledge base is more sensitive to proximity effects, co-localization and embeddedness than an analytical knowledge base, which should facilitate integration in global innovation networks. They show that an analytical knowledge base and MNC affiliation increase the geographical scope: the companies are less dependent on co-location and physical presence. In the case of a synthetic knowledge base, the presence of an affiliate in a specific region increases the likelihood of external collaboration in this region. International collaborative linkages are also less geographically dispersed.

In his chapter on the 'varieties of innovative impulse', Philip Cooke analyses the interaction between MNCs and smaller enterprises. He distinguishes two basic forms of relationships between regions and MNCs that he confronts in terms of a Porterian and a Jacobian perspective. In the first case innovation and competitiveness are the result of regional specialization. In the second case, which draws on the pattern ascribed to J. Jacobs, competitive advantage is also the result of diversification, regional variety of knowledge spillovers and 'transversality' thinking. The advantages of 'Jacobian' embedded skills, that is, especially the 'related variety' of regions, is a key motivation for the regional embeddedness of MNCs. Taking the example of four different Swedish clusters, the author describes three different types of regional embeddedness of MNCs among SME clusters: (1) single MNC-dominated clusters; (2) platforms in which

MNCs and specialist knowledge suppliers collaborate around their quest for 'related variety'; and (3) science excellence. In the next step these three types of MNC embeddedness are generalized on the basis of additional empirical evidence. The first type, which the author terms 'integrated supply chain model' (ISC), is characterized by a focal company that coordinates proximate suppliers of different inputs. The second type, the 'advanced aggregator model' (AA), is characterized by regionally embedded skills and 'systems integration' potential. The 'science excellence model' (SE) is typical of regions with high knowledge intensity and institutional innovation. The author concludes that distributed knowledge flows, related variety and regional transversality are cornerstones of the future innovation-centred economy.

Petra Ahrweiler, Michel Schilperoord, Nigel Gilbert and Andreas Pyka analyse the embeddedness of MNCs in innovation networks and the results of their involvement in collaborative R&D. They take the example of Ireland, a country that relies heavily on foreign-owned MNCs and their R&D, thus rendering involvement in innovation networks and cooperative research crucial for national innovativeness. Given the non-linear and complex dynamics of knowledge spillover effects, this requires complex assumptions on the technological capital ('kenes') of the firms, on market dynamics, on organizational learning, on partnerships and knowledge transfer, on networks and start-ups. Given the necessarily complex assumptions that the authors explain with reference to the respective literature, they use an agent-based simulation, that is, 'a theory running on a computer'. MNCs are modelled as larger companies. It can be shown that they have a beneficial effect on the capital and knowledge level of the economy. If they cooperate with their environment, this will raise the knowledge level and the stability of the whole economy. This shows not only the role of corporate embeddedness in a national system of innovation, but also the potential of agent-based modelling for a dynamic and detailed description of a complex system.

On the basis of in-depth interviews in German and British MNCs, Simona Iammarino, Jan-Philipp Kramer, Elisabetta Marinelli and Javier Revilla Diez analyse three different dimensions of the regional embeddedness of these companies: the interdependence of regional and organizational knowledge creation; the influence of the regional environment on corporate R&D strategies; and the types of industrial and scientific patterns of cooperation between the subsidiaries and other companies within and beyond the group. The authors show that MNCs 'make use of and provide skills to the local labour market [and] benefit from the presence of regional universities and research infrastructure'. Regional partners, especially in higher education, the regional availability of scientists and R&D

resources as well as regional cluster and network initiatives significantly influence the regional embeddedness of MNCs. Decentralized development activities facilitate their interaction with the environment. In general, German companies and employees are more regionally embedded than their UK counterparts.

The chapter by Simone Strambach and Benjamin Klement discusses the organizational decomposition of innovation processes, especially in the German software industry. It focuses on the knowledge interactions between different subsidiaries of an MNC and between subsidiaries and external companies, universities, research institutes, customers and knowledge-based business services. As a function of the available methods for decontextualizing the software production from the environment in which the software will be used, the authors distinguish between customized solution providers, cost-driven outsourcing firms and complex innovation process managers, highlighting the multi-local and multi-scalar character of organizationally decomposed innovation processes. On the one hand, the internationalization of software production in non-OECD countries is especially difficult in the software industry because the difficulties of separating knowledge-creating and knowledge-using activities limit the delegation of knowledge-creating activities to offshore partners. On the other hand, in cases where parts of the innovation process are outsourced, this significantly raises the levels of competences and the autonomy of the external subsidiaries. These subsidiaries establish their own linkages to their regional environment, for example to public and private knowledge-based services or research institutes. This shows that the degree of regional embeddedness is also linked to increased autonomy and advanced technological capabilities of the subsidiary.

The chapter by Knut Koschatzky and Elisabeth Baier asks whether European MNCs are equally spread over the European territory independently of regional endowment with knowledge resources or whether they are concentrated in innovative locations where they can exploit localized, context-specific knowledge in regional networks. Using European regional data supplemented by the locations of 700 research-oriented MNC HQ, the authors identify four clusters of economic regions in Europe (hubs of knowledge generation and innovation, lagging regions, public and service driven innovation centres and industry-driven innovation centres). MNCs prefer the first type as the location for their corporate headquarters. Therefore the hypothesis of an equal distribution that could be expected for footloose companies can be refuted: geography, and therefore the possibility of regional embeddedness, also matters for corporate headquarters.

Taking the example of seven European regions, Dieter Rehfeld observes a shift from 'spontaneous' to 'constructed' regional embeddedness for which the activities of foundations and social networks are also important. He analyses regional embeddedness according to four dimensions: human resources is the most important dimension of regional embeddedness, followed by innovation and quality of life, with finally sustainability playing only a minor role. He shows that bigger companies and those that are founded in the region are more regionally embedded than smaller and medium-sized companies and those with foreign origins. Similar to the results of Asheim et al., Rehfeld also shows that IT companies and financial and business services are less involved in the region than other companies. Four motives are crucial for the decision to rely on regional embeddedness: taking part in an innovative business milieu; making use of the local market; strengthening regional attractiveness; and building up social capital.

The chapter by Christoph Barmeyer and Katharina Krüth on the *pôles de compétitivité* (competitiveness clusters) analyses France's experience with cluster policies as an indicator of a fundamental transformation of the previous, centralized French governance model, characterized by a status-based logic and segmented social networks. They expect a shift from 'centralized and top-down mechanisms of political coordination by the state towards decentralized structures in terms of innovation policy [and from] personalized and homogeneous social networks as the basis of cooperative innovation activities towards multiple and heterogeneous cooperation structures' see p. 272 in this volume). On the basis of three case studies, the authors are able to demonstrate how bottom-up and top-down tendencies are combined and how heterogeneous partners cooperate, thus demonstrating a transformation of the previous Colbertist model of economic governance.

In his chapter, Bob Hancké discusses the origins of business coordination, a theoretical gap of the varieties of capitalism approach. Taking the example of Central and Eastern Europe, he analyses the emergence of interfirm coordination in the engineering sector. A specific feature of these countries is the important role of large foreign MNCs that have to cope with bottlenecks in the production of collective goods such as skills and regional technological capacity. In the process of rapid re-industrialization, which to a large extent was led and organized in these countries by MNCs, skills shortages and technical bottlenecks of suppliers led to collective action problems. This has forced these companies to build forms of interfirm coordination, often supported by international chambers of commerce that had the ability to enforce compliance with collective solutions to training bottlenecks. Therefore, even without public interventions, 'endogenous' forms of business coordination have emerged, because only in this way could the cooperation between MNCs faced with local bottlenecks be enforced. This shows that, even without historical precursors and under highly unlikely conditions, islands of institutionally embedded production can emerge in an open, co-evolutionary process, which in this case is driven by local subsidiaries of global companies.

Rajneesh Narula and José Guimón draw several political conclusions about the debate on corporate embeddedness. They begin with the observation that foreign direct investments by MNCs might play an ambivalent role in national innovation systems: they contribute either to the upgrading of domestic clusters or to the reduction of its long-run potential (e.g. by the 'crowding out' of innovative domestic firms or the downgrading of a foreign subsidiary's R&D mandate). The role of MNCs in the upgrading of national innovation systems also depends on the level of domestic innovative capacities. Only when these local competences are sufficiently developed can regions profit from the competences of foreign MNCs by integrating them in local clusters. This observation is especially important for the new member states of the EU, as the role of foreign subsidiaries in these countries is significantly higher than in the Western and Southern European countries. The authors conclude that innovation policies in the new member states should focus mostly on the embeddedness and upward evolution of existing MNC operations by creating linkages between the MNC subsidiary and local organizations and clusters. These countries should try to attract 'demand-driven' rather than 'supply-driven' R&D. Similar to Hancké (Chapter 12), they conclude that in this context the upgrading of human capital and public R&D are especially important. The concluding chapter by Jannika Mattes and Martin Heidenreich draws together some of the ideas presented in the previous chapters in order to systemize the dilemmas of corporate embeddedness, the role of external knowledge structures and the influence of strategic actions of policy makers and corporate actors.

Together, the 14 contributions in this volume suggest that national and regional embeddedness can be an important asset for augmenting the innovativeness and competitiveness of MNCs and their subsidiaries as well as the economic position of their home and host countries. However, corporate and regional embedding strategies first have to take into account the dilemmas that go along with such a strategy: lock-in effects, stronger subsidiaries and thus difficulties of integrating them in a global strategy (Part I). Second, the innovativeness of subsidiaries depends on the respective knowledge infrastructures, that is, on universities and R&D facilities as well as on the advanced technological and business competences of knowledge-based service providers and regionally concentrated corporate headquarters (Part II). Third, corporate embeddedness is becoming less and less a stable cultural feature of national and regional innovation systems and increasingly the result of entrepreneurial strategies and political decisions (Part III). These results show that research on the institutional embeddedness of MNCs can provide a basis for fruitful interchange among scholars interested in economic sociology, regional studies, national production and innovation models, and international management.

NOTES

1. Boyer (2005: 67) defines the 'complementarity of institutional forms (as) a configuration in which the viability of an institutional form is strongly or entirely conditioned by the existence of several other institutional forms, in such a manner that their conjunction offers greater resilience and possibly better performance compared to alternative configurations'.
2. This internal embeddedness of subsidiaries in the corporation is disregarded in this book because its conceptual inclusion would overstretch the embeddedness concept. The corresponding challenges are better analysed by conventional organizational sociological concepts such as integration and coordination.

REFERENCES

Andersson, U., Forsgren, M. and Holm, U. (2002), 'The strategic impact of external networks: subsidiary performance and competence development in the multinational corporation', *Strategic Management Journal*, **23** (11): 979–96.

Andersson, U., Forsgren, M. and Holm, U. (2007), 'Balancing subsidiary influence in the federative MNC. A business network view', *Journal of International Business Studies*, **38** (5): 802–18.

Asheim, B. and Isaksen, A. (2002), 'Regional innovation systems: the integration of local "sticky" and global "ubiquitous" knowledge', *Journal of Technology Transfer*, **27** (1): 77–86.

Bartlett, C.A. and Ghoshal, S. (1989), *Managing Across Borders: The Transnational Solution*, Boston, MA: Harvard Business School Press.

Bathelt, H., Malmberg, A. and Maskell, P. (2004), 'Clusters and knowledge: local buzz, global pipelines and the process of knowledge creation', *Progress in Human Geography*, **28** (1): 31–56.

Beckert, J. (2003), 'Economic sociology and embeddedness: how shall we conceptualize economic action?', *Journal of Economic Issues*, **37** (3): 769–87.

Boschma, R.A. (2005), 'Proximity and innovation: a critical assessment', *Regional Studies*, **39** (1): 61–74.

Bouquet, C. and Birkinshaw, J. (2008), 'Managing power in the multinational corporation: how low-power actors gain influence', *Journal of Management*, **34** (3): 477–508.

Boyer, R. (2005), 'Coherence, diversity, and the evolution of capitalisms. The institutional complementarity hypothesis', *Evolutionary and Institutional Economics Review*, **2** (1): 43–80.

Buckley, P.J. and Casson, M. (1976), *The Future of the Multinational Enterprise*, London: Macmillan.

Cantwell, J., Dunning, J.H. and Lundan, S.M. (2010), 'An evolutionary approach to understanding international business activity: the co-evolution of MNEs and the institutional environment', *Journal of International Business Studies*, **41** (4): 567–86.

Clark, E. and Geppert, M. (2011), 'Subsidiary integration as identity construction and institution building: a political sensemaking approach', *Journal of Management Studies*, **48** (2): 395–416.

Cooke, P., Asheim, B.T. and Boschma R. (eds) (2011), *Handbook of Regional Innovation and Growth*, Cheltenham, UK and Northampton, MA, USA: Edward Elgar.

Cooke, P., Heidenreich, M. and Braczyk, H.-J. (2004), *Regional Innovation Systems* (2nd edn), London; New York: Routledge.

Dunning, J.H. (1988), 'Toward an eclectic theory of international production: a restatement and some possible extensions', *Journal of International Business Studies*, **19** (1): 1–31.

Dunning, J.H. (1998), 'Location and the multinational enterprise: a neglected factor?', *Journal of International Business Studies*, **29** (1): 45–66.

Dunning, J.H. and Lundan, S.M. (2008), *Multinational Enterprises and the Global Economy* (2nd edn), Cheltenham, UK and Northampton, MA, USA: Edward Elgar.

Edquist, C. (2005), 'Systems of innovation – perspectives and challenges', in J. Fagerberg, D.C. Mowery and R.R. Nelson (eds), *The Oxford Handbook of Innovation*, Oxford: Oxford University Press, pp. 181–208.

Fligstein, N. (2001), 'Social skill and the theory of fields', *Sociological Theory*, **19** (2): 105–25.

Forsgren, M., Holm, U. and Johanson, J. (2005), *Managing the Embedded Multinational. A Business Network View*, Cheltenham, UK and Northampton, MA, USA: Edward Elgar.

Geppert, M. and Williams, K. (2006), 'Global, national and local practices in multinational corporations: towards a sociopolitical framework', *International Journal of Human Resource Management*, **17** (1): 49–69.

Geppert, M., Williams, K. and Matten, D. (2003), 'The social construction of contextual rationalities in MNCs: an Anglo-German comparison of subsidiary choice', *Journal of Management Studies*, **40** (3): 617–41.

Ghoshal, S. and Bartlett, C.A. (1990), 'The multinational corporation as an interorganizational network', *Academy of Management Review*, **15**: 603–25.

Giddens, A. (1990), *The Consequences of Modernity*, Cambridge/Oxford: Polity Press.

Grabher, G. (1993), 'Rediscovering the social in the economics of interfirm relations', in G. Grabher (ed.), *The Embedded Firm. On the Socioeconomics of Industrial Networks*, London and New York: Routledge, pp. 1–31.

Granovetter, M. (1985), 'Economic action and social structure: the problem of embeddedness', *American Journal of Sociology*, **91** (3): 481–510.

Hall, P.A. and Gingerich, D.W. (2009), 'Varieties of capitalism and institutional complementarities in the political economy: an empirical analysis', *British Journal of Political Science*, **39** (3): 449–82.

Hall, P.A. and Soskice, D. (2001), 'An introduction to varieties of capitalism', in P.A. Hall and D. Soskice (eds), *Varieties of Capitalism: The Institutional Foundations of Comparative Advantage*, Oxford: Oxford University Press, pp. 1–68.

Hancké, B., Rhodes, M. and Thatcher, M. (eds) (2007), *Beyond Varieties of Capitalism: Conflict, Contradiction, and Complementarities in the European Economy*, Oxford: Oxford University Press.

Heidenreich, M., Barmeyer, C. and Koschatzky, K. (2010), 'Product development in multinational companies', in P. Ahrweiler (ed.), *Innovation in Complex Systems*, London: Routledge, pp. 137–49.

Heidenreich, M., Barmeyer, Ch., Koschatzky, K., Mattes, J., Baier, E. and Krüth, K. (2012), *Multinational Enterprises and Innovation: Regional Learning in Networks*, London: Routledge.

Held, D., McGrew, A., Goldblatt, D. and Perraton, J. (1999), *Global Transformations*, Cambridge: Polity Press.

Hollingsworth, J.R. and Boyer, R. (1997), 'Coordination of economic actors and social systems of production', in J.R. Hollingsworth and R. Boyer (eds), *Contemporary Capitalism: The Embeddedness of Institutions*, Cambridge, UK: Cambridge University Press, pp. 1–47.

Holm, U., Malmberg, A. and Sölvell, Ö. (2003), 'Subsidiary impact on host-country economies. The case of foreign-owned subsidiaries attracting investment into Sweden', *Journal of Economic Geography*, 3: 389–408.

Kostova, T., Roth, K. and Dacin, M.T. (2008), 'Institutional theory in the study of multinational corporations: a critique and new directions', *Academy of Management Review*, 33: 994–1006.

Krippner, G.R. and Alvarez, A.S. (2007), 'Embeddedness and the intellectual projects of economic sociology', *Annual Review of Sociology*, 33: 219–40.

Krugman, P. (1991), *Geography and Trade*, Cambridge, MA: MIT Press.

Le Galès, P. and Voelzkow, H. (2001), 'Introduction: the governance of local economies', in C. Crouch, P. Le Galès, C. Trigilia and H. Voelzkow, *Local Production Systems in Europe. Rise or Demise?*, Oxford: Oxford University Press, pp. 1–24.

Lundvall, B.-Å. (1992), 'Introduction', in B.-Å. Lundvall (ed.), *National Systems of Innovation: Towards a Theory of Innovation and Interactive Learning*, London: Pinter, pp. 1–19.

Marshall, A. (1982), *Principles of Economics*, 9th edn, London: Macmillan (first edn 1890).

Mattes, J. (2010), *Innovation in Multinational Companies: Organisational, International and Regional Dilemmas*, Bern et al.: Peter Lang.

Mattes, J. (2011), 'Dimensions of proximity and knowledge bases: innovation between spatial and non-spatial factors', *Regional Studies* (forthcoming), DOI: 10.1080/00343404.2011.552493.

Maurice, M., Sellier, F. and Silvestre, J.-J. (1986), *The Social Foundations of Industrial Power. A Comparison of France and Germany*, Cambridge, MA and London: MIT Press.

Metcalfe, S. (1995), 'The economic foundations of technology policy: equilibrium and evolutionary perspectives', in P. Stoneman (ed.), *Handbook of the Economics of Innovation and Technological Change*, Oxford: Blackwell, pp. 409–512.

Meyer, K.E., Mudambi, R. and Narula, R. (2011), 'Multinational enterprises and local contexts: the opportunities and challenges of multiple embeddedness', *Journal of Management Studies*, **48** (2): 235–52.

Nelson, R.R. (1994), 'The co-evolution of technology, industrial structure, and supporting institutions', *Industrial and Corporate Change*, 3 (1): 47–63.

North, D.C. (1991), 'Institutions', *Journal of Economic Perspectives*, 3 (1): 97–112.

Ohmae, K. (1990), *The Borderless World: Management Lessons in the New Logic of the Global Market Place*, New York: Harper.

Patel, P. and Pavitt, K. (1991), 'Large firms in the production of the world's technology: an important case of "Non-Globalisation", *Journal of International Business Studies*, **22** (1): 1–21.

Peng, M.W. and Khoury, T.A. (2008), 'Unbundling the institution-based view of international business strategy', in A.M. Rugman (ed.), *The Oxford Handbook of International Business*, Oxford: Oxford University Press, pp. 256–68.

Phene, A. and Almeida, P. (2008), 'Innovation in multinational subsidiaries: the role of knowledge assimilation and subsidiary capabilities', *Journal of International Business Studies*, **39** (5): 901–19.

Piore, M.J. and Sabel, C.F. (1984), *The Second Industrial Divide. Possibilities for Prosperity*, New York: Basic Books.

Polanyi, K. (1944), *The Great Transformation*, New York: Holt, Rinehart.

Porter, M.E. (1998), 'Clusters and the new economics of competition', *Harvard Business Review*, November/December, 77–90.

Sölvell, Ö. and Birkinshaw, J. (2007), 'Multinational enterprises and the knowledge economy: leveraging global practices', in J.H. Dunning (ed.), *Regions, Globalization, and Knowledge-based Economy*, repr. Oxford: Oxford University Press, pp. 82–105.

Storper, M. (1997), *The Regional World: Territorial Development in a Global Economy*, New York and London: Guilford Press.

Streeck, W. (1991), 'On the social and political conditions of diversified quality production', in E. Matzner and W. Streeck (eds), *Beyond Keynesianism: The Socio-Economics of Production and Full Employment*, Aldershot, UK and Brookfield, US: Edward Elgar, pp. 21–61.

Sturgeon, T.J. (2002), 'Modular production networks: a new American model of industrial organization', *Industrial and Corporate Change*, **11** (3): 451–96.

Westney, E. and Zaheer, S. (2008), 'The multinational enterprise as an organization', in A.M. Rugman (ed.), *The Oxford Handbook of International Business*, Oxford: Oxford University Press, pp. 341–66.

Whitley, R. (1999), *Divergent Capitalisms: The Social Structuring and Change of Business Systems*, Oxford: Oxford University Press.

Whitley, R. (2002), 'Multiple market economies' in D. Sachsenmaier, J. Riedel and S.N. Eisenstadt (eds), *Reflections on Multiple Modernities*, Leiden, Boston and Köln: Brill, pp. 217–40.

Womack, J.P., Jones, D.T. and Roos, D. (1990), *The Machine That Changed the World*, New York: Rawson.

Yamin, M. and Andersson, U. (2011), 'Subsidiary importance in the MNC: what role does internal embeddedness play?', *Journal of Management Studies*, **20** (2): 151–62.

Zeitlin, J. (2008), 'The rediscovery of industrial districts: a disciplinary paradox', in G. Jones and J. Zeitlin (eds), *The Oxford Handbook of Business History*, Oxford. Oxford University Press, pp. 219–41.

PART I

Challenges and varieties of corporate embeddedness

2. Regional embeddedness of multinational companies and their limits: a typology[1]

Martin Heidenreich and Jannika Mattes

Multinational companies (MNCs) are important protagonists for the generation and international transfer of technological knowledge. They are responsible for most global R&D expenditure[2] and provide important channels through which technological competences can be transferred across national as well as cultural and institutional borders (OECD, 2009; Dunning and Lundan, 2009). MNCs are analysed as global networks in which internationally distributed subsidiaries produce innovations in a 'more distributed and open architecture of knowledge production and application' (Gerybadze, 2004: 123). Complementary to this international dimension of knowledge production, other authors stress the territorial embeddedness of MNCs that do not act as 'footloose companies' but are able to exploit specific regional competences due to the embeddedness of their subsidiaries 'in different local networks' (Andersson et al., 2002: 979). Cantwell and Iammarino (2003), for example, show that MNCs spread their competence base by exploiting diversified technological competences in spatially distinct institutional and organizational settings. Taking the example of US-based semiconductor firms, Phene and Almeida (2008) demonstrate that the external availability of competences and the capability of subsidiaries to exploit them are essential for the innovativeness of a company. MNCs are therefore geographically unbound and in principle transnational networks of knowledge production, while at the same time their competences are based on learning processes and knowledge exchange in specific local contexts (Kristensen and Zeitlin, 2005). In this sense an MNC uses and combines two types of learning that are based on international yet intra-organizational relations as well as on external regional linkages with other companies and regional institutions.

This picture of MNCs harmoniously combining regional and global knowledge is naturally oversimplified and ignores the difficulties of establishing and combining regional and corporate learning processes as well as the strategic options that are open to MNCs and regional actors. First, regional competences are not easily accessible to MNCs and MNCs have a broad spectrum of alternative options. Second, this is equally true for regions as it is also risky for them to focus on a specific MNC (which is often identical to a focus on a specific branch and technology) because it may lead to lock-in effects and reduce the diversity of technological competences, thus linking the destiny of a region to a specific company. As for MNCs, it is also not easy for regions to simultaneously provide competences and resources that are useful to MNCs and avoid the risks entailed by a targeted industrial policy.

In order to discuss the regional embeddedness of MNCs it is therefore necessary to carefully analyse the opportunities and resources that MNCs and regions can provide for each other. The following discussion will be based on insights from two, until now largely unrelated, debates: regional studies and international business studies (section 2.1). It will be shown that the innovativeness of MNCs and their subsidiaries may be based on their ability to exploit four different dimensions of regional embeddedness. However, such an embedding strategy is not always the best option for the involved companies. Besides intensive forms of embeddedness, MNCs may prefer more cautious forms (which we term 'exploitative embeddedness') or even completely renounce any form of regional embedding. Also for regions a specific focus on MNCs may be risky. Instead of specifically targeting MNCs and their fields of activity, regional policies may also choose a broader focus. On the basis of four case studies on innovation processes in German MNCs and their regional environments, we distinguish and analyse four different types of regional embeddedness as the combined result of corporate and regional strategies (section 2.2). We can show that an arms'-length relationship between subsidiaries and their regional environment (which we designate as 'mutual non-interference') can be a strategic choice that entails a beneficial situation for both MNCs and regions. In contrast, a close coupling (labelled 'mutual problem solving') of subsidiaries and their regional context creates significantly different opportunities and risks. The other two types, regional problem solving and MNC-induced problem solving, illustrate that the relationship between subsidiaries or regional institutions can be asymmetric and unbalanced. Our empirical account thus shows different dimensions and forms of regional embeddedness as a highly demanding strategic option for subsidiaries as well as for other regional actors. These findings are discussed in a brief conclusion (section 2.3).

2.1 REGIONAL EMBEDDEDNESS OF MNCS: INTEGRATING ORGANIZATIONAL AND REGIONAL PERSPECTIVES

Even if a major strength of MNCs is their ability to exploit heterogeneous competences, there are fundamental differences between inner-organizational and regional types of learning and networks. A crucial task is to understand these differences in order to analyse the challenges faced by both regions and MNCs in their attempts to support and enhance the innovativeness of companies. In the following we will first discuss the fundamental barriers between companies and their regional environment. While MNCs are hierarchically structured economic organizations, external regional relationships are neither hierarchical nor necessarily shaped by economic logics. Regional actors also belong to non-economic subsystems, for example social, scientific, political or educational subsystems (2.1.1). The related coordination difficulties that explain the crucial role of proximity and regional institutions in coordinating regional exchanges will be discussed on the basis of selected approaches in the fields of international business studies (2.1.2) and regional studies (2.1.3). In the next step we shall discuss the risks and limits of regional embeddedness for companies and for industrial policies (2.1.4).

2.1.1 Fundamental Differences between Organizational and Regional Relations

Contrary to the current debate, we assume that regional learning is fundamentally different from learning within an MNC. The differences between regions and MNCs are often downplayed, for example when both MNCs and regions are analysed as networks (Ghoshal and Bartlett, 1990; Saxenian, 2006) or when regions and MNCs are conceived as learning or knowledge-based communities (Becker-Ritterspach et al., 2010; Maskell and Malmberg, 1999; Cooke, 2002). The advantage of network approaches and knowledge-based views, namely that of analysing learning and exchange processes in and beyond MNCs with a unified and intuitively convincing framework, can turn into a disadvantage if the differences between organizational and regional networks and forms of learning are neglected.

Two different forms of networks between MNCs and their regional environment have to be at least analytically distinguished. The first scenario is when MNCs and their subsidiaries cooperate with other regional companies, especially with suppliers, customers or even competitors. In this case hierarchically structured economic organizations with partially competing goals have to agree on common aims, rules and courses of action. Although challenges are always linked with these types of inter-organizational cooperation ('not-invented-here' syndrome, opportunism, knowledge leakage etc.), even greater challenges exist with the second scenario in which regionally embedded subsidiaries interact with regional administrations and politicians, research labs, professional schools, development centres, intermediaries or individuals in order to benefit from their competences, contacts and resources. In this case MNCs (as economic organizations) have to take into account the different logics of economic, political, scientific, educational, technological or social subsystems. Each subsystem with its actors and organizations follows its own logics, standards, criteria, languages, problem definitions, regulatory structures, patterns of interpretations and success criteria. A direct transfer of knowledge, for example between universities, development centres and companies, is thus excluded because the criteria for scientific truth, technical functioning and economic success are inherently different. Thus, complementary to the advantages of 'open innovation' (Chesbrough, 2003), subsidiaries have to face the challenges of cooperating across the borders of different organizations and subsystems.

Regional institutions can support companies in dealing with the challenges of heterogeneous cooperation by bridging the gap between different organizations and societal subsystems. The existence of relatively stable patterns of interaction, obligations, sanctions and incentives is the major strength of regions. Regional ties may be characterized by personal, trust-based relations and by formally institutionalized patterns of interaction between regional companies and other actors, for example via business associations, chambers of commerce, industrial development or technology transfer agencies. These institutions can facilitate agreements on common rules in spite of conflicting interests, divergent definitions of the situation and different norms and patterns of behaviour because regions are social fields, characterized by actors, organizations and more or less informal rules: 'The theory of fields . . . offers a view as to how local orders are created, sustained, and transformed' (Fligstein, 2001: 109).

Regional institutions facilitate a (loose) coupling of different organizational or societal logics (Weick, 1976: 3). Using terminology inspired by Polanyi (2001 [1957]), this close coupling of different organizational or societal logics can be termed 'institutional embeddedness'. This concept was initially proposed by Karl Polanyi in order to distinguish traditional, institutionally embedded societies from modern, disembedded market societies (Hess, 2004). Granovetter (1985: 493) reintroduced the embeddedness concept in order to explain the dynamic, process- and experience-based production of trust and social order. According to

Beckert (2003: 769), '[e]mbeddedness refers to the social, cultural, political, and cognitive structuration of decisions in economic contexts'. We use the embeddedness concept in order to focus on 'bridging institutions' between different organizations or societal subsystems that structure the interaction of the respective actors by the provision of resources and rules. These institutions contribute to the reduction of uncertainties and problems of communication and cooperation that are the result of potentially conflicting interests ('opportunism'), different definitions of the situation and heterogeneous logics of action. They can be created and maintained both by companies (which may invest in regional training and research, in regional networks or in regional associations) and by political, administrative, scientific and educational actors. In the following the concept of regional embeddedness is discussed from both organizational and regional perspectives.

2.1.2 The Embeddedness of MNCs from the Organizational Perspective

It is assumed in the literature that research and development (R&D) is becoming increasingly internationally distributed in MNCs and ceases to be concentrated in the headquarters (HQ) or in another central location. The analytical focus in international business literature has thus been on the internal complexity of MNCs and different patterns of coordination and configuration, but generally not on the external environment (Westney and Zaheer, 2001; Holmqvist, 2003). The debate on innovation in MNCs has likewise mostly ignored the business environment (Andersson et al., 2007; Holm et al., 2003).

However, especially in the knowledge-based stream in international business studies (Kogut and Zander, 1993), MNCs are not only characterized by their capability to transfer technological and organizational competences across national borders (Monteiro et al., 2008). The question as to how these competences are being created hence gains importance. Besides internal innovation, the external dimension of innovativeness, that is, the capability to effectively use localized knowledge in specific national and regional contexts, comes to the fore (Anderson et al., 2007). Thus an MNC should be able to combine the advantages of geographical, social, institutional, organizational and cognitive proximity (Boschma, 2005) as the basis of interactive learning with the capability to organize internal innovation processes and the ability to transfer competences beyond the boundaries of a subsidiary, a region or a country. In the following we shall shortly discuss how the regional embeddedness of MNCs has been discussed in three prominent streams of international business literature (cf. Chapter 1).

In 'transaction cost approaches' the context of MNCs is shaped by external, mostly political, decisions, for example trade barriers, subsidies and other locational advantages (Dunning and Lundan, 2008).

In 'network-based approaches' the linkages within a MNC (between subsidiaries and HQ) and beyond are analysed as networks. Ghoshal and Bartlett (1990) had pointed out that intensive contact with external partners can enhance the internal autonomy of the subsidiary from the HQ and that more competent environments can hence increase the innovativeness of a site. In contrast to the internal network of subsidiaries and HQ, the linkages to customers, competitors and other external actors are designated as 'the external network'. A strong external embeddedness will generally increase the dispersal of productive resources among the different units of an MNC and reduce their specialization – and vice versa. This results in a potential 'contradiction between the high degree of embeddedness required in order to stimulate problem solving and arm's-length relationships needed to achieve greater standardization and cost efficiency' (Forsgren et al., 2005: 183).

An 'institutional perspective' assumes that 'strategic choices are not only driven by industry conditions and firm capabilities, but are also a reflection of the formal and informal constraints of a particular institutional framework that managers confront' (Peng et al. 2009: 66). The classical institutionalist assumption that institutions 'reduce uncertainty and provide meaning', however, is challenged by Kostova et al. (2008: 1001), who observe that 'MNCs are embedded in multiple, fragmented, ill-defined, and constantly evolving institutional systems'. Therefore MNCs have to face conflicting demands for legitimacy that will hardly reduce uncertainty. Given these conflicting environments and demands, Kristensen and Zeitlin (2005) challenge the assumption of the MNC as an integrated, coherent, rational actor and insist on the potential benefits of MNCs and their local presence for also 'the many local communities which they tap into and interconnect' (Kristensen and Zeitlin, 2005: 302).

To draw together these different perspectives in the field of international business studies, the regional environment of companies can be analysed as a pool of heterogeneous resources and competences that can be used also in inner-organizational negotiations (Cantwell and Mudambi, 2005, 'strategic dimension'), as an opportunity for learning ('cognitive dimension') and as a source of conflicting norms and demands for legitimacy ('regulative dimension'). If subsidiaries are able to exploit these resources and competences, they can increase their influence within the company. The most important sources of regional competences are linked to the availability of competent customers, suppliers and competitors. Regional embeddedness in international business studies is thus understood in general as external networks with regional companies. Cooperation with regional actors in other societal subsystems, for example research institutes, universities, politicians and administrations, employment offices, schools and training facilities or cooperation-enhancing institutions, plays a minor role. In the following we discuss the concept of embeddedness from the viewpoint of regional studies.

2.1.3   The Embeddedness of MNCs from the Regional Perspective

In early regional studies, regional embeddedness was analysed as the result of transportation and transaction cost advantages and the availability of natural resources (coal, ore, wood, sun, fertile land etc.). As a protagonist of the 'new economic geography', Krugman (1991) explains the emergence and consolidation of regional agglomerations by the reduction of procurement and distribution costs, that is, by cost advantages of territorially concentrated forward and backward linkages. In more recent studies the focus has shifted to learning and network advantages, that is, the possibility of exploiting the experience, knowledge and skills of proximate companies and institutions. In this perspective regional advantages are not only the result of transaction cost savings. They are also the outcome of mutual learning, facilitating the exchange of implicit, experience-based, uncodified knowledge, the recombination of existing knowledge and the possibility of establishing and stabilizing interaction-based trust relationships: 'knowledge creation is supported by the institutional embodiment of tacit knowledge' (Maskell and Malmberg, 1999: 167). An initial answer to the question concerning the forms and advantages of regional embeddedness is thus that spatial proximity eases mutual understanding and 'buzz', that is, 'learning processes taking place among actors embedded in a community by just being there' (Bathelt et al., 2004: 31).

Second, more formal regional institutions (e.g. business associations, unions, chambers of commerce) may contribute to the stabilization of inter-organizational patterns of cooperation and learning and to the emergence of local trust. According to Autio (1998), these institutions are the governance dimension of regional knowledge application and exploitation subsystem because they facilitate the emergence and stabilization of horizontal and vertical networks between firms.

Third, regional institutions can facilitate the provision of 'local collective competition goods' (LCCG; e.g. qualified employees, R&D services, technology transfer, reliable legal or technological norms, information on new markets and technologies, consultancy and other 'real services'; cf. Le Galès and Voelzkow, 2001). Autio (1998) designates these institutions as the knowledge generation and diffusion subsystem (universities, research

institutes, technology transfer agencies and both regional and local innovation support agencies) of regional innovation systems (RIS).

The fourth dimension of regional embeddedness, namely regional
networks with suppliers, customers and clients, is the crucial focus of the
debate on industrial clusters (Enright, 2000).

The core of regional policies is mostly the creation of institutions that
are essential for the creation of knowledge. Regional or national agencies
can provide collective goods by supporting an adequate regional 'knowledge infrastructure' (R&D, technology transfer infrastructures, education,
training). To some extent industrial policies can also support and facilitate
regional patterns of cooperation and competition, for example through
regional development agencies or competence centres involving business
associations, employee representatives and public authorities for specific
technological fields. In both dimensions the corresponding policies can
be initiated at the national level, at the regional level and at the level of
specific inter-organizational networks. In most cases these policies do
not focus on larger or MNCs but on small and medium-sized enterprises
(SMEs), which are the crucial backbone of regional economies. In general,
regional or cluster policies are designed as alternatives to classical, MNC-
centred policies that were accused of supporting national champions,
picking the winners or fostering so called next-generation technologies
that never entered the market successfully (Boekholt and Thuriaux, 1999).

In conclusion, in the regional debate at least four regional advantages
can be identified: first the advantages of regional proximity, which have
been designated as 'buzz', interactive learning, knowledge spillover and
exchange of tacit knowledge; second, the availability of regional institutions that facilitates inter-organizational patterns of cooperation and
communication; third, the institutional provision of local collective competition goods; fourth, the facilitated access to proximate customers,
competitors, suppliers and other service providers that may be the result of
reduced transaction costs and a common institutional and social context
(see Table 2.1).

2.1.4   The Advantages and Risks of Regional Embeddedness

As shown in the previous sections, although regional embeddedness may
offer many opportunities for corporate subsidiaries of MNCs as well as for
regions, it also implies major risks for both sides. Regional embeddedness
is not *per se* the best or even the only available option for increasing corporate and regional competitiveness and innovativeness. This is especially
true for MNCs that are not bound to the region but can to a large extent
decide strategically about their regional involvement. In the following we

will discuss the advantages and potential risks of regional embeddedness from these two complementary viewpoints.

For a subsidiary, external cooperation is a way of enhancing the technological capabilities of a group and exploiting specific external competences. However, companies also try to keep crucial competences and technologies within the company and minimize the loss of control due to external cooperation. There are thus good reasons for not cooperating in regional R&D projects (Häusler et al., 1994). This is especially true for very innovative companies: 'laggards have more to gain from knowledge spillovers, but leaders have more to lose from knowledge leakages' (Cantwell, 2009: 38). Innovation cooperation with external, for example regional, partners is therefore less likely than would be expected purely on the basis of learning and cost advantages of regional innovation processes since these advantages may be threatened by the involvement in regional clusters (Mattes, 2010). Strategies of regional embeddedness thus have to deal with conflicting interests of protecting proprietary knowledge and acceding additional competences. Regional learning processes involve the risk of a potential loss of corporate control over essential competences and the spread of knowledge to competitors (or to their suppliers). Therefore companies are very cautious in using the advantages of localized learning: while they may be interested in exploiting regional markets, regionally available competences, local proximity and learning advantages, they will also try to avoid the risks of knowledge spillovers to competitors and other companies.

Complementary to the ambivalent interests of MNCs, regions may also hesitate to focus their support and resources on MNCs and their technological fields of specialization – an ambivalent attitude already shaped very early in regional studies, which regarded MNCs as a threat to regional economies. The Central Italian districts, for example, were analysed as territorially distributed parts of a common value chain that is more flexible, more innovative and in some ways also more democratic than large Northern Italian companies. The emergence of larger companies in the industrial districts was thus seen as a threat to the economic vitality of these districts that could '"eat" local economies by internalizing everything as intra-firm trade, disconnecting it from the external, market-based local environment' (Storper, 2000: 154). However, other authors also analyse MNCs as potential sources of technological competences and global connections for regional economies (Kristensen and Zeitlin, 2005). Enright (2000), for example, shows that foreign MNEs can be 'at the heart of vibrant clusters that take on a life of their own and in which the cluster itself does not depend on any single foreign MNE' (Enright, 2000: 134). For Rugman and Verbeke (2008: 165) the question remains open as to '[w]hether MNEs will consistently enhance the upgrading of local knowledge clusters, rather than eliminate domestic expertise and reduce long-run cluster stability in host countries'. MNCs may thus strengthen regional clusters by way of a global signalling effect, by the international cross-fertilization of local clusters and by implanting new technological sectors in local economies. On the other hand, they may weaken a local economy by reducing its variety and by locking a region into a specific technological trajectory.

Given the strategic alternatives of MNCs to regional embeddedness and the ambivalent regional interests in supporting the regional embeddedness of MNCs by a targeted industrial policy, we can thus distinguish between different dimensions of regional embeddedness, as illustrated in Table 2.1.

Based on the theoretical considerations put forward in this section and summarized in Table 2.1, we will now derive a typology for analysing four different ways of dealing empirically with the advantages, interests and risks of regional embeddedness.

2.2   BETWEEN CORPORATE AND REGIONAL DYNAMICS: FOUR TYPES OF REGIONAL EMBEDDEDNESS

Our basic assumption is that regional embeddedness is not the 'one best way' for corporate subsidiaries or for regions. Given the structural differences between corporate and regional interests and logics, regional embeddedness is by no means an easy, automatic or purely beneficial strategy. Excluding the cases in which the MNC is completely detached from the region, we have identified four different dimensions of regional embeddedness that may stabilize and facilitate the interaction of MNCs and their regional environment. MNCs and regions individually and jointly develop their own ways of interacting. The resulting embeddedness may thus be selective and weak. This observation provides the starting point for our empirical account. Before examining the case studies, we shall therefore propose a typology of regional embeddedness that illustrates how MNCs and regions find their specifically tailored forms of interacting.

The ways in which MNCs interact with their regional environment can be categorized as either exploitative or augmentative (cf. also Kuemmerle, 1997, 1999, 2002). First, MNCs use regions as providers of resources by exploiting regionally available LCCGs (exploiting capabilities). By doing so, they render certain activities in the region more profitable than others and shape the regional focus. The involved strategy can be called 'exploitative embeddedness'. Second, MNCs can participate in shaping regional

Table 2.1 Four dimensions of regional embeddedness

Dimension of regional embedding	Examples	Potential chances and risks for MNCs	Potential chances and risks for regions	Role of regional industrial policy
Informal norms and rules based on geographical collocation and social proximity	Buzz, informal contacts, personal links	Informal contacts and information, but no means of controlling them	Creation of regional dynamics, but no means of strategic influence	Limited
Formal rules stabilizing regional patterns of interaction and cooperation	Business associations, chambers of commerce, unions etc.	Allows assessment of regional expectations, but no direct means of shaping them	Creation of regional frameworks, but danger of lock-in	Limited (support of 'bridging institutions')
Institutional provision of resources for knowledge generation and diffusion	Universities; technology transfer, education, politics and public administration providing local collective competition goods	Provision of resources and learning opportunities, but loss of control and proprietary knowledge	Emergence of an attractive regional infrastructure, but danger of depending on specific companies and sectors	Targeted industrial policies providing tailored public support for the MNC (R&D, qualified employees, legal and administrative framework, financial means)
Regional industrial networks	Privileged cooperation with local suppliers, service providers, customers and competitors	Availability of knowledge, enhanced innovativeness and power for the subsidiary, but possibility of internal conflicts in the MNC and knowledge spillover	Creation of regional cluster dynamics, but danger of dependence on one sector, lock-in effects	Mainly broad industrial policies (network brokerage)

Regional strategy of MNC \ Regional policy	Broad industrial policies (not focused on a specific company or sector)	Targeted industrial policies (focused on a specific company or sector)
Exploitative embeddedness (exploiting available regional capabilities; global orientation)	(1) Mutual non-interference (*IT-G*)	(2) Regional problem solving (*Auto1-G*)
Augmentative embeddedness (augmenting and exploring regional capabilities; local creation of global competence)	(3) MNC-induced problem solving (*Transport-G*)	(4) Mutual problem solving (*Auto2-G*)

Note: The codes in italics refer to four selected MNCs in the fields of information technology, automotive and transportation.

Figure 2.1   Embeddedness between corporate strategies and regional policies: a typology

development by investing in the region, often acting not only as an economic actor but also as a social and political actor in their regional context (augmenting capabilities). We call this strategy 'augmentative embeddedness'. At the same time the region assumes a certain position as to how it faces the MNC – a position mirrored in regional policies, the regional industrial structure, the set-up of the intermediaries and the scientific infrastructure. The region can opt to conduct 'broad industrial policies'; that is, it regards itself as a provider of LCCGs for all local companies. In some cases, however, the region conducts 'tailored industrial policies', concentrating specifically on a focal sector or company.

By combining exploitative and augmentative embeddedness of MNCs with broad and targeted industrial policies of regions, we have derived four types of embeddedness (see Figure 2.1). First, 'mutual non-interference' (1) results from the exploitation of available LCCGs on the part of the MNC and from broad industrial policies of the region. The MNC's main orientation is hence global; the region is only one of many sources of rules and resources on which it can draw. From the regional point of view, the MNC is one of a multitude of relevant actors and the region's policies are aimed at providing resources and infrastructure for all companies. The mutual relationship between regions and a specific subsidiary is 'at arm's length', that is, they are not essential for each other. Second, if the region develops specifically targeted industrial policies, the intensity of the relationship between the company and regional actors increases. The region then tries to provide the MNC with specific solutions, turning itself into a specialized resource pool for this particular company. In this sense the region renders itself useful to the company by providing externalized services for it in terms of 'regional problem solving' (2). Third, regional policies can maintain a broad focus while the MNC contributes to the augmentation of regional capabilities. As 'MNC-induced problem solving' (3), the company assumes a role in shaping regional dynamics, augmenting regional knowledge and constructing LCCGs itself. The MNC regards the region as the local source of its global competences and sets the pace for regional evolvement. Finally, in the constellation of 'mutual problem solving' (4), MNCs and regions both view each other as core influence factors with regard to how to organize their activities. The MNC assumes an active role in regional policies and contributes to regional resources and rules; the region tailors its activities to meet the MNC's needs. Both systems follow their own logics, but they cooperatively conduct activities and take each other's requirements into account. This results in the joint construction of a specialized region, characterized by a strong degree of embeddedness in which economic, scientific and political logics complement each other (cf. also Etzkowitz 2001).

In the following we shall illustrate these four forms of embeddedness on the basis of four case studies on the organizational and regional context of four innovation processes in German-based MNCs. We focus on systematic differences between inner-organizational and regional learning processes and on the challenges and opportunities arising from these heterogeneous embedding relationships. In this way we aim to illustrate how regional embeddedness is actively constructed in the interaction of corporate and regional actors and how these actors cope with the challenges and risks of embeddedness.

2.2.1 Mutual Non-interference: a Strong Global Company in a Multifaceted Region

The least intensive type of embeddedness between MNCs and regions is 'mutual non-interference' (1). In this case the MNC does not invest in its regional context but exploits the available resources at a very general level. The LCCGs on which the MNC may draw are qualified labour, suppliers and infrastructure. The region does not in turn focus its economic policies specifically on the MNC or on a particular sector; it is more interested in creating a generally positive industrial atmosphere. The case of a multinational IT company allocated in Swabia (IT-G) illustrates the main features of this ideal type.

From the MNC's point of view the region is a pool of resources on which it can draw. Qualified graduates from local universities are recruited to work in IT-G and to stay in the region; simultaneously, IT-G draws upon universities in other places. In some cases clients from the region are involved simply because informal aspects of geographic proximity ease communication and interaction. At the same time the region is not the only resource pool available for IT-G and it takes care not to render itself dependent upon these local structures:

> At this point of time, the [regional cooperation] was rather coincidental. . . . We have known them for a fair while, . . . so it is easy to approach them. . . . You can simply knock on their door and say 'Hi, I'd like to talk something through with you', and that's not possible at any door. This is why we have chosen them. If they are allocated here in Germany, in Europe, in Asia or in the USA, doesn't really matter. We hardly have a local orientation there. (Interview with project manager, IT-G: 5)

A particularly strong informal bond is established each time a professor from the local university directly participates in the initiation of a new technological project in IT-G. He spends his sabbatical in the company and works jointly with internal employees. This can be considered as personalized internalization of externally available, local knowledge. His contribution is that of an additional expert who introduces new triggers in the form of ideas and knowledge into the company.

The main driver for contact with the region is not the availability of resources as such but that of spatial and social proximity. Above all, regional cooperation provides a means of reinforcing the internal strength of the subsidiary in the corporate group.

> Of course, we are generally interested in [local cooperation], due to a mix of pragmatic and geopolitical reasons, to have 'local' clients with who we can do this as a prototypical development. . . . First, it's easier to handle if they are allocated locally, and second, it's always our wish to show the US that Germany is not the ghost driver of the world, but that there's actually quite a lot going on here. (Interview with project manager, IT-G: 17)

Regional policies do not in turn target the MNC directly. The regional industrial structure is very diversified and dominated by many SMEs in various branches, rendering the focus of regional politics a rather general one. The corporate world reflects this wide array of activities: regional firms are active especially in the automotive and mechanical engineering industry, and those who are interconnected with IT are small service providers rather than companies producing their own software. Economic policies define a number of competence networks in a variety of sectors with the aim of fostering the connectedness among allocated firms.

> Basically, we are the transmitter to all these networks, to the possibilities, how can I get informed as an innovating company, how to cope with these issues. . . . As the case arises, it's simply about finding out: which partner do they need? (Head of regional development, region IT-G: 8)

In the same vein, numerous scientific and academic institutes are allocated in the surroundings of IT-G, some of them with a specific focus on IT, but many in other areas. Universities remain independent and do not purposefully aim to create joint strategic plans with IT-G. The head of an institute for educating skilled IT workers formulates the relationship with the MNC as follows:

> It is not our aim to specifically consider one company. That's not the point, because then one is happy and the other ones are not. We have a public mission of education, and that ranks higher. . . . And this basic education has to be designed in a way which makes it transferrable to other structural conditions. (Interview with head of IT education institute, region IT-G: 4)

The situation of mutual non-interference is hence not characterized by the absence of regional interaction, cooperation and exchange, but only by the absence of stable, institutionalized patterns of embeddedness. For the MNC, regional competences and contacts are not systematically important and they only play a role when they can be used in company-internal struggles to obtain a better strategic position in the group. Regional policies focus in turn on supporting a vivid industrial atmosphere that is suitable for meeting the diverse needs of the various allocated firms. This form of embeddedness hence results in a situation where (mainly informal) interaction between MNC and region takes place occasionally, but not in a systematic, stable way.

This is not necessarily a handicap for the company or for the region. Instead, the MNC cherishes its independence from the region and regards itself as a strong company that does not depend on particular conditions in specific regions. Its strategy is global and the benchmarks for cooperation partners and resources are also set globally. The resulting situation is also not unfavourable for the region. Numerous companies in various sectors are allocated here and the very general focus of regional initiatives contributes to an atmosphere that does not exclude or disadvantage any of them. Mutual non-interference is hence not a situation of ignorance or even hostility. It is simply based on the understanding that regions and MNCs should both follow their own strategies and only occasionally exploit their mutual resources. The few spillover effects that we observe between them (as the local recruitment of qualified labour or technological cooperation) are not stabilized by regional institutions.

2.2.2   Regional Problem Solving: Accommodating MNCs as Regional Key Players

More specific than in the first type is the integration between MNCs and regional policies in the second type, which we term 'regional problem solving' (2). Here, the MNC maintains its exploitative approach towards the regional context. It is mainly interested in absorbing external knowledge and using the best available resources in its projects. In this case, however, the region implements targeted industrial policies that focus particularly on the MNC and its sector; available LCCGs match the needs of the MNC. The aim of regional policies is to accommodate the MNC in its surroundings and to support it comprehensively by creating synergies between the corporation and other regional companies and institutions. The following case of an automobile company illustrates how embeddedness emerges in this type.

Auto1-G regards the region as a pool of competences targeted according to its particular needs. Resources, labour, schools and R&D centres are available in a way that suits the MNC – a reason to make ample use of them. In this way the MNC collaborates for example with allocated universities for basic research activities. It also engages in an exchange with scientific institutes active in its own activity field.

> [Cooperation with universities takes place] where we still do . . . basic research. But that's selective. That's in all these cases in which we have basically come to dead-ends in our own technological development and say: 'Okay, we actually need another research approach. . . . We won't advance with what we have here.' (Interview with head of component producer, Auto1-G: 21)

Interaction runs largely mono-directionally. Regional actors perform tasks that are useful for the MNC and in some cases the MNC even defines necessities and requirements that the local authorities or scientific partners must meet. The company itself does not actively invest in the regional surroundings but allows them to be created externally.

> And they [enumerates engineers working for Auto1-G] also influence the scientific world, because they cooperate with these institutes, be it scientific institutes or universities. And they tell them: 'In this area and in this area, we need further research.' (Interview with employee in quality management, Auto1-G: 20)

A particularly striking example of how strongly Auto1-G's requirements influence its regional surroundings is the establishment of local subsidiaries by almost all of its major strategic suppliers. The aim here is not to enhance regional capabilities but to have these partners nearby in order to be able to use their resources more easily, to create a regional concentration of relevant capacities and even to absorb external competences into the internal corporate knowledge base. This again mirrors the fact that Auto1-G is not primarily interested in sustainable investments in regional strengths but in maximum exploitation, regional concentration and sometimes even in internalization of relevant knowledge.

Based on the strategic importance of the MNC for the region as a major employer and taxpayer, regional authorities accept the exploitative role of Auto1-G and arrange its regional surroundings accordingly. The region hence takes up technological topics that are of importance to the MNC and tries to accommodate and anticipate technological trends within the company.

> [This new technology] is of course somehow a bit of a spearhead for this region, because it's closely interlinked with automotives. We are an automobile city and hence naturally try to push forwards next generation technologies, because we know that they will be an important topic in the future. (Interview with employee in regional development, region Auto1-G: 7)

In order to foster regional dynamics relevant to Auto1-G, various regional networks and initiatives in relevant technological fields have emerged. They have the explicit vision of supporting SMEs and suppliers in the process of readjusting to the changing technological focus of Auto1-G:

> In connection with this new technology, we have a problem with the future. We as a rich region are endowed with this manifold automotive supply industry. How will this now change structurally if this technology changes the motor technology so fundamentally that we can talk of a fundamental revolution? . . . And hence, in this region, we have started a way of thinking which asks: How shall we, with our typical industrial culture, prepare ourselves for that? (Interview with head of scientific institute, region Auto1-G: 1)

There is a huge identification with the MNC and its focuses and latest strategies:

> The community and also the mayor identify with this. And from time to time, a delegate of a major political party drops in. There is also a certificate, signed by a minister, attesting the city a positive economic climate. There's a microclimate, that's simply part of things. (Interview with project manager, Auto1-G: 13)

Local universities establish special degrees that equip their graduates with competences in the new technological field, contributing to a dense infrastructure concentrating on this topic of interest for the MNC.

The case of regional problem solving hence reflects a huge imbalance. In a one-sided dependence, the RIS adapts to the MNC's needs. While the MNC regards the region as a pool of resources available for exploitation and internalization, the region allows itself to become dependent on Auto1-G. The region maintains its strength by investing in MNC-related infrastructure, with regional actors solving the problems defined by the company.

Regional problem solving reflects the region's decision to turn itself into a specialized pool of resources and rules for the dominant MNC. As this MNC is the central provider of labour, technological leadership, economic strength and even of reputation and identification for the region, this is not generally considered to be problematic. Instead, regional policies are focused on the industrial core of the region, despite the potential risks of such a strategy. The provision of external resources supports the MNC even though the company itself maintains a low-key approach: it does not need to get involved more closely. Everything that is relevant and necessary for MNC-internal activities is being created for it externally – a situation that reflects the dominant position of the company in the local economy. The MNC limits its own regional involvement by exploiting these specifically provided LCCGs but without investing in their evolution. Sometimes it even internalizes regional competences in order to back up its own global, non-regionalized strategy.

2.2.3   MNC-induced Problem Solving: MNCs as Regional Political Players

Contrary to the type of regional problem solving, the MNC itself can assume a driving role with regard to regional embeddedness. If it adopts an augmentative approach to its regional surroundings and treats them as a relevant entity for creating global competence, the MNC's interest in the region becomes more durable and sustainable. The MNC is then willing to invest in the region itself and to support the creation of a viable industrial atmosphere. If the region in turn conducts general industrial policies and provides general resources useful for a broad range of regional companies, this can be termed 'MNC-induced problem solving'. A company operating in the field of transportation provides a good example of such a case.

Transport-G takes an active interest in its regional surroundings and regards them as the focus of its strategic and industrial activities. It sees itself as responsible for forming the region to meet its own needs, for fostering activities in the relevant sector and for getting involved as closely as possible:

> There are a couple of engineering offices in the region which have evolved out of former Transport-G-areas. That's the usual procedure: Transport-G external-izes something. . . . It means, the colleagues are still there, they are just called differently. . . . You supply and nourish yourself, you somehow feed yourself. (Interview with electronics manager, Transport-G: 24–5)

Transport-G actively pushes former employees into leading positions in regional committees, with the explicit aim of maintaining an eye on regional political decisions as well as a say in such decisions. Furthermore, the MNC itself creates a regional policy network that engages in mutual dialogue and in enhancing the region's reputation. In this initiative Transport-G is the leading actor, even though it then purposefully steps back and involves regional political committees for the actual operation of its initiative:

> Transport-G bought all the shares, or financed all the shares, and then they gave 51 % of them to the municipality, and the university also got a part of it. (Interview with regional development employee, region Transport-G: 4)

While actively investing in the region and establishing regional institu-tions and rules itself, the MNC also seeks to draw on available regional resources. It buys from and cooperates with many regionally allocated firms. The following example shows how Transport-G designs a project to make it possible to use regional public subsidies.

> When choosing to do this with the university in Central Franconia, it was of course part of the considerations that it was a project financed by the Free State of Bavaria. And there were certain criteria to be met, so to speak, in order to get these funds at that point of time. . . . Of course such aspects also play a role, that it is being supported by public, political authorities and they want to strengthen regions and partly support that. (Doctorate engineer, Transport-G: 18)

With very similar dynamics and based on intense and far-reaching personal networks, Transport-G draws on complementary capabilities available in the nearby university. To foster such close relationships, Transport-G also establishes its own chairs at this university through former employees becoming involved in university teaching.

The region does not in turn shape its activities to meet the specific needs of Transport-G but maintains a more general focus that reflects the wide array of regional industrial activities. Start-up centres and general economic policies form the core of its programme. The region is also a European Metropolitan Region, an initiative regarded as a tool to enhance informal aspects of regional embeddedness, that is, to increase regional visibility and reputation.

However, the political focus on general regional infrastructure does not imply that it cannot fit Transport-G's needs. For example, the municipality gives the MNC support in how to draw on regional funds and a network initiative acts as a neutral mediator in recruiting additional partners for Transport-G's project.

> [The network initiative] has brought together the partners to be considered, and it has assumed a moderating role. And it has, above all, also collaborated in regard to the question whether the [federal state] should spend money on such a project or not. You just believe more of what an independent association tells you than what a company says, especially if the company has its own claims in it. (Interview with transportation cluster manager, region Transport-G: 1)

Based on the involvement of many players in regional policies and on the very informal basis of cooperation, redundancies emerge. Organization and coordination are not taken care of.

> There are projects carried through by the competence initiative, by the cluster. There are projects headed by regional development. It depends on where there is a trust relationship, where there are possibilities. From my point of view, it doesn't matter who conducts it. (Interview with head of regional development, region Transport-G: 6)

In this case the MNC and region follow different strategies but complement each other to a high degree. Transport-G acts as a political player that wants to get involved and the region is willing to have the MNC assume a shaping role. The region regards itself in turn as a host to the MNC's activities and its own contribution mainly refers to providing a reputation-oriented social interaction sphere. The MNC defines its involvement in the region as a way of shaping its own relevant surroundings. Based on its economic dominance, the region accepts the MNC as one of many political actors: although problems are defined among the MNC and region, it is up to the MNC to solve them.

What happens in this constellation is that the MNC itself creates and influences political activities, initiatives and networks in the region (at the incitement of the region, which we have termed elsewhere 'experimental regionalism'; cf. Heidenreich, 2005). In this sense the MNC redefines itself here as an actor that not only acts in economic and organizational spheres but also enters the field of political and social interaction in order to articulate its economic interests there. Transport-G does so by contributing to the creation of regional political institutions. For the region, this commitment of a dominant MNC is ambiguous. It is, of course, an asset to have a company bear risks and costs that would otherwise have to be assumed by regional politics. At the same time, regional authorities lose part of their political sovereignty and accept that an economically motivated actor takes part in decisions that follow a different set of logics. Therefore corporate-founded regional networks cannot fully substitute those created by independent regional actors, which in turn results in a multitude of uncoordinated, scattered and competing regional initiatives. Regional dynamics are hence lively and manifold but not always focused and neutral.

2.2.4   Mutual Problem Solving: the Development of Specialized Clusters

The embeddedness between an MNC and its regional environment is closer if both the MNC and regional policies choose a strategy of structured and institutionally stabilized cooperation and exchange. This case of 'mutual problem solving' occurs if the MNC invests in augmenting the assets in its regional surroundings, fostering the business climate and also getting involved in the political and scientific decisions of regional agencies. At the same time, the region reinforces the MNC's activities through the offer of coordinated regional resources and by creating opportunities for cooperation. Links between the MNC and its regional setting can become particularly strong, resembling a triple-helix-like structure with tight connections between universities, industry and governmental parties (cf. Etzkowitz, 2001). The following case of an automobile company illustrates these characteristics.

Auto2-G strongly shapes its regional surroundings. It is not only a member of various political and scientific committees and decision boards, but even establishes internal functions explicitly in charge of maintaining regional contacts. One of them is an official regional contact person. Additionally, a member of the board of directors is specifically responsible for the regional, active representation of the company. The company thus assumes responsibility for regional evolvement.

> Auto2-G is life donator for the region, and without Auto2-G the region would be finished. And on the other hand, Auto2-G also wants to represent a socially competent and good company. It has a somewhat familial relationship with the municipality, with the region. No-one in its surroundings would say: 'This is an exploiter!' (Interview with project leader, Auto2-G: 21)

In order to further increase regional viability, Auto2-G initiates a regional network at the political level, an idea explicitly aimed at achieving a higher level of interconnectedness between various municipalities in the region. This general idea of increasing the region's viability is in the MNC's interest as an indirect, future-oriented aspect of its internal operations. Similarly, Auto2-G encourages other MNCs to allocate nearby with the aim of creating complementary knowledge and also of easing the region's dependence on Auto2-G alone, hence anticipatorily preventing a lock-in situation. Auto2-G provides its own network opportunities.

The MNC's use of regional resources underlines its close links with the region. It fosters dense, long-established and intense relation networks to suppliers, subcontractors and service providers in the regional surroundings. In order to make the most of the close proximity of some partners, Auto2-G has established exclusive and preferential just-in-time supply mechanisms, the most visible being the shared use of transportation vehicles directly from the external suppliers onto the belts of Auto2-G's production (a 'logistical bridge'). Based on mainly local recruitment of employees, the identification of the company with its regional surroundings is extremely high.

In regard to scientific infrastructure, Auto2-G established its own university institute nearby which intensifies cooperation with the scientific world. The participating doctorate students work exclusively on Auto2-G's projects. This results in maximum interconnectedness between inner-corporate and scientific research topics. Furthermore, employees of the MNC teach seminars in the local university of applied sciences, backing up the corporate involvement in the steering committee of this scientific institution. The following quote illustrates how formal institutions back up regional embeddedness.

> Actually, Auto2-G could also get all of this another way, but not as effectively and not as elegantly and not as good in terms of efficiency. You can do this with universities that are further away, that's easily possible, and partly you can do that with your own research. The specific advantage here is that we have created framework conditions which are as simple and elegant as at all possible, and so we can fully concentrate on what we want to achieve with them in a very good context. (Interview with university professor, region Auto2-G: 16)

The region supports Auto2-G's activities in turn by providing complementary efforts. In order to make it easier for the MNC to establish lasting relationships with its regional partners, the municipality sets up mediating institutions, for example an industrial park structured exactly according to Auto2-G's specifications and needs. While the municipality assumes the risks and costs of this park, the MNC can formulate its expectations and requirements, which are then taken into account.

In order to facilitate even stronger embeddedness between Auto2-G and regionally allocated educational entities, the curriculum of the local university of applied sciences reflects the strength of Auto2-G and the importance of the automobile industry for the region.

> Those companies [allocated in the region] indirectly have a very strong influence, simply because history has shown that those universities that are strongly regionally rooted are the most successful ones. That is, it doesn't help you to offer study programmes in areas where we don't have companies in situ. . . . But the core has to fit into the region. (Interview with professor in the University of Applied Sciences, region Auto2-G: 18)

Additionally, the municipality establishes networks and platforms fostering industrial contacts, acting as a neutral mediator and connector between Auto2-G and other allocated companies. This is especially visible concerning small start-up firms where contacts can be granted via the involvement of a neutral third party.

> At that time, we had a company in [our start-up centre], an engineering company. And they wanted to get in touch with Auto2-G. And I knew that they wouldn't get access to them. So I said: 'What about that: You do an opening speech. And then the CEO of Auto2-G already has to listen. They are all sitting in the auditorium and you can take the stage and already introduce yourself.' And that's how we did it and it worked really well. This way, it's always possible to push contacts a little bit. (Interview with head of the start-up centre, region Auto2-G: 3)

In conclusion, the situation of mutual problem solving in this case is defined via interdependence and strong embeddedness. The MNC and region try to accommodate each other, meet each other's requirements and institutionalize their close links via formal contact persons backed up by personal networks. In this manner the evolution of a dense and specifically targeted regional infrastructure is mutually reinforced and turns into a circle of excellence. While the MNC regards the region as the backbone of its corporate viability, the region looks at Auto2-G as the elixir of life for its regional dynamics. The actors jointly define and solve problems, with their differing logics serving to back each other up: Auto2-G acts as a neutral networker between various communities and the municipality in turn provides neutral mediation between Auto2-G and its suppliers.

The structure we observe here is characterized by institutionalized, strong links between the corporate and regional systems. Both rely on each other and regard themselves as relevant for each other. However, this takes place without moving away from the inherent logics of the two systems. It is precisely their complementarity that makes the embeddedness beneficial. Based on this mutual understanding, the two systems not only both establish relevant structures for each other but actually build them jointly. This results in the orchestration of activities and helps to avoid redundancies, facilitated via a permanent dialogue between regional and corporate authorities. At the same time we can also observe that such a strong embeddedness between MNC and region is not very likely to be fully reciprocal. It is usually the MNC that defines the necessities, sets its claims and channels the regional development into the direction that best fits its own – in the end still economic – interests. Even if both the region and the company currently benefit from this close link, the economic decline of cities that once depended on one specific company points at the risk of a mutual lock-in. In addition, the difference between internal and external logics does not disappear. The example of a specific innovation project demonstrates this: in order to preserve proprietary knowledge, it was conducted completely within the company and did not incorporate regional partners at all (Heidenreich et al., 2012).

2.2.5 Summary

Based on a typology of regional embeddedness of MNCs, we have illustrated different patterns of regional coordination between companies and their regional surroundings in four case studies. Our findings show that embeddedness is by no means a uniform phenomenon. Instead, the four dimensions of regional integration identified in section 2.1 (see Table 2.1) do not always occur simultaneously but constitute a tool kit from which both MNCs and regional actors strategically extract selected bits and pieces to fit their needs. The resulting constellations are hence attempts to find a balance between the described advantages, challenges and risks of regional embedding. Table 2.2 summarizes the case study results.

On the basis of the empirical illustration of these ideal types, we were able to show that targeted industrial policy reflects the region's willingness to make itself dependent on the MNC or on a particular sector. In a similar vein, active involvement of the MNC in regional activities shows its disposition to establish global strength via local competences. If these two strategies of mutual consideration coincide, the two systems are coupled via strategies of 'mutual problem solving' (cf. also Forsgren et al., 2005). Regional investments then reinforce each other and induce a virtuous circle of competence development: both parties invest in the same direction, but as they do so jointly, they back each other up and reinforce each other's attempts. Kristensen and Zeitlin (2005: 317) analyse this constellation on the basis of Danish and Italian examples as 'engines of industrial

Table 2.2   Four types of regional embeddedness and their characteristics

Dimensions of regional embeddedness	Mutual non-interference (IT-G)	Regional problem solving (Auto1-G)	MNC-induced problem solving (Transport-G)	Mutual problem solving (Auto2-G)
Informal norms and rules	Selective personal contacts	Partly existent, but not decisive	Thick layer of personal contacts	Systematically developed as back-up for formal structures
Formal rules	No	Yes, mostly tailored to MNC	Partly as broad industrial policies	Yes, tailored to MNC's needs and very coordinated. Partly led by MNC itself
Institutional provision of resources	Only general goods (infra-structure etc.)	Targeted industrial policies provide MNC-tailored LCCGs	General goods that are strategically exploited by the MNC. MNC itself also provides regional goods	Targeted industrial policies provide MNC-tailored LCCGs. MNC itself also provides regional goods
Regional industrial networks	No	Cluster evolution, establishment of local subsidiaries of major suppliers	Cluster evolvement in the sector, exchange platforms initiated by MNC	Cluster evolvement in the sector, platforms and discussion networks

districts'. At the same time, this type of embeddedness intensifies the risk of local lock-ins based on very focused but not necessarily broad activities. Through the way these are applied, the differing underlying logics of MNCs and regions turn into an advantage.

Problems are, however, not always solved in such a close form of embeddedness. Instead, both MNCs and regions may also opt to solve their own problems in strategies of 'mutual non-interference' (1). In these cases a coordinated strategy of MNCs and other regional actors is difficult to develop and relatively unattractive. Such a combination can work well for all the participants: the MNC follows its global orientation and regional political actors take care of enhancing the general industrial dynamics for the region. Instead of facilitating each other's activities, subsidiaries focus on their roles in the corporate network and regional political actors on the development of a supportive broad industrial policy.

In contrast to these balanced strategies, embeddedness can also assume a non-reciprocal form. In these cases dominant problem solvers largely define the relevant joint issues and act accordingly in their own influence spheres. In 'regional problem solving' (2) the region dominantly provides integrating institutions and collective resources, anticipating the MNC's requirements and interests. On the other hand, in 'MNC-induced problem solving' the company acts as an additional political agent that not only tackles its own internal problems but also assumes responsibility and a dominant say in regional political evolvements. Both of these non-reciprocal forms of interaction easily result in parallel and inefficient institutions in which multiple actors initiate forms of interaction (networks, initiatives etc.) at the same time without being strongly bound to each other. The following conclusion will draw together the implications of these results.

2.3   CONCLUSIONS

Between regional and international business studies there is an emerging consensus that the innovativeness and competitiveness of companies might be increased by closer links between the MNC and its regional environment, especially by the utilization and advancement of context-specific, tacit knowledge in regional, institutionally stabilized communication and cooperation networks. A good regional infrastructure and innovative suppliers, buyers, customers and competitors are a considerable advantage in company-wide learning processes and in power and negotiation relations. The question remains open, however, as to if, how and to what extent MNCs also use the advantages of their regional embeddedness. As initially stated, the fundamental differences between internal and external networks and learning processes are ignored or underestimated. Our starting point is that regional and inner-organizational networks and the corresponding learning processes are fundamentally different and that their interrelationship can assume very different forms that are not fully grasped by simply talking of embeddedness. Based on insights from theories on international business and regional studies, we therefore described four dimensions of regional embeddedness and their respective advantages and disadvantages. In the next step we distinguished between exploitative and augmentative corporate strategies as well as between broad and targeted industrial policies. The combination of these alternatives resulted in four types of interaction between regional and organizational logics: mutual non-interference, regional problem solving, MNC-induced problem solving and mutual problem solving.

The relationship between MNCs and regions is hence complicated and demanding. The involved actors have to find a way of institutionalizing bonds between their different institutional frameworks but also need to find a common language in agreement with their distinct logics. The form of embeddedness that actually exists between the two systems depends on both the MNC's strategy in regard to its global or local orientation and on the focus of regional politics. It is not merely the company itself that decides about the strength, direction and content of integration.

These findings have important implications for the debate on regional embeddedness and learning in subsidiaries. We have to assess the interrelationship of MNCs and regions anew, starting from the assumption of its improbability in order to understand its difficulties and to avoid an overly optimistic picture of regional embeddedness. Although the use of regional resources and rules is certainly possible, it is not a necessary resource for MNCs, at least if the term is used in the broader sense to include not only relations with other economic organizations (suppliers, customers, competitors) but also scientific, educational, political and social actors in the region. Many of the processes that have been analysed as local embeddedness remain at arm's length and learning between various regional actors seems to occur less regularly than assumed in regional studies. The proclaimed 'free' regional spillovers are often not exploited in innovations. Regarding further research, we therefore need more studies on specific innovation projects that do not treat MNCs or regions as black boxes but instead provide concrete insights into the interaction between organizational and regional actors. This also suggests the need for closer collaboration between scholars working in regional and organizational sciences.

NOTES

1. The case studies upon which we draw in this chapter were performed within the framework of the project 'Regional Learning in Multinational Companies' (Mattes, 2010; Heidenreich et al., 2011). Interviews were conducted between May 2006 and August 2007 in the form of approximately ten interviews per subsidiary and per region. We would like to thank our interview partners as well as the Volkswagen Foundation for their support.
2. According to UNCTAD (2005: 119), 'the 700 largest R&D spending firms of the world – of which at least 98% are TNCs – accounted for close to half (46%) of the world's total R&D expenditure and more than two-thirds (69%) of the world's business R&D' in 2002. With $544 billion spent in 2007, the 1402 largest R&D spending firms of the world – which are also mostly MNCs – accounted for 61 per cent of the world's total R&D expenditure and 88 per cent of the world's business R&D (own calculations on the basis of OECD, 2009 and Guevara et al., 2009).

REFERENCES

Andersson, U., Forsgren, M. and Holm, U. (2002), 'The strategic impact of external networks: subsidiary performance and competence development in the multinational corporation', *Strategic Management Journal*, **23** (11): 979–96.

Andersson, U., Forsgren, M. and Holm, U. (2007), 'Balancing subsidiary influence in the federative MNC: a business network view', *Journal of International Business Studies*, **38**: 802–18.

Autio, E. (1998), 'Evaluation of RTD in regional systems of innovation', *European Planning Studies*, **6** (2): 131.

Bathelt, H., Malmberg, A. and Maskell, P. (2004), 'Clusters and knowledge: local buzz, global pipelines and the process of knowledge creation', *Progress in Human Geography*, **28** (1): 31–56.

Becker-Ritterspach, F., Saka-Helmhout, A. and Hotho, J.J. (2010) 'Learning in multinational enterprises as the socially embedded translation of practices', *Critical Perspectives on International Business*, **6** (1): 8–37.

Beckert, J. (2003) 'Economic sociology and embeddedness: how shall we conceptualize economic action?', *Journal of Economic Issues*, **37** (3): 769–87.

Boekholt, P. and Thuriaux, B. (1999), 'Public policies to facilitate clusters: background, rationale and policy practices in international perspective', in OECD (ed.), *Boosting Innovation: The Cluster Approach*, Paris: OECD, pp. 381–412.

Boschma, R.A. (2005), 'Proximity and innovation: a critical assessment', *Regional Studies*, **39** (1): 61–74.

Cantwell, J. (2009), 'Location and the multinational enterprise', *Journal of International Business Studies*, **40**: 35–41.

Cantwell, J. and Iammarino, S. (2003), *Multinational Corporations and European Regional Systems of Innovation*, London: Routledge.

Cantwell, J. and Mudambi, R. (2005), 'MNE competence-creating subsidiary mandates', *Strategic Management Journal*, **26** (12): 1109–28.

Chesbrough, H.W. (2003), *Open Innovation: The New Imperative for Creating and Profiting from Technology*, Boston, MA: Harvard Business School Press.

Cooke, P. (2002), *Knowledge Economies. Clusters, Learning and Cooperative Advantage*, London and New York: Routledge.

Dunning, J.H. and Lundan, S.M. (2008), *Multinational Enterprises and the Global Economy*, 2nd edn, Cheltenham, UK and Northampton, MA, USA: Edward Elgar.

Dunning, J.H. and Lundan, S.M. (2009), 'The internationalization of corporate R&D: a review of the evidence and some policy implications for home countries', *Review of Policy Research*, **26** (1–2): 13–33.

Enright, M.J. (2000), 'Regional clusters and multinational enterprises: independence, dependence or interdependence?', *International Studies of Management & Organization*, **30** (2): 114–38.

Etzkowitz, H. (ed.) (2001), *Universities and the Global Knowledge Economy. A Triple Helix of University–Industry–Government Relations*, London: Continuum.

Fligstein, N. (2001), 'Social skill and the theory of fields', *Sociological Theory*, **19**: 105–25.

Forsgren, M., Holm, U. and Johanson, J. (2005), *Managing the Embedded Multinational. A Business Network View*, Cheltenham, UK and Northampton, MA, USA: Edward Elgar.

Gerybadze, A. (2004), 'Knowledge management, cognitive coherence, and equivocality in distributed innovation processes in MNCs', *Management International Review*, **44** (3): 103–28.

Ghoshal, S. and Bartlett, C.A. (1990), 'The multinational corporation as an interorganizational network', *Academy of Management Review*, **15** (4): 603–25.

Granovetter, Mark (1985), 'Economic action and social structure. The problem of embeddedness', *American Journal of Sociology*, **91** (3): 481–510.

Guevara, H.H., Tübke, A. and Moncada-Paternò-Castello, P. (2009), *The 2009 EU Industrial R&D Investment Scoreboard*, Joint Research Centre, Institute for Prospective Technological Studies, Luxembourg: Office for Official Publications.

Häusler, J., Hohn, H.-W. and Lütz, S. (1994), 'Contingencies of innovative networks: a case study of successful interfirm R&D collaboration', *Research Policy*, **23**: 47–66.

Heidenreich, M. (2005), 'The renewal of regional capabilities. Experimental regionalism in Germany', *Research Policy*, **34** (5): 739–57.

Heidenreich, M., Barmeyer, C., Koschatzky, K., Mattes, J., Baier, E. and Krüth, K. (2012), *Multinational Enterprises and Innovation. Regional Learning in Networks*, London: Routledge.

Hess, M. (2004) '"Spatial" relationships? Towards a reconceptualization of embeddedness', *Progress in Human Geography*, **28** (2): 165–86.

Holm, U., Malmberg, A. and Sölvell, Ö. (2003), 'Subsidiary impact on host-country economies. The case of foreign-owned subsidiaries attracting investment into Sweden', *Journal of Economic Geography*, **3** (4): 389–408.

Holmqvist, M. (2003), 'A dynamic model of intra- and interorganizational learning', *Organization Studies*, **24** (1): 95–123.

Kogut, B. and Zander, I. (1993), 'Knowledge of the firm and the evolutionary theory of the multinational corporation', *Journal of International Business Studies*, **24** (6): 625–45.

Kostova, T., Roth, K. and Dacin, M.T. (2008) 'Institutional theory in the study of multinational corporations: a critique and new directions', *Academy of Management Review*, **33** (4): 994–1006.

Kristensen, P.H. and Zeitlin, J. (2005), *Local Players in Global Games. The Strategic Constitution of a Multinational Corporation*, Oxford: Oxford University Press.

Krugman, P. (1991), *Geography and Trade*, Cambridge, MA: MIT Press.

Kuemmerle, W. (1997), 'Building effective R&D capabilities abroad', *Harvard Business Review*, **75** (2): 61–70.

Kuemmerle, W. (1999), 'The drivers of foreign direct investment into research and development. An empirical investigation', *Journal of International Business Studies*, **30** (1): 1–24.

Kuemmerle, W. (2002), 'Home base and knowledge management in international ventures', *Journal of Business Venturing*, **17** (2): 99–122.

Le Galès, P. and Voelzkow, H. (2001), 'Introduction: the governance of local economies', in C. Crouch (ed.), *Local Production Systems in Europe. Rise or Demise?* Oxford: Oxford University Press, pp. 1–24.

Maskell, P. and Malmberg, A. (1999), 'Localised learning and industrial competitiveness', *Cambridge Journal of Economics*, **23** (2): 167–85.

Mattes, J. (2010) *Innovation in Multinational Companies: Organisational, International and Regional Dilemmas*, Bern et al.: Peter Lang.

Monteiro, L.F., Arvidsson, N. and Birkinshaw, J. (2008), 'Knowledge flows within multinational corporations. Explaining subsidiary isolation and its performance implications', *Organization Science*, **19** (1): 90–107.

OECD (2009), *Science, Technology and Industry Scoreboard. Innovation and Performance in the Global Economy*, Paris: OECD.

Peng, M.W., Sun, S.L., Pinkham, B. and Chen, H. (2009), 'The institution-based view as a third leg for a strategy tripod', *Academy of Management Perspectives*, **23** (4): 63–81.

Phene, A. and Almeida, P. (2008), 'Innovation in multinational subsidiaries: the role of knowledge assimilation and subsidiary capabilities', *Journal of International Business Studies*, **39** (5): 901–19.

Polanyi, K. (2001 [1957]), 'The economy as instituted process', in M.S. Granovetter and R. Swedberg (eds), *The Sociology of Economic Life*, 2nd edn, Boulder, CO: Westview Press, pp. 29–51.

Rugman, A.M. and Verbeke, A. (2008), 'Location, competitiveness, and the multinational enterprise', in A.M. Rugman and T.L. Brewer (eds), *The Oxford Handbook of International Business*, 2nd edn, New York: Oxford University Press, pp. 146–80.

Saxenian, A. (2006), *The New Argonauts: Regional Advantage in a Global Economy*, Cambridge, MA: Harvard University Press.

Storper, M. (2000), 'Globalization, localization, and trade', in G.L. Clark, M.P. Feldman and M.S. Gertler (eds), *The Oxford Handbook of Economic Geography*, Oxford: Oxford University Press, pp. 147–65.

United Nations Conference on Trade and Development (UNCTAD) (2005), *World Investment Report 2005, Transnational Corporations and the Internationalization of R&D*, New York and Geneva: UN.

Weick, K. (1976), 'Educational organizations as loosely coupled systems', *Administrative Science Quarterly*, **21** (1): 1–19.

Westney, D.E. and Zaheer, S. (2001), 'The multinational enterprise as an organization', in A.M. Rugman and T.L. Brewer (eds), *The Oxford Handbook of International Business*, New York: Oxford University Press, pp. 349–79.

3. The multi-home-based corporation: solving an insider–outsider dilemma

Örjan Sölvell

3.1 INTRODUCTION

Today most goods, services and factors of production, including capital, technology and skilled people, face global competition. Globalization has allowed for sliced-up value chains, where materials, components and products criss-cross world markets. A steel leg for a chair might begin in Sweden, go to the UK for assembly, go back to central warehousing in Sweden, and then return to the UK to be sold in the store. International transactions are carried out through efficient export–import markets, but a substantial part of global flows is managed by multinational corporations (MNCs). MNCs control networks of subsidiaries and manage webs of alliance partners and contract partners across the world. Thus the modern MNC is entangled in global value chains, with both in-house units and external partners carrying out headquarter (HQ) functions (strategy, legal, finance, human resource, public relations, communication, branding), R&D, design and engineering, manufacturing (components, subsystems, final products) and assembly/packaging, procurement, logistics and warehousing, and sales and service operations in multiple locations. Some units are highly integrated into a global whole, whereas other units are given considerable autonomy. Sometimes subsidiary units controlling strategic resources and capabilities, such as headquarter functions and/ or R&D, are given the status of 'centers of excellence' (see Holm and Pedersen, 2000, and Birkinshaw and Hood, 1998 for overviews), where subsidiaries take on, or are given, roles outside the confines of the local market. Such center mandates are typically driven by both internal and external factors (Frost et al., 2002).

Parallel to increased globalization we have also witnessed a process leading to an increasingly strategic role for particular regional/local environments, that is, world-class clusters. Clusters have become hotspots for innovation and economic prosperity. In a world of global flows the 'Hollywoods' or 'Silicon Valleys' of the world have increased their attraction for mobile resources – including talented people (students, researchers, entrepreneurs, inventors and other skilled people), technologies/patents, venture capital, portfolio investments and, last but not least, foreign direct investment (FDI) from MNCs. The more it is possible for resources and capabilities to move around the globe, the more specialized and differentiated we expect the world to become. Whereas certain regions and clusters will erode in this process, others will attract resources, leading to continued cluster growth and competitiveness. These structural changes create challenges for the modern MNC, which must handle both globalization and localization forces in order to stay on the competitive edge.

The modern MNC is often conceptualized as a collection of globally dispersed units possessing distinctive competences and knowledge (Cantwell, 1991b; Madhok, 1997). We would argue that one of the main strategic challenges facing top management in today's MNCs is to configure and coordinate resources and competences in such a way that the efficiency of global markets is combined with innovativeness and knowledge creation emanating from world-leading clusters (Mattes, 2006; Sölvell, 2003). Important strategic and organizational choices emerge: should more strategic subsidiary units be tightly interconnected or should the MNC allow for independent functional centers of excellence or even multiple home bases? Can the global firm tap capabilities and technologies from afar or must the MNC invest (e.g. through mergers and acquisitions – M&A) to become an insider in leading clusters? And what are the organizational implications of increased 'insiderization' into host clusters – will fully embedded units fit into a globally integrated MNC or is a dilemma perhaps emerging?

With parallel globalization and localization forces at play, MNCs face numerous strategic and organizational choices. MNCs typically benefit from globalization, selling their products worldwide and utilizing standardized markets for factors of production to enhance the overall efficiency of the firm. In addition to enhancing economies of scale, MNCs utilize global markets to access standardized low-cost labor through offshoring and sourcing of codified technology (through licensing and other agreements), financial capital and other tradable resources.

Localization forces, on the other hand, seem to be more challenging to corporate management. Tapping locally bound capabilities and gaining access to local networks from afar pose many challenges to an outsider but can be selectively tapped, for example through scanning units in host clusters (Sölvell and Zander, 1995). Some argue that MNCs can not only tap selectively but also have the ability to tap any resource or capability in every location. However, as we will expand on further below, an insider–outsider dilemma can arise for an MNC that utilizes global markets for innovation purposes. More critical technologies and skills are often not traded globally for competitive reasons and cannot be easily tapped from afar, due to their embeddedness and tacit nature (Malmberg et al., 1996). In order to circumvent these problems, MNCs can choose to build insider positions in clusters through long-term greenfield investment or M&A. However, with increased 'insiderization' of the subsidiary unit, a counterforce of 'outsiderization' is likely to emerge when subsidiaries control strategic and often unique resources and capabilities within the MNC (Sölvell and Zander, 1998).

In this chapter we postulate that there is a flaw in the popular argument that capabilities, knowledge and technology are now 'global goods' (Reiner and Halme, 2009), and that therefore innovation is a global process. Innovation processes cannot be equated with global value chains of standardized components, goods and services. In other words, the analysis of MNCs and their levels of efficiency and competitiveness should be separated from their innovation processes and degree of innovativeness. Furthermore, this chapter will propose a general model of the global MNC, encompassing both globalization and localization aspects: the multi-home-based corporation (MHC). The MHC solution, we argue, can mitigate the dilemma of increased insiderization in host clusters, leading to increased outsiderization of subsidiary units within the overall MNC.

3.2 GLOBALIZATION AND AN INCREASED ROLE OF CLUSTERS

In most industries today global markets offer a road to enhanced efficiency through improved economies of scale in varying parts of the value chain. Depending on homogeneity of demand, trade restrictions, transportation costs and homogenization of technology, global sales can involve more or less local adaptation and design, and more or less dispersion of packaging, assembly, testing and full production. The more a firm faces one homogeneous market with few or no trade barriers, and the lower the transportation costs (e.g. through digital media), the more one global source for development and production can be used. However, in many industries today fragmenting forces still prevail, forcing MNCs to run dispersed operations and often reducing some of the potential for global-scale advantages. However, for some scholars this element of localization is only a matter of time and the 'death of distance' is just around the corner (Cairncross, 2000). We would instead argue that with increased globalization, allowing for increased mobility of resources and capabilities around the world, an increased proliferation of clusters will follow, that is, an increased role for localization. Localization is thus not a counterforce to globalization; the two sets of forces are complementary.

Clusters are dynamic arrangements based on knowledge creation and innovation in a broad sense. Clusters are not only made up of physical flows of inputs and outputs, but also consists of intense exchange of business information, know-how and technological expertise in both traded and untraded forms. Such technological spillovers (Griliches, 1992) were at the core of Marshall's (1920) analysis in the early twentieth century but had been mostly forgotten until Paul Krugman (Krugman, 1991) and Michael Porter (Porter, 1990, 2003) brought them to the fore in the early 1990s. Several studies have confirmed knowledge externalities in clusters (Audretsch and Feldman, 1996; Jaffe et al., 1993).

The level of dynamism in clusters, such as the amount of and quality of linkages between cluster actors and external linkages to international markets, varies from cluster to cluster and within a cluster over time. Some agglomerations are more on the static side, that is, the 'Silicon Glens' as opposed to the more dynamic 'Silicon Valleys'. The level of networking and organization of collective action, factor mobility and general dynamism differs enormously across clusters. The level of sophistication also differs in that some clusters on the world scene are more oriented towards producing low-cost goods (e.g. the automotive cluster in Dogu Marmara, Turkey), while others offer highly differentiated products (e.g. the automotive cluster in southern Germany), including R&D, design and branding. If the quality of resources differs within a region, so does the flexibility with which the pieces can be assembled and reassembled. Similar to a Chinese puzzle, the shape of each component plays a role but it is also how the pieces fit together and how they are constantly rearranged to improve the productivity of available resources that is important (see Figure 3.1).

The main economic benefits for firms situated within clusters, as

Figure 3.1   Clusters facilitate easy and creative reshuffling of resources

outlined by Marshall (Marshall, 1920), include access to related industries (upstream and downstream), specialized pools of labor, efficient utilization of specialized machinery and technological spillovers (for recent overviews see Beaudry and Schiffauerova, 2009 and Lindqvist, 2009). Clusters offer resource and capability flexibility, creating the foundation for sophisticated firm strategies and for upgrading and innovation among incumbent firms. In summary:

1. Firms in dynamic clusters develop strategies, routines across the value chain and new capabilities in a process of prestigious back-yard rivalry.
2. Firms in clusters tend to share many activities involving innovative activities through cooperation. Clusters enhance the utilization of resource complementarities within a setting of a 'common language', trust and high social capital.
3. Firms in rich clusters can operate more efficiently, drawing on specialized assets, suppliers and buyers with short lead times. Critical resources and capabilities are often not within the firm but accessible through networks inside the cluster.
4. Firms in clusters can achieve higher levels of knowledge creation and innovation. Knowledge spillovers and close day-to-day interaction between buyers, suppliers and organizations lead to incremental improvements that form the foundation of both technical (product and process improvements) and non-technical innovations (business model improvements). Innovations diffuse fast within clusters.
5. Clusters offer a flexible environment where different resources (individuals, technologies, capital etc.) can be quickly reshuffled and restructured (spin-offs, labor mobility transferring skills across organizations etc.), allowing for new and better economic combinations of skills, capital and technology. The need for changing the strategy or recipe of the firm can be quickly accommodated within the cluster.
6. Clusters offer an environment where 'regional white spaces' can be quite easily organized (activities linking cluster actors such as firms, universities and public bodies), enhancing collective action and building a commons.
7. New business formation tends to be higher in dynamic clusters. Startups are reliant on close interaction with suppliers and buyers. The cost of failure is typically lower within a cluster where many alternative opportunities exist.
8. Clusters in many cases offer lead markets where sophisticated buyers pull technology development and innovation in close interaction with local suppliers.

The outcomes of firms, as manifested in the output of goods and services, will vary from cluster to cluster. There is no question that cars from Japan compete in the global marketplace with cars from Germany or the USA, and increasingly, Japanese-built cars in the USA compete with American cars built in Mexico. However, global markets are one thing and local clusters another. Products from one cluster will 'taste and smell' different from products from another cluster. They will cater to different consumer tastes; they will exhibit differences in cost levels, quality, features, energy efficiency and so on. MNCs have an important agenda in configuring strategic activities in relation to the strengths and weaknesses of different clusters around the world within their fields of technology.

3.3   FOUR STRATEGY ELEMENTS FACED BY THE MNC AND THREE SOLUTIONS

In a world of increased competitive pressures MNCs not only need to improve their operational efficiencies and cost position, that is, their competitiveness, but also to sustain and enhance their innovativeness. Global markets are central for an MNC's cost position, while insider positions in clusters are central for innovation processes, especially in open innovation processes where links to external actors, including users, are crucial. In the classic economics sense firms are competitive when they face relatively lower input costs (land, energy, taxes, wages etc.) compared to competitors in other nations. According to this view, government subsidies, favorable access to natural endowments and currency depreciation make indigenous firms more competitive. While such advantages are important to MNCs, increased competitiveness constitutes only a minor part of the fundamentals of sustaining competitive advantage. Sustained competitive advantage is first and foremost built on the firm's ability to continuously upgrade and create new products and processes to meet changes in demand, competition, and technology. Therefore MNCs must take both competitiveness and innovativeness into account as they configure and coordinate units around the world.

If we combine the two dimensions of efficiency-seeking and innovation-seeking strategies with global and local outlooks as outlined above, we obtain a matrix with four corners (see Figure 3.2), each representing a critical strategy element. The upper left-hand corner involves innovativeness emanating from clusters. The upper right-hand corner focuses on innovation as a global process, often referred to as the transnational solution, combining resources and capabilities from several locations. Here, tapping resources and capabilities in host locations is not seen to

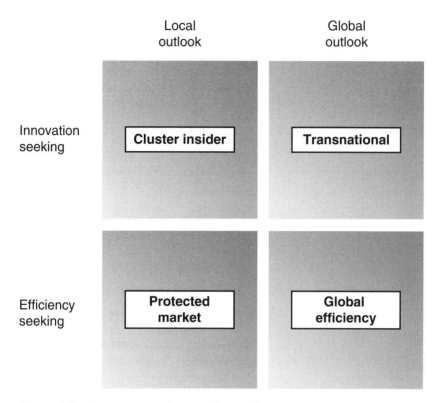

Local
outlook

Global
outlook

Innovation
seeking

Cluster insider

Transnational

Efficiency
seeking

Protected
market

Global
efficiency

Figure 3.2   Four strategy elements facing the MNC

pose severe problems. The lower left-hand corner covers strategies of cost efficiency with emphasis on the home market (often true for MNCs from large home markets), and the lower right-hand corner covers global efficiency and global cost leadership.

MNCs tend to combine different elements of the matrix and we will point to three important baseline models, each combining two elements. Two of these models are found in the mainstream literature on MNCs and the third is identified as a possible emergent model.

3.3.1   The Multi-domestic MNC

Leading MNCs from small home countries have been very successful in achieving high levels of competitiveness through global markets. By selling their products and systems across international markets they have been able to exploit advantages of scale comparable to firms from larger markets. MNCs from smaller countries have gradually managed

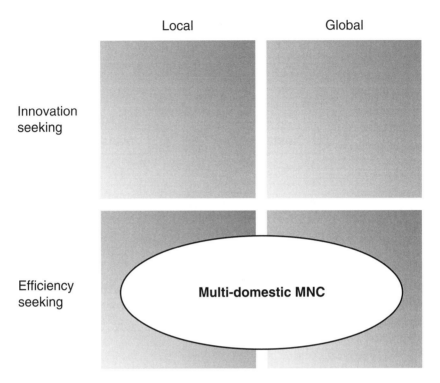

Figure 3.3   The multi-domestic MNC

to achieve further gains in cost-effectiveness by establishing assembly and production units in larger markets, sometimes also for reasons of protectionism or government demands. Instead of carrying one flag, these MNCs carry many flags and have many 'homes' (Zander, 1997). The strategy has been characterized as multi-domestic when the MNC seeks to combine efficiencies of global and local markets. In manufacturing industries, core components and subsystems are produced at a global scale in just a few locations, whereas assembly and local adaptation are performed on a country-by-country basis. Global outsourcing of products and components has also been a central feature of multi-domestic MNCs (see Figure 3.3).

3.3.2   The Transnational Corporation (TNC)

The transnational model (Figure 3.4) emerged as an answer to increased globalization. With the advent of more sophisticated MNCs in the 1980s, the model then included highly dispersed networks of subsidiaries

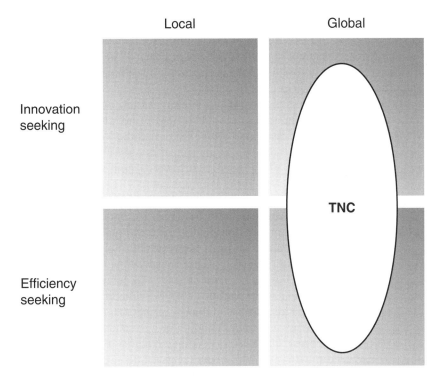

Figure 3.4   The transnational corporation (TNC)

(Bartlett and Ghoshal, 1989). A central feature of the model is that it not only involves global efficiency-seeking but also global innovation and tapping for global reach (Bartlett and Ghoshal, 1986).

The primary concern of the TNC strategy is how to foster the development and integration of internationally dispersed resources and capabilities on a worldwide scale. Exactly how TNCs should go about learning and creating new practices on a global scale was mainly theoretically derived and has been underpinned only by case studies. It is rather remarkable that in spite of the lack of empirical support, the transnational model has become mainstream within the international business field. A few empirical studies have tried to penetrate the issues of cross-border learning and transfer of skills on a broader basis, exposing the weaknesses of the model (de Meyer, 1992; Gerybadze and Reger, 1999). Innovation and the creation of new knowledge in cross-border settings tend to be costly and involve delays in time-to-market for new products (for a discussion of this see Sölvell and Zander, 1995).

In spite of their intuitive attractiveness, we would argue that transnational strategies have proven problematic. Attempts within TNCs to create new solutions through global teams have turned out to be miscalculations as a result of high costs and major delays (Ridderstråle, 1997). To learn and share across the globe is appealing but it involves large costs and organizational barriers.

We would argue that the majority of international business scholars today point to the advantages of global strategies and structures akin to the transnational model. Even though we see few studies of these globally linked innovators, many scholars argue that it is only a matter of time and of the sophistication of the MNC. However, a number of traditionally underemphasized factors should be considered when assessing the degree to which global innovation is or may become a major force in the MNC. First, the introduction of internationally integrated innovation projects requires the implementation of systems that reward involvement in projects that are temporary and fall between national organizational entities. These systems seem hard to come by spontaneously and many managers we have met testify that involvement in temporary projects without an organizational home does not help individual careers. Second, the cross-border context also adds complexity in that dispersed units tend to have their own identity and understanding of what constitutes an effective development process. Unless projects that cut across different national units are carried out with regular frequency, these differences will continue to have a negative effect on inter-unit collaboration and the effectiveness of cross-border innovation. Third, an important part of local knowledge creation and innovation is context dependent and therefore the absorptive capacity of other units of the MNC is limited (Foss and Pedersen, 2002). Fourth, at least one study suggests that information processing in the modern multinational is not necessarily based on objective data (Arvidsson, 1999) and thus the difficulties involved in agreeing what skills reside where and the lack of willingness to share it among subsidiaries (the not-invented-here (NIH) syndrome) will hamper any attempts at global innovation.

3.3.3 Multi-home-based Corporation (MHC)

The MHC model builds on the notion that innovation is a highly complex and localized process, and that corporate units (both local firms and MNC subsidiaries) in various ways are entangled within their local clusters (Malmberg et al., 1996). Clusters range from globally competitive to more regional ones and for MNCs it is critical to have major operations in world-leading clusters in their fields of technology. The model also builds on the notion that in order to stay competitive it is not enough to assign

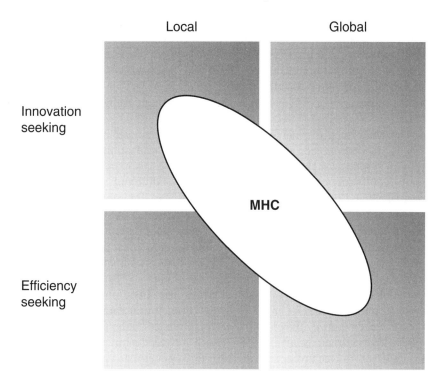

Figure 3.5   The multi-home-based corporation (MHC)

a center of excellence status along functional lines to particular subsidiaries (see discussion of subsidiary R&D roles in Ronstadt, 1978; Nobel and Birkinshaw, 1998). The MHC tends to co-locate strategic resources (divisional HQ functions, divisional R&D, design, manufacturing etc.) into home bases. Just as firms once emerged in their home market and built a home base for further expansion, the MHC model takes this one level further and combines the MNC into a set of rather autonomous divisional home bases (the role of the home base for MNCs was first discussed by Porter, 1986, and the multi-home-based model by Sölvell et al., 1991). We would hypothesize that this model is more attractive for MNCs from smaller home countries, where the original home base (i.e. home market) never had such a strong influence.

The strategy for success in an MHC is both to ensure innovativeness through insider positions in one or more leading clusters and to ensure efficiency by means of a global strategy for production, sourcing and sales (Figure 3.5). As most MNCs are diversified to a certain degree, each line of business needs to find its home base. These home bases become more or less independent centers, developing their own strategies and organizational models. The home base unit (with business HQ, R&D, design and in manufacturing industries core manufacturing operations) plays a global role. In addition, organizational resources, including sales subsidiaries and local partners involved in market penetration, are spread around the world to ensure maximum competitiveness through global efficiency and scale.

The MHC is a distinct model implying a certain set of strategic and organizational choices. It is different from the multi-domestic model in that it emphasizes the role of innovation. It is also different from the traditional home-country MNC as it allows for different home bases, not necessarily in the original home country. It is also different from the transnational model in that it downplays globally linked innovation projects and intense skill transfers and cross-country combinations. Instead of building more and more complex organizational forms, in order to integrate complicated processes of innovation around the world, the MHC model puts emphasis on simple organizational structures, with clear home bases for each line of business and a strict hierarchy between strategic activities critical for innovativeness (home base) and other activities critical for enhanced efficiency and competitiveness (sales subsidiaries and externally contracted partners). If there is a need for interaction between home bases, for technological or customer support reasons, the bases can be organized in such a way that dependences become sequential and each base has a clear mandate, for example for a part of the value chain. Simple interfaces are important in the MHC model to ensure that the baton is efficiently handed over.

It is often argued that MNCs invest abroad as a way to tap knowledge from local business contexts and that the competitive success of the MNC can be explained by its ability to accumulate and integrate knowledge from different parts of the world (Cantwell, 1991a; Dunning, 1988). One would thus argue that with increased tapping of world-leading clusters, the modern MNC would not need any particular home bases. There are many studies showing increased levels of foreign patenting (Zander, 1997; Almeida, 1996; Pearce, 1994; Cantwell, 1993). That could be interpreted to signify that knowledge creation in the MNC is now global. However, nothing is said as to whether (1) the new knowledge was later successfully exploited throughout the MNC and (2) the new knowledge was the result of cross-border innovation and learning. If the answers to these two questions are negative, foreign patenting can be interpreted as a result of home bases, particularly if there is little or no overlap in the patenting (i.e. technologies) across subsidiary units, a result that was shown by Zander (1997).

Figure 3.6   Two dimensions of cluster and corporate insiders/outsiders

3.3.4   Solving a Dilemma

The main argument for configuring and coordinating the MNC along the MHC model is to solve an apparent dilemma. Take the following example. A multinational firm is entering a foreign market and has developed some local sales and service capabilities. The subsidiary unit has the clear target of penetrating the market. Technology and strategic resources reside elsewhere in the MNC. In Figure 3.6 we would find this unit in the lower right-hand corner, depicted as an outsider in the host cluster and an insider within the corporation.

The outsider position in the host business environment means that the subsidiary and its staff are not part of core networks (social clubs etc.) and are less likely to be involved in innovation processes in the host cluster. For example, a European sales subsidiary in Tokyo for a car make is not at all integrated into the automotive clusters of Japan, including the famous 'Toyota City'. Over time the world's leading MNCs have built insider positions across a range of countries, either through long-term greenfield investments or through M&A. It is common in high-technology areas for world leaders to acquire smaller companies in leading clusters to access new technology and new customers.

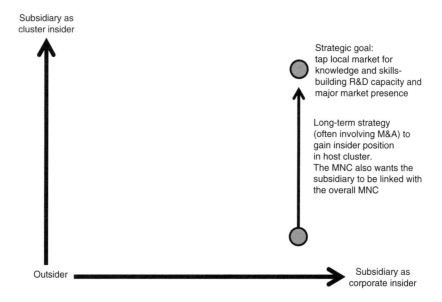

Figure 3.7   Building an insider position in a host cluster

So far this seems fairly unproblematic. Through increased commitment in the host country the MNC builds more of an insider position, opening up the potential for tapping host technology and skills (see Figure 3.7). To be an insider in a host cluster is essential to enjoy spillovers and the MNC will end up with embedded subsidiaries controlling unique capabilities and resources (Andersson et al., 2001, 2002). However, as has been argued by Sölvell and Zander (1998), subsidiary units possessing unique technologies, resources and capabilities are likely to build semi-autonomous positions within the corporation (see the four arguments against globally linked innovation processes in conjunction with the TNC model discussed above). To share and link units in various ways becomes more problematic and often involves increased coordination costs. We thus expect such embedded subsidiary units to end up in the upper left-hand corner rather than in the sought-after upper right-hand corner (Figure 3.8).

IBM can be seen as an example of what we mean by the MHC model. When the company was more of a technology and product firm, some technologies and products were based in the USA (mainframes), whereas others were concentrated in China (laptops). The laptop business was sold out to Chinese Lenovo in 2005. As a software and service company, IBM now has several bases, again one of which is in China.

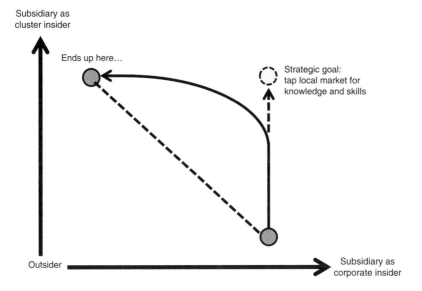

Figure 3.8   The insider–outsider dilemma

The IBM China Research Laboratory in Zhongguancun Software Park, in Beijing's academic cluster, specializes in speech and language technologies as well as cross-border e-business solutions for the whole of IBM.

In cases involving large mergers (Astra merging with Zeneca, Merck & Co. with Schering-Plough, Siemens with Nokia in the telecom network business etc.) we often have a duplication of home bases (R&D centers, regional HQ units etc.). With the MHC model we expect to see that duplication will diminish when certain units, often through a process of internal competition, become stronger and others weaker. Product and technology mandates are shifted around to facilitate simplification and leadership is transferred to one base. Finally we expect that the MHC model to be more common in industries where there are clear world-leading clusters, that is, 'Hollywoods', where the MHC model is an attempt to solve the insider–outsider dilemma presented above. There are of course advantages and disadvantages with such a strategy and organizational model but in the world of global competition facing MNC executives today we argue that this model has a great deal to offer in ensuring both high levels of efficiency and innovativeness. Maybe MNCs from small home countries with a less dominating original home base have been more prone to the MHC model and can thus act as inspiring examples.

REFERENCES

Almeida, P. (1996), 'Knowledge sourcing by foreign multinationals: patent citation analysis in the US semiconductor industry', *Strategic Management Journal*, **17**: 155–65.

Andersson, U., Forsgren, M. and Holm, U. (2001), 'Subsidiary embeddedness and competence development in MNCs – a multi level analysis', *Organization Studies*, **22**: 1013–34.

Andersson, U., Forsgren, M. and Holm, U. (2002), 'The strategic impact of external networks: subsidiary performance and competence development in the multinational corporation', *Strategic Management Journal*, **23**: 979–96.

Arvidsson, N. (1999), *The Ignorant MNE – The Role of Perception Gaps in Knowledge Management*, doctoral dissertation, Institute of International Business, Stockholm School of Economics.

Audretsch, D. and Feldman, M. (1996), *Location, Location, Location: The Geography of Innovation and Knowledge Spillovers*, Berlin: Wissenschaftszentrum für Sozialforschung, Forschungsschwerpunkt Marktprozeß und Unternehmensentwicklung.

Bartlett, C. and Ghoshal, S. (1986), 'Tap your subsidiaries for global reach', *Harvard Business Review*, **64**: 87–94.

Bartlett, C. and Ghoshal, S. (1989), *Managing Across Borders. The Transnational Solution*, Boston, MA: Harvard Business School Press.

Beaudry, C. and Schiffauerova, A. (2009), 'Who's right, Marshall or Jacobs? The localization versus urbanization debate', *Research Policy*, **38**: 318–37.

Birkinshaw, J. and Hood, N. (1998), *Multinational Corporate Evolution and Subsidiary Development*, London: Macmillan.

Cairncross, F. (2000), *The Death of Distance: How the Communications Revolution will Change our Lives*, Boston, MA: Harvard Business Press.

Cantwell, J. (1991a), 'A survey of theories of international production', in C. Pitelis and R. Sugden (eds), *The Nature of the Transnational Firm*, London: Routledge, pp. 16–63.

Cantwell, J. (1991b), 'The international agglomeration of R&D', in M. Casson (ed.), *Global Research Strategy and International Competitiveness*, Oxford: Basil Blackwell, pp. 104–32.

Cantwell, J. (1993), 'Corporate technological specialisation in international industries', in M.C. Casson and J. Creedy (eds), *Industrial Concentration and Economic Inequality*, Aldershot, UK and Brookfield, US: Edward Elgar, pp. 216–32.

de Meyer, A. (1992), 'Management of international R&D operations', in O. Granstrand, L. Håkanson and S. Sjölander (eds), *Technology Management and International Business. Internationalization of R&D and Technology*, New York: John Wiley & Sons, pp. 163–79.

Dunning, J.H. (1988), 'The eclectic paradigm of international production: a restatement and some possible extensions', *Journal of International Business Studies* (Spring), 1–31.

Foss, N.J. and Pedersen, T. (2002), 'Transfer of knowledge in MNCs: the role of sources of subsidiary knowledge and organizational context', *Journal of International Management*, **8**: 49–67.

Frost, T., Birkinshaw, J. and Ensign, P.C. (2002), 'Centers of excellence in multinational corporations', *Strategic Management Journal*, **23**: 997–1018.

Gerybadze, A. and Reger, G. (1999), 'Globalization of R&D: recent changes in the management of innovation in transnational corporations', *Research Policy*, **28**: 251–74.

Griliches, Z. (1992), 'The search for R&S spillovers', *Scandinavian Journal of Economics*, **94**: 29–47.

Holm, U. and Pedersen, T. (eds) (2000), *The Emergence and Impact of MNC Centres of Excellence – A Subsidiary Perspective*, London: Macmillan.

Jaffe, A.B., Trajtenberg, M. and Henderson, R. (1993), 'Geographic localization of knowledge spillovers as evidenced by patent citations', *The Quarterly Journal of Economics*, **108** (3): 577–98.

Krugman, P. (1991), *Geography and Trade*, Cambridge, MA: MIT Press.

Lindqvist, G. (2009), 'Disentangling clusters – agglomeration and proximity effects', unpublished doctoral dissertation, Center for Strategy and Competitiveness, Stockholm School of Economics.

Madhok, A. (1997), 'Cost, value and foreign market entry mode: the transaction and the firm', *Strategic Management Journal*, **18** (1): 39–61.

Malmberg, A., Sölvell, Ö. and Zander, I. (1996), 'Spatial clustering, local accumulation of knowledge and firm competitiveness', *Geografiska Annaler*, **78B** (2): 85–97.

Marshall, A. [1890] (1920), *Principles of Economics*, 8th edn, Book IV, London: Macmillan.

Mattes, J. (2006), 'Innovation in multinational companies – an empirical analysis of innovation networks between globalisation and localization', *Bamberger Beiträge zur Europaforschung und zur internationalen Politik*, 14.

Nobel, R. and Birkinshaw, J. (1998), 'Innovation in multinational corporations: control and communication patterns in international R&D operations', *Strategic Management Journal*, **19**: 479–96.

Pearce, R.D. (1994), 'The internationalization of research and development by multinational enterprises and the transfer sciences', *Empirica*, **21**: 297–311.

Porter, M.E. (1990), *The Competitive Advantage of Nations*, New York: The Free Press.

Porter, M.E. (2003), 'The economic performance of regions', *Regional Studies*, **37**: 549–78.

Reiner, R. and Halme, K. (2009), 'Open innovation in a globalised world – implications for innovation policies in Europe', Working Paper presented at the INNO-Views Policy Workshop.

Ridderstråle, J. (1997), *Global Innovation – Managing International Innovation Projects in ABB and Electrolux*, doctoral dissertation, Stockholm: Institute of International Business, Stockholm School of Economics.

Ronstadt, R.C. (1978), 'International R&D: the establishment and evolution of research and development abroad by seven U.S. multinationals', *Journal of International Business Studies*, **9**: 7–24.

Sölvell, Ö. (2003), 'The multi-home based multinational: combining global competitiveness and local innovativeness', in J. Birkinshaw, S. Ghoshal, C. Markides, J. Stopford and G. Yip (eds), *The Future of the Multinational Company*, Hoboken, NJ: John Wiley and Sons, pp. 34–44.

Sölvell, Ö., Zander, I. and Porter, M.E. (1991), *Advantage Sweden*, Stockholm: Norstedts Juridik.

Sölvell, Ö. and Zander, I. (1995), 'The dynamic multinational firm', *International Studies of Management & Organization*, **25**, (1–2): 17–38.

Sölvell, Ö. and Zander, I. (1998), 'International diffusion of knowledge: isolating mechanisms and the role of the MNE', in A.D. Chandler, Jr, P. Hagström and Ö. Sölvell (eds), *The Dynamic Firm*, Oxford: Oxford University Press, pp. 402–16.

Zander, I. (1997), 'Technological diversification in the multinational corporation – historical trends and future prospects', *Research Policy*, **26**: 209–27.

4. MNCs between the local and the global: knowledge bases, proximity and distributed knowledge networks

Bjørn T. Asheim, Bernd Ebersberger and Sverre J. Herstad

4.1 INTRODUCTION

The present stage of economic globalization is characterized by the emergence of widely distributed production and innovation networks (Coe et al., 2008; Gereffi et al., 2005; Sturgeon, 2003). These involve complex constellations of collaboration between independent enterprises and the globalization of R&D and innovation controlled administratively within the realm of multinational enterprises (UNCTAD, 2005). The key component in this is technological asset development and control, that is, knowledge and its diverse properties and geographies. However, research has yet to disentangle the relationship between basic characteristics of knowledge and the internationalization of innovation. For the purpose of theoretical conceptualization, this chapter links research on different industrial knowledge bases with research on the internationalization of innovation by means of MNC activity and external networking. For the purpose of first-step empirical analysis, we have used Norwegian community innovation survey data to investigate the following research questions:

1. To what extent are different knowledge bases and MNC affiliations associated with different degrees of spatial dispersion of innovation collaboration?
2. To what extent does presence in a foreign region by means of a daughter subsidiary influence the diversity of collaborative relationships maintained by Norwegian enterprises in the same foreign region?
3. To what extent is the impact of subsidiary presence contingent on the knowledge base of the firm?

4.2   MULTINATIONAL COMPANIES

Research within economics and political science has traditionally studied globalization as a process entailing the emergence of global supply chain linkages, driven by the availability of low-cost production in developing countries that can be linked to mass markets in developed countries. The ability to administratively coordinate activities across different national economies has led to multinational companies being assigned a key role in the development of these linkages. Two trends necessitate 'opening up' this focus. First, increasing product complexity, innovation-based competition and rates of technological change entail a shift away from innovation that relies primarily on the internal knowledge bases of firms or corporations towards innovation that becomes embedded in globally distributed knowledge networks. These may extend far beyond supply chain and MNC linkages. Recent empirical studies suggest that the ability to embed in such networks on an international scale is associated with increased innovativeness at the firm level (Cotic-Svetina et al., 2008; Herstad et al., 2008; Huang and Soete, 2008). Firms need to search for knowledge on a global scale and collaborate with partners located outside their home countries and regions.

Second, there is increasing evidence that access to knowledge, technologies and other highly localized capabilities shape FDI-based internationalization (UNCTAD, 2005). There is also evidence that linkages to international corporate networks may be vital channels for information and knowledge transfer to firms and territorial systems (Bathelt et al., 2004) and have impact on the formation of external linkages at home and abroad. Gertler et al. (2000) point to the predominance of the corporate network as a source of innovative ideas for foreign-owned enterprises in the Ontario region of Canada compared to the more extensive use of external information sources by endogenous firms. Goerzen and Beamish (2003) investigated the relationship between diversity in contexts of localization and MNC performance. They found that the interaction between asset dispersion and country diversity impacts positively. Similarly, Frenz et al. (2005; Frenz and Ietto-Gillies, 2005) find corporate network affiliation to be positively associated with innovativeness and point to a particularly strong impact of the degree of network multinationality on all their performance variables. In their different ways, these findings all reflect the importance of presence in numerous business contexts (Forsgren, 1996) and the exposure to diverse, localized information and knowledge.

The question of home- and host-economy impacts from FDI has been thoroughly scrutinized, not least through different econometric attempts to measure the extent to which technology is transferred in either direction and spill over into home and host contexts. The empirical evidence stemming from this is at best mixed (Görg and Greenway, 2004; Kvinge, 2007) and riddled with problems such as that of knowledge and information heterogeneity (Kaiser, 2002). This is combined with biases that are inherent in statistical models and available data (Döring and Schnellenbach, 2006; Henderson, 2007) and combined with the fact that its impact is mediated by the context itself into which knowledge and information may spill (Frenken et al., 2007). Attempts to identify the impact of MNC activity on different territorial systems using aggregate data should therefore be supplemented with a more fine-grained analysis of contextualized innovation behaviour. We suggest building the basis for such a framework on the recognition that the knowledge bases upon which firms draw are diverse (Asheim and Gertler, 2005) and that according to Potterie and Lichtenberg (2001) the type of MNC-based affiliation as well as its institutional origins may matter in shaping subsidiary embeddedness in global innovation networks.

Institutional origins can be related (a) to systematic differences in the internal workings of the MNC network with respect to control, coordination and communication towards their subsidiaries and external partners abroad (Doremus et al., 1998; Geppert et al., 2003; Pauly and Reich, 1997), (b) to the different properties of the transaction environments into which they enter in their host locations (Caryannis and Alexander, 2004; Herstad, 2005; Storper, 1997), and (c) to industrial systems in which the MNC's headquarters remain embedded. Work within international business studies has argued that the process of MNC-based internationalization entails that national institutional systems and national innovation systems are 'inserted into each other' by means of the MNC network (Doremus et al., 1998; Herstad, 2005) and that the internal workings of this network reflect patterns of preferences developed and institutionalized at home (Bartlett and Ghoshal, 1998; Morgan et al., 2001; Ruigrok and Tulder, 1995). Centralization, preferred by Japanese MNCs, implies that individual units are submitted to tight reporting requirements *vis-à-vis* headquarters, the latter assuming a lead role in the hierarchy coordinating their activities (Bartlett and Ghoshal, 1998; Lam, 2003). 'Formalization', traditionally preferred by US multinationals (Geppert et al., 2003; Pauly and Reich, 1997), allows a far larger degree of decentralization, but substitutes the direct intervention by the headquarters (HQ) with formal systems that are heavily oriented towards financial performance monitoring. This allows the MNC to maintain broader internal and external linkages without management overload or lost control, but may come at the cost of lost knowledge synergies between the constituent components. Contrasting knowledge synergies with operational synergies and linking this to different modes of control, Persaud (2005) finds that whereas such formalization increases operational synergy, its impact on knowledge synergies is negative as the latter presupposes dense social interaction among R&D unit personnel (Persaud, 2005). This is consistent with Bartlett and Ghoshal (1998), who suggest that control and communication through 'socialization', traditionally more prevalent among European multinationals but increasingly becoming established as the preferred mode on a broader basis, provide the strongest foundation for constructing communicative capacity. The aim of corporate socialization processes is to establish a shared set of values, objectives and belief systems across MNC units (Björkman et al., 2004) and link these to the build-up of inter-unit personal ties (Ghoshal et al., 1994; Szulanski, 1996, 2003). However, stronger internal communicative capacity may in turn come at the expense of attention towards external linkages (Blanc and Sierra, 1999).

Coordination, control and communication structure information and knowledge flow within the MNC, determining the extent to which the network of subsidiaries serves as others' extended ears and eyes. Such eyes and ears constitute search spaces (Katila, 2002; Katila and Ahuja, 2002). This may (a) trigger collaboration by means of identifying place-specific opportunities and partners with whom close interaction is required or (b) substitute the need for own physical presence by means of information and knowledge transfer through the MNC network. These effects will depend on the position of individual units within the network and the nature of knowledge involved. As several studies have pointed to the role of headquarters as 'nerve centres' (Gupta and Govindarajan, 2000; Persaud, 2005), we believe that those nodes with a tight and well-functioning relationship with the HQ enjoy the richest exposure to these information flows. These relationships include the formation of dense HQ–subsidiary personal networks, common world-views, social and institutional proximity conducive to less friction on communication (Ivarsson, 2002), shared managerial and R&D personnel labour markets and participation on common social and professional scenes. In sum, subsidiaries located in the same territorial system as corporate HQ are likely to have a more central position within the network, can establish denser communication channels towards the HQ and are therefore more likely to experience exposure to information and knowledge spillovers from the network (Ebersberger and Herstad, 2011). On the other hand, HQ location abroad may serve to bridge the Norwegian affiliate and the external innovation system in the HQ location. This means that the analysis must account for the fact that the structure and strategy of MNCs may differ according to their institutional origins and according to 'headquarter effects'. These may both mediate the impact of knowledge base characteristics and proximity on the global innovation network affiliation of firms.

4.3   DIFFERENTIATED KNOWLEDGE BASES

Work within organizational theory has found the nature of knowledge to be a strong determinant of organizational structure (Birkinshaw et al., 2002). Our own empirical research of FDI-based internationalization in Nordic countries suggests that engineering-based industries are associated with a strong home-base orientation resulting from 'sticky' knowledge bases, more selective external interfaces that are less geographically dispersed and co-patenting networks that converge on certain key locations (Asheim and Herstad, 2005; Herstad and Jonsodittir, 2006; Ebersberger, 2006). A recent survey of multinationals similarly found that sectors that rely more heavily on complex knowledge that is difficult to move had less dispersed innovation activities than those characterized by modularity and codifiability (Doz et al., 2006). At the regional level, Sturgeon's (2003) study of Silicon Valley found that modularity and codifiability enabled far more globally distributed linkages than those found within the distinctively regionalized, automotive industry (Sturgeon, 2003; Sturgeon et al., 2008). This all suggests that the nature of knowledge structures the spatial patterns of innovation and its degrees and patterns of regionalization versus globalization within and independent of MNCs.

In order to disentangle this issue it is necessary to go beyond the traditional distinctions between high-tech, medium-tech and low-tech industries, as these tend to conceal rather than capture fundamental knowledge-base characteristics. One way of doing this is to study the basic types of knowledge used as input in knowledge creation and innovation processes, and distinguish between 'synthetic', 'analytical' and 'symbolic' types of knowledge bases.[1] In the philosophy of science, an epistemological distinction can be identified between two more or less independent and parallel forms of knowledge creation, 'natural science' and 'engineering science' (Laestadius, 2000). Johnson et al. (2002: 250) refer to the Aristotelian distinction between *episteme*, that is, knowledge that is universal and theoretical, and *techne*, that is, knowledge that is instrumental, context specific and practice related. The former corresponds with the rationale for 'analysis', referring to understanding and explaining features of the (natural) world (natural science/know-why), and the latter with 'synthesis' (or integrative knowledge creation), referring to designing or constructing something to attain functional goals (engineering science/know-how) (Simon, 1969). A main rationale of activities drawing on symbolic knowledge is the creation of alternative realities and the expression of cultural meaning by provoking reactions in the minds of consumers through transmission in an affecting, sensuous medium. The fundamental analytical–synthetic dimension of the typology that we applied in the empirical analysis is specified below. We stress that the underlying idea behind the differentiated knowledge base approach is not to explain the level of competence (e.g. human capital)[2] or the R&D intensity (e.g. high tech or low tech) of firms but to characterize the nature of the specific (or critical) knowledge input on which the innovation activity is based (hence the term 'knowledge base') (Moodysson, 2007). According to Laestadius (2007), this approach also makes it less relevant to classify some types of knowledge as more advanced, complex and sophisticated than other knowledge or to consider science-based (analytical) knowledge as more important for innovation and competitiveness of firms and regions than engineering-based (synthetic) knowledge. This is once again a question of contingency with respect to the firm, industries and regions in focus.[3]

4.3.1   Analytical Knowledge Base

An analytical knowledge base refers to economic activities where scientific knowledge based on formal models and codification is highly important. Examples are biotechnology and nanotechnology. University–industry links and respective networks are important and more frequent than in the other types of knowledge bases. In this type of knowledge base, inputs and outputs are more often codified than in the other types. This does not imply that tacit knowledge is irrelevant, since both kinds of knowledge are always involved and needed in the process of knowledge creation and innovation (Nonaka et al., 2000; Johnson et al., 2002). The fact that codification is more frequent is due to several reasons: knowledge inputs are often based on reviews of existing studies, knowledge generation is based on the application of scientific principles and methods, knowledge processes are more formally organized (e.g. in R&D departments) and outcomes tend to be documented in reports, electronic files or patent descriptions. These activities require specific qualifications and capabilities of the people involved. In particular, analytical skills, abstraction, theory building and testing are more often needed than in the other knowledge types. The workforce, as a consequence, more often needs some research experience or university training. This means that a certain proportion of the firm's workforce are members of epistemic communities of professionals maintained independently of the firm and have a common language for signalling and communicating knowledge, including over large distances. Knowledge creation in the form of scientific discoveries and (generic) technological inventions is more important than in the other knowledge types. These inventions may lead to patents and licensing activities. Knowledge application takes the form of new products or processes and there are more radical innovations than in the other knowledge types. An important channel for knowledge application is new firms and spin-off companies that are formed on the basis of radically new knowledge or inventions.

4.3.2 Synthetic Knowledge Base

A synthetic knowledge base refers to economic activities where innovation takes place mainly through the application or novel combinations of existing knowledge. Often this occurs in response to the need to solve specific problems arising in the interaction with customers and suppliers. Distinct industry examples include plant engineering, specialized advanced industrial machinery and shipbuilding. Products are often 'one-off' or produced in small series. R&D is generally less important than in the first type (especially 'R') and normally takes the form of applied research, more often taking the form of product or process development. Although university–industry links are relevant, there are clearly more of them in the field of applied R&D than in basic research. Knowledge is created less in a deductive process or through abstraction but more often in an inductive process of testing, experimentation, computer-based simulation or through practical work. Knowledge embodied in the respective technical solution or engineering work is, however, at least partially codified. Tacit knowledge is more important than in the analytical type, in particular due to the fact that knowledge often results from experience gained at the workplace and through learning by doing, using and interacting (Lorenz and Lundvall, 2006). Compared to the analytical knowledge type, more concrete know-how, craft and practical skills are required in the knowledge production and circulation process. Such skills are also provided by professional and polytechnic schools or by on-the-job training in addition to technical universities. Moreover, problem solving often takes place in local communities of practice. Overall, this leads to a rather incremental way of innovation, dominated by the modification of existing products and processes. Since these types of innovations are less disruptive to existing routines and organizations, most of them take place in existing firms, whereas spin-offs are relatively less frequent.

Table 4.1 provides a summary of the main differences between the knowledge bases. The knowledge bases contain different mixes of tacit and codified knowledge, codification possibilities and limits, qualifications and skills that represent specific innovation challenges and pressures as well as strategies of turning knowledge into innovation to promote

Table 4.1   Differentiated knowledge bases: a typology

	Analytical (science based)	Synthetic (engineering based)
Rationale for knowledge creation	Developing new knowledge about natural systems by applying scientific laws: *know why*	Applying or combining existing knowledge in new ways to solve problems: *know how*
Knowledge development and use	Scientific knowledge, models, deductive	Cross-disciplinary, experience based, inductive
Interplay between actors	Collaboration within and between research units	Interactive learning with customers and suppliers
Knowledge content	Strong codified knowledge content, highly abstract, universal codes, available in professional epistemic communities	Partially codified knowledge, strong tacit component, local codes, more context specific, communities of practice
Sensitivity to geographical distance	Travels well. Meaning relatively constant between places	Sticky. Meaning may vary substantially between places
Examples	Drug development	Mechanical engineering

Sources: Asheim and Gertler (2005); Asheim et al. (2007).

competitiveness. The distinction between knowledge bases takes account of the rationale of knowledge creation, the way knowledge is developed and used, the criteria for successful outcomes and the interplay of actors in the processes of creating, transmitting and absorbing knowledge. This in turn helps to explain their different sensitivity to geographical distance and, accordingly, the importance of spatial proximity for localized learning. As this distinction refers to ideal types,[4] most activities in practice comprise more than one knowledge base. However, the degree to which certain knowledge bases dominate varies and is contingent on the characteristics of firms and industries as well as between different types of activities (e.g. research and production).

4.4   PROXIMITY AND DISTRIBUTED NETWORKS

There seems to be a generic and global trend towards integration and collaboration in the area of firms' knowledge creation and innovation processes. The development towards more and more distributed knowledge networks can, for example, be traced in several biotechnology clusters over the last 10–15 years. In fact, due to the strong growth of potential biotechnology applications, particularly in life science, it has been increasingly hard for firms as well as regions to host all necessary competences within its boundaries. This points to the importance of the external 'search space' of MNCs, that is, the linkages by which new challenges and opportunities are identified at a global level. It is commonly recognized that the more diverse the information sources used, the higher the likelihood of innovating (see, e.g., Laursen and Salter, 2006). It also points to how the search is reflected in subsequent collaboration network formation (see, e.g., Hansen, 1999). This takes place because relevant collaboration partners must be identified and because the transfer or integration of knowledge from identified sources (through search) may require their direct participation in the process (due to the often tacit nature of knowledge). Thus the impact of knowledge bases and MNC affiliation must be understood within the context of how they influence the interplay of search spaces and collaboration networks.

The dominance of one knowledge base arguably has different spatial implications for the knowledge interplay of actors compared to another knowledge base. The analytical knowledge base tends to be less sensitive to distance-decay facilitating global knowledge networks as well as dense local collaboration. The process of identifying opportunities and potential collaboration partners is enabled by the flow of information in global epistemic communities, whereas subsequent processes of collaboration are eased by knowledge codified in a manner that is understandable to all insiders of such communities, that is, members of academic or professional disciplines existing independently of firms and regions. The synthetic knowledge base, on the other hand, has a tendency to be relatively more sensitive to proximity effects. Its cross-disciplinary, experience-based nature makes the process of searching for opportunities and partners far less straightforward, as it is less obvious where relevant knowledge can be found and not necessary signalled extensively. Information flows communicating relevant knowledge are less tied to global epistemic communities and more tied to local communities of practices, making the innovation search more dependent on physical co-presence. Similarly, context-specificity and tacitness may mean that the process of establishing and maintaining collaborative relationships is more dependent on face-to-face contact.

The MNC enters this picture by extending the internal search space of affiliated units (through the corporate group network) into foreign contexts. Different group units, located in different contexts, may, depending on the communicative skills of the corporation, cross-fertilize each other with ideas and information that partly originate from their respective external networks and that may signal the existence of potential partners and new venues to explore. Furthermore, the existence of a parent group HQ or subsidiary in a foreign country may serve as a platform for the establishment and subsequent execution of complex collaborative project work.

All in all, this leads us to expect (a) that enterprises operating based on synthetic knowledge have less geographically dispersed collaboration patterns than enterprises operating based on an analytic knowledge base and (b) that the external collaboration patterns of enterprises operating based on synthetic knowledge in any given region are more contingent on a physical presence in the same region than for enterprises operating based on analytical knowledge. Lastly, we expect (c) that affiliation with a multinational corporate group gives access to internal search spaces that ease the identification of opportunities for collaboration abroad, hence resulting in more geographically dispersed collaboration patterns while keeping open the option that this effect may be contingent on knowledge base characteristics.

4.5   DATA AND METHODOLOGY

4.5.1   Norwegian Innovation Survey

The empirical analysis was conducted using Norwegian community innovation survey data. The fourth round of the innovation survey (CIS4) was carried out in 2005 and covers innovation activities, networking and output in Norwegian enterprises during the three-year period from 2002 to 2004. In contrast to most other European countries, participation in the Norwegian survey is compulsory and non-respondents are fined. This results in a comparatively large data set that is not plagued by a non-response bias. Community innovation survey data allow for investigating patterns of innovation across a wide range of industries and have been used increasingly for analysis in industrial organization (Cassiman and Veugelers, 2006, 2002; Cefis and Marsili, 2006; Czarnitzki et al., 2007) and management studies (Laursen and Salter, 2004, 2006).

The total data set contains 2843 observations from the mining and quarrying, manufacturing and knowledge-intensive service sectors. Of these we shall use only the innovation-active enterprises for which all required information on the dependent and the independent variables is available. This restriction reduces the sample to 1506 companies. Table 4.2

Table 4.2 Sectoral breakdown of the total sample (sector figures in percentages)

	Small < 50 empl.	Medium 50–250 empl.	Large > 250 empl.	Total
Number of observations	1739	897	207	2843
Innovation active comp.	799	559	148	1506
Sectors				
Mining & quarrying	3	2	11	4
Food, beverages & tobacco	4	11	18	8
Textiles, leather	12	18	11	14
Chemicals, rubber & paper	6	6	9	7
Basic metal	9	13	12	11
Machinery & equipment	8	10	5	8
Electronics & instruments	12	8	7	10
Manufacturing nec.	11	16	14	13
Knowledge-intensive services	34	16	13	25
Total	100	100	100	100

shows its distribution across the sectors. Table 4.3 provides a summary of variables used and Table 4.4 provides descriptive statistics.

4.5.2 Dependent Variables: International Network Scope and Regional Network Diversity

Global innovation networks are operationalized using the information available on external innovation collaboration (i.e. collaboration with actor groups not part of the parent MNC) and its geography. This is defined strictly to include only committed, direct interaction (Fey and Birkinshaw, 2005) and excludes a number of linkages such as purchases of components and machinery (Hauknes and Knell, 2009) as well as patents and contract R&D (Granstrand et al., 1992). Collaborative relationships result from strategic decisions to engage in knowledge exchanges with different actor groups and are therefore a good proxy for the strength of embeddedness in networks of various forms.

To capture degrees of network embeddedness we construct measures of diversity along two dimensions. First, given the type of innovation collaboration – vertical along the value chain or scientific with partners in

Table 4.3   Variables

Variable name	Description
D_SYN	Dummy variable indicating synthetic (= 1) or analytic (= 0) knowledge bases
DGEO_VER	Variable capturing the geographical diversity (number of world regions) of customer and supplier collaboration
DGEO_SCI	Variable capturing the geographical diversity (number of world regions) of science system collaboration
DGEO_NO	Variable capturing the number of different collaboration partners used in Norway
DGEO_ND	Variable capturing the number of different collaboration partners used in other Nordic (Norway excluded) countries
DGEO_EU	Variable capturing the number of different collaboration partners used in other (non-Nordic) European countries
DGEO_US	Variable capturing the number of different collaboration partners used in the USA
S_NO	Variable indicating the existence of a collaborative relationship with a parent group unit in Norway
S_ND	Variable indicating the existence of a collaborative relationship with a parent group unit in another Nordic country
S_EU	Variable indicating the existence of a collaborative relationship with a parent group unit in another (non-Nordic) European country
S_US	Variable indicating the existence of a collaborative relationship with a parent group unit in the USA
LEMP	Size control, log of number of employees
PROPAT	Patenting propensity
INTMARKT	Share of sales on foreign markets
EXPSHR	Export share
APP	Sector-level appropriability conditions, measured as share of innovating companies in a sector indicating that competitors provide important information input to innovation
HAMNO	Dummy indicating that no factors hampering innovation activities are stated
ORG_DM	Dummy indicating affiliation with a domestic (Norwegian) multinational corporate group
ORG_FO	Dummy indicating affiliation with a foreign corporate group
ORG_FO_ND	Dummy indicating affiliation with a Nordic (Norway excluded) corporate group
ORG_FO_EU	Dummy indicating affiliation with a European (Nordic countries excluded) corporate group
ORG_FO_US	Dummy indicating affiliation with a US corporate group
ORG_FO_OT	Dummy indicating affiliation with a corporate group based in other countries

Table 4.4   *Analytical versus synthetic knowledge bases and average diversity of networks*

	Sample		Functional diversity of collaboration network in different world regions				Geographical diversity of vertical and science system collaboration	
	Fre-quency	%	DGEO_NO	DGEO_ND	DGEO_EU	DGEO_US	DGEO_VER	DGEO_SCI
Analytical knowledge base	101	6.71	2.366	0.505	0.772	0.287	1.356	1.485
Synthetic knowledge base	1405	93.29	1.071	0.314	0.380	0.138	0.959	0.466
Total	1506	100.00	1.158	0.327	0.406	0.148	0.985	0.535

Note: Innovation active companies only.

the science system – we measure the geographical scope of the collaboration network. The geographical scope of the network determines its exposure to diverse localized information buzz and knowledge but reinforces the problems of search, coordination and knowledge transfer (Hansen, 1999, 2002). These in turn are assumed to be further reinforced (synthetic) or counteracted (analytic) by different knowledge base characteristics. The variables DGEO_VER and DGEO_SCI capture the number of different locations in which value chain or science system collaboration is maintained. As the geographical breakdown of the location is given by five different regions and both vertical and scientific collaboration involve two types of partners (clients and suppliers, universities and research organizations), the geographical scope of the networks can take values between 0 and 10.

Second, a collaboration network is more functionally diverse the more different are the partners with which a company collaborates. The diversity of collaborative relationships maintained within a given region indicates the strength of the embeddedness in this region. This follows from the recognition that identifying numerous different collaboration partners in a foreign region presupposes a strong search capacity in that region and the increasing diversity of collaboration partners means that the complexity of the collaborative network increases exponentially (Owen-Smith and Powell, 2004). This challenges the absorptive capacity of the firm and thus reflects a high degree of commitment to innovation system linkages in the specific region. This is captured by our indicators DGEO_NO,

DGEO_ND, DGEO_EU and DGEO_US, giving the number of partners of different types with which the Norwegian respondent enterprise
collaborates within the specified regions of Norway (NO), other Nordic
countries (ND), other European countries (EU) and in the USA (US). As
the survey differentiates between a total of seven different external partner
groups, this indicator can take on values between 0 and 7.

4.5.3   Independent Variables: Knowledge Bases

To differentiate between analytical and synthetic knowledge bases (see
Table 4.3 for variables) we use the information on search channels.
Different channels are assessed on a four-level scale (3 = 'high importance', 2 = 'medium importance', 1 = 'low importance', 0 = 'not relevant'). Our approach builds on the assumption that the composition of
the external search space reflects the internal knowledge base composition
of the searching enterprise. As the use of a specific information source is
a question of discrete choice rather than an outcome of investments in
relation-specific trust and contractual arrangements, and this use assumes
the existence of internal competences and knowledge systems conducive
to absorption, a strong orientation towards external sources of science-
based information is assumed to reflect the predominance of an internal
analytical knowledge base.

   We similarly assume that strong orientation towards sources of
application-oriented, context-specific knowledge (customers, suppliers)
reflects the predominance of a synthetic knowledge base. Observations
that report a higher (average) valuation of information originating from
scientific sources than information from industrial sources are consequently classified as relying on an analytical knowledge base, whereas
companies reporting a higher (average) valuation of non-science knowledge sources (customers, suppliers, competitors) are classified as relying
on a synthetic knowledge base. A dummy variable (D_SYN) captures the
reliance on synthetic knowledge sources. As would be expected against the
background of previous research (see, e.g., Laursen and Salter, 2004) and
the nature of the Norwegian economy, firms purely relying on an analytical knowledge base are rare and account for just below 7 per cent of our
sample (see Table 4.4).

4.5.4   Independent Variable: Proximity

Our key assumptions are that presence in specific geographical contexts
may be necessary to tap into the innovation systems of these contexts and
that this necessity is contingent on the knowledge flows into which one

wishes to tap. Hence dummy variables (S_NO, S_ND, S_EU, S_US) are included to indicate whether or not the respondent enterprise has established collaborative relationships with subsidiaries of its own corporate group in Norway, other Nordic countries, other EU countries and the USA respectively.

The international ownership structure of the companies is captured by ORG_DM, indicating domestic, Norwegian multinational companies. ORG_FO indicates foreign-owned enterprises, which are further broken down by the home country into ORG_FO_US, ORG_FO_EU and ORG_FO_ND, where the first indicates US-owned, the second EU-owned and the third Nordic-owned companies. An additional dummy variable ORG_FO_OT is included to capture foreign ownership originating outside these specified regions. The reference in the regressions is enterprises not affiliated with corporate groups and enterprises affiliated with groups that are not MNCs. These dummies allow us to control for effects of multinationality as such, while simultaneously accounting for possible impacts of institutional origins and headquarter location. Specifically, the ORG_DM dummy allows us to single out possible impacts stemming from being part of a multinational corporate group based in Norway, whereas the foreign ownership dummies allow us to control for headquarter location effects on collaboration within the region of the headquarter location. If headquartered in a foreign region, the HQ is likely to be more embedded in territorial innovation systems of that region. If headquartered in Norway, the HQ and respondent enterprise are likely to be better integrated with each other and the enterprise is thus better integrated with the international corporate network of the parent (Ebersberger and Herstad, 2011).

4.5.5 Methodology

Knowledge base characteristics and proximity dummies are used as explanatory variables in OLS (ordinary least squares) regressions, with network scope and diversity measures as dependents. Although negative binomial regressions yield structurally the same results, the OLS set-up was chosen as it allows for direct interpretation of coefficients and interaction terms. We include controls for sector groups, size measured by the log of the number of employees (LEMP) and for the share of exports (EXPSHR). We also include variables capturing the share of its total sales on international markets (INTMKT), its utilization of formal protection instruments such as patents (PROPAT) and the absence of perceived factors hampering the innovation activities (HAMPNO). Descriptive statistics on the entered variables are given in Table 4.5.

Table 4.5   Descriptive statistics and correlations (innovating companies N =
1506)

	Variable	Mean	Std dev.	Min.	Max.	1	2	3	4	5	6
1	DGEO_VER	0.985	1.746	0	10	1.00					
2	DGEO_SCI	0.535	1.117	0	10	0.62	1.00				
3	DGEO_NO	1.158	1.866	0	7	0.76	0.72	1.00			
4	DGEO_ND	0.327	0.865	0	7	0.69	0.60	0.50	1.00		
5	DGEO_EU	0.406	1.059	0	7	0.76	0.68	0.51	0.62	1.00	
6	DGEO_US	0.148	0.587	0	7	0.60	0.52	0.35	0.40	0.61	1.00
7	S_NO	0.106	0.307	0	1	0.42	0.35	0.41	0.30	0.33	0.21
8	S_ND	0.052	0.222	0	1	0.33	0.29	0.28	0.37	0.32	0.18
9	S_EU	0.060	0.237	0	1	0.40	0.33	0.30	0.34	0.43	0.25
10	S_US	0.037	0.189	0	1	0.33	0.33	0.26	0.22	0.33	0.35
11	D_SYN	0.933	0.250	0	1	−0.06	−0.23	−0.17	−0.06	−0.09	−0.06
12	LEMP	3.900	1.176	2.303	9.320	0.22	0.30	0.21	0.23	0.22	0.12
13	PROPAT	0.228	0.420	0	1	0.25	0.24	0.17	0.21	0.29	0.19
14	INT-MARKT	0.634	0.482	0	1	0.22	0.16	0.13	0.15	0.22	0.17
15	EXPSHR	0.349	0.390	0.000	1.000	0.11	0.10	0.00	0.06	0.17	0.14
16	APP	0.055	0.037	0	0.400	0.08	−0.01	−0.03	0.03	0.05	0.08
17	HAMNO	0.147	0.354	0	1	−0.14	−0.11	−0.12	−0.09	−0.08	−0.08
18	ORG_DM	0.056	0.231	0	1	0.41	0.28	0.29	0.36	0.35	0.20
19	ORG_FO*	0.152	0.359	0	1	0.08	0.13	0.05	0.10	0.13	0.09

Note: * correlations of the indicators of variables breaking the foreign ownership further down
into country groups (ND, US, EU and others) can be obtained from the authors upon request.

4.5.6   Findings

We first investigated the impact of knowledge base characteristics on the
geographical diversity of collaboration. Table 4.6 shows that whereas
analytical and synthetic knowledge are not associated with any significant
differences in the geographical diversity of value chain collaboration,
analytical knowledge is associated with far more geographically dispersed
patterns of science system collaboration. Taken together, this means that
the analytical knowledge base is associated with collaborative networks
that are substantially more geographically dispersed than the networks
maintained by companies operating based on synthetic knowledge.

7	8	9	10	11	12	13	14	15	16	17	18
1.00											
0.22	1.00										
0.26	0.33	1.00									
0.16	0.19	0.44	1.00								
−0.08	−0.03	−0.04	−0.09	1.00							
0.22	0.24	0.22	0.21	−0.07	1.00						
0.13	0.15	0.20	0.15	−0.08	0.18	1.00					
0.10	0.12	0.15	0.13	−0.07	0.10	0.21	1.00				
0.02	0.05	0.13	0.14	−0.05	0.16	0.14	0.25	1.00			
0.03	−0.02	0.00	0.03	0.04	0.08	0.00	0.01	0.12	1.00		
−0.06	−0.06	−0.05	−0.07	0.06	0.00	−0.04	−0.12	−0.07	−0.07	1.00	
0.28	0.49	0.45	0.24	0.00	0.22	0.15	0.13	0.09	0.04	−0.07	1.00
−0.01	0.20	0.27	0.28	−0.06	0.23	0.10	0.16	0.12	−0.01	−0.01	−0.10

All else being equal, we also find that the effect of affiliation with multinational corporate groups affects the geographical diversity of both vertical and science system collaboration at the individual enterprise level. This holds for all forms of MNC affiliation, except for those headquartered in other Nordic countries. Consistent with the notion that presence eases search and provides a platform for collaboration, this suggests not only that MNC networks provide linkages between their subsidiaries by means of their internal network but also that they trigger collaborative linkages between subsidiaries in one country and external partners in another.

To disentangle the relationship between knowledge bases, proximity and global innovation network linkages, we investigated the extent to

*Table 4.6   Regression of the geographical diversity of vertical and
scientific networks*

	Geographical diversity of vertical collaboration		Geographical diversity of science system collaboration	
	Coef.	Std err.	Coef.	Std err.
D_SYN	−0.186	0.159	−0.827	0.104***
LEMP	0.148	0.038***	0.197	0.025***
PROPAT	0.645	0.099***	0.348	0.065***
INTMARKT	0.400	0.088***	0.100	0.058*
EXPSHR	−0.008	0.107	−0.024	0.070
APP	1.697	1.187	−1.367	0.775*
HAMNO	−0.433	0.112***	−0.239	0.073***
ORG_DM	2.652	0.180***	0.998	0.117***
ORG_FO_ND	−0.010	0.183	−0.031	0.120
ORG_FO_EU	0.413	0.171**	0.287	0.111**
ORG_FO_US	0.585	0.220***	0.380	0.143***
ORG_FO_OT	1.310	0.540**	0.708	0.353**
No. of obs.	1506		1506	
F	30.04***		25.25***	
Adjusted R^2	0.247		0.215	

Note: *** (**, *) indicate significance at the 10% (5%, 1%) level. Regressions include ten
sector dummies, which are jointly significant.

which the diversity of external (i.e. outside the parent MNC) collaboration in any given region outside Norway is contingent on collaboration internal to the corporate network with a subsidiary in the same region; whether or not this impact in turn is contingent on knowledge base characteristics; and whether or not the location of the MNC headquarter matters either because it is located in Norway or because it is located in the foreign region of collaboration. Thus the dependent variables indicating the functional diversity of collaboration networks in the different specified regions (DGEO_NO, DGEO_ND, DGEO_EU, DGEO_US) is regressed on the dummy variable indicating active innovation collaboration with a firm's subsidiary in these same regions (S_NO, S_ND, S_EU, S_US) and the dummy variable indicating synthetic knowledge. We also include interaction terms measuring the extent to which the impact of this subsidiary collaboration in the region on the external collaboration diversity in the same region is contingent on knowledge base characteristics (D_SYN*S_NO, D_SYN*S_ND, D_SYN*S_EU, D_SYN*S_US). Table 4.7 provides a summary of the regression results.

Table 4.7 Regression of the network diversity within a given geography

Dep var.	DGEO_NO		DGEO_ND		DGEO_EU		DGEO_US	
	Coef.	Std err.	Coef.	Std err.	Coef.	Std err.	Coef.	Std err.
S_xx^+	1.140	0.405***	0.188	0.290	0.009	0.310	0.886	0.186***
D_SYN	−1.130	0.187***	−0.149	0.084*	−0.339	0.099***	−0.032	0.059
$D\_SYN * S\_xx^+$	0.885	0.429**	0.719	0.300**	1.359	0.321***	−0.005	0.198
LEMP	0.139	0.041***	0.068	0.019***	0.066	0.022***	0.010	0.013
PROPAT	0.336	0.105***	0.246	0.050***	0.407	0.059***	0.169	0.035***
INTMARKT	0.152	0.094	0.117	0.045***	0.197	0.052***	0.096	0.031***
EXPSHR	−0.295	0.114**	−0.074	0.054	0.138	0.064**	0.085	0.038**
APP	−3.600	1.261***	0.513	0.602	1.072	0.706	0.971	0.418**
HAMNO	−0.421	0.119***	−0.129	0.057**	−0.092	0.066	−0.050	0.039
ORG_DM	1.372	0.196***	0.761	0.104***	0.735	0.121***	0.215	0.066***
ORG_FO_ND	−0.077	0.195	0.065	0.097	−0.018	0.109	−0.032	0.065
ORG_FO_EU	0.165	0.182	0.161	0.087*	0.033	0.110	−0.052	0.061
ORG_FO_US	0.529	0.234**	0.081	0.112	0.216	0.132	−0.019	0.087
ORG_FO_OT	1.148	0.574**	0.245	0.274	0.079	0.322	−0.107	0.191
No. of obs.	1506		1506		1506		1506	
F	26.94***		19.54***		27.65***		15.44***	
Adjusted R^2	0.259		0.213		0.280		0.174	

Note: *** (** , *) indicate significance at the 10% (5%, 1%) level. Regressions include ten sector dummies, which are jointly significant. +xx = NO for regression of DGEO_NO, xx = ND for regression of DGEO_ND, xx = EU for regression of DGEO_EU, xx = US for regression of DGEO_US.

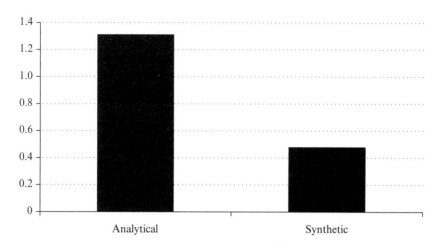

Figure 4.1   Geographical scope of science system network

Within the Nordic countries as well as within the EU, maintaining active innovation collaboration with a subsidiary in the region does not have a significant effect on the diversity of the external collaboration network, which is independent of knowledge base characteristics. We also note, interestingly, that whereas the impact from various forms of foreign group affiliations is distinctively positive on the diversity of collaboration maintained by Norwegian enterprises within Norway, the impact on foreign collaboration diversity is largely non-existent. However, it is distinctively positive both within and outside Norway for affiliation with domestic corporate groups. This means that it is not inward but outward FDI that triggers the richest linkages between Norwegian enterprises and collaboration partners abroad (see, e.g., Potterie and Lichtenberg, 2001). This could be explained partly by denser informal communication patterns and social networks between enterprise and HQ, allowing more strategic leeway for the enterprise, and partly by proximity to the information gravitation role of HQ, making the network serve as a richer search space for affiliated enterprises located in the same country (Ebersberger and Herstad, 2011).

Enterprises with a synthetic knowledge base reveal a far less geographically broad collaboration network than enterprises with an analytical knowledge base (see Figure 4.1). Yet for companies with a synthetic knowledge base, having an active collaboration with a subsidiary in a given region triggers a distinct increase in the diversity of collaboration in the same region, which, all else being equal, raises it well above the level of companies with an analytical knowledge base (see Figure 4.2). This

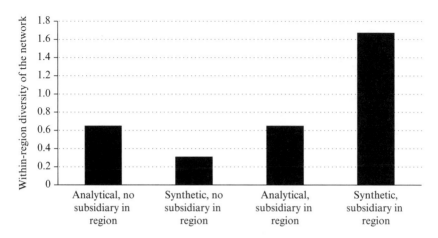

Figure 4.2   Diversity of collaborative network

means that presence in the region, and thus proximity to information flows communicating opportunities and proximity to the actors and networks towards which one may establish collaborative relationships, has a strong, positive impact on the likelihood that companies operating based on synthetic knowledge will embed themselves in such external linkages. Conversely, for companies operating primarily based on analytical knowledge, it means that collaborative networks form independently of a subsidiary presence. This is again consistent with the notion that analytical knowledge travels well and does so within international 'epistemic communities' that are far less sensitive to distance-decay effects on information and knowledge than the communities of practice within which synthetic knowledge is contained.

Contrary to the case of the Nordic countries and the EU, established collaborative linkages with a daughter subsidiary in the USA have a strong and positive impact on the diversity of external collaboration in the USA maintained by Norwegian enterprises. This holds regardless of the knowledge base that the company relies on. This suggests that whereas it is the knowledge base characteristics that trigger the impact of subsidiary presence outside the USA, it is the institutional context itself that triggers this impact in the USA. It should be noted that the explanatory power of our model is reduced substantially in the USA. While it explains a strong 28 per cent of the variation in collaboration diversity within the EU, it explains only 18 per cent of the variation in the USA.

4.6 CONCLUSION: PROXIMITY, NETWORKS AND KNOWLEDGE BASES

It is still common to characterize sectors by means of their R&D intensity, to analyse internationalization as the extent to which this R&D is conducted at home or abroad and to consider MNC affiliation merely as a question of foreign ownership. Instead of these traditional means of classification, our analysis shows that it is more useful to speak of how different knowledge bases and forms of MNC affiliation condition the nature of international innovation network affiliation. The increased complexity and knowledge intensity in firms' knowledge creation and innovation processes imply that distributed knowledge networks transcend industries, regions and the common taxonomies of high or low tech. Multinational companies are key actors in this, not only because they develop and maintain internal cross-subsidiary information diffusion and inter-subsidiary collaboration networks but also because association with such enterprises triggers broader international collaboration patterns external to the MNC network itself. This points to the role of the MNC network as a search space for affiliated organizations (Ebersberger and Herstad, 2011) through which potential collaboration partners abroad are identified and collaborative relationships are maintained once established.

MNC affiliation has an overall positive impact on the geographical scope of value chain and science system collaboration. However, once we consider the embeddedness within specific regions, measured as the diversity of collaboration patterns maintained, the impact of multinationality as such disappears and is replaced by a strong impact of affiliation with a corporate group located in Norway, that is, outward FDI. Even when the foreign owner is located in the same world region, this does not appear to trigger richer collaboration patterns. These results indicate that institutional and social proximity between enterprise and the enterprise group's HQ – facilitated by co-location – is associated with richer information spillovers from the HQ and with a higher degree of commitment on the part of the HQ regarding the subsidiary group's embeddedness in foreign locations. Expanding one's own corporate network abroad builds the richest search spaces (Ebersberger and Herstad, 2011) and triggers the broadest collaboration patterns.

Knowledge spillovers take place in and around distributed knowledge networks between firms with complementary knowledge bases and competences (i.e. related variety). This is especially facilitated where the knowledge spillover takes place across industries involving generic technologies (such as IT, biotech and nanotech) (Frenken et al., 2007) and operating based on an analytical knowledge base. In these cases opportunities are more easily signalled across space. This makes the process of searching for and identifying opportunities over large distances easier and less dependent on the co-presence in regions for tapping into place-specific information flows (Katila and Ahuja, 2002). Information is essentially less sensitive to distance-decay effects. The actual process of transferring knowledge (Hansen, 1999) through collaborative interaction is similarly less dependent on co-location and physical presence, enabling broader search patterns to translate into geographically more dispersed collaborative relationships. Enterprises operating based on analytical knowledge therefore reveal a broader scope of collaboration, driven primarily by their higher propensity to interact with science system actors on an international scale. Behind this interaction are search processes that target the information buzz of global epistemic communities as well as the relative ease of collaboration over large cultural and physical distances stemming from knowledge codified in universal codes.

Enterprises that depend on synthetic knowledge are found to be more sensitive to their spatial proximity to the communities and partners with which they collaborate. Information flows are to a larger degree specific to places rather than epistemic communities and are thus sensitive to distance-decay effects. This makes the process of identifying potential partners as well as establishing and maintaining collaborative relationships far more dependent on physical co-presence. As a result, international collaborative linkages are less geographically dispersed. Within most world regions the diversity of the maintained collaboration patterns is highly sensitive to physical presence in the form of a corporate group subsidiary with which a collaborative relationship is established. Behind the collaboration patterns established by synthetic knowledge based enterprises lies the 'buzz' of territorial systems and thus a stronger need for face-to-face interaction with collaboration partners once they have been identified.

NOTES

1. The distinction between analytical and synthetic knowledge bases was originally introduced by Laestadius (1998, 2007) as an alternative to the OECD's classification of industries according to R&D intensity (e.g. high, medium and low tech), arguing that knowledge intensity is more than R&D intensity (e.g. that engineering-based industries such as paper and pulp are also knowledge intensive, even if they do not show up as high-tech industries in statistics). This has been further developed by Asheim and Gertler (2005) and Asheim and Coenen (2005) to explain the geographies of innovation for different firms and industries using knowledge bases to show the broader organizational and geographical implications of different types of knowledge (e.g. how innovation processes are organized, patterns of cooperation, locational aspects and importance of proximity). The idea of distinguishing between analytical and synthetic knowledge bases

in this way was developed at a workshop in Lund in November 2001, organized by Björn Asheim and also involving Gernot Grabher, Aage Mariussen and Franz Tödtling, in preparation for a TSER project entitled 'TEMPO' within the 5th Framework Program of the EU. At this workshop the original analytical–synthetic distinction was expanded by a third category, the symbolic knowledge base, to cater for the growing importance of cultural production (Asheim et al., 2007). We acknowledge our debt to the abovementioned colleagues in the process of developing the concepts and analytical approaches. In this chapter only the analytical–synthetic part of the typology is used in the analysis.

2. Guiliani (2005) and Guiliani and Bell (2005) confusingly refer to 'level of competence' as 'knowledge base' instead of using the term 'competence base' to avoid misunderstanding.

3. The differentiated knowledge-base approach has been used in several empirical studies (Asheim and Coenen, 2005; Moodysson et al., 2008; Asheim and Hansen, 2009), but more work is still needed to develop methods for measuring the concept. However, various strategies have already been applied (especially qualitative approaches) and more are under construction: analytical knowledge bases can be identified in general purpose technologies (no one–one relation) and measured by, for example, scientific publications and patents; the synthetic knowledge base is more directly product/process oriented and can be measured by both patents and trademarks, while the symbolic knowledge base manifests itself in context-specific products and performances and can be measured by copyrights and brands. On the level of firms and organizations the patent/publication ratio could be applied by making use of keywords in the analyses (a high share of publications indicating an analytical knowledge base); furthermore, patent citations where the differentiation between analytical and synthetic knowledge bases would refer to the patent citing other patents (synthetic) or scientific publications (analytical); if the impact of patterns is generic (analytical knowledge) or specific (synthetic); and lastly more qualitative approaches (which have been mostly applied so far) such as innovation biographies and interviews and surveys could be used. Finally, on a regional level, in addition to using interviews and surveys, register-based statistics could be applied. In Asheim and Hansen (2009) occupation-based data categorized by the Swedish nomenclature on occupational codes (ISCO) was used to classify occupations into analytical, synthetic and symbolic knowledge bases. While occupational data help us to identify people with different knowledge bases, they do not allow any differentiation between the industries in which these people work. Thus ISCO data combined with data on industrial groups (NACE) on a detailed level (a three-digit level or more) would be ideal for constructing a knowledge base index. Having NACE and ISCO data separately would not provide the opportunity to upgrade the quality of such data by testing ISCO for NACE. In any case such an index could so far probably only be constructed in countries with a well-developed tradition of statistical information (e.g. the Nordic countries), but it would be well worth of trying to see if it would be possible to transcend the traditional statistics in use today. However, secrecy requirements would make this hard to achieve.

4. Ideal types are a mode of conceptual abstraction where the empirical input constituting the ideal types exists in reality but the ideal types as such do not.

REFERENCES

Asheim, B. and Coenen, L. (2005), 'Knowledge bases and regional innovation systems: comparing Nordic clusters', *Research Policy*, **34**: 1173–90.

Asheim, B.T. and Gertler, M.S. (2005), 'The geography of innovation: regional innovation systems', in J. Fagerberg, D.C. Mowery and R.R. Nelson (eds), *The Oxford Handbook of Innovation*, New York: Oxford University Press, pp. 291–317.

Asheim, B. and Hansen, H.K. (2009), 'Knowledge bases, talents, and contexts: on the usefulness of the creative class approach in Sweden', *Economic Geography*, **85**: 425–42.

Asheim, B.T. and Herstad, S.J. (2005), 'Regional innovation systems, varieties of capitalisms and non-local relations: challenges from the globalising economy', in R.A. Boschma and R.C. Kloosterman (eds), *Learning from Clusters: A Critical Assessment for an Economic-Geographical Perspective*, Dordrecht: Springer.

Asheim, B., Coenen, L., Moodysson, J. and Vang, J. (2007), 'Constructing knowledge-based regional advantage: implications for regional innovation policy', *International Journal of Entrepreneurship and Innovation Management*, **7**: 140–55.

Bartlett, C. and Ghoshal, S. (1998), *Managing across Borders: The Transnational Solution*, London: Random House.

Bathelt, H., Malmberg, A. and Maskell, P. (2004), 'Clusters and knowledge: local buzz, global pipelines and the process of knowledge creation', *Progress in Human Geography*, **28**: 31–56.

Birkinshaw, J., Nobel, R. and Ridderstråle, J. (2002), 'Knowledge as a contingency variable: do the characteristics of knowledge predict organization structure?', *Organization Science*, **13**: 274–89.

Björkman, I., Barner-Rasmussen, W. and Li, L. (2004), 'Managing knowledge transfer in MNCs: the impact of headquarter control mechanisms', *Journal of International Business Studies*, **35**: 443–55.

Blanc, H. and Sierra, C. (1999), 'The internationalization of R&D by multinationals: a trade-off between external and internal proximity', *Cambridge Journal of Economics*, **23**: 187–206.

Caryannis, E. and Alexander, J. (2004), 'Strategy, structure and performance issues of precompetitive R&D consortia: insights and lessons from SEMATECH', *IEE Transactions on Engineering Management*, **51**: 226–32.

Cassiman, B. and Veugelers, R. (2002), 'Cooperation and spillovers: some empirical evidence from Belgium', *American Economic Review*, **9**: 1169–84.

Cassiman, B. and Veugelers, R. (2006), 'In search of complementarity in innovation strategy: internal R&D and external knowledge acquisition', *Management Science*, **52**: 68–82.

Cefis, E. and Marsili, O. (2006), 'Survivor: the role of innovation in firms' survival', *Research Policy*, **35**: 626–41.

Coe, N.M., Dicken, P. and Hess, M. (2008), 'Global production networks: realizing the potential', *Journal of Economic Geography*, **8**: 271–95.

Cotic-Svetina, A., Jaklic, M. and Prodan, I. (2008), 'Does collective learning in clusters contribute to innovation?', *Science and Public Policy*, **35**: 335–45.

Czarnitzki, D., Ebersberger, B. and Fier, A. (2007), 'The relationship between R&D collaboration, subsidies and R&D performance: empirical evidence from Finland and Germany', *Journal of Applied Econometrics*, **22**: 1347–66.

Doremus, P., Keller, W., Pauly, L. and Reich, S. (1998), *The Myth of the Global Corporation*, Princeton, NJ: Princeton University Press.

Döring, T. and Schnellenbach, J. (2006), 'What do we know about geographical knowledge spillovers and regional growth? A survey of the literature', *Regional Studies*, **40**: 375–95.

Doz, Y., Wilson, K., Veldhoen, S., Goldbrunner, T. and Altman, G. (2006), *Innovation: Is Global the Way Forward?*, Paris: INSEAD.

Ebersberger, B. (2006), *Innovation Activities of Domestic Multinational Companies*, Oslo: NIFU STEP.

Ebersberger, B. and Herstad, S. (2011), 'Go abroad or have strangers visit? On organizational search spaces and local linkages', *Journal of Economic Geography*, doi: 10.1093/jeg/lbq057.

Fey, C.F. and Birkinshaw, J. (2005), 'External sources of knowledge, governance mode and R&D performance', *Journal of Management*, **31**: 597–621.

Forsgren, M. (1996), 'The advantage paradox of the multinational corporation', in I. Björkman and M. Forsgren (eds), *The Nature of the International Firm*, Copenhagen: Copenhagen Business School Press, pp. 69–85.

Frenken, K., Oort, F.V. and Verburg, T. (2007), 'Related variety, unrelated variety and regional economic growth', *Regional Studies*, **41**: 685–97.

Frenz, M. and Ietto-Gillies, G. (2007), 'Does multinationality affect the propensity to innovative? An analysis of the Third Community Innovation Survey', *International Review of Applied Economics*, **21**: 99–117.

Frenz, M., Girardone, C. and Ietto-Gillies, G. (2005), 'Multinationality matters in innovation: the case of the UK financial services', *Industry & Innovation*, **12**: 65–92.

Geppert, M., Williams, K. and Matten, D. (2003), 'The social construction of contextual rationalities in MNCs: an Anglo-German comparison of subsidiary choice', *Journal of Management Studies*, **40**: 617–40.

Gereffi, G., Humphrey, J. and Sturgeon, T.J. (2005), 'The governance of global value chains', *Review of International Political Economy*, **12**: 78–104.

Gertler, M.S., Wolfe, D.A. and Garkut, D. (2000), 'No place like home? The embeddedness of innovation in a regional economy', *Review of International Political Economy*, **7**: 688–718.

Ghoshal, S., Korine, H. and Szulanski, G. (1994), 'Interunit communication in multinational corporations', *Management Science*, **40**: 96–110.

Goerzen, A. and Beamish, P.W. (2003), 'Geographic scope and multinational enterprise performance', *Strategic Management Journal*, **24**: 1289–306.

Görg, H. and Greenway, D. (2004), 'Much ado about nothing? Do domestic firms really benefit from foreign direct investment?', *The World Bank Research Observer*, **19**: 171–97.

Granstrand, O., Bohlin, E., Oscarsson, S. and Sjöberg, N. (1992), 'External technology acquisition in large multi-technology corporations', *R&D Management*, **22**: 111–33.

Giuliani, E. (2005), 'The structure of cluster knowledge networks: uneven and selective, not pervasive and collective', DRUID Working Paper 2005-11.

Giuliani, E. and Bell, M. (2005), 'The micro-determinants of meso-level learning and innovation: evidence from a Chilean wine cluster', *Research Policy*, **34**: 47–68.

Gupta, A.K. and Govindarajan, V. (2000), 'Knowledge flows within multinational corporations', *Strategic Management Journal*, **21**: 473–96.

Hansen, M.T. (1999), 'The search–transfer problem: the role of weak ties in sharing knowledge across organizational subunits', *Administrative Science Quarterly*, **44**: 82–111.

Hansen, M.T. (2002), 'Knowledge networks: explaining effective knowledge sharing in multiunit companies', *Organization Science*, **13**: 232–48.

Hauknes, J. and Knell, M. (2009), 'Embodied knowledge and sectoral linkages: an input–output approach to the interaction of high- and low-tech industries', *Research Policy*, **38**: 459–69.

Henderson, J.V. (2007), 'Understanding knowledge spillovers', *Regional Science and Urban Economics*, **37**: 497–508.

Herstad, S. (2005), *Utenlandsk direkte eierskap* (Foreign Direct Ownership), Oslo: University of Oslo.

Herstad, S., Bloch, C., Ebersberger, B. and Velde, E. van der (2008), *Open Innovation and Globalization: Theory, Evidence and Implications*, Helsinki: VISION Eranet.

Herstad, S. and Jonsodittir, A. (eds) (2006), *National Innovation Systems and Domestic Multinational Corporations*, Report, Nordic Innovation Center.

Huang, C. and Soete, L. (2008), 'The global challenges of the knowledge economy: China and the European Union', *Science and Public Policy*, **35**: 771–81.

Ivarsson, I. (2002), 'Transnational corporations and the geographical transfer of localized technology: a multi-industry study of foreign affiliates in Sweden', *Journal of Economic Geography*, **2**: 221–47.

Johnson, B, Lorenz, E. and Lundvall, B. (2002), 'Why all this fuss about codified and tacit knowledge?', *Industrial and Corporate Change*, **11**: 245–62.

Kaiser, U. (2002), 'Measuring knowledge spillovers in manufacturing and services: an empirical assessment of alternative approaches', *Research Policy*, **31**: 125–44.

Katila, R. (2002), 'New product search over time: past ideas in their prime?', *The Academy of Management Journal*, **45**: 995–1010.

Katila, R. and Ahuja, G. (2002), 'Something old, something new: a longitudinal study of search behaviour and new product introduction', *Academy of Management Journal*, **45**: 1183–94.

Kvinge, T.J. (2007), 'Essays on foreign direct investments and host country effects', doctoral dissertation, Oslo: University of Oslo.

Laestadius, S. (1998), 'Technology level, knowledge formation and industrial competence in paper manufacturing', in G. Eliasson et al. (eds), *Microfoundations of Economic Growth*, Ann Arbor: The University of Michigan Press, pp. 212–26.

Laestadius, S. (2000), 'Biotechnology and the potential for a radical shift of technology in forest industry', *Technology Analysis & Strategic Management*, **12**: 193–212.

Laestadius, S. (2007), 'Vinnväxtprogrammets teoretiska fundament', in S. Laestadius et al. (eds), *Regional växtkraft i en global ekonomi. Det svenska Vinnväxtprogrammet*, Stockholm: Santerus Academic Press, pp. 27–56.

Lam, A. (2003), 'Organizational learning in multinationals: R&D networks of Japanese and US MNEs in the UK', *Journal of Management Studies*, **40**: 673–703.

Laursen, K. and Salter, A. (2004), 'Searching high and low: what types of firms use universities as a source of innovation?', *Research Policy*, **33**: 1201–15.

Laursen, K. and Salter, A. (2006), 'Open for innovation: the role of openness in explaining innovation performance among UK manufacturing firms', *Strategic Management Journal*, **24**: 131–50.

Lorenz, E. and Lundvall, B. (2006), *How Europe's Economies Learn: Coordinating Competing Models,* Oxford: Oxford University Press.

Moodysson, J. (2007), 'Sites and modes of knowledge creation: on the spatial organization of biotechnology innovation', Lund: Department ⌐ ⌐⌐⌐⌐ and Economic Geography, Lund University.

Moodysson, J., Coenen, L. and Asheim, B. (2008), 'Explaining spatial patterns of innovation: analytical and synthetic modes of knowledge creation in the Medicon Valley Life Science Cluster', *Environment and Planning A*, **40**: 1040–56.

Morgan, G., Kristensen, P.H. and Whitley, R. (eds) (2001), *The Multinational Firm: Organizing across Institutional and National Divides*, New York: Oxford University Press.

Nonaka, I., Toyama, R. and Konno, N. (2000), 'SECI, ba and leadership: a unified model of dynamic knowledge creation', *Long Range Planning*, **33**: 5–34.

Owen-Smith, J. and Powell, W.W. (2004), 'Knowledge networks as channels and conduits: the effects of spillovers in the Boston biotechnology community', *Organization Science*, **15**: 5–21.

Pauly, L.W. and Reich, S. (1997), 'National structures and multinational corporate behavior: enduring differences in the age of globalization', *International Organization*, **51**: 1–30.

Persaud, A. (2005), 'Enhancing synergistic innovative capabilities in multinational corporations: an empirical investigation', *Journal of Product Innovation Management*, **22**: 412–29.

Potterie, B. van P. de la and Lichtenberg, F. (2001), 'Does foreign direct investment transfer technology across borders?', *The Review of Economics and Statistics*, **83**: 490–97.

Ruigrok, W. and Tulder, R. van (1995), *The Logic of International Restructuring*, London: Routledge.

Simon, H. (1969), *The Sciences of the Artificial*, Cambridge, MA: MIT Press.

Storper, M. (1997), *The Regional World*, New York: Guilford.

Sturgeon, T.J. (2003), 'What really goes on in Silicon Valley? Spatial clustering and dispersal in modular production networks', *Journal of Economic Geography*, **3**: 199–225.

Sturgeon, T.J., Biesebroeck, J.V. and Gereffi, G. (2008), 'Value chains, networks and clusters: reframing the global automotive industry', *Journal of Economic Geography*, **8**: 297–321.

Szulanski, G. (1996), 'Exploring internal stickiness: impediments to the transfer of best practice within the firm', *Strategic Management Journal*, **17**: 27–43.

Szulanski, G. (2003), *Sticky Knowledge: Barriers to Knowing in the Firm*, London: Sage Publications.

UNCTAD (United Nations Conference on Trade and Development) (2005), *World Investment Report 2005: Transnational Corporations and the Internationalization of R&D*, New York: United Nations.

5. MNCs, clusters and varieties of innovative impulse

Philip Cooke

5.1 INTRODUCTION

The aim of this chapter is to examine the interaction between MNCs and smaller enterprises, notably those in clusters that in a supposed regime of 'open innovation' become more, not less, important to corporate fortunes. By reference to exemplary cases the analysis proceeds to show that without clusters MNCs can no longer survive since their attenuated knowledge dynamics mean that they are now largely dependent upon laboratory or enterprise research of an extra-mural nature or on other external competences and experiences. This presentation will analyse rationales for continued MNC involvement in home or host bases in advanced economies. More specifically, the chapter deals with three important relationships. The first is that between the implications of a hydrocarbon and a post-hydrocarbon global economic paradigm and associated shifts in organizational focus and interactions. The second concerns the manner in which innovation regimes and styles among large and smaller firms will change. The third concerns varieties of relations between multinationals and clusters, which often house knowledgeable small and medium-sized enterprises (SMEs), and how these change under these important macroeconomic shifts. Utilizing empirical case material and also touching somewhat on the 'open innovation' literature and critique, the presentation will offer three models for consideration and comparison by which MNC domestic and developed host-country implanting is currently understandable.

The first of these, termed the integrated supply chain (ISC) model, is evidenced from the comparison cases of automotive parts clusters in south Ontario, Canada and Konya, Turkey. In these somewhat traditional exemplars, a range of distinctive but related suppliers of metallurgical and engineering inputs co-locates in geographical proximity and, in complex and cross-cutting ways, serves the global automotive assembly industry. The second relational type is termed the advanced aggregator (AA) model and refers to regional contexts with 'Jacobian' embedded skills, that is, significant 'related variety' whose aggregation or 'systems integration' potential is attractive for inward investment as well as rapid indigenous firm growth, notably in 'clean-tech' industry (see also Cooke, 2010). Denmark supplies the regional exemplar here. Finally, we examine a packaging industry exemplar (from Sweden), a process- and policy-rich test of the thesis of growing MNC dependence on regional innovation platforms. These are found where related variety among industry subsectors exists and has been recognized, and transversal interactions among cluster members in distinct industries operate. The exemplary case discussed below is in a moderately developed peripheral region with high knowledge intensity, institutional innovation and path-dependent 'branching' centred upon the science and technology of forestry, including clean and bioforestry applications. Accordingly, this 'science excellence' (SE) regional model has its base close to both biotechnology (fibres) and nanotechnology (adhesives) and the science excellence element still informs MNC options as the knowledge imperative driving geographical and relational proximities, respectively. It is concluded that 'variety', notably 'related variety' assisting broad or narrower knowledge aggregation 'platforms', is a key motivator of MNC 'proximity capital' (Crevoisier, 1997) in the contemporary era.

In the chapter, we utilize a number of related filters through which to analyse the highly complex and varied processes under examination. It is important to recognize, first, the specialization–diversification debate that nowadays tends to question the supremacy of Porterian over Jacobian conceptual models of successful innovation. The specialization emphasis of the former is clearly a high-risk strategy for regional evolution, while the diversity emphasis in the latter is less risk-prone and, as evidence shows, a superior developmental model accordingly. This colours the perspective and empirics of this chapter. Second, the current era is one of turbulence caused by ecological and financial economic crises. Shifts away from hitherto dominant technological paradigms and socioeconomic regimes are clearly evident but of such scale that they are more in the form of developments of strategic niches and mentalities than achieved objectives. Some 'transition regions' lead the world in eco-innovation and one of these is highlighted by the AA model, although its principles are not confined to eco-innovation.

Conventional wisdom has been that an interactive (user–producer) model has replaced a traditional linear model of innovation in theory and practice. However, a moment's thought demonstrates that both are wrong. Innovation processes must vary over time and according to market. Sometimes the producer is more influential than the user and vice versa. The neoliberal era, which has just passed, was characterized by 'supply-side' innovation based on deregulation and the primacy of 'efficient markets'. In many industries, notably investment banking, innovations proliferated to the ultimate detriment of investors. To some extent such market 'efficiency' is also stressed in what is known as user-driven or customer-driven innovation (von Hippel, 2005) but it mainly applies to leisure market niches such as snowboards and mountain bikes. Critique of this perspective on innovation comes from the likes of Verganti (2006), who shows how many market niches, but not all, are characterized by design-driven innovation where the customer simply chooses the often radical innovation offered by design-intensive large or small firms. Finally, and returning to the current crises of ecology and economy, innovations to supersede hydrocarbon consumption or save global financial institutions from bankruptcy and shift industrial trajectories towards, for example, eco-innovation require large-scale Keynesian demand management by the state. This is what is denoted by demand-driven innovation. Thus innovation takes numerous forms that may relate or not: design-driven innovation may be necessary to achieve demand-driven innovation, for example. It is the core thesis of this chapter that innovation drives competition, that it affects multinational and small firms equally since they must all compete to survive, and that these complex innovation impulses drive yet another form of innovation – 'open innovation', whereby multinationals increasingly come to depend on global outsourcing, even for research and innovation. Open innovation builds on traditions of open science in academia and open source in software engineering (Linux). It differs in that it is subject to transaction costs between firms or firms and research whereas the others are publicly available (Chesbrough, 2003). Open innovation is thus much misunderstood, being a synonym for outsourcing, in this case of innovation, usually by MNCs or large firms to smart SMEs. The chapter simply explores three models of this, the ISC, the AA and the SE models in anticipation that future research will reveal more.

5.2   EVOLUTIONARY ECONOMIC GEOGRAPHY: RELATED-VARIETY THEORY

It has been stated that 'specialization' is inferior to 'diversification' in the achievement of regional innovation and growth. So much of the dominant literature disagrees with this view that space must be devoted to a discussion of the virtues of Jacobian 'variety' so that the innovative platforms that are so crucial for multinational competitiveness can have their attractions to the latter properly explained. Evolutionary economic geography has made interesting progress in understanding regional development processes in a context framed by globalization of multinational capital and its crisis. Foremost among the concepts associated with this perspective is the dimension of geographic proximity that addresses 'neighbourhood effects' between industries displaying related variety in the evolutionary sense. The basic argument is that in contrast to the 'specialization' thesis of innovation and competitive advantage associated with neoclassical writers like Porter (1990, 1998), variety is a better predictor of regional economic accomplishment. Thus evolutionary economic geography is aligned with the 'diversification' position developed by Jane Jacobs (Jacobs, 1969). She argued that cities, and by extension regions, with a mix of industrial activity, among which were related industries where (lateral) absorptive capacity for knowledge spillovers was high, were economically more accomplished than specialized urban (or regional) economies. Subsequent empirical research supports Jacobs over Porter (Audretsch and Feldman, 1996; Feldman and Audretsch, 1999; Cantwell and Iammarino, 2003; Boschma and Frenken, 2003; Frenken et al., 2007). Relatedly, and from a different part of the evolutionary economic geography landscape, is the regional innovation systems literature, which also recognizes related variety as a valuable platform on which innovative cross-fertilizations or cross-pollinations of innovative knowledge can be found (Braczyk et al., 1998; Cooke et al., 2004; Asheim and Gertler, 2005). Here, the latest thinking shows successful regional innovation systems to have related variety in industry terms and in firm structure terms. Thus large, possibly multinational, firms with localized elements to otherwise globalized supply chains contribute to an integrated regional platform. Clusters of SMEs in creative, bioscientific, environmental or software and ICT industries can coexist, and importantly, cross-fertilize, as the empirics that follow will show.

Finally, regional innovation system analysis nowadays draws attention to different emphases in regional and larger-scale innovation processes. There are four of these, written about to varying degrees and intensities thus far. First we can identify the era from approximately 1980 to the present as a 'supply-driven' innovation era. This means that most economies experienced business-friendly governance, deregulation and a withdrawal of the state from industry policy generally. This was seized upon enthusiastically in financial innovation, where important and extremely fast-growth parts of the financial services industry were effectively unregulated, non-transparent and only moderately accountable. Accordingly, great losses accrued to multinational financial services firms such as Lehman Brothers, AIG and Bear Sterns when the whole global financial innovation eco-system unravelled (Tett, 2009; Lewis, 2010; Lowenstein, 2010). Second, an interesting debate opened up in the middle of the first decade of the 2000s between those who see the rise of user-driven or customer-driven innovation as an important corollary of the supply-driven innovation environment. At its extreme, Von Hippel (2005) has written extensively on the increasing importance to consumption markets of user-driven innovations such as mountain bikes, snowboarding, bungee jumping and other outgrowths of the modern tourism and leisure industry. Others, like Verganti (2006, 2009), are critical of the limited niche market focus of such a perspective, its conservatism and, in innovation terms, its incrementalism. Contrariwise, the focus in this alternative design-driven innovation perspective is considered to be the real and systematic market innovation that occurs when new products and product lines enter markets. This is said to be transformational of sociocultural meanings, radical and concerned not with market research but design-led evolution of new propositions by inclusive circles of design experts. This analysis is also extended to regional innovation strategizing, notably in the design-intensive region of Lombardy in Italy, centred on Milan. Interestingly, Verganti (2009) claims inspiration from the innovation systems literature, particularly that referring to technological paradigms and the technology-push radicalism of innovation in markets, after Dosi (1982). Another innovation perspective we shall touch on that claims inspiration from a radical technology paradigm shift is the field of co-evolutionary transitions research that focuses on the current ecological crisis.

In different ways and in different contexts it will be shown how our three 'principal–agent' MNC platform models draw upon related variety as the 'evolutionary fuel' of their global–local relatedness.

5.2.1 Co-evolutionary Transitions

Given that the imperatives for change away from opaque financial innova-tiveness, on the one hand, and the continued pollution associated with the consumption of fossil fuels, on the other, are so great in relation to MNCs (notably the oil and gas industry) and their platforms of suppliers, theories of how this is to be done must be explored. This is because such a situation conditions the organization of global industry, stimulating further and further open innovation by MNCs towards globally leading, knowledge-intensive platforms of innovation, including eco-innovation. The idea of co-evolution is closely associated with the innovation systems perspec-tive (Nelson, 1994, 2008; Cantwell et al., 2009). The Netherlands-based multi-level perspective (MLP) school of 'Co-evolutionary Transitions' focuses on eco-innovation from a viewpoint that aligns neatly with the literature on innovation systems and technological paradigms or regimes that are at the core of the thinking behind this chapter (Kemp et al.,

1998; Kemp et al., 2001; Geels, 2004, 2006; van den Bergh and Bruinsma, 2008). Criticized for a tendency to underplay the importance of systems of innovation rather than individual firm 'strategic niche management' as the way innovations enter markets (Hekkert et al., 2007; Negro et al., 2007) and the absence of any economic geography in transitions thinking (Cooke, 2009, 2010), this is nevertheless a valuable framework with which to analyse meta-economy change at the level above that of the technological regime or socio-technical paradigm beloved of celebrated innovation theorists such as Dosi, Freeman and Perez (Dosi, 1982; Freeman and Perez, 1988). This is important in terms of the fourth 'neo-linear innovation' model, which is 'demand-driven innovation'. This refers to the kind of neo-Keynesian, transition management with state orchestration that is needed to meet wide societal needs for sustainable development, non-fossil fuels, renewable energy and a low-waste economy.

Finally, an intermediate perspective between co-evolutionary transition theory and, for example, design-driven innovation theory but at the same time seeking to unify understanding of macro-change of the kind the world is experiencing after the 2008–9 financial crisis is supplied by 'big shift' thinking. This is more a theory of knowledge flow and transfer than a theory about innovation, but it nevertheless encompasses elements of value to an innovation discourse framed by relationships between MNCs and clusters. It is new enough to be currently available mainly on websites emanating from XeroxPARC, erstwhile home to John Seeley Brown, author with Paul Duguid of an influential book on the information economy (Seeley Brown and Duguid, 2001). This approach, which presages a 'big book' before long, is summarized as 'big shift' analysis (Hagel and Seeley Brown, 2009). Here, ideal types are the preferred method for contrasting the immediate past with the pressing future. Equally, there is no economic geography in the analysis. However, in terms of taking account of knowledge dynamics in the new socio-technical landscape, it is useful and instructive as a broad orientation device.

5.2.2 'Big Shift' Theory

'Big shift' theory focuses on that which is occurring globally in the macroeconomy according to transitions thinking by experts with connections to respected future-oriented business thinking such as the Xerox PARC facility in Palo Alto, California (Silicon Valley) (Seeley Brown and Duguid, 2001). Now Seeley Brown, like others (see VINNOVA, 2010), sees the world in a 'big shift' in thinking and practice, occasioned by a number of crises such as climate change, energy, finance and associated economic recession, even the ageing crisis. In this big shift, environments

BOX 5.1   THE BIG SHIFT IN KNOWLEDGE
             PARADIGMS

- Knowledge stocks
- Knowledge transfer
- Codified knowledge
- Transactions
- Push programmes
- Scalable efficiency
- Stable environments

- Knowledge flows
- Knowledge creation
- Tacit knowledge
- Relationships
- Pull programmes
- Scalable learning
- Turbulent environments

Source: Hagel and Seeley Brown (2009).

for business that were stable, even embracing the emergence of China as a signatory of World Trade Organization liberal market norms, have now turned turbulent. What were once relatively straightforward technology 'push' environments have become 'pull' environments caused by user- or demand-driven innovation. Knowledge flows and sources are more distributed and more knowledge must be created than simply transferred in a linear manner. Innovation that was once dependent upon the large client firm's requirements bringing forth subcontracting of production through the supply chain evolves into user-led innovation in which the SME itself finds markets for its capabilities in relation to the demands of an exacting customer. Knowledge has to be gathered from multiple global, external sources as well as from inside the firm and the cluster. Accordingly, firms may be dynamic and innovation disruptive rather than incremental. As Box 5.1 makes clear, market pull rises over technology push as the key innovation driver, suggesting that innovation is perceived as likely to be incremental rather than allow for radical change under the new regime. As was indicated, authors from Dosi (1982) to Verganti (2006, 2009) conceive of 'pull' as market-driven and incremental, whereas technology 'push' can have radical innovation outcomes.

In the following we shall exemplify important aspects of transition, related variety and 'transversality' thinking. Transversality is the term capturing lateral knowledge interactions among actors in related variety clusters resulting in innovation that in turn creates regional growth and competitiveness (Cooke, 2011). This is demonstrated in the frame of some carefully selected exemplars of new process and policy practice concerning relations between MNCs and clusters. The outcome is recognition, drawn from numerous different settings of the central importance of distributed knowledge flows, related variety and regional transversality as cornerstones of the future evolving economy. These are the macro-scale 'landscape' shifts that confront MNCs, which require 'strategic niche management', much of the knowledge for which lies in platforms of regional innovation composed of knowledgeable clusters of firms large and small characterized by 'related variety'.

5.3   CORPORATE MODELS OF STRATEGIC NICHE MANAGEMENT

What role, if any, exists for large, even multinational, companies in processes of co-evolutionary transition? They are by no means negligible and occur with force in socioeconomic contexts characterized by corporate relational proximity to government, notably the Nordic countries, which in general have an exemplary record in stimulating 'green innovation' in their economies and abroad. Much of the empirical material in the following is drawn from this leading 'green economy' georegion. In the subsequent four sketches we are looking for regional embeddedness of MNCs among SME clusters or platforms as they aim to innovate. To highlight some strong findings beforehand, we see first that the Processum bioethanol cluster has expertise in numerous related-variety economic activities which produce eco-innovations ultimately for MNCs such as AkzoNobel. In the Robotdalen cluster of various robotics product innovations it is clear that the MNC Asea Brown Boveri (ABB) is quite dependent on the expertise of numerous firms as suppliers of inputs and producers of innovative designs, notably Giraff for healthcare robotics. The Skåne agro-food cluster displays coexistence of MNCs and smart SMEs but not their strong integration because the former retain laboratory expertise in house while for the latter it is externalized to university research networks. Finally, Uppsala BIO, a cluster of biotechnology firms, has had its trajectory turned towards medical biotechnology 'theranostics' because MNC GE Healthcare has such a large and important presence, replacing the global biopharmaceuticals expertise of cluster firms that were suppliers to Pharmacia until it was closed after purchase by US MNC Pfizer. In this case we thus observe a rather rare occurrence, namely the switching of an evolutionary, path-dependent innovation trajectory through the disembedding and embedding activities of MNCs in a science-driven industrial cluster. The lesson of these sketches is how diverse MNC–SME interdependences can be. From these insights the final empirical section formalizes the present stage of research and analysis into the three ISC, AA and SE model categories.

5.3.1 Sweden's Bioethanol Cluster and Market

Sweden has become a world leader in the development and processing of renewable fuels, primarily low-blended ethanol in petrol with a leading-edge tax subsidy and globally leading research programmes. Due to policy evolution over a number of years, Sweden is one of the largest markets for ethanol fuels used in vehicles. Only Brazil is more advanced in terms of development, and Brazil and the USA in terms of volume. All ethanol used for fuel is processed from wood or other renewable sources, a defining feature of 'biofuel'. Thus Sweden has had buses running on pure ethanol for more than 20 years, and approximately 34 000 cars run on low-ethanol blends (e85). Low-ethanol blends reached 6.2 per cent of the petrol used by vehicles in 2006. Elsewhere in Europe there are some test cars but few buses running on pure ethanol.

A new cluster initiative, comparable in concept to Kalundborg's (Denmark) industrial symbiosis (industrial ecology) urban recycling model, is the Processum Biorefinery Initiative at Örnsköldsvik at the Processum Technology Park. The member companies operate in manufacturing, consultancy and R&D in the pulp, paper, chemical and energy industries. At the heart of the initiative is a large pulp and paper plant whose lignocellulosic waste is utilized as feedstock for the production of biochemicals, a biorefinery producing bioethanol and a biomass-burner combined heat and power plant. This initiative is led by a large-firm consortium, but it differs in that it is conceived as a cluster project (Processum Technology, 2007). The cluster concept in a heavy industry context such as forest products is somewhat innovative. It brings together processing industry companies, the municipality and universities such as Umeå with expertise in tree biotechnology and Lulea with expertise in large-scale processing plant control technology (Figure 5.1).

Thus the northern Swedish town of Örnsköldsvik has become a cluster of ethanol processing and R&D. Sekab, Etanolteknik (Etek) and the BioAlcohol Fuel Foundation (BAFF) are all based there. Other user firms in the cluster include AkzoNobel (water-based paints), Domsjö Fabriker (bioethanol, substitute organic cotton), Övik Energi (energy) and Kvaerner Power (energy from pulp and paper). In May 2004 a pilot plant for industrial-scale ethanol production was inaugurated in Örnsköldsvik. An ethanol cluster arose in Örnsköldsvik due to a pre-existing sulphite pulp mill processing sulphite for sugar as a by-product from which ethanol is produced. Etek, for example, is locally involved in a research project on New Improvement of Lignocellulosic Ethanol (NILE) funded by the EU and budgeted at €12.8 million. Lund University of Technology was one of the initiators of this project encompassing 21 universities, institutes and

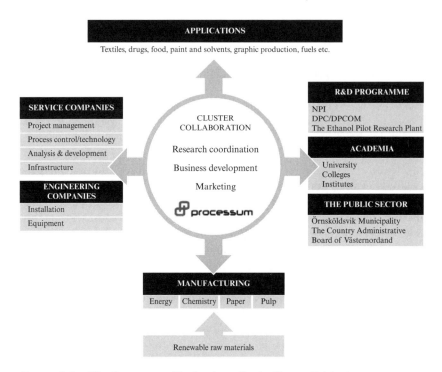

*Figure 5.1   The Processum Technology Park Cluster Initiative,
                Örnsköldsvik, Sweden*

companies, coordinated by Institut Français du Pétrole. The Etek role
in the project is primarily to conduct verification of laboratory process
development tests on a large scale. Etek's pilot plant produces 13 000 m³
of cellulose-based ethanol. Sekab and Agroetanol are leading producers in
Sweden and its customers are global oil companies. Despite these exports,
ethanol fuel is also imported from Brazil and the USA. Thus Sweden is
also a substantial market for ethanol fuel. In 2006 a total of 377 petrol
stations supplied e85 and the number is increasing by some 200 per year
based on existing trends. Although the ethanol fuel market is strong in
Sweden, biodiesel is less evolved, accounting for only 1 per cent of total
Swedish diesel consumption. Sweden's few biodiesel pumps are concentrated in the three biggest cities and very few vehicles are driven by this
product alone.

In 2005 some 9000 m³ of low-blended biodiesel and 1600 m³ of pure
biodiesel were sold in Sweden. This approximated to 2000 ordinary
cars, according to Miljöfordon in Gothenburg, an organization working
towards a more environmentally friendly vehicle stock in the city. Similar

organizations exist in Stockholm and Malmö financed by each municipality respectively. Hence it is anticipated that the supply of biodiesel will increase in Sweden, since two new processing plants were opened by 2007. Tax incentives mean that expectations for further companies to utilize biodiesel in future are positive. In 2004 the Swedish government allocated €133 million in their tax strategy for alternative fuels. In 2006 it announced tax reliefs for 20 Swedish companies retailing fuels with ethanol or biodiesel. These companies gain relief from CO_2 and energy taxes when producing or importing biofuels. The Swedish government further announced that biofuels would continue to receive supportive biofuel tax relief until 2013.

Hence it can be seen that such clusters are dominated by large firms in typically large-scale industries in pulp and paper or petrochemicals with downstream recycling. These are all large firms, often MNCs dominated by firms such as Körsnas of Sweden and Stora Enso of Finland. However, this is not wholly the norm, but more so than in some high-tech industries where the technology (e.g. biotechnology) is not large-firm but SME-dominated. To some extent ICT has been like this, although scale has entered the sector very much in recent years, while nanotechnology has no real large multinational corporate champion but rather myriad SMEs. We can conclude that, in pursuit of demand-driven innovations in the renewable energy, waste recycling and pulp and paper industries, MNCs formed themselves into an interactive cluster to which a few small specialist suppliers in the private and public sectors were attracted. The embedding process was thus multi-MNC inspired.

5.3.2 Robotdalen – Robotics Valley

Here, unlike the previous case, there is little collaboration among the MNCs even though they are scarcely in competing segments of the heavy engineering market. The robotics industry is dominated by Asea Brown Boveri (ABB), which has numerous regional sub-divisions specializing in distinct robotics market segments such as industrial robots, field robots and so on. Its role is therefore crucial to its cluster but the cluster management team want to innovate, mainly in a design-driven way, to create new niches for robotic products, such as healthcare, which can use small robots, or robots that clean awkward industrial spaces, for example in ships. In this case the cluster embeds itself around ABB in particular. This is part of the 'big shift' that creates the following future challenges and opportunities for clusters of smart engineering firms, large firms (such as ABB, Atlas Copco, Volvo and ESAB) and small firms in a specialist robotics cluster like Robotdalen (Robotics Valley) in Sweden. This exists in the Örebro to Västerås axis to the west of Stockholm. Foremost among

---

**BOX 5.2   IMPLICATIONS OF THE 'BIG SHIFT':
ROBOTDALEN TO ROBOTICS VALLEY**

- Public funding
- Subcontracting
- Standard solutions
- R&D driven
- Compliance
- Dependent
- Internal focus & mobilization
- Hydrocarbons

- Market funding
- 'Star' start-ups
- Creative, market focus
- User-driven innovation
- Trust
- Independent
- External focus & mobilization
- Green economy

---

current challenges are the changes introduced by the cluster management team to shift the balance of funding from public to private while keeping public stakeholders among key supporters. Of significance will be the ending of Sweden's national innovation agency financial support to the robotics cluster in 2013.

More effort is to be focused on supporting the regular emergence of serial start-up businesses, among which there will have to be some star firms. These will show creativity, not only in meeting user demand but in solving the financial support problem for firms moving from start-up to production stage. Here, the already existing inward investment 'star' firm Giraff may act as an exemplar, model or mentor. However, others such as the Dry-ice Blaster sea-container cleaning robotics firm can also serve as exemplars of how to identify gaps in global markets and fill them swiftly. The key reason for this will be the requirement for Robotdalen firms to become increasingly more outward facing, represented by the shift from Robotdalen to Robotics Valley in its identity and branding. As part of this, 'green robotics' may also find an important niche in relation to the two other key global niches in which Swedish 'lead markets' exist, notably Ambient Healthcare Robotics and Robotics for SMEs (Box 5.2).

What are the 'lessons learnt' from this cluster description? To conclude, the MNC creates the cluster that then builds identity by both supplying ABB and innovating in 'lead markets' where new niches are explored. If successful, ABB then acquires the firms that collaborate on the innovation and markets it globally. In this way, ABB and to a lesser extent the other robotics MNCs get cheap, subsidized, yet novel research and innovation from the cluster embedded around it.

We next pay attention to two completely different industries that involve both large, global corporations on the one hand and SME cluster businesses on the other.

5.3.3 The Skåne Food Innovation Network

Here we examine a quite strongly user-driven innovation system in which the virtues of transversality are understood by large firm actors, are being realized in cluster cross-fertilization manoeuvres but have yet to be fully understood by the majority of small supplier firms. The first comments focus on the Skåne Food Innovation Network (SFIN). This is a Swedish Innovation Agency-supported (VINNOVA; VinnVäxt programme) cluster of agro-food firms, many of which are large, often international, businesses, firms that serve the Swedish market or smaller firms and spin-outs at various stages of maturity from the university system in Lund. They include Unilever, Nestlé, TetraPak, Danisco, Danone and Findus. A first-stage VinnVaxt support winner, SFIN has realized that it is at a crucial turning point in its evolution and is already considering necessary changes in its business model with some urgency. Foremost here is the necessity for internationalization, specialization and marketization of SFIN services to augment the network beyond the end of the VinnVaxt funding in 2013.

This transition issue represents the SFIN equivalent of the big shift discussed above in the Robotdalen and below in the Uppsala BIO cases. As well as the need for a shift towards a more entrepreneurial stance, the requirement to access further project funding from public projects and membership services is pronounced. The overall organization of SFIN in relation to local enterprise and innovation support services requires some attention. The number, range and relatively low threshold of project support allocation and the relationships of SFIN within the Skåne Region innovation system also need closer attention.

Figure 5.2 is a representation of SFIN in the broader Skåne Region innovation system. It is a stylized rather than a complete picture. Even so, it is noteworthy that the SFIN subsystem is a rich one, with numerous network links both to clients providing financial support and those in receipt of services such as projects, test-beds and so on. Accordingly, it is a multi-level governance system with funding at all levels from municipal to EU and through projects and membership. 'Innovation at Interfaces' is the name of the VinnVaxt project, funded at some €1 million per year for ten years.

Noteworthy is the presence of at least a further six officially recognized and supported regional clusters in the Skåne innovation system. Most of

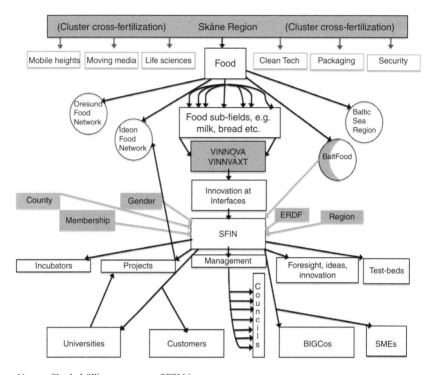

Note: Shaded fillings represent SFIN income streams.

Figure 5.2   The SFIN subsystem in the Skåne Region innovation system

these, ranging from mobile telephony (Mobile Heights) to packaging and
security, display characteristics of 'related variety' with SFIN's core field
of agro-food production and services. Large multinationals such as Sony
Ericsson and Ericsson Mobile Platforms orchestrate Mobile Heights, for
example. Life Sciences already has a bridge to SFIN through functional
food research and applications. CleanTech, which is an industry of great
potential, is already the subject of an SFIN project focused on the packaging industry. These links are noteworthy in representing advanced innovation system practice. The idea of the regional development authority
assisting such cross-pollination efforts more widely is already embedded
in the practices of SFIN and also a worthy achievement, recognizing as
it does the greater transversality in knowledge flows that may support
regional innovation. Here we see yet another kind of innovation, quite
user-driven in markets where MNCs must be responsive to customer
concerns. The cluster supports technology-focused innovation, especially

in functional foods reliant upon experimentation and exploitation of findings from agro-food bioscience. It thus coexists with, does not compete with and does not supply the MNCs that coexist in the broad agro-food innovation platform. Green concerns are felt by niche and global players. TetraPak, for example, is a project partner with other firms, small and large, in a cluster-funded initiative on green packaging and recycling. However, many smaller firms are independently innovating healthy foods, utilizing organic rather than biotech-derived food ingredients, ranging from seaweed to Omega 3 oils for bread and other edible products. Genetically modified (and inedible) potatoes are intensively grown for their starch, an input into green packaging, bioplastics and other clean intermediary products.

5.3.4 Uppsala BIO in Transition

This is a science-driven, user-focused, occasionally radical innovation setting. A radical 2009 innovation was the breakthrough in battery technology for large-scale electrical energy storage-utilizing algae, hitherto seen as mainly of value as a renewable fuel (Zhang and Cooke, 2010). In the early years of the present century Uppsala lost its corporate driver Pharmacia, which was acquired by Pfizer and almost completely closed down at the Uppsala cluster site. Only Phadia, the former Pharmacia diagnostics plant, survives. Large corporate influence is now wielded by GE Healthcare, which acquired UK medical equipment firm Amersham and now animates a significant supply chain of subcontractors in the cluster. Hence the cluster had to shift its focus from drug discovery to diagnostics, but now finds that markets have ceased to make such distinctions and the 'theranostics' industry has emerged with the evolution of knowledge in the global biopharmaceuticals industry.

The transition issues and contextual big shift discussed in Robotdalen and SFIN apply equally to Uppsala BIO. In particular, the need for a shift towards a more entrepreneurial stance is pronounced. Furthermore, in line with norms emerging in the world of 'big pharma', the role of learning from clinical data and analyses means knowledge transfer is probably only useful in a few contexts. Creativity in reflection upon combined diagnostics and therapeutics or 'theranostics' is seen as an important future direction for which Uppsala BIO scientists and firms are well qualified. Equally, the rise of user demand for customized rather than generic solutions to health problems marks a change in focus for biopharmaceuticals. Research on rare and possibly expensive compounds will thus be disruptive as well as incremental, and market segmentation will accordingly be a feature of some significance in the therapy targeting of the future.

BOX 5.3   FROM UPPSALA BIO TO BIO UPPSALA–STOCKHOLM

- Public funding
- Subcontracting
- Raise competences
- Science driven
- Uppsala focus
- Local cluster
- Small budget
- Internal mobilization
- Limited growth
- Balanced board

- Market funding
- 'Star' start-ups
- Creative, market focus
- Entrepreneur/user driven
- Global niches/mobilization
- Wider cluster (Stocsala)
- Attract global talent
- Enhanced budget
- VenCap increased
- Business-led board

The equivalent of the 'big shift' for RIS set-ups is the move from an 'institutional' (largely public; IRIS) to a more entrepreneurial (ERIS) innovation system management approach (Cooke et al., 2004). We can observe that the impulse towards the transition from 'institutional' to 'entrepreneurial' in the nature of the innovation system is accompanied by a contextual 'big shift' in the nature of competitive innovation in biopharma. Accordingly, public funding, already alarmingly small in Uppsala BIO, needs drastic augmentation from new, including private, sources to replace the terminating VinnVaxt funding (2013) and supplement it further. Probably some funding from EU Structural Funds can make up some of the deficit, but Uppsala BIO itself may wish to consider becoming a revenue raiser from its own activities in Uppsala, Sweden and beyond (see Box 5.3).

Accordingly, BIO Uppsala–Stockholm will rapidly need a task force to focus on raising the rate at which start-up businesses appear on the scene. Good exemplars already exist but may be hamstrung by insufficient research project or investment capital. It is worth considering the possibilities and prospects of creating a local public–private venture capital fund that, if successful, could in future be 'privatized' as a full market performer.

More global talent will be attracted to such a major, collaborating pole, augmenting the local recruitment from schools and colleges that are well embedded in the local innovation system. This would release Uppsala BIO from the inevitably time- and resource-consuming business of spreading the word about biopharma to educators – something too important to be done mostly by an innovation system-building agency. Finally, to provide strong underpinnings to the ambitions listed above, the board of BIO Uppholm is to be re-engineered to be more business biased than it has been hitherto, reflecting the evolution in priorities as the cluster moves from its 'institutional' to its more 'entrepreneurial' phase. Representation from dynamic SMEs as well as accomplished officers of major local business performers will be required to sit alongside academic leaders and those in governance in a new, dynamic and future-friendly innovation support organization.

The clear contrast in these exemplars is that SFIN has multinational food companies that engage with but do not dominate regional innovation policy. Instead, they are involved and supportive, learning of specific industry perspectives that, as large firms, they may not have taken seriously enough due to corporate 'group-think'. Thus TetraPak's CEO is key to SFIN strategy but absorptive of the multifold demand for, on the one hand, regional produce in local supermarkets and 'green packaging' on the other. SFIN projects and initiatives respond swiftly to user-driven innovation of these and other kinds. In the Uppsala biotechnology cluster in contrast, the loss of Pharmacia was that of a regional and local 'champion'. The cluster has become more inclined to biotech tools and devices than it was, even though 'theranostics', as the neologism implies, integrates therapeutics (drug treatments) and diagnostics (testing devices). This is not unconnected with the somewhat passive role of the cluster management board chair occupied by GE Healthcare's R&D director. Accordingly, it is having to seek intellectual leadership and scale from the Stockholm biotechnology cluster, even though its few innovation projects and spin-out businesses are moderately successful.

We thus see the interesting variety in terms of innovation impulses: demand-driven innovation in Sweden's bioethanol platform; Robotdalen is more design-driven in its innovation profile; SFIN is clearly quite user-driven in the emphasis given to producing local, organic but also more global biofoods deriving from university laboratory research; Uppsala's biotechnology cluster is science-based and relatively user-driven in its core field of theranostics and with a single major multinational customer embedded in close geographical proximity. A second basis for comparison is the embedding impulse, which also differs between each platform. Thus the bioethanol cluster groups together numerous related variety-seeking MNCs, securing private and public business and research expertise. Robotdalen is in essence a single MNC-driven cluster (although other MNCs are involved, they are in different market niches and geographically non-proximate) that has attracted suppliers who nevertheless value less reliance on ABB and seek innovation in which its dominant customer might also be interested, if successful. SFIN is a cluster of non-integrated MNCs in a single large geographical space. Innovation is customer-focused and user-driven as well as being technologically advanced. However, technological sophistication and its applications are mainly initiated by SMEs, although MNCs and SMEs may collaborate on 'co-evolutionary transition' projects such as green packaging, as was noted. Finally, Uppsala BIO is somewhat akin to Robotdalen in largely serving a single multinational. However, the interest here lies in cluster-branching from biopharmaceuticals when Pharmacia dominated to theranostics now GE Healthcare is the dominant MNC.

In the empirical part of this chapter we now move into exemplifications of the relational geography of three key MNC–cluster relational types. Models of innovation distinctiveness are highlighted in the broader context of our two macrotheoretical frames concerning eco-dynamics and knowledge dynamics in the currently changing global politico-economic context. The key connection between the foregoing illustrative accounts of distinctive types of cluster embeddedness and innovation impulse towards MNCs is that the following are clear types, distilled from the same broad reasoning but applied in different countries and their regions, on the one hand, and different industries on the other. It will be recalled that the four Swedish exemplars actually devolved into three types on close analysis. These can be summarized as (1) single MNC-dominated cluster nevertheless evolving 'related variety' (Robotdalen with ABB; Uppsala BIO with, first, Pharmacia then GE Healthcare); (2) platforms in which MNCs and specialist knowledge suppliers collaborate around their quest for 'related variety' (Processum eco-innovation cluster in Sweden); and (3) science excellence (SFIN; Uppsala BIO). The three models discussed below are fundamentally derived from these insights and underscore the value of the categorizations.

5.4   MODELS OF MNC–CLUSTER INTERACTION

Here we are concerned with two traditional supply-chain clusters in automotive engineering, both quite design-driven in their innovation model but facing the pressures of co-evolutionary transition because of their position in the highly emissions-producing automotive industry. We see no general model of the MNC–cluster and even less the MNC–SME isolate relationship in the foregoing. The sector is less important than it was and innovation platforms have become more pronounced as knowledge dynamics have 'shifted' from the vertical to a more horizontal disposition. Hence in the following we shall report on three model types that seem worthy of further testing, since each is drawn from recent empirical research. The first of the models in question is an integrated supply chain model such as is frequently found in the global automotive industry. However, despite different levels of development both are vertically organized MNC-dominant clusters. The MNC assemblers are global with no direct presence in these automotive parts clusters, or more accurately, related variety platforms. Accordingly, platforms of suppliers concentrate in specific spaces and supply the global car industry according to their competences and accomplishments. Konya in Turkey is one of these, supplying majors such as Toyota from their low-cost base. Ontario is another, with vast knowledge-processing and talent-formation potential. Each in different ways is a relatively balanced MNC–SME cluster supplying what was once a stable global market, but which has of late become more turbulent with unclear implications as a consequence of co-evolutionary and big shift change management pressures. The second is the advanced aggregator (AA) model and the third is based in research (science excellence), applied not in a frontier science field like biotechnology but the more design- and user-driven innovation context of the packaging industry.

5.4.1 MNC-dominated Platforms (ISC Model)

We examine these two integrated supply chain clusters from the environmental and innovation perspectives to indicate the dependent mindset of producers in Konya, unreflective of 'green engineering' and somewhat complacent about the innovation potential of the local university. This compares with the more developed, knowledge-intensive and 'green' market conscious innovation cluster in southern Ontario.

5.4.2 Konya – Energy and Environment

The Turkish government, with EU assistance, embarked on a national cluster strategy in 2009. The following analysis draws on documents and interviews conducted during a lengthy evaluation of the country's ten cluster roadmaps. These were widely examined but for simplicity only their environmental and innovation content are assessed here. Much of the writing of the cluster roadmaps was done by consultants involved in The Competiveness Institute, an offshoot of Michael Porter's Global Competitiveness Institute at Harvard Business School.

The global automotive industry is experiencing its biggest crisis ever and the market has turned aggressively against traditional designs in favour of 'green' or low-emissions designs. As an ISC model, the future Konya cluster will thus probably become an expert in producing parts for low-emissions vehicles. At the end of 2009 there was no sign that these realities had yet impinged upon the Turkish authorities or their panel of international cluster-building advisers. The global automotive crisis affecting general market demand, specific issues concerning hydrocarbon-fuelled vehicles, the loss of demand for typical large products (e.g. SUV and pick-up trucks) and the rise of consumer interest in hybrids and other low-emission technologies has enormous implications for the Konya cluster in its Global Innovation Network (GIN). Indeed, it is no exaggeration to say that it has to re-tool substantially and in an innovative manner. From what is observed below regarding innovation in the cluster, this seems *a priori* unlikely.

Since the cluster roadmap makes no mention of the core crisis of the contemporary automotive industry, it has now had to be re-thought and re-cast with 'green engineering' more at the forefront of the analysts' minds.

5.4.3   Konya – Innovation

The presence of Selçuk University, Turkey's largest, near Konya may or may not be of particular advantage to the cluster. However, an incentive structure needs to be put in place to secure the university's active involvement in upgraded R&D, innovation and technology transfer. The automotive parts industry and the cluster roadmap process could usefully consider the specific kinds of innovation needed from Selçuk University.

In most studies of supply chain innovation in advanced automotive producer regions and countries the upgrading of knowledge requirements coming from original equipment manufacturer (OEM) (e.g. FDI) customers is incremental, but usually of very great importance to modernizing such clusters.

Arguably less innovation is required for aftermarkets, given that by definition these satisfy yesterday's models. Contrariwise, it may be expected that the cluster's aftermarket status locks it into a trajectory where it is hard to move into advanced (e.g. 'green') automotive technologies.

As can be seen, the competitor exemplar is exceedingly well provided with knowledge centres and advanced training courses. Numerous well-known and less-well-known supplier firms are present and they constitute a relatively complete value chain or even value star. It is both the second largest global auto-parts cluster and number 4 in North America in relation to research on renewable fuels. While this is by no means an independent cluster, since it is still reliant on orders from large firms like GM, Chrysler, Ford and Toyota, it is nevertheless a more anticipatory cluster, blessed with foresight from advanced knowledge, research and innovation that the Konya cluster can only dream of. Either way, a globally leading

---

BOX 5.4   THE ONTARIO AUTO-PARTS CLUSTER

The Competition: TORONTO REGION IS . . .

- The #2 automotive cluster in North America with large assembly plants for major OEM companies
- Location of a strong supplier base of more than 280 companies, including: ABC Group, ArclelorMittal Dofasco, Bridgestone/Firestone, Burlington, Denso Manufacturing Canada, Linamar Corporation, Magna International, Mahle, Martinrea International, Meritor Suspension Systems, Mobiletron Electronics, NTN Bearing Mfg, OMRON Dualtec Automotive Electronics, Showa Canada, TS Tech Canada, Tsubaki of Canada, Westcast Industries, Woco, Woodbridge Group, and Yazaki North America
- Home to 89 science and engineering university programmes
- 30 steel and materials science research institutes
- Producing a highly educated and highly skilled workforce – over 4300 engineering graduates per year
- A leading research location; for example, the region is ranked #4 in North America for renewable fuels

Source: Centre for Advanced Studies.

---

parts cluster like that south-west of Toronto warrants benchmarking to inform aspiring cluster strategies elsewhere (see Box 5.4).

5.4.4   The Advanced Aggregator Model: North Jutland Clean Technologies Support

In this case we see a region of Denmark that has grasped the opportunities offered by the green economy over a period of some 30 years. It is a design-driven, co-evolutionary transition regional model. This began with the first experimental wind turbines, production of which began in the early 1970s. Utilizing technical knowledge from related and traditional regional industry such as the manufacture of agricultural equipment and propeller-making for the shipbuilding industry, the Danes produced a superior, more innovative new-technology solution to the problem of energy generation

---

**BOX 5.5   THE FLEXENERGIE ADVANCED
            AGGREGATOR MODEL OF COMPLEX
            SYSTEMS INTEGRATION**

Flexenergie Knowledge-sharing Network, Denmark

- Strategy to design and build 40–50 renewable energy local power stations
- 5 design projects – one in Thisted
- Geothermal, wave, waste, biogas, biomass, engineering etc. firms
- Partners include Vatenfall (Swedish energy generator), Aalborg University, Exergi (local energy design consultancy), Velux-Arcon (local heating & cooling systems)
- Key markets – Emirates, Spain, Russia, E. Europe
- Local power generation projects include:
  - Brøndeslev township (Vatenfall's natural gas + biogas mix)
  - Jammerbugt (Geothermal + biogas energy mix)
  - Thisted (solar, wind and wave energy)

Source: Centre for Advanced Studies.

---

from wind turbines than the main competitor region, which was, at that time, California. The Californian model came from propeller-driven aircraft design while the Danes modelled theirs on the shapes of ploughs, milk coolers and ships' propellers. Learning to point three blade propellers downwind rather than two blades upwind – as typically occurred with Californian technology – proved the superior design. Now local business Vestas is the biggest in the world, with a 40 per cent global market share. The next steps were the evolution of specialized skills in related industries such as solar energy, biomass and biogas, wave and other marine energy and geothermal energy. The Danish Ministry of Education instituted several new interdisciplinary engineering degree courses in recognition of the different engineering knowledge mixes involved in transversal industries like renewable energy. There were also subsidies, often to consumers, to invest in renewable energies in these times. These consumer subsidies lasted 30 years but subsequent tax revenue from sales have more than paid the subsidy back to the Treasury (see Box 5.5).

There are three reasons why this model is of relevance to this discussion of the MNC in relation to the cluster in the region. First, Denmark, particularly North Jutland, is a region dominated by SMEs that can often be found in clusters. Thus the wind turbine industry, though by now dominated by large local firms like Vestas or inward investors like Siemens, began as numerous geographically proximate SME districts. Second, and subsequently, established firms like Grundfos and Danfoss, both in engineering, began experimenting with and then producing green engineering products. In Grundfos's case this also involved lobbying the EU to get tougher standards on the energy efficiency of products like industrial heating and cooling pumps. Other specialist firms such as Velux (windows) and Logstor (pipework) began to pay attention to the renewable energy sector and by the 2000s a network of firms with many complementarities had evolved. This network is now called Flexenergie and specializes in the manufacturing of district heating and cooling systems. These are produced for the local market and export markets. They burn combinations of biomass or biogas in combination with solar, with wind, sea or geothermal power. Such flexibility is required because solar or wind energy may be inadequate at particular periods and the customized package can compensate for this by bringing other energy forms on line as required. Third, as shown in the next section, this was a mix of top-down responsiveness and a bottom-up business initiative. The governance process, involving representation of industry needs to government and the EU, was largely industry-led but required government responsiveness regarding changes to regulations and standards (i.e. facilitating green production niches).

Markets have expanded to the Middle East, India and China as well as to Southern and Eastern Europe. Recently a regional consortium won a €4 million contract with the regionally managed Danish VaxtFonden (User-driven Innovation Fund) initiative to conduct five advanced projects into renewable energy combinations (Figure 5.7). The approach very much sprang from the firm side rather than from government. Thus there was only moderate government support, mainly through consumer subsidies, which enabled, for example, farmers to invest in renewable energy in the form of early wind turbines. The opening of interdisciplinary engineering training similarly followed rather than led the processes described above. Nowadays there is more regional influence following the establishment of Denmark's five regions in 2007. North Jutland region manages the 'User-driven Innovation Fund' that allows Flexenergie to design next-generation renewable energy mixes for district heating and cooling schemes.

It is important to understand that this exemplar emphasizes more the successful identification of the green economy by firms than the leading role of governance and policy in achieving the described outcome. However, firms were hampered in their implementation of plans by regulatory standards and financial constraints. Accordingly the role of government has to be recognized in three important ways. First, early renewable energy experimentation and production were subsidized by consumer grants that enabled firms to produce and sell new products like wind turbines to individual consumers, notably farmers. Second, firms alone were not able to fund sufficient pre-competitive research and innovation preparation. More recently the new regional governance system in Denmark, with devolved control over regional budgets of the national User-driven Innovation Fund, is a stimulant to this innovative network in local district heating and cooling systems, for which there is a rapidly growing global market. Finally, as is shown below, efforts by localities of up to 50 000 people to become entirely dependent only on renewable energy have borne fruit. A considerable commitment of political leadership and vision was demonstrated at the early stages of development. However, leaders with action capabilities were forthcoming and, despite community scepticism, strategy was developed and actions implemented. Thisted is North Jutland's second community after the island of Samsø to become wholly independent of fossil fuels in its energy use. It also has firms producing for renewable energy supply chains, so it is sustainable in production and consumption. As noted above, farmers in some cases have diversified into energy production from biogas, the surplus energy from which they sell to the national electricity grid. Most of this effort in Samsø and Thisted is at the initiative of the local communal government but its appeal is worldwide, as recent study visits from the Mayor of Toronto, the Pentagon, and the Venezuelan, Indian and Bangladeshi embassies testify.

Evidently, the achievements of the North Jutland renewable energy sector and, more recently still, the rise of wholly or largely sustainable communities rest upon three things. First, a vision was formed by community leaders and entrepreneurs of the 'green economy' and 'green community'. Second, strategy was formulated at the firm and community level to pursue this vision. On important occasions this involved interacting with government to get better business conditions in support of green innovation. Third, much of the strategic niche management that allowed the industry to grow and the communities to be laboratories for renewable energy was due to a 'golden thread' of policy that began in 1970, or possibly earlier, recognizing the power and importance of demand-driven innovation from public bodies, in many cases through public procurement, consumer subsidy and regulatory change.

5.4.5 MNCs Dependent on Clusters (Science Excellence) Model: Värmland Region's Packaging Arena

This is a highly user-driven and design-driven innovation platform model that is highly attuned to 'transversality' and empowering local SME platforms to secure strong positions as innovative suppliers to global packaging users. In this respect it is one of the more interesting post-cluster complexes. It is the Swedish region of Värmland, home to the Packaging Arena, a complex cluster of packaging, paper and graphics firms that are indispensable to the MNCs they supply, including in Asian markets (see Figure 5.8). In this peripheral region university science and technology have been focused on the needs of MNCs in the packaging, paper, steel and ICT platform, while advanced college expertise in flexography and packaging media more generally has been conducted simultaneously by SMEs and educational or research institutions. Among the MNCs active in the region are IKEA, TetraPak and Lofbergs Lila coffee. To show how the MNC embedding in the regional platform works, we find the coffee company utilizing the services of The Packaging Arena (TPA) to 'rehearse' customer response to new flexographic designs to its packaging. This entails market research from the TPA-based Karlstad University Services Research Centre, customer eye-tracking equipment in TPA's Packaging Media Laboratory and design input from SMEs spun out of the flexographics training centre at Broby College (see below). Other MNCs from Japan, China and India take advantage, for a fee, of TPA's expertise in the design and networking of packaging businesses and expertise in the regional platform (Figure 5.8).

TPA is a functioning cluster of 45 members that supplies services ranging from guidance and process support, to consumer testing and innovation support. One strength is its engagement with consumer, paper and graphics research at Karlstad University and Broby College of Cross Media in Sunne. TPA is one of many clusters operating in the Värmland regional innovation system. Importantly this displays considerable relatedness among the clusters, enabling knowledge spillovers and joint working to occur. This aspect of joint working is evident in TPA's strategic plan document, discussed at greater length below. The process management team is well qualified and team members have distinct competence areas that result in the whole group being able to manage sometimes complex work-related tasks. Perhaps uniquely, TPA displays a number of related facilities, notably the Packaging Media Lab, the Packaging Greenhouse, DoTank Design Studio, Swedish Flexography Institute and the Graphics Institute at Broby College. Consideration is being given to creating an incubator at the downtown Karlstad head office.

TPA adopts a modern, conceptualized approach to management. Members are allocated to a Value Star that covers each part of the supplier base. New memberships are encouraged mainly from candidates who offer functions that strengthen the Value Star. The CEO is male but the other seven staff are female, each with a particular sub-unit such as the Japan desk (Japanese national) or the Packaging Media Lab to manage. In this facility eye-tracking analysis is managed, a function that enables the consumer's eyeline to be tracked when confronted with substantial amounts of visual information such as in a supermarket where choices are made about which products to buy. Such consumer information is made available to retail outlets, which utilize the Packaging Media Lab as a living laboratory for testing out new product displays, for example. The Packaging Greenhouse, by contrast, is a place where ideas can be proposed, discussed, analysed and adopted or rejected by members from retailing and the packaging supply chain. Inputs to such ideas sessions are enriched by the presence of representatives of the Service Research Centre at Karlstad University and the Graphics Institute at Sunne. The Japan desk is important because of the close knowledge transfer links established with the Japanese packaging industry. Representatives of the latter are regular visitors to several of the facilities of TPA, as they are to major trade exhibitions such as TokyoPac.

Of significance in understanding management style is the Strategic Plan for 2010–12. This is animated by a vision of TPA as 'the most innovative environment for consumer-driven sustainable packaging management'. To this end, five strategic goals are listed: knowledge and competence development; physical and functional facility provision; a regional innovation platform; sustainable packaging solutions; and international actor cooperation. Each of these translates into projects (discussed below) and a 'logic for regional growth'. Accordingly, under 'knowledge and competence', the latter involves: sustainable materials, consumer-driven innovation, co-production, and knowledge interactions between universities and industry. Regarding 'physical and functional facilities', the following are indicated: strengthening technical infrastructure, providing test-beds and demonstrator facilities, and establishing a functional cooperation meeting place (e.g. Karlstad University's Service Research Centre is to move into TPA HQ). 'Innovation platform' will promote knowledge-driven innovation based on companies knowing better what consumer markets require of products and services (research projects by Service Research Centre on needs-driven innovation). 'Sustainable Packaging' involves technical research on fibre, (potato) starch, paper surfaces, green packaging and renewable energy, among other subjects. These projects will involve Karlstad and other universities as well as Broby College, itself a low-emissions educational facility. Firms like TPA members FlexPartner and Exonera contribute to 'green packaging' through innovation in flexible substrate graphics and nanotechnology for releasable adhesives. Finally, under 'internationalization', aims are to make Värmland visible as a leading packaging research, design and production centre, opening doors both ways for international cooperation and stimulating FDI into the region. Hence the strategy moves smoothly from global vision to regional innovation, something that is well regarded and supported in the Värmland regional plan and the favourable views of national agencies towards TPA.

In line with the internationalization imperative, TPA has secured a €50 000 project from Tillväxtverket (Swedish Economic Development Agency) to promote the building up of Chinese, Indian and Japanese markets. This in turn will require growing support for innovative research groups in Värmland who will work with the clusters and identify cluster needs. This is a key part of Värmland Region's regional development strategy. To that end, it was recently announced that the Region and Karlstad University will fund ten new cluster professors in consumer studies, energy efficiency, production systems, service science, the public sector (including leadership and regional development) and renewable energy. There will be cooperation with Norwegian silicon solar firm REC's energy centre located in Värmland and the Printed Electronics cluster in regard to some of these projects. With the Paper Surface Centre and Service Research Centre at Karlstad University there is a 'Food for the Elderly' research project involving research partners from the Faraday Packaging Centre at Leeds University (UK), the CRIT at Bologna, Italy and universities from Japan and China.

TPA's own project plans for the 2010–12 period involve joint research on consumer-driven innovation with the Service Research Centre of Karlstad University, now sharing premises with TPA, developing durable methods for co-production, and communication of research results for consumers, producers and students. The project to combine research, testing, showroom and office accommodation is nearly complete and thought is being given to an IncuPac incubator space for four start-up companies (e.g. Exonera) on site. The Innovation Platform projects involve developing tools and methods for joint business development, market communication and Pacsem, the largest Swedish packaging industry exhibition and trade fair. Sustainable Packaging solutions will be focused on research into fibre-based materials for packaging and improving co-production among supplier firms in the Value Star. Finally, projects on developing international cooperation, raising the Värmland Region's international profile and securing inward investments will be pursued.

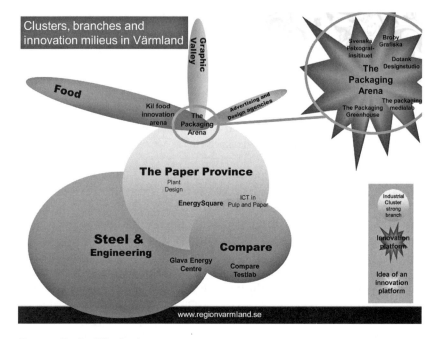

Source: Region Värmland.

Figure 5.3   The Packaging Arena in the Värmland RIS

Communication tends to be effective, notably within TPA head office, which is open-plan and around it has the presence of the Packaging Media Lab, Service Research Centre and possibly an IncuPac incubator in the same complex in the heart of Karlstad's shopping centre. Communications abroad are very strong in Japan, growing in India, where the TPA agent was a visitor in early February 2010, and emerging in China.

As a key part of the Värmland regional innovation system, TPA contributes immensely to the cohesion of the regional economy, as shown in Figure 5.3. TPA can be seen to occupy a position at the heart or cross-roads of the leading clusters in the region of Värmland and to be very closely involved with many such initiatives and facilities, notably 'Graphics Valley' in Sunne where the Swedish Flexography Institute and Broby College are located alongside firms like Flexigraph. Broby College is a school for graphic media, especially printing, although it now runs courses in packaging design, photography, scriptwriting, graphic research, web design and digital media arts that are no longer primarily aimed at packaging alone. It is important for Sweflex, an association of over 100 Swedish flexography firms. The Paper Province, another well-established cluster of paper manufacturers, also has close links with TPA.

Markets are principally in Sweden and some neighbouring Nordic countries like Norway and Finland. Member firms are seeking markets in other nearby EU countries too, such as Germany and the UK. TPA is represented at packaging fairs such as those in Gothenburg and Stockholm in Sweden and in Tonsberg, Norway. In Asia, where the cluster is active, as has been discussed, South Korea (Kitech) has hosted seminars at which TPA presented and were also hosted back in Karlstad. Accordingly a 'memorandum of understanding' was signed by representatives of both parties. These visits complement those of the Japan Packaging Institute, which has involved exhibition attendance at TokyoPac. Japanese packagers were also hosted by TPA in return. The Governor of Värmland signed a collaboration agreement with Hirosaki University and a memorandum of understanding with the Japan Packaging Federation in late 2008. Shortly afterwards, the China Packaging Federation was visited with another memorandum of understanding being signed. Closer to home, comparable exchanges have occurred with the UK Faraday Centre and CRIT in Italy. Presence at the world's biggest packaging trade fair, the Düsseldorf Interpack trade show, was also arranged in 2008. Hence, from a strong and established base in Sweden, TPA has become active in communication and market penetration in European and Asian markets. If there is a 'soft spot' regarding such activities, it is that they could usefully have occurred sooner since many of these are among the largest in the world and ready for business.

As may be seen from the existence of the 2010–12 Strategic Plan, TPA is clearly highly future-oriented. We have seen that previous plans such as the Packaging Media Lab have come to fruition and new plans to house university research in the head office are being implemented. The IncuPac incubator idea seems likely to be fulfilled. This means TPA has many key cluster elements involving retailer display rooms, customer psychological and product testing, research and possible accommodation for four start-up firms under one roof with good links to other parts of the institutional 'Value Star' complementing the company 'Value Star' with which TPA works. Platform links outside the packaging cluster are strong, especially towards print, paper, packaging and ICT (Compare) as well as printed ICT industries that themselves form an innovation platform in the region. This is expected to continue given the substantial investments made by national agencies and Värmland Region.

The region is a driver in the forward thinking of the cluster. Mention has been made of the appointment of ten new professors in each cluster area. However, the Regional Growth Programme also deserves mention. In line with good international practice, the region conducted a 'global megatrends' analysis, identifying ten key trends of relevance to the region's industry and society. In this each cluster organized action plans in response. Areas such as 'innovative environments (living environment)', 'entrepreneurship', 'clustering', user-driven innovation, competences and information and communications closely echo many of TPA's own strategic plan targets. These were exposed to a scenario analysis process and the results informed the regional development programme. Of importance here is the vivid manner in which the interlocking nature of Värmland's clusters was revealed, this being an important source of future economic welfare given the high degree of knowledge and innovation interactively transferring from research to industry in the region and beyond it. The Regional Development Programme was approved in 2008, during which year the Glava Energy Centre and Kil Innovative Food Arena initiatives were established, followed in 2009 by Karlstad University setting up a Care & Wellness Centre and in 2010 by the ten regionally funded cluster professorships in Karlstad University. In future orientation, innovative thinking and interest in the consumer Värmland Region, its regional innovation system and its clusters are exemplary elements by no means widely practised yet elsewhere. Thus Värmland may be said to have created or 'constructed regional advantage' to benefit its firms' quests for 'competitive advantage' in global markets.

5.5   CONCLUSIONS

Multinational companies are nowadays quite interactive with and even dependent upon clusters for certain kinds of organizational and business knowledge for innovation. In a world of increasing user-, demand- and design-driven innovation the presence of knowledgeable 'circles' of expertise regarding diverse aspects of markets gives knowledge advantage to both industrial organizational forms. For knowledge acquisition MNCs have become more embedded. Macro-leverage is exerted on them by ecological and knowledge paradigm impulses, and it is noticeable that the distributed knowledge flows identified in 'big shift' thinking are being practised, especially within the clusters or broader platforms, further advantaging the innovative knowledge capabilities of embedded multinationals. Accordingly the shape of the future economy looks increasingly transitional and transversal, with innovation impulses coming more from the demand and design sides than from the supply-side deregulation that preceded the presently emergent paradigm.

This chapter has thus been an exercise in iterative conceptualization in which exemplars of different innovation and transition aspects of regional development are taken to indicate possible leading-edge trends as informed by theory – in this case transitions, related-variety and transversality perspectives that have differing but complementary aims in understanding regional innovation. The main thesis under inspection was that MNCs become more dependent on SMEs and especially clusters of specialist knowledge in this era of 'open innovation', 'open source' and 'open science' that constitute the new GIN. The thesis holds up in general fairly well. However, it is clear that in some industries (process industries, utilities, even automotive) MNCs continue to dominate and there is not much room for strategic niche management for SMEs. Design-driven innovation is top-down, delayed and transition dependent on corporate judgements or previous misjudgements.

In the final section model types were compared that bore out the thesis that MNCs are more dependent than they were on GIN clusters. However, the MNC–cluster relational proximity model is equally a strong pointer to the vitality of large-firm dominated sectors.

The rise of both user-driven and design-driven innovation in a context of crisis and transition (the big shift) casts a clarifying light upon the complex processes and policy responses under inspection. Nevertheless, the positive account of a complex, cluster-focused region supplying strategic goods and services in Värmland, Sweden was instructive of a regional innovation system possessed of several remarkable industry clusters that display the modern characteristic of cross-fertilization or cross-pollination of knowledge – transversality – among them to a highly advanced degree. Centrally placed in this system is TPA, which is an innovation platform (Figure 5.8) that commissions, networks and markets scientific and technological knowledge to paper, packaging, steel, electronics and food cluster members of the regional platform. Much of its work has been ambitious and apparently effortlessly achieved.

However, it was noted above that a possible 'soft spot' that needs addressing, perhaps belatedly, is internationalization. It was not clear whether large bites are being taken out of foreign markets yet, and while good evidence of exploration of other European and Asian markets was evident, it is all rather recent. Two other 'soft spots' are worthy of comment. The packaging industry is resolutely male and little evidence was available to indicate that TPA could claim to have been a leader in re-balancing gender divisions in the workplace. However, it was clear that design-driven innovation platform Broby College now has females as a majority of its students, but many of these have to seek work in other Swedish regions. Such mismatches warrant attention. Finally, the effects of climate change and rising energy costs from fossil fuels had only recently begun to attract attention in TPA. While some firms visited revealed themselves to be 'green', this was mainly in their adherence to ISO 14000 norms that were set nearly 20 years ago. There was little evidence that the advantages of green production, consumption and service were being clearly understood in a systematic way, yet alone exploited. This too needs immediate attention, not least because packaging is widely perceived by consumers to be too much, too difficult to open and contributing to food waste of many kinds. If the industry fails to respond innovatively to such negative perceptions, many regional ambitions may be thwarted, with undesirable effects on the regional labour market.

REFERENCES

Asheim, B. and Gertler, M. (2005), 'The geography of innovation: regional innovation systems', in J. Fagerberg, D. Mowery and R. Nelson (eds), *The Oxford Handbook of Innovation*, Oxford: Oxford University Press, pp. 291–317.
Audretsch, D. and Feldman, M. (1996), 'Knowledge spillovers and the geography of innovation and production', *American Economic Review*, **86**: 630–40.
Boschma, R. and Frenken, K. (2003), 'Evolutionary economics and industry location', *Review of Regional Research*, **23**: 183–94.
Braczyk, H., Cooke, P. and Heidenreich, M. (eds) (1998), *Regional Innovation Systems*, London: UCL Press.
Cantwell, J. and Iammarino, S. (2003), *Multinational Corporations & European Regional Systems of Innovation*, London: Routledge.
Cantwell, J., Dunning, J. and Lundan, S. (2009), 'An evolutionary approach to understanding international business activity: the co-evolution of MNEs and the institutional environment', *Journal of International Business Studies*, **41**: 567–86.
Chesbrough, H. (2003), *Open Innovation*, Boston, MA: Harvard Business School Books.
Cooke, P. (2009), 'Transition regions: green innovation and economic development', presented at DRUID Conference, Copenhagen, Denmark, 17–19 June.
Cooke, P. (2010), 'Jacobian cluster emergence: wider insights from "green innovation" convergence on a Schumpeterian "failure"', in D. Fornahl, S. Henn and M. Menzel (eds), *Emerging Clusters*, Cheltenham, UK and Northampton, MA: USA: Edward Elgar, pp. 17–42.
Cooke, P. (2011), 'Transversality and regional innovation platforms', in P. Cooke et al. (eds), *The Handbook of Regional Innovation & Growth*, Cheltenham, UK and Northampton, MA, USA: Edward Elgar, pp. 303–14.
Cooke, P., Heidenreich, M. and Braczyk, H.-J. (eds) (2004), *Regional Innovation Systems*, 2nd edn, London and New York: Routledge.
Crevoisier, O. (1997), 'Financing regional endogenous development: the role of proximity capital in the age of globalization', *European Planning Studies*, **5**: 407–16.

Dosi, G. (1982), 'Technological paradigms and technological trajectories: a suggested interpretation of the determinants and directions of technical change', *Research Policy*, **11**: 147–62.

Feldman, M. and Audretsch, D. (1999), 'Innovation in cities: science-based diversity, specialisation and localised competition', *European Economic Review*, **43**: 409–29.

Freeman, C. and Perez, C. (1988), 'Structural crisis of adjustment, business cycles and investment behaviour', in G. Dosi et al. (eds), *Technical Change & Economic Theory*, London: Pinter, pp. 38–66.

Frenken, K., van Oort, F. and Verburg, T. (2007), 'Related variety, unrelated variety and regional economic growth', *Regional Studies*, **41**: 685–97.

Geels, F. (2004), 'From sectoral systems of innovation to socio-technical systems', *Research Policy*, **33**: 897–920.

Geels, F. (2006), 'Co-evolutionary and multi-level dynamics in transitions', *Technovation*, **26**: 999–1016.

Hagel, J. and Seeley Brown, J. (2009), 'Defining the big shift', *Harvard Business Review*, http://blogs.hbr.org/bigshift/.

Hekkert, M., Suurs, R., Negro, S., Kuhlmann, S. and Smits, R. (2007), 'Functions of innovation systems: a new approach for analysing technological change', *Technological Forecasting & Social Change*, **74**: 413–32.

Jacobs, Jane (1969), *The Economy of Cities*, New York: Random House.

Kemp, R., Schot, J. and Hoogma, R. (1998), 'Regime shifts to sustainability through processes of niche formation: the approach of strategic niche management', *Technology Analysis & Strategic Management*, **10**: 175–96.

Kemp, R., Rip, A. and Schot, J. (2001), 'Constructing transition paths through the management of niches', in R. Garud and P. Karnoe (eds), *Path Dependence & Creation*, Mahwah, NJ: Lawrence Erlbaum Publishers, pp. 269–99.

Lewis, M. (2010), *The Big Short*, London: Penguin.

Lowenstein, R. (2010), *The End of Wall Street*, New York: Penguin.

Negro, S., Hekkert, M. and Smits, R. (2007), 'Explaining the failure of the Dutch innovation system for biomass digestion', *Energy Policy*, **35**: 925–38.

Nelson, R. (1994), 'The co-evolution of technology, industrial structure, and supporting institutions', *Industrial and Corporate Change*, **3**: 47–63.

Nelson, R. (2008), 'What enables rapid economic progress: what are the needed institutions?', *Research Policy*, **37**: 1–11.

Porter, M.E. (1990), *The Competitive Advantage of Nations*, New York: Free Press.

Porter, M.E. (1998), *Clusters and Competition: New Agendas for Companies, Governments, and Institutions, on Competition*, Boston, MA: Harvard Business School Press.

Processum Technology (2007), *The Biorefinery of the Future*, Örnsköldsvik: Processum.

Seeley Brown, J. and Duguid, P. (2001), *The Social Life of Information*, Boston, MA: Harvard Business School Books.

Tett, G. (2009), *Fool's Gold*, London: Little Brown.

Van den Bergh, J. and Bruinsma, F. (2008) (eds), *Managing Transition to Renewable Energy*, Cheltenham, UK and Northampton, MA, USA: Edward Elgar.

Verganti, R. (2006), 'Innovating through design', *Harvard Business Review*, Reprint R0612G, 1–9.

Verganti, R. (2009), *Design Driven Innovation*, Boston, MA: Harvard Business Press.

VINNOVA (2010), *The Matrix: Post-Cluster Innovation Policy*, Stockholm: VINNOVA.

Von Hippel, E. (2005), *The Democratisation of Innovation*, Cambridge, MA: MIT Press.

Zhang, F. and Cooke, P. (2010), 'Hydrogen and fuel cell development in China: a review', *European Planning Studies*, **18**: 1085–110.

PART II

Knowledge infrastructures as embedding devices

6. Simulating the role of MNCs for knowledge and capital dynamics in networks of innovation

Petra Ahrweiler, Michel Schilperoord, Nigel Gilbert and Andreas Pyka

In this chapter we investigate the effects of the presence and embeddedness of multinational corporations (MNCs) in networks of innovation. New products and processes can result from the ongoing interactions of innovative organizations such as universities, research institutes, firms such as MNCs and small and medium-sized enterprises (SMEs), government agencies, venture capitalists and others. These organizations generate and exchange knowledge, financial capital and other resources in networks of relationships, which are embedded in institutional frameworks on the local, regional, national and international level (Ahrweiler, 2010). Innovation is an emergent property from these interactions on the micro level, providing the combination of actors and organizations, their capabilities and their cooperative behaviours match.

By looking at knowledge flows and capital stocks, we investigate whether the mere presence of MNCs is beneficial for innovation networks and whether there is an additional advantage if these MNCs are engaged in collaborative R&D with other players in the network. We examine the role of MNCs for innovation networks from the perspective of their subsidiaries' host countries by applying the agent-based SKIN model (Simulating Knowledge Dynamics in Innovation Networks; see Ahrweiler et al., 2011). The simulation is grounded in the empirical example of Ireland, enabling us to analyse the role of MNCs in the Irish indigenous industry.

Before Ireland was particularly hard hit by the economic and financial crisis, foreign direct investment (FDI) in the country produced a very high GDP growth rate. Since the 1970s there has been a growth in the high-tech industry sectors but this has only been fostered by foreign-owned MNCs. The MNCs are still poorly integrated into Irish networks, clusters and innovation centres. Accordingly, Ireland has something that approaches a dual economy, composed of SMEs with weak R&D and innovation performance, and MNCs with cutting-edge technology providing a substantial contribution to the wealth of the country. To prevent MNCs from leaving Ireland in favour of competing manufacturing locations and to help the indigenous industry benefit from MNCs, Irish policy makers have been trying to persuade MNCs to locate their R&D in Ireland and to cooperate with Irish organizations (SMEs, universities etc.) in innovation networks. In this chapter we contribute to assessing the impacts and effects of these policies by modelling scenarios that correspond to Irish MNC policy options.

6.1   MNCS AND KNOWLEDGE DYNAMICS

What is the role of big multinational enterprises in the dynamics of knowledge production? MNCs increasingly organize their R&D internationally, which means that subsidiaries become R&D-intensive and have to relate, coordinate and cooperate with R&D activities at the headquarters and at other subsidiaries. The forward transfer of knowledge to overseas subsidiaries has long been established as an important function of MNCs (Dunning, 1958; Vernon, 1966). MNCs are capable of relying on go-it-alone strategies because they find the sources of technological competence and innovation within their own organizational boundaries. They thus act as international network firms that coordinate intra-organizational learning activities (Kogut and Zander, 1993; Gupta and Govindarajan, 2000). This is not a one-way street: the headquarters also benefits from the knowledge of its subsidiaries (cf. Håkanson and Nobel, 2000) and relies on the procedural knowledge its subsidiaries might have about manufacturing details (cf. Phene and Almeida, 2008) or on contextual knowledge about local markets. 'MNCs . . . have continuously extended their network of R&D locations and knowledge centers across the world. They are moving away from a single, self-contained, in-house center of knowledge towards a more distributed and open architecture of knowledge production and application' (Gerybadze, 2004: 123). MNCs can also learn from partners such as universities or small and medium dedicated technology firms in inter-organizational innovation networks.

Tension exists between the remaining importance of the place of origin, which is where most R&D activities are still located (cf. Heidenreich et al., 2010), and internationalization, which demands that R&D is transferred to various domestic settings with spillover and learning opportunities for indigenous industries and periphery learning for the MNC (Doz and Santos, 1997; Schlegelmilch and Chini, 2003). From the perspective of the MNC, the subsidiaries' geographical location can be an important source of value (Frost, 2001; Foss and Pedersen, 2002; Pearce et al., 2008; Song and Shin, 2008); 'the technological abilities of subsidiaries depend above all on the national context and hardly at all on company-wide knowledge flows' (Heidenreich et al., 2010: 138). The attractiveness of the host country is an important factor: 'MNCs can take advantage of local capacities of host countries in terms of technology stocks, research programmes and trajectories and creative human capital' (Narula and Michel, 2010: 123). The innovation networks they tap into consist of heterogeneous organizations such as local universities, research institutes, technology-oriented indigenous firms, suppliers and customers.

From the perspective of the host countries, MNCs are seen as important contributors to the innovation landscape and infrastructures of the indigenous industries. To attract them into the country, national and local governments provide tax incentives and other financial benefits for MNCs: locating R&D in the host country may be subsidized and participation in local educational and research networks is encouraged.

6.2   THE IRISH CASE

Ireland's inward investment promotion agency, IDA Ireland (Industrial Development Agency Ireland), is responsible for attracting and developing foreign investment in Ireland. The original reasons for locating in Ireland used to be a cheap labour force for manufacturing and low tax rates. Additionally, Ireland was attractive to FDI because it offered a European, English-speaking environment. In the 1990s the IDA's success in attracting foreign-owned MNCs to Ireland produced very high growth rates (Cogan, 2000). In 2008, their home countries were reported by the IDA as 47 per cent USA, 11 per cent UK, 10 per cent Germany, 5 per cent France, 17 per cent rest of Europe and 10 per cent other. The economic impact of the foreign-owned MNCs is still very large. However, Ireland has only a small home market; the MNCs produce mainly for export. Their interaction with and integration into the host country industry is weak (Cogan, 2004).

6.2.1   Business R&D in Ireland

Although the Irish policy agencies emphasize the requirement for all industry actors to engage in R&D activities and to move up the value chain through innovation, the actual situation is not as they might wish. Business R&D in both the MNCs and the indigenous industry is still below the EU average. 'Despite its tremendous success in attracting high-tech

Table 6.1   Irish patents in the period 1979–2006

	Patents	%
Irish-owned	911	32
Foreign-owned	1925	68
Total	2836	100

Source: USPTO patent database.

industries, Ireland lags behind in cutting-edge R&D' (Charnitzki, 2007: 323). There is a strong reliance on imported innovation via MNCs (Cogan, 2004) because most of the R&D of Irish-based MNCs is still performed in their home countries. 'Ireland heavily relies on R&D performed by foreign affiliates. This may have several implications for further productivity growth' (Charnitzki, 2007: 324). The relevance of foreign subsidiaries for the Irish national innovation system is indicated by the proportion of R&D expenditure of foreign subsidiaries to the total R&D business expenditure of the country, in 2007 this was 72.4 per cent (source: OECD–AFA Database, 2007). Looking at the owners of patents in Ireland, the heavy reliance on the MNCs again becomes obvious (see Table 6.1). The indigenous SMEs do not experience much benefit from the Irish-located MNCs; they are rather low-tech on average, operate in local markets and do not engage in R&D themselves (Cogan, 2004).

Foreign-owned MNCs no longer look at Ireland as the most attractive location for cheap manufacturing and attractive tax rates, and even Irish-based MNCs are starting to look for other locations to move to (the most well-known example in the recent past was the exit of DELL from Limerick in Ireland to Poland). In past years the number of MNCs with units in Ireland indicated a clear decrease (cf. IDA Ireland, 2008). The IDA and other Irish policy agencies and business associations are trying to retain and attract MNCs by promoting Ireland's young and well-educated qualified employees, and its competitive economy, modern infrastructure, supportive regulations for intellectual property and R&D environment.

6.2.2   Embedding Foreign-owned MNCs in Irish Innovation Networks

To prevent MNCs from leaving Ireland in favour of competing manufacturing locations and to help the indigenous industry to benefit from MNCs, Irish policy makers have been trying to persuade MNCs to locate their R&D in Ireland and to cooperate with Irish organizations (SMEs,

Table 6.2   Collaboration for innovation activities of Irish and foreign-owned companies (2004–06)

Nationality	Size	Collaboration in innovation activities?		
Irish	S3	Yes	19	32%
	250+ employees	No	40	68%
	S2	Yes	73	21%
	50–249 employees	No	273	79%
	S1	Yes	103	10%
	10–49 employees	No	959	90%
TOTAL			**1467**	
Foreign	S3	Yes	52	48%
	250+ employees	No	56	52%
	S2	Yes	58	26%
	50–249 employees	No	166	74%
	S1	Yes	30	17%
	10–49 employees	No	145	83%
TOTAL			**507**	

Source: CIS 2008.

universities etc.) in innovation networks. This agenda of embedding MNCs in innovation networks with indigenous actors is perceived by Irish policy makers to be very urgent. Not only is the Irish economy suffering particularly badly from the effects of the economic and financial crisis, but the indigenous industry also needs an innovation boost for economic recovery. Embedding MNCs and indigenous firms in collaborative R&D and innovation activities is seen as a crucial issue for the future of the Irish economy. The benefits for the local environment of having MNCs as knowledge hubs and financial magnets are, however, heavily intertwined with the benefits for the MNCs themselves in profiting from the Irish R&D context. Due to their home orientation, the MNCs still show a low R&D integration into networks, clusters and innovation centres in Ireland. This picture is confirmed by the CIS data for Ireland on collaborative innovation activities for foreign-owned companies in comparison to the domestic Irish innovation network. Table 6.2 shows the answers of 1467 Irish-owned companies and 507 foreign-owned companies to question 7.1[1] (Collaboration in innovation activities: Yes/No) of the CIS for each employment size class.

Table 6.3 shows the answers of the Irish-owned big companies to a question about the type of collaboration (from question 7.2 of the CIS).

*Table 6.3   Collaboration for innovation activities of Irish-owned size S3
companies (2004–06)*

	Type of collaboration	
ENT-IE	Other Irish enterprises within enterprise group	15%
SUP-IE	Irish suppliers	15%
UNI-IE	Irish universities or other HEIs	14%
CON-IE	Irish consultants, commercial labs, or private R&D institutes	12%
SUP-EU	European suppliers	12%
GOV-IE	Irish government or public research institutes	8%
CLI-IE	Irish clients or customers	7%
CON-EU	European consultants, commercial labs, or private R&D institutes	7%
CLI-EU	European clients or customers	2%
	Other	8%
		100%

Source: CIS 2008.

Types are ENT, SUP, CLI, CON, UNI, GOV, as explained in the table. Locations are Ireland (IE), Northern Ireland (N-IE), Europe (EU), the USA (US), China or India (CI) and OTHER. Irish-owned firms show strong integration into the indigenous network – collaborations mainly happen within the country.

If we look at the cooperation partners of Irish-owned big companies (250+ employees) compared to the cooperation partners of foreign-owned big companies (Table 6.4), we see, however, that foreign-owned big companies tend to tap into knowledge from the indigenous environment, even though they are not strongly embedded in the domestic firm network. There is a strong orientation towards the headquarters and other parts of their own enterprise group, and a broad outreach to the international supplier and service network when it comes to innovation collaboration with other companies.

However, it is the embedding of MNC innovation activities into the Irish firm network that policy makers trust will yield knowledge flows and innovation diffusion to boost the indigenous economy: expected are spillover effects (cf. for criticizing the 'fairytale of spillovers' Pyka et al., 2009), spin-offs for the Irish economy and a skilled workforce that could move permanently into the country. Last but not least, there would be subcontract and sub-supply linkages to increase the innovation capacity of Irish firms (Cogan, 2004).

*Table 6.4   Collaboration for innovation activities of foreign-owned size S3
companies (2004–06)*

	Type of collaboration	
ENT-US	Other US enterprises within enterprise group	24%
UNI-IE	Irish universities or other HEIs	21%
ENT-EU	Other European enterprises within enterprise group	20%
SUP-EU	European suppliers	19%
SUP-IE	Irish suppliers	18%
SUP-US	US suppliers	18%
CLI-EU	European clients or customers	16%
ENT-IE	Other Irish enterprises with enterprise group	14%
CON-IE	Irish consultants, commercial labs, or private R&D institutes	10%
CLI-IE	Irish clients or customers	10%
CON-EU	Other European consultants, commercial labs, or private R&D institutes	9%
CLI-US	US clients or customers	9%

Source: CIS 2008.

The data show that this is not yet happening on a big scale. So, how important are MNCs and their host-country subsidiaries for the indigenous industry? Are these policy efforts correctly targeted? The innovation networks around MNCs consist of many heterogeneous actors following diverse rule sets and are located in a large parameter space of environmental conditions: to identify single knowledge-related parameters as responsible for economic impact is difficult in a setting full of non-linear dynamics. Conventional econometric analysis finds this difficult. 'Attempts at identifying the impact of MNC activity on different territorial systems, using aggregate data, should therefore be supplemented with a more fine-grained analysis of structurally contextualized innovation behavior' (Asheim et al., 2010: 4).

To shed light on the assumed beneficial relationship between MNC subsidiaries and their host countries' indigenous industry, we shall investigate how important the knowledge hub and financial magnet functions of MNCs are for innovation networks. By capturing the non-linear dynamics of innovation networks in a model and experimenting with this, it becomes possible to understand what is happening and what can happen on the macro level in order to assist regional decision makers with evidence-based innovation policy strategies. Over the last few years the methodology of agent-based modelling (ABM) (Gilbert and Troitzsch, 2005; Gilbert, 2007;

Tesfatsion, 2001) has frequently been adopted. Using agent-based simulation informed by empirical research allows us to set up artificial 'innovation networks' and to experiment with them to find out what emerges from their dynamics.

6.3   AGENT-BASED SIMULATION WITH SKIN

In this chapter we model the networking behaviour of innovative actors focusing on MNCs and analyse their contributions by building on prior work (e.g. Gilbert et al., 2007) with the SKIN simulation. SKIN is a multi-agent model of innovation networks in knowledge-intensive industries grounded in empirical research and theoretical frameworks from innovation economics and economic sociology. The agents represent innovative firms in a region that try to sell their innovations to other agents and end users but who also have to buy raw materials or more sophisticated inputs from other agents (or material suppliers) in order to produce their outputs. This basic model of a market is extended with a representation of the knowledge dynamics in and between the firms. Each firm tries to improve its innovation performance and its sales by improving its knowledge base through adaptation to user needs, incremental or radical learning, and cooperation and networking with other agents.

6.3.1   The Agents

A SKIN agent is a firm that owns technological capital, that is, 'the portfolio of scientific resources (research potential) or technical resources (procedures, aptitudes, routines and unique and coherent know-how, capable of reducing expenditure in labour or capital or increasing its yield) that can be deployed in the design and manufacture of products' (Bourdieu, 2005: 194). This technological capital is the individual knowledge base of a firm. It is called the firm's 'kene' (Gilbert, 1997) and it consists of a number of units of knowledge.

Each unit is represented as a triple consisting of a firm's capability C in a scientific, technological or business domain (e.g. biochemistry), represented by an integer randomly chosen from the range of 1–1000, its ability A to perform a certain application in this field (e.g. a synthesis procedure or filtering technique in the field of biochemistry), represented by an integer randomly chosen from the range 1–10, and the expertise level E the firm has achieved with respect to this ability (represented by an integer randomly chosen from the range 1–10). The firm's kene is its collection of $C/A/E$ triples (Figure 6.1).

$$\left\{ \begin{array}{c} C \\ A \\ E \end{array} \right\}, \left\{ \begin{array}{c} C \\ A \\ E \end{array} \right\}, \left\{ \begin{array}{c} C \\ A \\ E \end{array} \right\}, \left\{ \begin{array}{c} C \\ A \\ E \end{array} \right\}, \left\{ \begin{array}{c} C \\ A \\ E \end{array} \right\}, \ldots$$

Figure 6.1   The kene of an agent

Firms apply their knowledge to create innovative products that have a chance of being successful on the market. The special focus of a firm, its potential innovation, is called an 'innovation hypothesis'. In the model the innovation hypothesis (IH) consists of a subset of the firm's kene triples.

6.3.2   The Market

Given that actors in empirical innovation networks of knowledge-intensive industries interact on both the knowledge and the market levels, we need a representation of market dynamics in the SKIN model. Agents are therefore characterized by their capital stock. Each firm, when it is set up, has a stock of initial capital. It needs this capital to produce for the market and to finance its R&D expenditures; it can increase its capital by selling products. The amount of capital owned by a firm is used as a measure of its size and additionally influences the amount of knowledge (measured by the number of triples in its kene) that it can maintain. In many knowledge-intensive industries we find the coexistence of large and small actors (e.g. the large pharmaceutical firms and biotech start-ups, and the former national monopolists and high-tech specialists in the ICT industries; cf. Pyka and Saviotti, 2005). We assume that large diversified firms are characterized by a larger knowledge base as compared to smaller specialized companies (cf. Brusoni et al., 2001).

Firms apply their knowledge to create innovative products that have a chance of being successful on the market.

> Most technology is specific, complex . . . [and] cumulative in its development . . . It is specific to firms where most technological activity is carried out, and it is specific to products and processes, since most of the expenditures is not on research, but on development and production engineering, after which knowledge is also accumulated through experience in production and use on what has come to be known as 'learning-by-doing' and 'learning-by-using'. (Pavitt, 1987: 9)

The probability for an agent to form an innovation hypothesis is proportional to the kene length, whereas the proportionality is derived from the average kene length.

The underlying idea for an innovation, modelled by the innovation hypothesis (IH), is the source an agent uses for its attempts to make profits within the market. Due to the fundamental uncertainty of innovation (Knight, 1921), there is no simple relationship between the innovation hypothesis and product development. To represent this uncertainty we developed the following mechanism: the innovation hypothesis is transformed into the simulation of a product through a mapping procedure in which the capabilities and abilities of the innovation hypothesis are used to compute an index number that represents the product. The particular transformation procedure applied allows the same product to result from different kenes, which is not too far from reality where the production technologies of firms within a single industry can vary considerably (Winter, 1984).

A firm's product, P, is generated from its innovation hypothesis as

$$P = \sum_{IH} (C_i A_i) \bmod N$$

(where N is a constant representing the maximum number of different possible products).

A product has a certain quality, which is also computed from the innovation hypothesis in a similar way, by multiplying the abilities and the expertise levels for each triple in the innovation hypothesis and normalizing the result. In order to realize the product, the agent needs materials. These can either come from outside the sector (raw materials) or from other firms that have generated them as their products. Which materials are needed is also determined by the underlying innovation hypothesis: the kind of material required for an input is obtained by selecting subsets from the innovation hypothesis and applying the standard mapping function above.

These inputs are chosen so that each is different and differs from the firm's own product. In order to be able to engage in production, all the inputs need to be obtainable on the market, that is, provided by other firms or available as raw materials. If the inputs are not available, the firm is not able to produce and has to give up this attempt to innovate. If there is more than one supplier for a certain input, the agent will choose the one at the lowest price and, if there are several similar offers, the one with the highest quality. If the firm can go into production, it has to find a price for its product, taking into account the input prices it is paying and a possible profit margin. While the simulation starts with product prices set at random, as the simulation proceeds a price adjustment mechanism following a standard mark-up pricing model increases the selling price if there is much demand and reduces it (but no lower than the total cost of production) if there are no customers. Some products are considered to be destined for the 'end user' and are sold to customers outside the sector: there is always a demand for such end-user products provided they are offered at or below a fixed end-user price.

A firm buys the requested inputs from its suppliers using its capital to do so, produces its output and puts it on the market for others to purchase. Using the price adjustment mechanism, agents are able to adapt their prices to demand and in doing so learn by feedback. In making a product, a firm applies the knowledge in its innovation hypothesis and this increases its expertise in this area. This is the way that learning by doing/using is modelled. The expertise levels of the triples in the innovation hypothesis are increased.

Thus, in trying to be successful on the market, firms are dependent on their innovation hypotheses, that is, on their kenes. If a product does not find any demand, the firm has to adapt its knowledge in order to produce something else for which there are customers (cf. e.g. Duncan, 1974). A firm has several ways of improving its performance, either alone or in cooperation, and in either an incremental or a more radical fashion.

6.3.3 Learning and Cooperation: Improving Innovation Performance

In an earlier publication (Gilbert et al., 2007) we showed how these learning features of the SKIN model are theoretically grounded in the body of literature known as 'Organizational Learning' (OL). After Dewey (1938) introduced the concept of experiential learning as a permanent activity cycle and started a discussion among educationalists about feedback learning and learning by doing, Michael (1973) coined the term organizational learning. Argyris and Schön's influential monograph *Organizational Learning* (1978; newly edited including further work as *Organizational Learning II*, 1996) proposed that a learning organization is one that is permanently changing its interpretation of the environment. In doing so, the organization learns new things. Drawing on their background as action theorists, Argyris and Schön show how these interpretations are gained and how they are connected to different organizational behaviours. They distinguish between three types of learning, rooting them in an understanding of organizational agency that targets growth and effectiveness:

- *Single-loop learning*: this is adjustment learning, referring to the rational use of one's own means and instruments to adapt to environmental requirements given a set of organizational goals, strategies and behaviours. It targets an improvement of the 'theory in use' of an organization using a simple action–outcome feedback and follows the heuristic 'maximize gains and minimize loss'.

- *Double-loop learning*: this is turnover learning with respect to the meta-level of goals, strategies and behaviours of an organization, and aims to adapt them to environmental requirements. The learning process includes un-learning of redundant knowledge to clear space for new behaviours. Furthermore, cooperation, including assumption and benefit sharing with collaborators, is seen as a vehicle for learning.
- *Deutero learning*: this is meta-level learning of the highest order where the organization reflects on its own identity. Here, the learning process itself is the object of learning ('to learn how to learn'). The organization's norms and values are subject to critique and change.

The SKIN model takes many of the ideas of the Argyris and Schön framework and uses them to examine the assumption that, in the words of de Geus (1997), the greatest competitive advantage for any firm is its ability to learn. Experiments concerning the effects of different combinations of learning activities on the agent population are reported in Gilbert et al. (2007). In the SKIN model firms predominantly engage in single- and double-loop learning activities. Deutero learning may appear when new agents are created intentionally by collaborating actors due to the success of the network.

In respect of single-loop learning, firm agents can:

- use their capabilities (learning by doing/using) and learn to estimate their success via feedback from markets and clients (learning by feedback) as already mentioned above;
- improve their own knowledge incrementally when the feedback is not satisfactory in order to adapt to changing technological and/ or economic standards (adaptation learning, incremental learning).

If a firm's previous innovation has been successful, that is, it has found buyers, the firm will continue selling the same product in the next round, possibly at a different price depending on the demand it has experienced. However, if there were no sales, it considers that it is time for change. If the firm still has enough capital, it will carry out 'incremental' research (R&D in the firm's labs). Performing incremental research (cf. Cohen and Levinthal, 1989) means that a firm tries to improve its product by altering one of the abilities chosen from the triples in its innovation hypothesis while sticking to its focal capabilities. The ability in each triple is considered to be a point in the respective capability's action space. To move in the action space means to go up or down by an increment, thus allowing for two possible research directions. The new triple learnt is added to the firm's kene.

Alternatively, firms can radically change their capabilities in order to meet completely different client requirements (innovative learning, radical learning). A SKIN firm agent under serious pressure and in danger of becoming bankrupt will turn to more radical measures by exploring a completely different area of market opportunities. In the model an agent under financial pressure turns to a new innovation hypothesis after first 'inventing' a new capability, that is, adding a randomly chosen new triple, for its kene and then generating a new innovation hypothesis.

Firms may also be active on the double-loop learning level of the model. They can:

- decide on their individual learning strategies themselves (e.g. incremental or radical learning), constructing and changing the strategies according to their past experience and current context. The context consists of external factors such as the actions of clients, competitors and partners and the availability of technical options, as well as internal factors such as their capital stock and the competencies available to them;
- engage in networking and partnerships to absorb and exploit external knowledge sources, to imitate and emulate, and to use synergy effects (participative learning).

An agent in the model may consider partnerships (alliances, joint ventures etc.) in order to exploit external knowledge sources. The decision whether and with whom to cooperate is based on the mutual observations of the firms that estimate the chances and requirements coming from competitors, possible and past partners, and clients. Bolton et al. (2005), writing from a theoretical viewpoint, and Michelet (1992), using empirical evidence, both show that greater mutual information, where firms know their partner's history of cooperation, improves the conditions for cooperation. In the SKIN model a marketing feature provides the information that a firm can gather about other agents: to advertise its product, a firm publishes the capabilities used in its innovation hypothesis. Those capabilities not included in its innovation hypothesis, and thus not in its product, are not visible externally and cannot be used to select the firm as a partner. The firm's 'advertisement' is then the basis for decisions by other firms to form or reject cooperative arrangements.

In experimenting with the model we can choose between two different partner search strategies (Powell et al., 2005), both of which compare the firm's own capabilities as used in its innovation hypothesis and the possible partner's capabilities as seen in its advertisement. Applying the conservative strategy, a firm will be attracted to a partner that has similar capabilities; using a progressive strategy, the attraction is based on the difference between the capability sets. Previously good experience with former contacts generally augurs well for renewing a partnership. This is mirrored in the model: to find a partner, the firm will look at previous partners first, then at its suppliers, customers and finally at all others. If there is a firm sufficiently attractive according to the chosen search strategy (i.e. with attractiveness above the 'attractiveness threshold'), it will stop its search and offer a partnership. If the potential partner wishes to return the partnership offer, the partnership is set up.

The model assumes that partners learn only about the knowledge being actively used by the other agent. Thus, to learn from a partner, a firm will add the triples of the partner's innovation hypothesis to its own. Once the knowledge transfer has been completed, each firm continues to produce its own product, possibly with greater expertise as a result of acquiring skills from its partner.

If the firm's last innovation was successful, that is, the value of its profit in the previous round was above a threshold, and the firm has some partners at hand, it can initiate the formation of a network. In the biotechnology-based pharmaceutical sector, for example, a network of firms often forms an independent legal entity. An example is Genostar, a French bio-informatics company that emerged from a public–private innovation network between the Institut Pasteur, INRIA (French National Institute for Research in Computer Science and Control) and the firms Genome Express and Hybrigenics.[2] The formation of a legal entity enables actions and exploits advantages that are only available to companies and can be considered as a particular form of deutero learning.

This is why networks are autonomous agents in the SKIN model. Of course, the participating members stay autonomous agents themselves and thus have a chance of double profit: the distributed rewards if the network is successful and the returns they get from their own successful innovation projects that they undertake outside of the network. Networks are 'normal' agents; that is, they get the same amount of initial capital as other firms and can engage in all the activities available to other firms. The kene of a network is the union of the triples from the innovation hypotheses of all its participants. If a network is successful, it will distribute any earnings above the amount of the initial capital to its members; if it fails and becomes bankrupt, it will be dissolved.

6.3.4 Start-ups

If a sector is successful, new firms will be attracted to it, representing Schumpeterian competition by imitation. This is modelled by adding a new firm to the population when any existing firm makes a substantial profit. The new firm is a clone of the successful firm, but with its kene triples both restricted to those in the successful firm's advertisement and set to a low expertise level.

This models a new firm that copies the characteristics of those seen to be successful on the market. As with all firms, the kene may also be restricted because the initial capital of a start-up is limited and may not be sufficient to support the copying of the whole of the successful firm's innovation hypothesis.

The SKIN model is the result of a number of projects that combined empirical research into innovation networks with agent-based simulation (see for the empirical grounding of the SKIN model Ahrweiler et al., 2010). In the following we shall describe the additional features that we have implemented to model the role of MNCs for innovation networks.

6.3.5 MNC Agents

In the adapted model MNCs are normal SKIN agents producing (manufacturing) and selling products to customers with inputs from suppliers. They can employ all the learning and networking activities usually available to SKIN agents. In addition to these attributes, MNC agents have two individual characteristics that give them a better chance of entering foreign markets and marketing new technologies due to their commercialization experience and distribution networks.

The amount of capital owned by a firm is used as a measure of its size and additionally influences the amount of knowledge (measured by the number of triples in its kene) that it can maintain. Compared to common SKIN agents, MNC agents have:

- large knowledge bases (dependent on capital stock; defined by a capital–knowledge ratio giving the proportionality between kene length and capital);
- high capital stocks (initial capital 50 times higher than usual SKIN agents).

We have flagged the MNCs in the model to distinguish them from enlarged SMEs in order to track them and analyse their properties and behaviour.

6.3.6   New Indicators

For the experiments we created and compared two scenarios: one with and the other without MNC agents. To measure the amount of knowledge k of firm agents, we used a measure calculated from a firm's kene.

$$k_i = \|k_i\|$$

where k_i is the length of the kene vector. From this, the average knowledge per firm can be derived as

$$\bar{k} = \frac{1}{nFirms} \sum_{i \in \{Firms\}} k_i$$

and the deviation of knowledge among the firms is

$$\sigma_k = \sqrt{\frac{1}{nFirms} \sum_{i \in \{Firms\}} (k_i - \bar{k})^2}$$

Using these indicators, we can model knowledge flows. The knowledge flow (kf) is the total increase of knowledge over all firm agents arising from their learning from partners. Let k_i^{t-1} be the knowledge of a firm agent before learning from partners and k_i^t be the knowledge of a firm after learning from partners. The knowledge flow is

$$kf = \sum_{i \in partnering\ Firms} (k_i^t - k_i^{t-1})$$

6.4   EXPERIMENTS

We can now return to the policy questions outlined above in relation to the Irish economy. How important is the knowledge integration function of MNCs as knowledge hubs and financial magnets for regional innovation networks? Does a firm population containing MNCs perform better in terms of knowledge diffusion and innovation performance than a uniform-size population of small and medium firms? What are the effects of MNC presence and activities on the knowledge level of the firm population? To deal with these questions we constructed two different comparisons. First, we compare a model with MNC agents to a model without MNC agents.

The following indicators are evaluated for the first comparison (distinguishing between SMEs and MNCs):

On the capital level:

- Increase of innovation performance:
  - We compare the two populations in terms of success (i.e. *reward above a certain success threshold*).
- Increase of capital:
  - We compare the two populations in terms of capital amount.
- Increase of sales of the industry:
  - We compare the two possible model variants in terms of the sales of the firms.

On the knowledge level:

- Increase knowledge flow (knowledge diffusion):
  - We use an adjacency matrix that contains the knowledge flow for each cooperation.

Second, we compare a model containing MNC agents in R&D cooperation with the indigenous industry to a model where MNCs just follow go-it-alone innovation strategies while all other firms in that scenario can cooperate with each other. Go-it-alone innovation strategies are the features described above as incremental and radical learning, which can be performed in the R&D labs of a firm without having to cooperate with external partners. Cooperation includes all features described above as partnerships and networks.

For the second comparison the following indicators are evaluated (distinguishing between SMEs and MNCs):

On the knowledge level:

- Increase of knowledge:
  - We compare the two populations in terms of knowledge amount.
- Increase knowledge flows (knowledge diffusion):
  - We use an adjacency matrix that contains the knowledge flow for each cooperation.

On the capital level:

- Sustainability of industry:
  - We compare the two possible model variants in terms of the lifetime of the firms.

The go-it-alone scenario shows a picture of MNCs without any R&D cooperation in the host country and MNCs that are innovation-active. Empirically, this means for most MNCs that their dominant R&D location is at the headquarters of their home country, while small parts of R&D are performed by their subsidiaries in host countries. In that sense, the go-it-alone scenario is a way of modelling the R&D location for MNCs as being completely headquarters based, that is, from the perspective of the host country, foreign based.

The starting configuration of the experiments was set up to simulate the agents of the Irish innovation system. Modelling results will be validated against empirical findings from Irish data. The initial parameter setting for the firm population mirrors the conditions in the Irish economy (Forfás Central Statistics Office, Statistical Release March 2009).

We begin with about 200 R&D-active MNCs and about 1000 R&D-active SMEs. We then measure the values after 200 ticks where the simulation has settled down into a more or less dynamic equilibrium or provides smooth curves for the evaluated indicators. For the more volatile indicator of innovation performance where the model has to deal with the true uncertainty (Knight, 1921) of the underlying processes (resulting in the *number of innovations*, i.e. the average numbers of products brought to market for firm agents), we measure the average number of successes over intervals of ten ticks.

6.5   RESULTS

To obtain reliable results from our experiments, we used 30 runs per scenario, that is, 90 runs in total. Table 6.5 summarizes our results for the first scenario comparison (model with and without MNCs).

To compare the two scenarios we used an independent two-sample *t*-test with equal sample sizes and unequal variance. Comparisons that are statistically significant are those with values less than 0.05 in the last column.

The indicator for the innovation performance of SMEs and MNCs shown in Table 6.5 is the percentage of successful SMEs/MNCs over their total numbers, where 'success' means that their last reward in the market was above a certain threshold. This indicator shows that the innovative performance of SMEs gets better when MNCs are in the population. MNCs have stable supplier requirements, that is, they offer a stable market for the products of the indigenous industry of SMEs.

Furthermore, MNCs provide a constant flow of products to satisfy the demands of SMEs and thus enable SMEs to deliver their products to the

Table 6.5   Results for first scenario comparison

Indicator	Without MNCs		With MNCs		*t*-test 1/2
	mean1	sd1	mean2	Sd2	
Innovative performance SMEs	37.8	10.5	56.7	4.7	**0.000***
Innovative performance MNCs			58.1	4.6	–
Sales SMEs	9477	777	10213	443	**0.000***
Sales MNCs			10370	664	–
Capital stock SMEs (average)	5.48	0.09	5.60	0.04	**0.000***
Capital stock MNCs (average)			5.92	0.03	–
Capital stock SMEs (median)	5.61	0.08	5.74	0.03	**0.000***
Capital stock MNCs (median)			5.91	0.03	–
Knowledge flow	2939	733	3509	492	**0.001***

Note: * indicates effects significant at the 5% level.

market. This is shown in the value of the sales of the SMEs, which improve in a scenario with MNCs, and the indicator for their capital stock, which follows along the same lines. The knowledge flow is significantly better in a scenario with MNCs, even though the big firms are not cooperating. This means that the mere presence of MNCs in the population somehow increases the cooperative behaviour of the indigenous industry. More research needs to be done to explain this result.

Table 6.5 shows that there is a statistically significant difference between scenarios for all the indicators measuring SME performance. Having MNCs in the innovation network raises the 'innovation performance' of the SMEs in the population. This is related to the 'capital stock' generated and available in this network, which provides a significant stability for the whole industry population. Checking simply for the averages of these indicators on the population level could lead to the conclusion that the results are created by design: one-fifth of the firms are MNCs with ten times the capital; that is, it is not surprising that the results show a larger amount of capital in the MNC scenario. However, we measured the indicators for SMEs separately and they have also changed positively in the MNC scenario. This means that the whole population of firms benefits from the presence of MNCs, that is, also the SMEs. MNCs not only concentrate

Table 6.6   Results for second scenario comparison

Indicator	MNCs go-it-alone		MNCs cooperating		*t*-test 2/3
	mean2	sd2	mean3	sd3	
Knowledge SMEs (average)	466.8	37.8	494.2	38.0	**0.007***
Knowledge MNCs (average)	373.6	34.3	651.2	84.9	**0.000***
Knowledge SMEs (median)	151.9	10.0	160.4	13.6	**0.008***
Knowledge MNCs (median)	149.5	8.3	220.4	63.1	**0.000***
Sustainability SMEs (average)	16.89	3.07	19.26	3.08	**0.004***
Sustainability MNCs (average)	51.8	67.4	125.9	34.4	**0.000***
Sustainability SMEs (median)	8.15	0.95	8.23	0.65	**0.693***
Sustainability MNCs (median)	51.8	67.4	128.9	36.5	**0.000***
Knowledge flow	3509	492	3962	631	**0.003***

Note: * indicates effects significant at the 5% level.

the capital and are 'too big to die'; their presence is beneficial for the whole population of firms.

MNCs give stability to the market structure by reliably providing input products and using products from the local providers. This enables the firms of the indigenous industry to grow, to learn from each other and to form sustainable local knowledge networks. To sum up, the most interesting result is the surprisingly beneficial effects on the capital and knowledge level that the mere MNC presence has for the indigenous industry.

Table 6.6 presents results for the second scenario comparison (a model where MNCs have R&D cooperations with the surrounding innovation network compared with a model where MNCs just follow go-it-alone strategies and only the host country agents collaborate with each other).

Here, we can see that when MNCs cooperate with the local environment in terms of R&D, the competence level of the whole population is raised. There are significant spillover effects when MNCs are actively engaged in R&D cooperations with the host country's industry.

The assumption that having MNCs in the cooperating population of agents will raise the 'Knowledge' or competence level of the whole population is confirmed by the experiments. At the population level, it would not be surprising that the amount of knowledge is larger on average in a population where MNCs are present because big firms can hold more knowledge by design (they have longer kenes). However, the values for the SMEs show that SMEs benefit more than proportionally from the cooperation with MNCs on the knowledge level.

Cooperating MNCs provide a significant degree of stability for the whole population. There are significantly fewer exits and firms survive longer in an environment where MNCs are present and well integrated into the indigenous innovation network. A population with cooperating MNCs is more sustainable than a population where cooperation is missing; this also applies to the median of SMEs in this population.

6.6 EMPIRICAL EVIDENCE FOR THE SIMULATION FINDINGS

The SKIN simulation is a theory running on a computer – it produces data as the outcome of the processes and mechanisms implemented in the artificial world. To test and possibly falsify the computational theory we need to validate it by confronting the model results with real-world data. For example, we could check how the simulated MNC effects will actually materialize in the empirical world for the case study we took as our example, the Irish economy. As outlined in section 6.2, policy agencies such as Science Foundation Ireland (SFI) have tried to encourage collaborative R&D between Irish universities, MNCs and indigenous firms for research-intensive science and technology, mostly in the ICT sector and the life sciences. Table 6.7 shows the most recent results of these efforts of the well-funded CSET Programme of SFI.

However, the newly released CIS data for the period 2006–08 (Table 6.8) do not show a strong increase in collaborative behaviour (cf. Table 6.2).

Also, the comparison between Irish-owned big companies and foreign-owned big companies (Tables 6.9 and 6.10) concerning integration into the indigenous network does not show any improvement in comparison to the former situation (Tables 6.3–6.4).

Table 6.7 Participation of foreign subsidiaries in CSETs (2010)

Number of funded projects	10
Number of participant firms	74
Indigenous firms	25 (34%)
Foreign subsidiaries	49 (66%)

Source: http://www.sfi.ie.

Table 6.8   Collaboration for innovation activities of Irish and foreign-owned companies (2006–08)

Nationality	Size	Collaboration in innovation activities?		
Irish	S3	Yes	13	22%
	250+ employees	No	47	78%
	S2	Yes	68	18%
	50–249 employees	No	318	82%
	S1	Yes	93	8%
	10–49 employees	No	1120	92%
TOTAL			**1659**	
Foreign	S3	Yes	42	46%
	250+ employees	No	49	54%
	S2	Yes	52	23%
	50–249 employees	No	174	77%
	S1	Yes	26	13%
	10–49 employees	No	179	87%
TOTAL			**522**	

Source: CIS 2010.

Table 6.9   Collaboration for innovation activities of Irish-owned size S3 companies (2006–08)

	Type of collaboration	
ENT-IE	Other Irish enterprises within enterprise group	8%
SUP-IE	Irish suppliers	8%
CON-IE	Irish consultants, commercial labs, or private R&D institutes	8%
CLI-IE	Irish clients or customers	8%
CLI-EU	European clients or customers	8%
UNI-IE	Irish universities or other HEIs	7%
SUP-EU	European suppliers	7%
GOV-IE	Irish government or public research institutes	7%
CON-EU	European consultants, commercial labs or private R&D institutes	5%

Source: CIS 2010.

Table 6.10 *Collaboration for innovation activities of foreign-owned size S3 companies (2006–08)*

	Type of collaboration	
UNI-IE	Irish universities or other HEIs	25%
ENT-EU	Other European enterprises within enterprise group	23%
ENT-US	Other US enterprises within enterprise group	18%
SUP-EU	European suppliers	16%
SUP-IE	Irish suppliers	15%
CON-EU	Other European consultants, commercial labs or private R&D institutes	14%
SUP-US	US suppliers	12%
CLI-EU	European clients or customers	12%
CON-IE	Irish consultants, commercial labs or private R&D institutes	11%
CLI-US	US clients or customers	11%
ENT-IE	Other Irish enterprises with enterprise group	9%
CLI-IE	Irish clients or customers	9%

Source: CIS 2010.

Table 6.11 *Irish patents in the period 2006–10*

	Patents	%
Irish-owned	459	31
Foreign-owned	1009	69
	1468	100

Source: USPTO patent database.

Looking at patents as one of the performance indicators and bearing in mind that the majority of patents listed in Table 6.1 were produced during the last four to five years of the measured period, we can see that the situation has also not improved at the output end (Table 6.11).

The heavy reliance on foreign MNCs for patents remains, as shown in Table 6.12.

However, the indigenous industry has caught up a little and is more innovative. Our simulation shows the same tendency (Table 6.13) and suggests that this is due to learning and knowledge flows through MNC presence and cooperation.

Table 6.12   Relevance of foreign subsidiaries in national innovation systems

	Patents with domestic inventor but foreign owner (% of total patents registered in USPTO), 2005-2010[a]
Austria	61.3
Belgium	62.4
Denmark	36.5
Finland	12.6
France	37.9
Germany	24
Greece	84.9
Ireland	**68.9**
Italy	39.1
Luxembourg	80.8
The Netherlands	35
Portugal	61.9
Spain	56.4
Sweden	27.2
UK	58.3
EU-15[b]	49.8

Notes:
a. *Source:* own calculations through patent counts in the US PTO (http://www.uspto.gov), following the methodology proposed by van Pottelsberghe de la Potterie and Guellec (2001).
b. The EU-15 figure is the arithmetic average for the member states.

Table 6.13   Number of patents with Irish inventor in the period 2005–10

	No. of companies	No. of patents	
Irish companies	157	358	(27.9%)
Irish universities	7	37	(2.9%)
Non-Irish companies	196	796	(61.9%)
Non-Irish universities	9	9	(0.7%)
Other[a]		85	(6.6%)
TOTAL		**1285**	

Note: a.   No specific data for assignee.

Source: USPTO patent database.

6.7   CONCLUSIONS

Experimenting with MNC links in knowledge-intensive industry scenarios has provided interesting insights. Our experiments compared a SKIN population with and without MNC agents, and a scenario with and without cooperating MNCs. Our results strongly confirm the current Irish MNC policy strategies. Just attracting and retaining MNCs provides increasing capital availability and innovation performance for the indigenous industry. Surprisingly, even the mere presence of MNCs in the indigenous economy raises the knowledge flows in the host country's industry because firms can more safely engage in R&D and market activities. This is certainly intensified when MNCs engage in local learning activities and embed themselves into the R&D network of regional innovation. The agent-based simulation confirms that MNCs in R&D collaboration with the indigenous innovation network improve the knowledge and competence level of the whole industry and the innovation diffusion and collaborative arrangements in the host country.

The aim of simulation modelling is not primarily to reproduce statistical observations but rather to gain a dynamic and detailed description of a complex system where we can observe the consequences of changing features and parameters. Such simulations serve as a laboratory to experiment with social life and test our theories in a way that cannot be done empirically for methodological reasons.

Our model has provided some answers to policy makers' 'what-if' questions, such as what would have been the impact if the Irish innovation policy strategies to attract MNCs into the country and embed them in R&D collaborations with the indigenous industry had been successful? Our research strategy highlights the twofold advantages offered by agent-based modelling for this kind of analysis. On the one hand, comparing different scenarios as we did in the simulation can never be done in the real world. On the other hand, the ABM (agent-based model) allows the generation of simulated data concerning innovation performance, knowledge development and so on necessary for the intended analysis but which is not empirically or only incompletely available. Further development of the model will be needed to recognize the heterogeneity of Irish MNCs as integrated players, global innovators, implementers and local innovators (Gupta and Govindarajan, 1991, 1994). Adding this will probably help to further advance our understanding of the complex processes of innovation in knowledge-intensive sectors.

NOTES

1. CIS survey question 7.1 answered by Irish-located firms: 'During the three years 2004 to 2006, did your enterprise co-operate on any of your innovation activities with other enterprises or institutions? Innovation co-operation is active participation with other enterprises or non-commercial institutions on innovation activities. Both partners do not need to commercially benefit. Exclude pure contracting out of work with no active co-operation'.
2. See http://www.genostar.com/en/about-genostar/history1.html.

REFERENCES

Ahrweiler, P. (ed.) (2010), *Innovation in Complex Social Systems*, London: Routledge.

Ahrweiler, P., Pyka, A. and Gilbert, N. (2011), 'A new model for university–industry links in knowledge-based economies', *Journal of Product Innovation Management*, **28**: 218–35.

Argyris, C. and Schön, D. (1978), *Organizational Learning: A Theory of Action Perspective*, Reading, MA: Addison-Wesley.

Argyris, C. and Schön, D. (1996), *Organizational Learning II: Theory, Method and Practice*, Reading, MA: Addison-Wesley.

Asheim, B., Ebersberger, B. and Herstad, S. (2010), 'MNCs between the local and the global: knowledge bases, proximity and distributed knowledge networks', paper presented at the MNC Conference, University of Oldenburg, Germany, February.

Bolton, G.E., Katok, E. and Ockenfels, A. (2005), 'Cooperation among strangers with limited information about reputation', *Journal of Public Economics*, **89**: 1457–68.

Bourdieu, P. (2005), *The Social Structures of the Economy*, Cambridge: Polity Press.

Brusoni, S., Prencipe, A. and Pavitt, K. (2001), 'Knowledge specialisation, organizational coupling and the boundaries of the firm: why do firms know more than they make?', *Administrative Science Quarterly*, **46** (4): 597–621.

Charnitzki, D. (2007), 'The value of using microdata and microdata linking to investigate innovation impacts', presentation in joint NESTI–TIP Workshop on Innovation Indicators for Policy Making and Impact Assessment, Paris, June.

Cogan, J. (2000), 'Science, technology and innovation policy and science & technology policy evaluation: the Irish experience', paper presented at the CISEP Workshop on Innovation and Diffusion in the Economy: The Strategy and Evaluation Perspectives, Lisbon, January.

Cogan, J. (2004), 'Building a system of innovation: reflections on the Irish experience', Science Policy Research Centre, UCD.

Cohen, W.M. and Levinthal, D.A. (1989), 'Innovation and learning: the two faces of R&D', *The Economic Journal*, **99**: 569–96.

De Geus, A. (1997), *The Living Company*, Boston, MA: Harvard Business School Press.

Dewey, J. (1938), *Experience and Education*, New York: Collier Books.

Doz, Y. and Santos, J.F.P. (1997), 'On the management of knowledge: from the transparency of collocation and co-setting to the quandary of dispersion and differentiation', INSEAD working paper series (97/119/SM), Fontainebleau.

Duncan, R. (1974), 'Modifications in decision structure in adapting to the environment: some implications for organizational learning', *Decision Sciences*, **5** (4): 705–25.

Dunning, J.H. (1958), *American Investment in British Industry*, London: Allen and Unwin.

Foss, N.J. and Pedersen, T. (2002), 'Transferring knowledge in MNCs: the role of sources of subsidiary knowledge and organisational context', *Journal of International Management*, **8** (1): 49–67.

Frost, T.S. (2001), 'The geographic sources of foreign subsidiaries' innovations', *Strategic Management Journal*, **22**: 101–23.

Gerybadze, A. (2004), 'Knowledge management, cognitive coherence, and equivocality in distributed innovation processes in MNCs', *Management International Review*, **44** (3): 103–28.

Gilbert, N. (1997), 'A simulation of the structure of academic science', *Sociological Research Online*, **2** (2), http://www.socresonline.org.uk/2/2/3.html (accessed 17 August 2010).

Gilbert, N. (2007), *Agent-based Models*, London: Sage Publications.

Gilbert, N. and Troitzsch, K.G. (2005), *Simulation for the Social Scientist*, Milton Keynes: Open University Press.

Gilbert, N., Ahrweiler, P. and Pyka, A. (2007), 'Learning in innovation networks: some simulation experiments', *Physica A – Statistical Mechanics and Its Applications*, **378** (1): 100–109.

Gupta, A.K. and Govindarajan, V. (1991), 'Knowledge flows and the structure of control within multinational corporations', *Academy of Management Review*, **16** (4): 768–92.

Gupta, A.K. and Govindarajan, V. (1994), 'Alternative value chain configurations for foreign subsidiaries: implications for coordination and control within MNCs', in H. Thomas, D. O'Neal and R. White (eds), *Building the Strategically Responsive Organization*, Chichester, UK: John Wiley, pp. 375–92.

Gupta, A.K. and Govindarajan, V. (2000), 'Knowledge flows within multinational corporations', *Strategic Management Journal*, **21** (4): 473–96.

Håkanson, L. and Nobel, R. (2000), 'Technology characteristics and reverse technology transfer', *Management International Review*, **40** (1): 29–47.

Heidenreich, M., Barmeyer, C. and Koschatzky, K. (2010), 'Product development in multinational companies. The limits for the internationalization of R&D projects', in P. Ahrweiler (ed.), *Innovation in Complex Social Systems*, London: Routledge, pp. 137–49.

IDA Ireland (2008), *IDA Annual Report 2008*, Dublin, http://www.idaireland.com/news-media/publications/annual-reports/2001-present/pdf, accessed 21 September 2011.

Knight, F.H. (1921), *Risk, Uncertainty, and Profit*, New York: Kelley and Millman.

Kogut, B. and Zander, U. (1993), 'Knowledge of the firm and the evolutionary theory of the multinational corporation', *Journal of International Business Studies*, **24**: 625–45.

Michael, D.N. (1973), *On Learning to Plan and Planning to Learn*, San Francisco, CA: Jossey Bass.

Michelet, R. (1992). 'Forming successful strategic marketing alliances in Europe', *Journal of European Business*, **4** (1): 11–15.

Narula, R. and Michel, J. (2010), 'Reverse knowledge transfer and its implications for European policy', in P. Ahrweiler (ed.), *Innovation in Complex Social Systems*, London: Routledge, pp. 122–36.

Pavitt, K. (1987), *Technology, Management and Systems of Innovation*, Aldershot, UK and Brookfield, USA: Edward Elgar Publishing Ltd.

Pearce, R., Dimitropoulou, D. and Papanastassiou, M. (2008), 'The locational determinants of FDI in the European Union: the influence of multinational strategy', in J. Dunning and P. Gugler (eds), *Foreign Direct Investment, Location and Competitiveness*, Progress in International Business Research 2, EIBA, Oxford: Elsevier, pp. 51–79.

Phene, A. and Almeida, P. (2008), 'Innovation in multinational subsidiaries: the role of knowledge assimilation and subsidiary capabilities', *Journal of International Business Studies*, **39**: 901–19.

Powell, W.W., White, D.R., Koput, K.W. and Owen-Smith, J. (2005), 'Network dynamics and field evolution: the growth of inter-organizational collaboration in the life sciences', *American Journal of Sociology*, **110** (4): 1132–205.

Pyka, A. and Saviotti, P.P. (2005), 'The evolution of R&D networking in the biotech industries', *International Journal of Entrepreneurship and Innovation Management*, **5** (1–2): 49–68.

Pyka, A., Ahrweiler, P. and Gilbert, N. (2009), 'Agent-based modelling of innovation networks: the fairytale of spillovers', in A. Pyka and A. Scharnhorst (eds), *Innovation Networks. New Approaches in Modeling and Analyzing*, Berlin and New York: Springer, pp. 101–26.

Schlegelmilch, B.B. and Chini, T.C. (2003), 'Knowledge transfer between marketing functions in multinational companies: a conceptual model', *International Business Review*, **12** (2): 215–32.

Song, J. and Shin, J. (2008), 'The paradox of technological capabilities: a study of knowledge sourcing from host countries of overseas R&D operations', *Journal of International Business Studies*, **39**: 291–303.

Tesfatsion, L. (2001), 'Structure, behavior, and market power in an evolutionary labor market with adaptive search', *Journal of Economic Dynamics and Control*, **25** (3–4): 419–57.

Van Pottelsberghe de la Potterie, B. and Guellec, D. (2001), 'The internationalisation of technology analysed with patent data', *Research Policy*, **30** (8): 1256–66.

Vernon, R. (1966), 'International investment and international trade in the product cycle', *Quarterly Journal of Economics*, **80**: 190–207.

Winter, S.G. (1984), 'Schumpeterian competition in alternative technological regimes', *Journal of Economic Behavior and Organization*, **5**: 287–320.

7. Technological capabilities and the regional embeddedness of multinational companies. A case study of Germany and the UK[1]

Simona Iammarino, Jan-Philipp Kramer, Elisabetta Marinelli and Javier Revilla Diez

7.1 INTRODUCTION

The regional embeddedness of multinational companies (MNCs) has been increasingly addressed in the economics and international business literature (e.g. Phelps et al., 2003; McCann and Mudambi, 2004, 2005; Arregle et al., 2009; Dunning, 2009; Mariotti et al., 2010; Mudambi and Santangelo, 2010). In particular, empirical research has confirmed a strong regional focus of MNC research networks in Europe (e.g. Cantwell and Iammarino, 2000, 2003; Cantwell and Piscitello, 2005; Revilla Diez and Berger, 2005; Narula and Santangelo, 2009). MNCs appear to have clear geographical preferences, with R&D strategies aimed at tapping into different regional innovation systems to feed new knowledge into intra-firm global networks.

In this study we look closely at the way in which MNCs become regionally embedded. We focus on leading UK and German MNCs operating in technology-intensive sectors and apply the concept of firm-level and regional-level technological capabilities. Following recent contributions (von Tunzelmann and Wang, 2003, 2007; von Tunzelmann, 2009), firms' technological capabilities are seen as the results of adaptive learning processes that are sustained through a variety of external connections and sources for innovation, at least partially embedded in the local environment of the firm. Notably, regional capabilities are more than the sum of capabilities of each individual firm, as they rely on many systemic elements that are external to the firm but internal to the specific region (von Tunzelmann, 2009).

In what follows, in order to understand to what extent and how geography matters for the innovation strategies of MNCs, we consider the link between firm-level (micro) and regional-level (meso) technological capabilities, focusing on three key aspects: first, we look at how MNCs build the skills necessary for knowledge creation; second, we explore how they organize their research structure; third, we analyse the way in which they build relationships for innovation within and outside the corporate group.

The chapter is organized as follows: section 7.2 reviews briefly the theoretical background and defines the research objectives; section 7.3 describes the methodology and the framework for the empirical analysis; section 7.4 provides information on the regions in which the interviewed MNCs operate; section 7.5 presents and discusses the results of the analysis, and section 7.6 concludes, indicating future research directions.

7.2   TECHNOLOGICAL CAPABILITIES: FIRMS AND REGIONS

Scholars in the economics and international business literature are increasingly focusing on the regional embeddedness of MNCs (see, among others, Phelps et al., 2003; McCann and Mudambi, 2004, 2005; Arregle et al., 2009; Dunning, 2009; Iammarino and McCann, 2010; Mariotti et al., 2010; Mudambi and Santangelo, 2010). Indeed, empirical evidence has found a strong regional concentration of MNC innovation networks in Europe, reflecting their attempt to tap into the local knowledge base of centres of excellence and feed it into intra-firm global networks (e.g. Cantwell and Iammarino, 2000, 2003; Cantwell and Piscitello, 2005; Revilla Diez and Berger, 2005; Narula and Santangelo, 2009). In other words, the skills embedded in the regional labour force, the local industry structure and knowledge networks, and the critical mass of innovative actors represent a major locational advantage that MNCs are able to exploit. MNCs are in fact able to benefit from the dynamic economies of scope that derive from the technological complementarities emerging in spatially distinct institutional and economic environments. In doing so, they not only build and reinforce their global competitiveness, but they simultaneously spread their competence base, acquire new technological assets and contribute to the local innovation system. They do so first by offering a 'package' of technical knowledge, organizational skills and management capabilities to their local customers, suppliers and collaboration partners; second by providing access to complementary streams of knowledge that are being developed in other regions (e.g. Cantwell and Iammarino, 2000, 2003; Santangelo, 2002; Ambos, 2005; Cantwell, 2009).

In other words, through their innovative activities, MNCs may become strongly spatially embedded.

The aim of this chapter is to explore such regional embeddedness through the concept of technological capabilities. At the firm level, technological capabilities are defined as the knowledge and skills that the enterprise needs to acquire, use, adapt, improve and create technology (e.g. Lall, 1992, 1993; Malerba, 1992; Bell and Pavitt, 1993). These technological capabilities represent unique intangible assets (IAs) that allow the firms controlling them to generate higher returns (Mudambi, 2008). The literature has highlighted that such capabilities arise both through interactions within the firm and between the firm and external actors, such as other enterprises, universities and research centres, local governments and public agencies. Capabilities thus involve learning and accumulation of new knowledge on the part of the firm, and also the integration of behavioural, social and economic factors into a specific set of outcomes.

Consequently, capabilities are seen as the results of adaptive learning processes that, in their collective dimension, can be highly localized, giving rise to 'system' capabilities, that is, referring to a specific spatial and industrial setting (von Tunzelmann and Wang, 2003, 2007; Iammarino et al., 2008; von Tunzelmann, 2009). Regional capabilities are defined as the knowledge and skills embedded in individuals, organizations and institutions located in a geographically bounded area and conducive to innovative activity. Therefore regional capabilities are not simply the sum of individual capabilities developed in isolation (Lall, 1992), as a region includes systemic elements that are exogenous to any local actor yet are endogenous to the region itself (e.g. Cooke et al., 1997; Howells, 1999). For instance, the overall supply of local high-skilled labour or the number of technologically active firms is external to each individual enterprise, yet it emerges from the activities and interactions among local actors. Despite these differences, however, the processes of capability building at the regional and firm level share some important similarities: they are long, uncertain and costly processes, showing high path dependence and cumulativeness.

These characteristics underpin the spatial agglomeration of knowledge creation, as the complexity of the innovation process often makes knowledge transfer and exchange difficult to achieve: in other words, it makes knowledge stick to people and places. As a consequence, our analysis can be framed within the regional innovation systems approach (e.g. Cooke, 1992; Doloreux and Paarto, 2005; Iammarino, 2005), derived from a spatial application of the broader concept of systems of innovation (among others, Freeman, 1987; Edquist, 1997). This body of research stresses three main issues: (1) that innovation is an interactive process among public and private actors and institutions; (2) that the regional system is defined in a specific context where networks of such actors and institutions act and interact for generating, importing, modifying and diffusing new knowledge and technologies; and (3) that all the economic and knowledge processes created inside and outside the firms are 'embedded' in the local environment (Cooke et al., 1997). Latest applications of the technological capabilities framework to regional innovation systems have emphasized that regions can be considered as spatial congregations of suppliers, producers, consumers and so on, each with their own unique level of capabilities (von Tunzelmann, 2009). Shifting the logic from mere co-location to co-evolution, it is argued that for a region to be progressive, its capabilities need to be interactive – that is, those of its producers, suppliers and customers need to be to some degree aligned and complementary – and dynamic – that is, able to cope with the continuous change of the actors' needs and abilities (von Tunzelmann, 2009).

Looking at the process of MNCs' regional embeddedness through the lenses of technological capabilities means, first of all, to understand how MNCs carry out their innovative activity within the firm and the region and how, in so doing, they rely upon and contribute to regional knowledge creation. Drawing on the literature summarized above, in what follows we focus on three main aspects:

1. How MNCs support and upgrade their employees' skills
2. How MNCs organize their R&D activity
3. How MNCs establish knowledge networks within the firm and with actors outside the firm.

In particular, for each of these three aspects we first identify the mechanisms through which technological capabilities are built within the firm; second, we highlight how the process of capability creation at the firm level interacts with that at the regional level.

7.3   METHODOLOGY AND FRAMEWORK FOR THE ANALYSIS

We study six MNCs belonging to the ICT (information and communication technologies), automotive and life science industries (two for each sector) operating in both Germany and the UK. Our investigation in the automotive sector includes two MNC headquarters, one UK-owned and one German-owned, as well as one respective subsidiary in both Germany and the UK. Similarly, in the life science (pharmaceutical and agrochemical) industry we study two MNC headquarters (one in the UK and one in Germany) and their respective subsidiaries in the aforementioned countries. For the ICT sector, we were not able to include UK-based MNCs in our sample.[2] Therefore we interviewed two German MNC headquarters and their respective UK subsidiaries. The analysis is based on 44 semi-structured interviews with senior managerial and technical personnel from different business units: R&D, human resources, production, communications/government relations and corporate development. The interview guides contained both some general questions common to all the interviewees[3] and some specific questions related to the function of the interviewee in the firm. These primary data are, in turn, supported with information from corporate publications, press releases and scientific literature.

As outlined above, to conduct our analysis we focus separately on human resources, the organization of R&D and the relationships for innovation within and outside the MNC, distinguishing between the process of capability building internal and external (i.e. involving the region) to the MNC, as explained below:

7.3.1 Capabilities and Human Resources

In order to understand how the knowledge and skills embodied in the MNCs' employees contribute to the firm's technological capabilities, our interviews focused on the following aspects: employee profile (academic and professional background); recruiting procedures and channels; intra-firm and inter-firm labour mobility; modes of training and up-skilling; professional development and talent management.

To understand the extent and modes in which the MNC relies and affects on regional technological capabilities, the following factors were examined: availability of relevant skills in the local labour market; extent of employee mobility across firms in the region; reliance on local providers of training; involvement with education and qualification networks.

7.3.2 Capabilities and the Organization of R&D Activities

To analyse how the organization of R&D affects the firms' technological capabilities, our interviews explored the following aspects: modes of internal organization of innovative activities; role of different company departments supporting innovation; role of spatial proximity and organizational modes to secure face-to-face contact.

To investigate the extent and modes in which the MNC relies and affects the regional innovation base we looked at: the role of regional innovation policies; the presence of relevant public and private actors; the functions of MNCs in industry and innovation networks; the characteristics of the regional business environment.

7.3.3   Capabilities and Innovation Networks

To explore how the ability of the firm to build relationships internally and externally contributes to technological capabilities, in our interviews we considered the following dimensions: the existence and modes of research collaborations with other firms and universities; the evolution of such collaborations; their spatial distribution; the advantages and problems of these collaborations.

To evaluate how firm-level interactive capabilities build upon and contribute to the regional ones we looked at the presence of a critical mass of interacting agents involved in R&D and the collective governance of such interactions.

The interviews provided a large amount of information regarding both the process of regional embeddedness in general terms as well as its sectoral and national (i.e. Germany versus the UK) specificities.

7.4   THE REGIONAL LOCATION OF MNCs

To answer the above questions it is necessary to provide a brief picture of the regional context in which the selected MNCs operate and the key actors involved in the creation of regional technological capabilities.

In Germany, four of the six investigated MNCs (i.e. the two ICT headquarters and two UK-owned subsidiaries from the automotive and life science industries) located the majority of their operations in the high-tech agglomerations of the south, in the regions of Baden-Württemberg and Munich. Baden-Württemberg is one of Germany's most prosperous areas, characterized by flagship mechanical engineering firms and a highly developed network of SMEs specialized in supplying components, production and development. Stuttgart and Karlsruhe, industrial centres of the Federal State of Baden-Württemberg, are leading high-tech agglomerations in Germany, comprising approximately 12.3 per cent of all employees in industrial research and 12.9 per cent of all patent applications in Germany.[4] The overall regional innovation system is supported by strong vocational education and excellent universities (such as Heidelberg and Karlsruhe University), an advanced regional infrastructure for technology transfer (e.g. the Steinbeis Foundation's region-wide network of tech-transfer offices)[5] and active local producer associations.

Similarly, Munich is one of the leading business and research regions in Europe, with an innovation system characterized by a high density of knowledge-intensive SMEs and MNCs, operating in ICT, bio-tech and mechanical engineering. The area comprises roughly 13 per cent of all employees in industrial research and 8.6 per cent of patent applications in Germany.[6] It is characterized by a high concentration of excellent scientific institutions, including several Max-Planck and Fraunhofer research institutes, and two of the nine elite universities selected by the 'Exzellenzinitiative' of the German Federal Ministry of Education and Research.[7]

The other two German-owned firms, operating in the automotive and life sciences industry, have their headquarters in the lower Rhine area of North-Rhine Westphalia (with branches also in Berlin) and in the south-east of Lower Saxony, respectively. North-Rhine Westphalia is a region strongly specialized in the chemical and healthcare industry, whilst Lower Saxony is one of the main German automotive clusters in terms of employees in knowledge-intensive industries and, as of 2005, comprised 10.6 per cent of the patent applications in the industry.[8]

In the UK, most of the MNCs interviewed (i.e. both the automotive and pharmaceutical UK headquarters and the ICT and life sciences German subsidiaries) have the core of their operations in the Greater South-East, a meta-region spanning 150 miles around London, from Cambridgeshire in the north-east, to Dorset in the south-west, and around the south-east coast. This area largely outperforms the rest of the country in terms of economic and productivity growth; it accounts for over a third of the national R&D and has the highest concentration of universities and public research institutions. Within this broad region there are several key technological clusters to which some of the interviewed companies belong, including the electronics and life science clusters in Cambridge and the ICT agglomeration in the Thames Valley. The former is characterized by a large share of small high-tech companies (over 60 per cent of bio-tech firms located there have fewer than ten employees).[9] Its success is largely linked to the presence of the University of Cambridge, which, as of 2005, had the highest research income in the country and which, by funding spin-outs and science parks, had a key role in the industrialization of the area (Minshall and Wicksteed, 2005). The Thames Valley encompasses the M4 corridor of IT and life sciences companies in Reading, Slough, Bracknell, Maidenhead, Newbury, High Wycombe, Windsor and Basingstoke. It is characterized by a large presence of foreign-owned firms (over 2000) and by strong links with the nearby universities in Reading and Oxford. In both cases regional public and private initiatives have been crucial in sustaining innovation: the Thames Valley Economic Partnership and the Cambridge Partnership, for instance, both gather the private sector, government agencies and educational institutions to facilitate innovation and develop the talent pool in the two areas.

Both automotive firms interviewed in the UK (i.e. the UK-owned MNC and the subsidiary of the German MNC) operate in the historical cluster centred in the West Midlands and spanning to the North-East of England. However, whilst the German subsidiary has its main site there, the UK firm has only some of its facilities in this area (having most of branches in the South-East, as seen above). The West Midlands hosts 1500 auto companies, has a total turnover of around £13 billion per year and employs 115000 people.[10] The North-West is home to 450 automotive companies, 200 of which are major automotive supply chain companies, has an annual business turnover of £9 billion and employs 43000 people.[11] The industry has experienced dramatic shifts in the past decades with a reduction of the manufacturing base, and the regional innovation system has witnessed increasing public and private partnerships to support competitiveness and innovation, such as the West Midlands PARD (Premium Automotive R&D) or the North-West automotive Alliance.

7.5   CASE STUDY RESULTS

The research has produced a detailed picture of technological capability building. In what follows we report separately the results related to human resources, the organization of R&D and the networks for innovation. Unless otherwise stated, the analysis applies both to Germany and the UK and covers both MNC headquarters and subsidiaries abroad across sectors.

7.5.1   Capabilities and Human Resources

7.5.1.1   The firm level
Investment in human resources is at the core of MNCs' efforts to increase competitiveness as the high pace of technological progress and scientific developments requires continuous education and qualification efforts. Overall, strategies to attract, retain and develop talent are quite common across sectors, despite the fact that industries face different skills constraints on the supply side. In this respect MNCs' strategies broadly fall into three categories: (1) talent management and individual up-skilling; (2) strategic skills forecast; and (3) engagement with higher education.

Talent management and individual up-skilling   Facilitated by their global network, MNCs are able to capture international trends in human resource management and education far better than locally operating companies (e.g. Harvey et al., 2000; De Cieri and Dowling, 2006); indeed our analysis shows a remarkable sophistication of hiring methods and talent management processes. As for the former, traditional strategies (specialist press, head-hunters etc.) are being complemented by social network software systems to attract especially the youngest highly qualified segments of the labour market. As for the management of talent, firms are investing increasingly in leadership programmes for high-profile candidates, developing systems to define clearer career paths with individually tailored training. Surprisingly, while it is generally acknowledged that intra-firm mobility is valuable, structured programmes to exploit this source of knowledge exchange more systematically are often not in place: intra-firm mobility tends to occur on an *ad hoc* basis. The only exception is that of new young employees enrolled in graduate programmes, which offer the possibility to work in other facilities abroad.

Strategic skills forecast Human resources, as a critical asset of the firm, need to be managed with a long-term view, therefore awareness of future skills demand and supply (both in the long and middle terms) is crucial. The interviewed MNCs are especially active in monitoring human capital supply in the medium to long run and showed awareness and concern for the insufficient future availability of scientific skills. In the UK, for example, one of the firms in the automotive sector produced a report to estimate the existence and cost of the future skill-gap, advocating urgent action from the government. Indeed, precisely to tackle long-term skills gaps, science awareness programmes, which encourage primary and secondary school pupils to enrol in scientific education, are pursued by many of the interviewed MNCs, especially in their home-base country.

On the other hand, skill needs in the short and middle term are in some cases forecasted through specific tools (such as the Development Needs Analysis) that evaluate human resources requirements in relation to business trends. The same tools are also used to identify intra-firm and extra-firm talent pools that could be employed to meet such requirements. In some German-owned MNCs based in their home country the engagement goes even further, with coordinated efforts with regional educational institutions. For instance, the human resources unit of one German automotive firm reported being actively engaged with a regional chamber of commerce, particularly by initiating specialized educational programmes in fields where demand was expected to grow (such as electromechanical engineering). Additionally, this firm established a corporate university at its headquarter location to secure the lifelong learning of its employees. In this university the firm conducts basic research in fields such as production technologies, coordinates collaboration with regional university partners and implements its PhD programme. For similar reasons, one of the pharmaceutical MNCs was involved in establishing a polytechnic in the vicinity of its German headquarters, offering training in technical and pharmaceutical chemistry.

Engagement with higher education Corporate investment in human capital relies strongly on the higher education sector both for training and (mostly) for graduate recruitment. The latter is given strategic priority by all firms (except one firm in the life science sector, for which it has a less vital role) and is sustained through structured graduate programmes. All our interviewees highlighted the importance of such schemes from different perspectives. For instance, those from HR departments valued graduate programmes as a means of talent identification that can then be developed through talent management and talent retention initiatives. On the other hand, interviewees from R&D units pointed out that these programmes are crucial to integrate graduates, and particularly PhDs, into indus-trial research, for instance by offering the opportunity to conduct small research projects on site. As for the former, universities provide training to MNCs in two ways: first they are one of the elements of the educational portfolio (which includes polytechnics, industry associations etc.) offering courses to enhance 'soft skills'; second, universities occasionally engage in long-term scientific training partnerships. In these initiatives, which tend to be international in scope, university and industry exchange capabilities through lectures and/or sharing facilities on a regular basis. In both cases the majority of interviewed MNCs find that identifying the right academic collaborator can be a slow process: not only do the different incentive structures between academia and industry constitute an obstacle, but there are also no efficient communication channels in place to identify the strengths of each university and the scope of potential collaborations.

7.5.1.2   The firm–region interaction

Having identified the mechanisms through which firms' capabilities are enhanced, we now explore how such mechanisms become territorially embedded, focusing on the two-way relationship between the region and the firm and vice versa.

From the MNC to the region   There are several ways in which firms' capa-bilities merge with regional ones. For instance, MNCs often have strong collaborative ties with regional partners from higher education. These include investments in polytechnics and support of scientific and technical education in the vicinity (both financially and through seminar series, or in-kind donations). In some cases, especially in German-owned MNCs operating in Germany, local skills are improved through collaborations with regional policy makers by supporting regional talent management and talent retention initiatives. For instance, the investigated automotive MNC, operating in Lower Saxony, collaborates actively with state and city government officials in a 'Study and Stay' programme, a place branding and talent management initiative designed to retain university graduates in the regional labour market.

From the region to the MNC The regional availability of scientists and of innovative industries has important consequences for MNCs' human resources and, therefore, technological capabilities. Indeed, although international recruiting is a key priority for all of the analysed MNCs, sourcing of regional scientific personnel and recruitment of graduates remains a central objective in the development of strategic partnerships with local universities. In some cases the local availability of scientists has in fact directly driven R&D investment decisions of MNCs. Moreover, in a regional labour market with a high density of innovative actors, MNCs' human capital also benefits from high inter-firm interregional mobility. According to our interviews in the UK, MNCs located in the Cambridge Cluster and in the Thames Valley have high inter-firm mobility in which outflows generally balance inflows. This process makes, *ceteris paribus*, recruiting talent easier across sectors and is reinforced by the fact that higher quality of life in the two locations facilitates attraction and retention of globally mobile talent. On the other hand, companies located in the Midlands reported more difficulties in recruiting. The picture is very similar in Germany, with high levels of inter-firm mobility in the ICT clusters of Munich and Karlsruhe as well as in the automotive cluster in the Stuttgart area, and relatively greater difficulties in recruiting for (automotive) companies in northern Germany.

7.5.2 Capabilities and the Organization of R&D

7.5.2.1 The firm level
To understand how capabilities are built in relation to R&D organization we need to focus on three aspects: (1) the infrastructure assisting R&D decision making; (2) the internal knowledge transfer processes; and (3) the management practices for interdisciplinary projects. These are explored in detail below.

Organizational infrastructure for innovation – R&D network decentralization and balance of top-down/bottom-up knowledge flows The organization of R&D infrastructure shows and embodies the mechanisms through which strategic decisions are taken and implemented. In our analysis we identified two dimensions of R&D infrastructure that critically affect the knowledge creation process: the degree of decentralization of both R&D units, and the way in which top-down corporate strategies are balanced with bottom-up knowledge flows from subsidiaries or decentralized units.

On the basis of our interviews we have identified two quite distinctive models. In some firms highly centralized basic research facilities are used in order to catalyse economic resources and capabilities. This strategy is followed for instance by one German-owned MNC in the automotive sector, in which the central research facilities serve the network of globally spread subsidiaries, carrying out strategic R&D for the whole group. A similar approach is taken by a German pharmaceutical company that consolidated its pre-clinical research in its headquarters while continuing to carry out clinical research in several major markets. In these cases, whilst strategic R&D decisions are taken in the headquarters, development activities are highly decentralized and spread across various locations, as emerged, for example, in the case of the subsidiaries of the German automotive MNC in the UK. It is precisely through development units that these MNCs tap into the different local knowledge by operating in strict contact with clients, suppliers, regulators and policy makers in each host region.

On the other hand, some MNCs are developing highly decentralized and entrepreneurial R&D units with large budget and planning autonomy. This model is chosen as it makes it possible to manage the research portfolio more efficiently by accessing external knowledge at earlier stages of the innovation process. In fact, such decentralized approaches are being developed in order to expand the spread and scope of R&D collaboration with industrial or scientific partners. Moreover, they are often complemented by (globally operating) venture capital units that support the identification and development of new growth opportunities. At the same time, intense interaction of such R&D centres with local business and service delivery units ensures inflow of relevant market information into the corporate R&D network. The risk of a decentralized infrastructure, however, is that it might result in an incoherent corporate strategy, and MNCs have developed different approaches to avoid this threat. For instance, one UK-owned pharmaceutical firm has introduced new managerial positions to coordinate globally independent research units and their collaborative strategies; other MNCs have established specific departments that manage internal knowledge transfer from the R&D units to the rest of the company and vice versa. Similarly, research portfolio offices have been set up by one ICT firm to evaluate and match internal and external research findings: supported by intense and structured communication processes, these units secure the transfer and utilization of research through intra-firm channels.

Knowledge transfer structures (intra-firm)   On the basis of the interviews we identified three main channels through which internal knowledge transfers are managed. First, face-to-face contact has emerged as the most important mechanism of internal and external communication for all interviewed MNCs. This is especially the case at the beginning of tech-nologically complex projects, where knowledge gaps with collaborators (internal or external) or clients are larger. Second, IT-based support struc-tures, such as workshare platforms, directories, intranet-based document systems or wikis are broadly used across the interviewed MNCs. Third, as mentioned above, some companies have developed specialized business units or positions focusing on intra-firm knowledge transfer, collecting and evaluating all internal research results and comparing them against external sources.

New management tools for interdisciplinary projects   Innovative activ-ity relies on a diversified mix of skills, therefore adequate organizational approaches for managing knowledge exchange across different disci-plines are critical. Indeed, a wide range of coordination and management methods has emerged from our analysis. These include the implementa-tion of a 'product life continuous management approach' in which dif-ferent teams that traditionally operated in separate stages of product development are jointly involved throughout the project life, streamlining the whole process. In this approach team integration is achieved through cross-functional review forums and meetings as well as specific software packages. Alternatively, interdisciplinarity is achieved by making team members work together in the same physical space as a separate project-based and mostly temporary unit of the company. This strategy, referred to as 'project house', allows the firm to pool specific competences for R&D tasks from several nationally and internationally located business units. Finally, a third interesting example occurs where MNCs, particularly from the ICT sector, pilot new research products with lead users in a real-life environment – an approach adapted from clinical research in the pharma-ceutical industry.

7.5.2.2   The firm–region interaction
In this section we explore the institutions and policies that facilitate the process of knowledge creation, diffusion and organization at the territorial level. MNCs are, on the one hand, a key element of such a system; on the

other hand, they are influenced by it as they respond to the local incentives and business opportunities. These bi-directional links are explored below.

From the MNC to the region   Most obviously, the impact of MNCs on the regional organization of innovation occurs through their R&D network infrastructure, especially when firms follow a decentralized approach with the aim of interacting with the local knowledge base. As this aspect has already been covered in other research efforts (see, e.g., Boutellier et al., 2008), we focus here on three additional channels.

First, inter-industry initiatives sponsored by MNCs are used to stimulate local and cross-industry knowledge spillovers: a relevant example is provided by a regional research and transfer platform developed by an ICT firm that funded inter-industry spin-outs and invested in new interdisciplinary research lines in Germany. A second type of influence occurs through MNCs' institutional participation as active stakeholders in regional cluster initiatives, chambers of commerce or science advisory boards. Through such participation MNCs can affect coordinated investments in quality of place, regional talent management projects or schemes to financially support star scientists in regional universities. There are several examples of such participation. For instance, in the UK the Thames Valley Economic Partnership, to which one of the interviewed MNCs (a German ICT subsidiary) belongs, established the TV Investment Network, a 'business angel network' that funds high-tech start-ups in the region. Third, regional organizational capacity benefits from corporate venture capital units that are often found in knowledge centres. Such units, present in Germany across the three sectors, foster commercialization of regionally created knowledge and intellectual property (IP) by supplying local innovative partners (universities, SMEs etc.) not only with venture capital but also with access to the MNC knowledge network.

Overall, the analysis reveals that the direct corporate influence on local organizational capital tends to be higher in firms operating and headquartered in Germany. In the UK, the impact occurs mostly indirectly through the activities of industry or regional associations to which the MNCs belong. This finding is largely unexpected and warrants further investigation. Specifically, it raises questions as to whether the origins of such differences are to be found in the more liberal Anglo-Saxon business culture or in the relatively weaker relationship between business and academia in the UK (as indicated, among others, by Cosh et al., 2006).

From the region to the MNC   The regional organization of innovation can have important effects on the degree of regional embeddedness of MNCs' operations. In particular we identify three key aspects that strengthen MNCs' regional integration: the presence of networking platforms and cluster initiatives, the presence of regional policy incentives for innovation; and, most importantly, a critical mass of innovative actors. In other words, our evidence suggests that the presence of scientific excellence is a necessary yet not sufficient condition for MNCs to become spatially embedded. As multinationals can easily access global scientific knowledge, regional policy initiatives also need to support innovation, cluster development and public–private networking in order to enable MNCs to access the regional knowledge repository and enhance their regional embeddedness.

In this respect, another interesting difference emerged among MNCs operating in the two countries: interviewees in the UK (regardless of the country of ownership of the MNC) were overall less aware of local incentives and initiatives. When asked about their relationship with regional institutions and government bodies, several of them reported low levels of interaction. Of those that reported being involved in regional development or other local policy initiatives, only some had adopted a proactive approach (e.g. by applying for regional funding streams or by sitting on regional boards). Others reported learning of and participating in regional initiatives only after being contacted by the relevant institution. On the other hand, employees in MNCs headquartered or subsidiaries operating in Germany declared themselves more often to be actively involved in regional initiatives. Although such differences certainly deserve further validation, they reflect none the less regional innovation systems' specific characteristics already highlighted in the literature on MNC location of innovative activities (see, e.g., the findings on the UK case by Cantwell and Iammarino, 2000; and on the German case by Cantwell et al., 2000).

7.5.3 Capabilities and Innovation Networks

7.5.3.1 The firm level

In our analysis we identify three key dimensions of MNCs' innovation networks that help shape technological capabilities. These relate to: (1) the identification of partners; (2) the creation and exchange of knowledge; and (3) the support to continuous collaboration. The mechanisms and rationale differ according to the nature of the collaborator: whilst industrial collaborations tend to occur mostly in applied research and their value is thus more closely related to the market, collaborations with academic partners occur in basic research and are sought to explore completely novel ideas. For these reasons we separate the analysis between industrial and scientific networks.

Industrial networks

1. Identification of industrial partners – *establishing knowledge networks*
The ability of the MNC to identify where external know-how can be accessed, what skills a potential partner offers and to which market such skills are most suited is crucial for technological development. Based on our interviews we identify two types of sources for the selection of potential research collaborators: those internal to the MNC and those external. The MNC itself provides the first internal avenue for selecting potential partners: not only R&D centres in the headquarters, other branches and subsidiaries are obvious and common options for collaborations. In certain cases, the R&D facilities of the parent company also act as a 'repository' of partners by guiding subsidiaries in the choice of collaborators within and beyond the corporate boundaries. As for external sources of partnerships, these can be found with competitors, customers and suppliers or contract research organizations. The identification of these collaborators relies on active and constant participation in industry activities (conferences, publications, innovation competitions) and organizations (industry boards). Although partnering options are scanned on a national and, especially, global level, a regional environment rich in industrial partners is critical to support networking activity.

Our interviews show that when selecting and establishing partnerships, sectoral differences are extremely relevant. In the ICT business services sector, R&D networks with clients and suppliers are very common. On the other hand, collaborations in the pharmaceutical industry tend to be mostly with bio-tech companies and seldom with direct competitors. Finally, MNCs in the automotive sector actively source external knowledge from development partners/suppliers, for instance by establishing supplier parks.

2. Knowledge creation and diffusion – *capacity to produce knowledge in networks and create value from networks*   The type of processes through which knowledge is exchanged in networks differs depending on the stage of product development and the nature of the partner. Generally speaking, two types of industrial collaboration can be identified: first technology partnerships, which focus primarily on early-stage R&D at the pre-competitive level; and second, product specific collaborations, which focus on later stages of the product/service development processes. These collaborations can either be bilateral or multilateral (e.g. in joint EU projects involving both academic and industrial members) and are generally supported and coordinated through dedicated MNCs' departments. Generally, industrial partnerships are highly formalized by means of clear milestones, deliverable lists and participation of the high-level management. In pre-competitive research, a shared research agenda accompanied by shared facilities and personnel mobility are the most used mechanisms to promote knowledge flows.

3. Support for continuous collaboration   The value of a network lies particularly in the continuity of the relationship with partners as this ensures that the accumulated knowledge spills over to future collaborations. To this end, some of the investigated MNCs utilized specialized management teams, such as R&D alliances or R&D liaison management. Moreover, the communication and management of intellectual property rights is crucial to support continuous collaboration capacity. Clear accountability of roles and responsibilities is key to prevent and/or manage conflicts that arise from IP disputes and corporate differences in culture and agenda.

Scientific networks

1. Identification of academic partners – *establishing knowledge networks* R&D collaborations with academia are highly valued and efforts are made across industries to increase them at the global as well as regional scale. Scientific partners are normally met at conferences and industry-related events or, as especially stressed in the pharmaceutical industry, by active participation in the scientific community (e.g. producing and/or publishing high-quality research results). These methods are mainly organic and *ad hoc*, and the majority of the MNCs, indeed, strive to find more efficient ways to identify partners. Other, less common mechanisms to identify academic partners relate to the acquisition of new firms with already established collaborations (e.g. university spin-offs) or (temporary) institutional cross-moves from industry to science and vice versa.

One of the major obstacles to network formation is the inability of academic institutions to adequately advertise their skills (they rely mostly on peer-reviewed publications or conference participation). As a consequence, several MNCs are trying to devise new mechanisms to identify the strengths of universities and design a more efficient way to interact with them. For instance, a UK firm from the pharmaceutical industry employs specialized scouting groups to identify promising partners from academia. Similarly, a German MNC, also from the pharmaceutical sector, reported close interaction with patent exploitation offices (either privately or publicly/university owned). Furthermore, corporate venture capital units have been implemented, especially in the ICT and pharmaceutical industry, as a means of systematically identifying qualified collaboration partners from scientific institutions.

2. Knowledge creation and diffusion – *capacity to produce knowledge in networks and create value from networks*   Collaborations with universities and research institutes are, in most cases, at the very early stage of the innovation stream (blue sky). Universities often act as a filter mechanism for the MNC to identify new targets as well as to validate and evaluate whether an idea has commercial potential. In doing so, these collaborations help the MNC to develop a basic understanding of new research findings and strengthen its absorptive capacity by re-integrating these findings into the intra-firm R&D network. To this end, for instance, one of the UK-owned pharmaceutical firms operating in Germany established a research advisory board composed of selected senior academics from leading universities to ensure high-level scientific management decisions (such as clinical study protocols).

Another major motivation for MNC collaboration with academic partners is early access to human capital, including the possibility to support talent creation. This is most commonly achieved through research contracts, shared facilities, PhD funding, access to industrial data and, less often, by sponsoring professorships and through in-kind donations of instruments to departments. Publicly funded joint research projects are another interesting mode of collaboration in which most MNCs were involved. In such projects the inflow of complementary knowledge from a range of industrial and academic partners was reported to be beneficial over and beyond the actual financial R&D incentive.

3. Support for continuous collaboration   As for industrial collaborations, cultural differences, legal issues and the synchronization of expectations are the main obstacles to successful collaborations (e.g. Broström and Lööf, 2006). All the MNCs interviewed reported difficulties in engaging with the academic community, mostly related to its partial understanding of business and industrial R&D processes (including its legal requirements) and to the differences in professional incentive structures: for instance academic publication needs might interfere with confidentiality protocols; moreover, universities' specific funding requirements (needed, e.g., to accommodate a PhD degree) could not always be met by MNCs. To overcome the differences in incentive structures, collaboration programmes with universities are often led by managers with a strong academic background (usually a PhD graduate) and try to incorporate academic incentives by, for instance, facilitating peer review publishing. IPR management is also critical in academic collaborations, especially concerning joint IP and the temporary exclusion of competitors from the newly created knowledge. Finally, it is acknowledged that continuity in the relationship ensures successful collaborations and, although partnerships are initially developed *ad hoc*, this is done with the long-term objective of establishing a durable contact. To that purpose, in some cases funding streams are deliberately distributed over time to the same university, rather than on a one-off basis.

7.5.3.2   The firm–region interaction

In this section we explore the capacity of the regional actors to engage with each other in order to exploit the advantages of physical proximity for knowledge transfer, creation and accumulation. On the one hand, MNCs can be active in promoting regional networks; on the other, they might be just participants and recipients of other regional initiatives. Both directions are explored below.

From the MNC to the region   Although knowledge flows are facilitated by geographical proximity, MNCs are not spatially constrained in their choice of partners and, indeed, in the majority of cases they do not explicitly differentiate among regional and global collaborators. Nevertheless, the need for spatial proximity in specific types of collaborations has strongly influenced, if not driven, the R&D investment strategy of some MNCs. Those firms with a decentralized R&D infrastructure (as described in section 7.5.2 above) have devised their strategy on the basis of the local availability of a critical mass of other innovative public and private actors. As such, they have built research facilities in different areas across the world in close proximity to local universities and research centres. For instance, one of the ICT firms based its R&D centres in outstanding engineering campuses worldwide and developed joint PhD programmes with the university. In so doing, it has institutionalized and made permanent pre-existing R&D relationships. In these cases geographical proximity is seen as instrumental in attenuating the conflicts that may arise due to the institutional distance between business and academia (e.g. Boschma, 2005; D'Este and Iammarino, 2010). Other firms across sectors and countries have invested in science parks (e.g. supplier parks, partner ports) close to their major R&D location to benefit from local knowledge and/or established strategic research partnerships with top universities. As reported by one ICT firm, future opportunities for regional network creation are also seen in fostering spin-outs or start-ups. Furthermore, MNCs can act as global antennas opening up international networks and knowledge inflows for SMEs in the region. For instance, an ICT firm reported that involving regional SMEs (and potential customers) in innovative product developments, such as technology or service delivery platforms, would particularly enable the local system to access global markets.

From the region to the MNC   As MNCs are not necessarily engaged in regional networks in order to exploit spatial knowledge flows, other institutions with a specific regional mandate need to be in place to support such processes. In the UK and Germany several organizations carry out these tasks. Many of the interviewed MNCs have taken part in regional network initiatives, which broadly fall in two categories: (1) activities financing R&D collaborations among regional actors, which include funding streams from national governments or the EU; and (2) activities aimed at creating networks across regional actors with the specific target of exchanging knowledge. In the UK these include, for example, sectoral knowledge transfer networks (where regional development agencies have a strong involvement). Similarly, some of the firms located in Germany were, or are, actively involved in the Clusters of Excellence initiative, funded by the German Federal Ministry of Education and Research. Whilst generally such initiatives are highly valued by MNCs, it was reported by several UK interviewees from different sectors that they are not adequately communicated by the competent government body and that often the bureaucratic demands are onerous and discouraging.

7.6   CONCLUSIONS

The aim of this chapter was to analyse MNCs innovation processes and their regional embeddedness by focusing on firm-level and regional-level technological capabilities. The research was based on an original survey of over 40 in-depth interviews with senior members of leading German and UK MNCs: by means of such primary data we have identified the processes through which technological capabilities are built within the firm, benefiting from and contributing to regional knowledge creation.

It has emerged that for technological capabilities to arise and upgrade, pervasive efforts and strategies are required. For instance, whilst the organizational support to innovation rests mainly on the R&D and knowledge transfer infrastructure and on the management practices for interdisciplinary projects, working through innovation networks requires identifying the right partners, managing knowledge creation and exchange among them, and supporting continuous collaboration capacity. Last but not least, ensuring that MNCs' employees are able to support innovation requires a long-term view of the scientific and managerial skills needed by the firm, a sustained training process and strong relationships with higher education institutions.

The analysis has also confirmed that MNCs' technological capabilities are, to some extent, spatially embedded in advanced regional innovation systems. Indeed, throughout their innovative activities MNCs benefit from and contribute to the local knowledge creation processes. For instance, they make use of and provide skills to the local labour market, benefit from the presence of regional universities and research infrastructure, and provide laboratories and other resources. Furthermore, MNCs can contribute to regional scientific networks by participating in regional governance boards, sponsoring cross-industry innovation initiatives and financing promising research or business ideas through venture capital units. At the same time, the regional governance mechanisms that support knowledge creation (such as policy incentives, clustering and networking initiatives) and, more generally, the critical mass of regional innovative actors also contribute to geographically embed the firm. These findings not only show how MNCs become regionally integrated but also that the concept of advanced technological capabilities is itself a fruitful way to systematically analyse such embeddedness.

To conclude, the limitations of this study should be addressed. Empirically, the study had an explorative character, making use of qualitative evidence that should be complemented with quantitative data in future research. This would for instance allow a more detailed comparative investigation of the weaker regional engagement of MNCs operating in the UK as opposed to Germany. Furthermore, whilst this research has mostly focused on the firm as a unit of analysis, future research should focus mainly on the region, its systemic interactions and their evolution. In particular, through a case study approach we should analyse different spatial innovation systems and identify their specificities with regard to both the dynamic and interactive nature of technological capabilities to be able to complement the approach followed here and disentangle more deeply the local–global nature of knowledge creation.

NOTES

1. The authors gratefully acknowledged the financial support received from the European Community's Seventh Framework Programme (FP7/2007–2013) under grant agreement no. 216813.
2. For details on firm selection and extensive methodology, see Kramer et al. (2009).
3. The general questions cover innovation activities and strategies of the analysed MNCs, external collaboration with science and industry, regional business environment for innovation (including human capital needs) and recommendations for long-term competitiveness.
4. Source: SV-Wissenschaftsstatistik (2010) and Deutsches Patent- und Markenamt (German Patent and Trademark Office) (2006).
5. The Steinbeis Foundation for Economic Development offers several activities related to knowledge and technology transfer (e.g. consulting, market and transfer-orientated R&D), thereby fostering partnership and knowledge sharing between academic institutes and businesses.
6. SV-Wissenschaftsstatistik and Deutsches Patent- und Markenamt (German Patent and Trademark Office) (2006).
7. Within the framework of the Initiative of Excellence, the federal government is promoting top-class university research with €1.9 billion, aiming to establish international visible research institutions in Germany (Wissenschaftsrat 2009).

8.   Source: Deutsches Patent- und Markenamt (German Patent and Trademark Office) (2006).
9.   Source: Greater Cambridge Partnership (2007).
10. Source: Advantage West Midlands (2007).
11. Source: North East Development Agency (2007).

REFERENCES

Advantage West Midlands (2007), 'Automotive Cluster, 3 Year Plan: 2008–11', AWM, Birmingham.

Ambos, B. (2005), 'Foreign direct investment in industrial research and development: a study of German MNCs', *Research Policy*, **34**: 395–410.

Arregle, J.-L., Beamish, P.W. and Hebert, L. (2009), 'The regional dimension of MNCs' foreign subsidiary localization', *Journal of International Business Studies*, **40**: 86–107.

Bell, M. and Pavitt, K. (1993), 'Technological accumulation and industrial growth', *Industrial and Corporate Change*, **2**: 157–209.

Boschma R. (2005), 'Proximity and innovation: a critical assessment', *Regional Studies*, **39**: 61–74.

Boutellier, R., Gassmann, O. and von Zedwitz, M. (2008), *Managing Global Innovation: Uncovering the Secrets of Future Competitiveness*, Berlin: Springer.

Broström, A. and Lööf, H. (2006), 'What do we know about firms' research collaboration with universities? New quantitative and qualitative evidence', Working Paper Series in Economics and Institutions of Innovation 74, Royal Institute of Technology, Centre of Excellence for Science and Innovation Studies, Stockholm.

Cantwell, J.A. (2009), 'Location and the multinational enterprise', *Journal of International Business Studies*, **40**: 35–41.

Cantwell, J.A. and Iammarino, S. (2000), 'Multinational corporations and the location of technological innovation in the UK regions', *Regional Studies*, **34**: 317–32.

Cantwell, J.A. and Iammarino, S. (2003), *Multinational Corporations and European Regional Systems of Innovation*, London: Routledge.

Cantwell, J.A. and Piscitello, L. (2005), 'Recent location of foreign-owned research and development activities by large multinational corporations in the European regions', *Regional Studies*, **39**: 1–16.

Cantwell, J.A., Iammarino, S. and Noonan, C. (2000), 'Inward investment, technological change and growth: the impact of multinational corporations on the UK economy', in N. Pain (ed.), *Inward Investment, Technological Change and Growth*, Basingstoke: Palgrave Macmillan, pp. 210–39.

Cooke, P. (1992), 'Regional innovation systems: competitive regulation in the new Europe', *Geoforum*, **23**: 365–82.

Cooke, P., Gomez Uraga, M. and Etxebarria, G. (1997), 'Regional innovation systems: institutional and organisational dimensions', *Research Policy*, **26**: 475–91.

Cosh, A., Hughes, A. and Lester, R. (2006), 'UK plc: just how innovative we are? Findings from the Cambridge–MIT Institute International Innovation Benchmarking Project', Industrial Performance center, MIT Working Paper series MIT-IP6-06-009.

D'Este, P. and Iammarino, S. (2010), 'The spatial profile of university–business research partnerships', *Papers in Regional Science*, **89**: 335–50.

De Cieri, H. and Dowling, P.J. (2006), 'Strategic international human resource management in multinational enterprises: developments and directions', in G.K. Stahl and I. Björkman (eds), *Handbook of Research in International Human Resource Management*, Cheltenham, UK and Northampton, MA, USA: Edward Elgar, pp. 15–35.

Deutsches Patent- und Markenamt (German Patent and Trademark Office) (2006), *Patentatlas Deutschland: Regionaldaten der Erfindungstätigkeit*, München.

Doloreux, D. and Paarto, S. (2005), 'Regional innovation systems: current discourse and unresolved issues', *Technology in Society*, **27**: 133–53.

Dunning, J.H. (2009), 'Location and the multinational enterprise: a neglected factor?', *Journal of International Business Studies*, **40**: 5–19.

Edquist, C. (1997), *Systems of Innovation: Technologies, Institutions, and Organizations*, London: Pinter.

Freeman, C. (1987), *Technology Policy and Economic Performance: Lessons from Japan*, London: Pinter.

Greater Cambridge Partnership (2007), Greater Cambridge annual profile, GCP, Cambridge.

Harvey, M.G., Novisevic, M.M. and Speier, C. (2000), 'An innovative global management staffing system: a competency-based perspective', *Human Resource Management*, **39**: 381–94.

Howells, J. (1999), 'Regional systems of innovation?', in D. Archibugi, J. Howells and J. Michie (eds), *Innovation Policy in a Global Economy*, Cambridge: Cambridge University Press, pp. 67–93.

Iammarino, S. (2005), 'An evolutionary integrated view of regional systems of innovation. Concepts, measures and historical perspectives', *European Planning Studies*, **13**: 495–517.

Iammarino, S. and McCann, P. (2010), 'Multinationals and economic geography. Location, technology, and innovation', mimeo.

Iammarino, S., Padilla-Perez, R. and von Tunzelmann, N. (2008), 'Technological capabilities and global–local interactions: the electronics industry in two Mexican regions', *World Development*, **36**: 1980–2003.

Kramer, J., Marinelli, E., Iammarino, S. and Reviella Diez, J. (2009), 'Intangible assets, multinational enterprises and regional innovation in Europe', Deliverable 1.3b WP1, available at: http://www.iareg.org/index.php?id=91.

Lall, S. (1992), 'Technological capabilities and industrialization', *World Development*, **20**: 165–86.

Lall, S. (1993), 'Understanding technological development', *Development and Change*, **24**: 719–53.

Malerba, F. (1992), 'Learning by firms and incremental technical change', *The Economic Journal*, **102**: 845–59.

Mariotti, S., Piscitello, L. and Elia, S. (2010), 'Spatial agglomeration of multinational enterprises: the role of information', *Journal of Economic Geography*, doi:10.1093/jeg/lbq011.

McCann, P. and Mudambi, R. (2004), 'The location behaviour of the multinational enterprise: some analytical issues', *Growth and Change*, **35**: 491–524.

McCann, P. and Mudambi, R. (2005), 'Analytical differences in the economics of geography: the case of the multinational firm', *Environment and Planning A*, **37**: 1857–76.

Minshall, T. and Wicksteed, B. (2005), *University Spin-out Companies: Starting to Fill the Evidence Gap*, London: The Gatsby Charitable Foundation.

Mudambi, R. (2008), 'Location, control and innovation in knowledge intensive industries', *Journal of Economic Geography*, **8**: 699–725.

Mudambi, R. and Santangelo, G. (2010), 'From shallow resource pools to proto-clusters: the role of MNC subsidiaries in peripheral regions', mimeo.

Narula, R. and Santangelo, G.D. (2009), 'Location, collocation and R&D alliances in the European ICT industry', *Research Policy*, **38**: 393–403.

North East Development Agency (2007), *Global Winner: Auto Industry Delivers Model Performance*, Newcastle upon Tyne: NEDA.

Phelps, N.A., Mackinnon, D., Stone, I. and Braidford, P. (2003), 'Embedding the multinationals? Institutions and the development of overseas manufacturing affiliates in Wales and North East England', *Regional Studies*, **37**: 27–40.

Revilla Diez, J. and Berger, M. (2005), 'The role of multinational corporations in metropolitan innovation systems: empirical evidence from Europe and Southeast Asia', *Environment and Planning A*, **35**: 1813–35.

Santangelo, G.D. (2002), 'The regional geography of corporate patenting in information and communications technology (ICT): domestic and foreign dimensions', *Regional Studies*, **36**: 495–514.

SV Wissenschaftsstatistik (ed.) (2010), *Forschung und Entwicklung in der Wirtschaft. Bericht über die FuE-Erhebungen 2007, 2008*, Essen. Available at www.stifterverband.info/ statistik_und_analysen/publikationen/fue_datenreport/fue_datenreport_2010.pdf (accessed 3 September 2011).

von Tunzelmann, N. (2009), 'Regional capabilities and industrial regeneration', in P. McCann, M. Farshchi and O. Janne (eds), *Technological Change and Mature Industrial Regions: Firms, Knowledge and Policy*, Cheltenham, UK and Northampton, MA, USA: Edward Elgar, pp. 11–28.

von Tunzelmann, N. and Wang, Q. (2003), 'An evolutionary view of dynamic capabilities', *Economie Appliquée*, **6**: 33–64.

von Tunzelmann, N. and Wang, Q. (2007), 'Capabilities and production theory', *Structural Change and Economic Dynamics*, **18**: 192–211.

Wissenschaftsrat (2009), Excellence Initiative, German Council of Science and Humanities. Available at www.wissenschaftsrat.de/exini-engl-start.html.

8. The organizational decomposition of innovation and territorial knowledge dynamics: insights from the German software industry

Simone Strambach and Benjamin Klement

8.1 INTRODUCTION

In OECD countries, in particular, changes in the organization of innovation became obvious in the mid-1990s. Indicators are the internationalization of business R&D, which in itself is not a new phenomenon but seems to be occurring at a much faster pace and is becoming more widespread. Often discussed as the new dimension of globalization, one major change in the spatial distribution of innovation is the integration of non-OECD countries, including developing countries, in R&D investments, particularly in India and China to even larger extents (OECD, 2008; UNCTAD, 2005). A shift towards more open innovation environments and the growing importance of external knowledge in innovation processes have been observed in different strands of innovation research. MNCs are important actors that shape knowledge dynamics across spatial and cultural borders, contributing heavily to the internationalization of innovation along their global value chains. However, we shall not focus on them exclusively, but place the organizational decomposition of innovation processes (ODIP) and its spatial implications at the centre of our chapter by answering the question: how does the organizational decomposition of innovation in OECD countries influence territorial knowledge dynamics?[1]

The debate on this question is quite controversial. On the one hand, there seems to be a consensus in the literature that the major share of MNCs' R&D in India and China comprises routine activities geared towards adapting existing designs or towards providing more standard parts in innovation processes that are transformed and integrated in innovative products and processes by firms in OECD countries (Bruche, 2009).

On the other hand, scholars active in global value chains and subsidiary research point to fast learning processes and the build-up of innovation capabilities of firms in non-OECD countries. These authors identify a far-reaching transition and assess the scattered empirical evidence as an indication of China's and India's change from production to innovation (cf. Altenburg et al., 2008; Lema, 2010; Quadros, 2009). It is argued that these countries are taking advantage of new opportunities to organize global value chains by investing strategically in their national innovation systems and stepping up their innovation efforts to constantly renew their competitive advantages. The catching up of several industries as well as an increase in the innovation capabilities of firms combined with the increasing offshoring of knowledge-intensive services is considered to be an indication of a new global dynamic and a shift in innovation activities.

While the rise of a new geography of innovation is discussed, the assessment of territorial knowledge dynamics, unfold and go along with distributed innovation processes, is still an open question. Obviously the offshoring of business R&D and knowledge-intensive service activities to low-cost countries indicates a higher degree of complexity in the international division of labour. As the organizational decomposition in the sphere of production is an ongoing process, ODIP is not a static phenomenon either. Some forms of ODIP might have existed for many years, but others have not emerged until recently, leading to an increase in diversity. Yet relatively few insights are available regarding the linkages and impacts of organizationally and geographically dispersed innovation processes as well as differences and commonalities between sectors.

This chapter seeks to provide deeper insights into the modes of organizationally decomposed innovation processes by arguing that it is necessary to open up the black box of knowledge interactions and to take into account the mutual reinforcement of linkages between actors, knowledge interactions and their territorial embeddedness. To this end we shall explore ODIP in the German software industry and its territorial organization.

The following section 8.2 provides the analytical framework that helps us to explore different types of ODIP. Drawing on several approaches such as systems of innovation, global value chains and research on knowledge-intensive business services (KIBS), we show that the organizational decomposition of innovation processes can occur in different ways. Section 8.3 elaborates on the sector-specific organization of innovation processes in the software industry. The empirical analysis of ODIP in the software industry starts in section 8.4, which also contains the methodological issues. The empirical results of the case studies are presented in section 8.5. We analyse the occurrence of ODIP, the practised modes and the types of actors involved in these processes. One major outcome of the study in Germany is that the strongly pronounced global/local dichotomy in the innovation debate falls short of the complexity and spatial differentiation of innovation processes. Especially the multi-local and multi-scalar character of organizationally decomposed innovation processes is significant in the software sector. In section 8.6 we put the micro-level results into the broader macro-level perspective by returning to the initial question of whether the organizational decomposition of innovation processes in OECD countries influences territorial knowledge dynamics. On the basis of our results we reflect on the debate regarding a qualitative shift or a changing geography of innovation.

8.2 THE ORGANIZATIONAL DECOMPOSITION OF INNOVATION – ACTORS, PROCESSES AND THE TERRITORIAL DIMENSION

Innovations in products, processes and services are the visible results of interactions between heterogeneous actors from inside and outside the firm who are embedded in spatially distributed networks. To gain insights into actors, processes and the territorial dimensions of innovation processes, we proposed the analytical framework of 'ODIP' (Schmitz and Strambach, 2009). Its aim is to capture the decomposition of innovation, compare these processes between sectors and to understand dynamics in the spatial organization shaped by these processes.

The literature strands on systems of innovation, MNCs, global value chains (GVCs) and KIBS (knowledge-intensive business services) show that organizational decomposition can occur in different ways and can involve a variety of different types of actors (cf. Schmitz and Strambach, 2009). Research on innovation systems emphasizes the importance of tight linkages between firms and research institutes or universities for the generation of knowledge in innovation processes (Cooke, 2001; Asheim and Gertler, 2005). Furthermore, subsidiaries that have been primarily concerned with the production of goods and services increasingly play a prominent role in intra-organizational innovation networks (Frost et al., 2002; Zander, 2002; Zanfei, 2000). Research on GVCs and global production networks (GPNs) points out that external suppliers are often expected to generate the knowledge that is required to produce improved or new components or systems (Jürgens, 2000, 2001; Humphrey, 2003). Additionally, the literature strand on KIBS outlines that KIBS have important roles as carriers and traders of knowledge and foster knowledge dynamics at multiple levels.

Table 8.1   Actor types according to the ODIP framework

Organizational Functional	Intra-organizational	Inter-organizational
Knowledge creating (exploration)	Actor Type 1 Decentralizing the R&D department; setting up knowledge communities	Actor Type 3 Commissioning research from universities or other organizations
Knowledge using (exploitation)	Actor Type 2 Delegating the development of new products to subsidiaries; setting up centres of excellence	Actor Type 4 Engaging suppliers of products and services (KIBS) in developing new products or processes

Source: Adapted from Schmitz and Strambach (2009).

Drawing on these insights, we define ODIP as the process by which firms shift parts of their innovation processes from their headquarters and centralized R&D department to decentralized R&D departments, subsidiaries, public/private research organizations and suppliers or KIBS.

The added value of the ODIP framework is the conjunction of these three different strands. Similar to the approach to 'systems of innovation', all actors that play an important role in the innovation processes are analysed. Not just the actors directly included into the GVCs of MNCs are analysed, but also the regional context and the relationships between local actors such as universities, research institutes, customers and KIBS are seen as important parts of global innovation processes. However, to capture the geographic dispersal of innovation processes we do not *a priori* conceive territories as a fixed geographical sphere bounded by the borders of a certain 'innovation system' but aim to cover the entire territorial scope of a firm's distributed innovation processes.

The ODIP framework consists of four actor types and four ODIP modes. Actor types are assigned to the actors participating in innovation processes with regard to their belonging to organizational and functional dimensions (Table 8.1). The organizational dimension relates to whether or not the participating actor is within the case study firm (intra-organizational) or external to the sample firm. The functional dimension refers to the business function that an actor has. Innovation can be delegated to those who are primarily concerned with knowledge creation and have only a loose connection with the production of goods and services or to actors who are primarily active in knowledge-using

Table 8.2 Modes of ODIP

Characteristics / ODIP modes	Organizational dimension: intra-/inter- organizational	Functional dimension: knowledge creating/using	Spatial dimension: same/different scale
I	Actors from one organizational dimension	Actors from one functional dimension	Regional/ national/ international
II	Actors from both organizational dimensions	Actors from one functional dimension	Regional/ national/ international
III	Actors from one organizational dimension	Actors from both functional dimensions	Regional/ national/ international
IV	Actors from both organizational dimensions	Actors from both functional dimensions	Regional/ national/ international

activities that are tightly connected to the production of goods and services.

The constellation of different actor types involved in an organizationally decomposed innovation process distinguishes the ODIP mode that a firm follows. These four ODIP modes (see Table 8.2) stand for four different settings in organizationally decomposed innovation processes. By ODIP modes we understand relatively stable patterns of diverse actor types and their networks in knowledge interactions. Decomposed innovation processes imply a labour division in knowledge production. While innovation research in particular is focused on the importance of knowledge sources in innovation processes, such as customers, suppliers, cooperation partners or research organizations, little is known about the complex constellations of such actors and their labour division in knowledge interactions.

The distinction between the four modes of ODIP is based on the suggestion that these differ in their level of complexity, influenced by the organizational and functional boundaries that have to be bridged, by the scope of external relationships that have to be managed and by the diversity of actors with distinct knowledge bases who collaborate. The diversity of actors with heterogeneous knowledge bases and the level of common knowledge heavily influence the scope of knowledge being integrated in distributed innovation processes (Grant, 1996). Thus an empirical case is related to the most complex mode of ODIP, mode IV, if actors from intra- and inter-organizational dimensions and knowledge-creating as well as knowledge-using actors are part of the innovation process.

This case appears complex because the organizational and cognitive proximity of involved actors is low. Organizational proximity may be regarded as a form of common knowledge between actors created by informal and formal routines that facilitate knowledge integration. Referring to the conventional tension between production and R&D, cognitive distance between actors professionally engaged in similar functional fields may be smaller. In turn, cognitive proximity facilitates communication, mutual understanding and knowledge integration (cf. Nooteboom et al., 2007; Boschma, 2005).

We use this developed framework of ODIP to examine and compare the different empirical forms of decomposed innovation processes and their territorial shaping. It is widely acknowledged that innovation processes have significant sector and industry-specific characteristics. Hence, in the following we shall present some sector specificities that may influence the way innovation is decomposed in the software industry.

8.3   INNOVATION AND PRODUCTION IN THE SOFTWARE INDUSTRY

It is meanwhile widely acknowledged in the interdisciplinary field of innovation research that innovation processes have significant sector- and industry-specific features (e.g. Pavitt, 1984; Malerba, 2002, 2005). Compared to many mature industrial and manufacturing industries, the evolution of the software industry to an autonomous sector is a relatively recent development. From a technological point of view, software can be seen as a cross-sectoral technology. From a sectoral point of view, it is a knowledge-intensive service industry. Insights into innovations in the software industry are still scarce due to the fact that there is no sharp line between production and innovation in the industry. While in manufacturing industries the production and innovation systems are organizationally differentiated and innovation processes imply a deviation from the usual operational working procedure, in KIBS industries such as the software industry both are closely interwoven. Innovation is not a separate activity; it takes place mostly in an *ad hoc* manner in the client interaction processes and in the production of customer-specific problem solutions (Djellal et al., 2003; Hipp and Grupp, 2005; Muller and Doloreux, 2007; Strambach, 2008). The internal processes of knowledge creation are only weakly formalized, as has been shown by empirical research (Hauknes, 2000; Sundbo, 2000; Marklund, 2000). In contrast to manufacturing firms, most KIBS firms do not systematically distinguish R&D activities in organizational terms as R&D departments or R&D management structures. Knowledge exploration and exploitation often overlap and take place simultaneously (cf. Friedewald et al., 2002; Holl et al., 2006; Segelod and Jordan, 2004).

Project-based work is the dominant form of work organization in software development to produce client-specific problem solutions. Innovation is inherently defined by novelty; however, in these knowledge-intensive industries every project implies a certain degree of uniqueness and is thus in a sense new. Due to the customer-specific context in which knowledge is applied, the individual task varies significantly. In the software industry innovation measures have to be geared to uncover routine problem solving from innovative problem solving. Traditional innovation statistics, input as well as throughput measures like patents, are often not appropriate for achieving this. Miles and Green (2008), for instance, point out that many innovation activities of knowledge-intensive service industries such as the software industry are likely to remain hidden from innovation researchers.

Distinct characteristics of innovation in the software industry are short innovation cycles and a high dynamic. As a considerable body of literature shows, the software industry increasingly relies on external knowledge sources, especially inter-firm linkages (cf. Grimaldi and Torrisi, 2001; Segelod and Jordan, 2004; Friedewald et al., 2002; Tödtling et al., 2006). Yet there is broad variation regarding the importance of different types of knowledge sources and their spatial dimension. Even though there is no clear-cut outcome of the complex architecture of different types of actors' linkages in innovation processes, a common finding of all studies is the importance of the relationships to customers in all phases of software development. Clients seem to be the main trigger for knowledge creation. Feedback from customers becomes important not only in the idea phase but also in the design, development and commercialization phases to align the end product to customer needs and demands as these are made increasingly explicit (Segelod and Jordan, 2004). In the software sector, in particular, the knowledge domains in which the firms operate shape both the development of the specific knowledge base of the firm itself and the expertise of their professionals in a co-evolutionary way (cf. Løwendahl et al., 2001: 914).

Recent research within a macro-level perspective indicates that institutions are potentially important, given that the evolution of the software sector very much depends on complex, often long-term relationships with client firms in other sectors of the economy (cf. Grimshaw and Miozzo, 2006). As shown in the development of the German software industry, the interplay of the institutional context of the national innovation system and the pattern of demand over time contributes to the specialization and competences of this industry (Strambach, 2010). The social embeddedness of economic transactions is crucial in the dynamic production of knowledge-intensive services (Tödtling et al., 2006). Furthermore, the software industry seems to be an example for the implementation of industrial methods such as standardization and modularization into service production. The outsourcing and offshoring processes gain more importance in the software industry, raising the question of whether we can observe a vertical disintegration in knowledge-intensive activities comparable with the organizational decomposition of production in manufacturing industries.

8.4   METHODOLOGY

Accessing information that clarifies and explains the organization of innovation processes in software companies required a number of case studies. They were achieved by semi-structured interviews, with actors playing a significant role in the innovation processes of firms in the software industry. We selected a number of software-producing subsidiaries of MNCs in the software and automotive industry (Baden-Württemberg as region of origin of MNCs, preferably with foreign subsidiaries in India).

The development of each case study was accompanied by intense desktop research including publicly available data on R&D facilities, R&D organization and important innovation-oriented collaborations. In-depth interviews were then undertaken with senior managers in charge of innovation management and/or innovation project managers.

Thirteen case studies were conducted, all comprising software firms with headquarters or significant development units in Baden-Württemberg. The firms were active in the development of internet business portals, business software, database solutions and embedded software. Basically, we analysed specific innovation events to capture the actors and their activities in ODIP. However, since each innovation event may feature different actor constellations, additional firms have been analysed to capture changes in general innovation process management and territorial organization. The Indian subsidiaries are represented by three case studies based on in-depth desktop research and interviews in Bangalore (India) and Germany. Furthermore, interviews with three regional support organizations in Baden-Württemberg and India focusing on networking and technology transfer contributed to the examination of ODIP in software firms from Baden-Württemberg. In the following empirical analysis all firms are anonymized unless information is publicly available through articles, papers, websites, databases and so on. The abbreviations indicate the products of the firms. NET stands for firms active developing internet portals or web services, BS stands for business software firms, providing solutions for finance services (BS_FIN), outsourcing (BS_OUT), databases (BS_DAT), customer relation management (BS_CRM), automobile manufacturing (BS_AUTO) and business simulations for e-learning (BS_SIM).

8.5 EMPIRICAL RESULTS

8.5.1 Actors and Processes in ODIP of the Software Industry

As mentioned in section 8.2, in the ODIP framework actors are typified according to their organizational characteristics. On the one hand, the organizational decomposition of innovation can take place within or between organization(s). On the other hand, it may involve actors active in the creation or the using of knowledge. This typology allows the determination of the organizational and functional borders that have to be crossed within an innovation process, providing important information about the different forms of distance and proximity that the innovating firm has to take into account. Table 8.3 reflects the occurrence of actor types in the analysed case studies.

Furthermore, we also analysed the software-producing subsidiaries located in India of three large MNCs active in embedded software (AUTO_IT), telecommunication solutions (COMM_IT) and business software (BS_GLOB). They are not included in Table 8.3, since they were not been analysed by the depiction of a specific innovation event (see section 8.4).

It will come as no surprise that customers play a role in every case since they are important as co-creators and co-producers of knowledge-based solutions (Bettencourt et al., 2002; Gallouj, 2002; Grimshaw and Miozzo, 2006; Muller and Doloreux, 2007; Strambach, 2008). Furthermore, organizationally decomposed innovation processes are characterized by limited presence of suppliers, public KIBS and R&D departments. However, we did find that several software firms involve knowledge-using subsidiaries in their innovation processes.

8.5.1.1 Modes of ODIP
As can be seen, software firms do not follow one single mode of ODIP. While there are some firms that engage all types of actors in their innovation processes, there are also firms that show very few linkages to external actors. In the following we introduce our typology of modes of ODIP that are differentiated by actor constellations (cf. section 8.2).

Table 8.3 Overview of the case studies – actors in ODIP

Actor type	Case study Actors	NET1	NET2	BS_DAT1	BS_FIN1	BS_OUT	BS_DAT2	BS_CRM	BS_AUTO	BS_SIM	BS_FIN2
4	Customers	X	X	X	X	X	X	X	X	X	X
	Suppliers/private KIBS						X		X		
3	Public KIBS						X			X	X
2	Subsidiaries					X		X	X	X	X
1	Decentralized R&D										X

Source: Own research.

Three groups of firms can be identified following the distinct ODIP modes above: 'customized solution providers' referring to mode I, 'cost-driven outsourcing firms' relating to modes II and III, and 'innovation process managers', which practise ODIP mode IV. We merged firms that practise ODIP modes II and III into one group because we are unable to find distinct differences in their patterns of knowledge interactions (see Table 8.4).

'Customized solution providers' are firms (e.g. NET1, NET2, BS_DAT1, BS_FIN1) whose sole external contribution to the innovation process results from intense interaction between the software firm and the customer. Their relation to public knowledge-creating organizations is limited to the sourcing of highly skilled personnel. Another feature is that they do not possess subsidiaries involved in innovation processes. In the KIBS literature these firms and their behaviour have been thoroughly investigated. The second group of firms (BS_OUT, BS_CRM, BS_AUTO, BS, DAT2), which will be called 'cost-driven outsourcing firms', has established subsidiaries that are also involved in innovation processes and source knowledge from research institutes and universities, public KIBS as well as private KIBS or suppliers. This means an increase in complexity for the management of innovation processes in comparison to firms of group 1, as the scope of knowledge integration is higher. Nevertheless, the firms' knowledge creation efforts are instead aimed at the absorption of new technologies (out of external sources such as publications or incorporated in human resources from universities and colleges). However, to whatever extent new knowledge is created, it is not represented by a decentralization of the firm's R&D efforts in the form of a formal organizational unit. The third group in our typology is formed by 'innovation process managers' (BS_SIM, BS_FIN2, BS_GLOB), who decentralize their R&D activities. Their subsidiaries not only carry out knowledge-using tasks during the innovation process but contribute to the knowledge-creating efforts of the firm. Furthermore, the complexity of knowledge interactions in their innovation processes is very high, involving several intra- and inter-organizational actors with specialized knowledge bases spread over several functions. Their innovation process design is characterized by the inclusion of a flexible mix of internal and external actors at different stages of the innovation process, thereby complementing knowledge using functions with systematic knowledge creation within intra- and inter-organizational settings.

8.5.1.2 Labour division in knowledge production along the value chain

Following the identification of actors involved in distributed innovation processes, a further insight into the processes and tasks assigned by the innovating firm to various actors is necessary to clarify at which stage of

Table 8.4 Modes of ODIP, differentiated by actor constellations

Characteristics / Modes of ODIP	Organizational dimension: intra-/ inter-organizational	Functional dimension: knowledge creating /using	Spatial dimension	Firms	Group
I	Actors from one organizational dimension	Actors from one functional dimension	Regional/ national/ international	NET1, NET2, BS_DAT1, BS_FIN1	Customized solution providers
II	Actors from both organizational dimensions	Actors from one functional dimension	Regional/ national/ international	BS_OUT, BS_CRM, BS_AUTO	Cost-driven outsourcing firms
III	Actors from one organizational dimension	Actors from both functional dimensions	Regional/ national/ international	BS_DAT2	Cost-driven outsourcing firms
IV	Actors from both organizational dimensions	Actors from both functional dimensions	Regional/ national/ international	BS_SIM, BS_FIN2, BS_GLOB	Innovation process managers

the value chain software firms delegate parts of their innovation processes to internal or external actors. Through the investigation of value chains we were also able to gain insights into the activities that are subject to organizational decomposition.

The 'customized solution providers' of group 1 not only show a low level of decomposition of innovation processes into external actors; their internal innovation processes can also hardly be represented as value chains. Basically they cannot be termed 'multinational companies' but we have nevertheless included them in our analysis. The differences between software MNCs and these firms may indicate the factors limiting the international decomposition of innovation processes in the software industry.

In firms of group 1, knowledge-using and knowledge-creating activities are closely interwoven. A common practice of these firms is to carry out knowledge processing in interdisciplinary project teams composed of both client staff and their own staff. As is typical for KIBS industries (Strambach, 2008; Gallouj, 2002; Muller and Doloreux, 2007), the nature of their innovations can be characterized as '*ad hoc* innovation'. They are unplanned by-products of innovative projects that the firm carries out in frequent interaction with their customers, taking place at all stages of product development. Hence, even though the firms' products may be highly innovative, they do not maintain R&D departments. They may not even have formalized any organizational routines for the management of innovations. Their 'innovation management' can often be described as the fostering of ideas and their communication in a working atmosphere, which one interview partner entitled 'coffee-table culture' ('Kaffeetischkultur').

The weakly formalized knowledge creation process and the lack of organizational routines such as a formalized innovation management (see also Friedewald et al., 2002) do not necessarily reflect a low degree of innovativeness. They point to re-contextualization as an important mechanism of knowledge creation in the software sector. Re-contextualization can be understood as the process of direct contextualization of individual or collective tacit knowledge without it being transformed through codification (Strambach, 2008). Codification processes themselves are context-dependent (Cohendet and Meyer-Krahmer, 2001) and the discontinuous and temporary nature of innovative projects acts as a significant brake on knowledge codification. These software firms act in highly volatile knowledge markets and the systematic knowledge generated as an activity 'far' from the customer context may turn out to be economically useless after a relatively short time-span.

In group 2, however, there are 'cost-driven outsourcing' software firms that have defined value chains and are able to involve several actors in their innovation processes. Their most prominent feature is the establishment

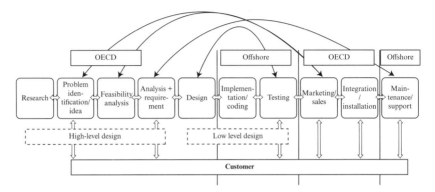

Source: Own figure, based on Segelod and Jordan (2004); Royce (1970).

Figure 8.1   Product development process of 'cost-driven outsourcing firms'

of a subsidiary – mostly in a developing country – that executes certain parts of the value chain to reduce costs and increase flexibility. The typical model of ODIP in group 2 is characterized by close interaction between the innovating firm and its customer in the initial and final phases of an innovation event, visualized in Figure 8.1. The initial phase in which the problem framing takes place is crucial for the design of software architecture; misunderstandings in this phase can cause the whole project to fail. Even in this early stage these software firms activated external actors (e.g. research institutes, consultants, software component suppliers) to integrate highly specialized knowledge bases for the specification of the required knowledge architecture to develop the complex problem solution. Offshore subsidiaries are usually involved in a later stage, mostly in the middle of the innovation process.

According to our research and the existing literature, a product development model can be identified for the 'cost-driven outsourcing firms' (see Figure 8.1). It shows the different activities and their characterization as a high-or low-level design based on the increasing share of knowledge creation activities compared with knowledge-using activities. The tasks assigned to offshore subsidiaries of the case study software firms in group 2 comprise mainly the coding and testing of software, which are easy to specify and communicate and hence spatially transferable. However, subsidiaries are hardly involved in the final, direct customer interaction in which the product is implemented in the complex customer context and its existing software environment. Hence, similar to those of other authors, our results show that in distributed innovation processes activities with a high level of knowledge-creating activities remain to be conducted in Germany. Decomposition of such activities involves high efforts in knowledge integration, coordination and governance due to the process character of knowledge and the uncertainty with regard to the quality and the appropriateness of the knowledge product. Subject to delegation to actors in non-OECD countries are mainly those parts in the innovation process that are characterized by a high degree of knowledge-using activities. However, we noted that in some cases, due to learning processes over time, the tasks assigned to offshore subsidiaries are extended towards activities comprising a higher level of knowledge creation, such as design and analysis/requirements.

In the following analysis the innovation event 'ePep' of the firm BS_AUTO will be presented in order to give an example of the practice of ODIP mode II along the typical product development process.

In this case the innovation was the highly sophisticated software 'ePEP', which supports all stages of the production process of the customer, the Trucks Europe/Latin America department of a German automaker. The entire engineering and manufacturing process at different sites had to be streamlined by the new software solution, replacing more than ten heterogeneous legacy systems. The development of this software was conducted by BS_AUTO, located in Ulm, Baden-Württemberg, which delegated parts of the software development to its subsidiary BS_AUTO Malaysia in Kuala Lumpur. BS_AUTO decided to achieve a higher degree of capacity utilization of its offshore resources to increase its profitability. It therefore purchased a software solution developed by business software provider BS_OUT2, located in Freiburg, Baden-Württemberg, which facilitates offshore working models through the standardization and specification of software components. Furthermore, this firm acted as a consultant for the customization and application of the product.

As shown in the value chain visualization in Figure 8.2, in the initial phase of the project the architectural design was accomplished with close interaction between the customer, the German headquarters of BS_AUTO and BS_OUT2. The role of the last was to kick-start the process, support architecture development, train employees and consult BS_AUTO in the transformation of the legacy systems. The use of BS_OUT2's software enabled BS_AUTO to outsource the component design to its Malaysian subsidiary at a relatively early stage of the innovation process. Thus the subsidiary's tasks have been extended upstream in the value chain. After a verification of the components developed in Malaysia by the HQ of BS_AUTO and the customer, the Malaysian subsidiary of BS_AUTO implemented the components and tested them. The originally existing different skill levels remained intact to a certain extent. In the last steps of the innovation process BS_AUTO Germany interacted closely

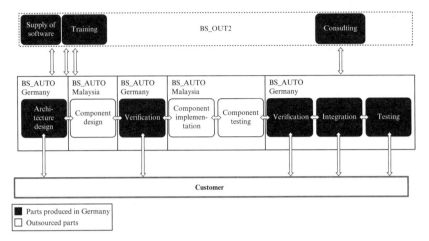

Source: Own figure.

Figure 8.2   Modularized software development process at BS_AUTO

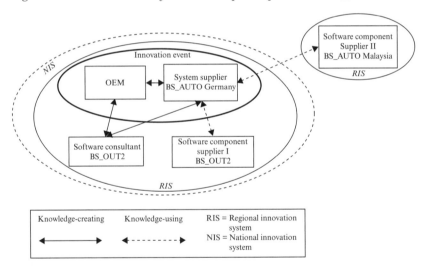

Source: Own figure.

Figure 8.3   Spatial dimension of the innovation event of BS_AUTO

with the customer and the software supplier BS_OUT2 during the verification, integration and final testing of the developed software.

The case of BS_AUTO (see Figures 8.2 and 8.3) shows how technological solutions can support the decomposition of innovation processes,

thereby upgrading the quality of tasks assigned to a software firm's subsidiary upstream in the value chain. Nevertheless, the subsidiaries of these 'cost-driven outsourcing' firms are assigned to knowledge-using tasks for the most part. This group of software firms shows that the development of organizational routines to dissolve the close connection between knowledge exploitation and knowledge exploration is a precondition for decomposing innovation.

The third group of software firms covers the 'innovation process managers' that practise ODIP mode IV and are organizationally very close to MNCs of manufacturing industries. Their value chains are determined and their innovation management is strongly institutionalized. There are several formalized organizational routines established to coordinate knowledge production within the firm and even for joint cooperation with customers.

What distinguishes these firms from the other cases is particularly the role that their subsidiaries play in decomposed innovation processes. Their subsidiaries show a high degree of autonomy by carrying out own knowledge creation activities and possessing independent relationships with customers. They have established networks with different actor types in their local context that support them in knowledge creation processes. Thus the main organizational capability of 'innovation process managers' is to utilize the accumulated knowledge base of the subsidiaries in innovation processes. For example, BS_FIN2 has established a separate organizational unit, the 'technology office', which is responsible for the de-contextualization of generic knowledge parts from the locally accumulated context-specific knowledge of its subsidiaries to make it available for use in innovation projects in distant places.

8.5.2 The Territorial Shaping of ODIP

Since we have so far approached the spatial dimension in an indirect way, in this section we address the territorial shaping of ODIP more directly, first by examining the location of actor types participating in decomposed innovation processes. Second, we shall focus on foreign-based subsidiaries to explore their changing role in ODIP over time. The importance of territoriality in knowledge processes is discussed mainly under two dimensions: proximity and embeddedness. With the following analysis we seek to gain insights into how these dimensions are related to ODIP.

Independent of the kind of innovation and the practised mode of ODIP, the empirical findings indicate that particular types of actors are found on the same spatial scale (Table 8.5). While the relations to customers, public and private KIBS are mainly regionally and nationally located,

Table 8.5 Overview of the spatial distribution of actors in ODIP

Actor type	Actors	Customized solution providers				Cost-driven outsourcing firms				Innovation process managers		
		NET1	NET2	BS_DAT1	BS_FIN1	BS_OUT	BS_DAT2	BS_CRM	BS_AUTO	BS_SIM	SAP	BS_FIN2
4	Customers	NIS	NIS	NIS	South Africa	NIS	RIS	RIS	RIS	NIS	Global	NIS
	Suppliers/private KIBS						RIS		RIS		Global	
3	Public KIBS					India, Sweden	RIS			RIS		
2	Subsidiaries							Egypt	Malaysia	India	Global	Hungary, Spain, Brazil
1	Decentralized R&D										Global	India

Note: RIS = regional innovation system; NIS = national innovation system.

the linkages to subsidiaries and R&D centres cross national borders. The linkages to customers, public and private KIBS imply a high level of knowledge-creating activities, such as problem framing or collaboration on research activities. To achieve the integration of diverse and specialized knowledge bases of these actors a certain degree of spatial proximity appears to be required. By overcoming cognitive distance, intensive and rich communication processes develop in order to build a level of common knowledge and establish mutual understanding on the required 'knowledge architecture' as well as to articulate procedures for knowledge exchange during the creation process. Co-presence, frequent face-to-face interactions and the necessity of temporary geographical proximity among the actors play an important role. It is particularly the flexibility of spontaneous and situation-dependent face-to-face communication and interaction processes that are enabled and facilitated by spatial proximity.

Geographical proximity is often combined with other forms of proximity (Boschma, 2005; Gertler, 2003) such as cultural, institutional or organizational proximity and therefore the impacts can hardly be considered as isolated. This is very significant in cases where knowledge-creating activities took place across national borders in innovation processes. The simultaneous absence of organizational, spatial and also cultural proximity turned out to be very inefficient in innovation projects. Nearly every firm could report experiences with failed projects in conducting distant knowledge-creating activities, especially across national borders with independent external actors. Thus, in successful projects the lack of spatial proximity was compensated by other kinds of proximity, mostly organizational proximity.

The findings also reveal that the spatial organization of software firms' innovation processes may not be typified according to a local–global dichotomy. No single firm was acting in distributed innovation processes exclusively on a certain scale, either locally nor globally. Instead, knowledge interactions processes are characterized by their multi-scalarity. During the innovation process actors on the regional, national and international scale were included depending on the required complementary knowledge. Even firms acting as customized solution providers are not bound to their regional innovation system. These firms also obtain innovation projects of customers in spatial distance through reputation or referrals because they are considered experts in a particular knowledge domain. The necessary high level of in-depth interaction in the innovation process is achieved through arrangements of temporary on-site working phases and replaced by on-site meetings, supported by information and communication technologies. These firms draw mostly on developed organizational models based on procedural knowledge gained in former projects in order to handle distant knowledge interactions. In all case studies, irrespective of which mode of ODIP was practised, the dynamic and temporary use of spatial proximity in the process of knowledge production was apparent. The necessity for moments of geographical proximity (Torre, 2008) remains of considerable importance in organizationally decomposed innovation processes of the software industry.

Turning to the question of embeddedness, we can state that an increasing degree of global division of labour in knowledge production does not necessarily indicate a decrease in the regional embeddedness of a firm. Our results underline the point that those firms that practise highly complex modes of ODIP are at the same time more embedded in global *and* local contexts than other software firms.

Even for the firms of group 2, which offshore parts of their innovation processes, evidence for regional embeddedness as well as an international division of labour can be found. While the knowledge-using activities are executed in non-OECD countries, these firms maintain regional/national relations to customers, suppliers and public/private KIBS. There is a pretty clear distinction between knowledge-creating actors in OECD countries and knowledge-using activities in non-OECD countries. The internationally organized 'innovation process managers' also remain deeply rooted in the innovation system of their home region. The distinctive features of these firms are the independence and autonomy of their offshore subsidiaries, responsible for their own customer relations. Global actors have a high significance in their innovation processes, since not only knowledge-using activities are conducted in non-OECD countries but also activities similar to those of the German headquarters.

Yet this fact did not lead to a diminished significance of relations within the home region of Baden-Württemberg. On the contrary, 'cost-driven outsourcing firms' and 'innovation process managers' show institutionalized relationships with regional actors such as public research organizations, universities, specialized KIBS and lead customers. They have established and continuously invest in regional knowledge networks that they mobilize in a flexible way in the respective innovation processes. For instance, BS_FIN2 collaborates in dynamic, content-specific contexts with several universities and research institutes. In these cases the content is mainly focused on basic research, concerning software engineering methods and framework generation. Hence software firms like BS_FIN2 can limit the build-up of their own expensive R&D capacities. As pointed out by these firms, without such regional, often highly personalized relations established over time, in innovative projects it would be difficult to gain access to the necessary expertise and competences in specialized knowledge domains and to combine this in a flexible, timely manner. Software firms act in highly fluid knowledge markets and have to respond to the increasing requirements in software development due to growing complexity and the increasingly different application domains. In turn, firms state an increasing demand for expertise in interdisciplinary knowledge fields combining IT know-how with vertical and/or horizontal domain knowledge. By providing highly specialized, knowledge-intensive expertise and comprehensive problem solving simultaneously, the integration of particular but diverse knowledge fields into one innovative solution constitutes the competitive advantage in developed markets. Software firms of group 3, in particular, leverage their innovation system (be it national or regional) and their global value chains to deliver innovative systemic solutions. It seems that the headquarters in Baden-Württemberg have gained the organizational capabilities to de-contextualize and re-contextualize knowledge that is accumulated and located in dispersed sites of the firm and flexibly combine it with external knowledge to create a complementary knowledge base.

8.5.3 Territorial Knowledge Dynamics – the Role of Subsidiaries

Over the course of the last ten years an evolution in the scope of the capabilities of subsidiaries can be noted in many cases of the analysed firms. As pointed out in research on MNCs, foreign-based subsidiaries in particular are increasingly involved in the use and generation of knowledge (Zanfei, 2000; Zander, 2002; Frost et al., 2002). In the case studies of AUTO_IT, COMM_IT and BS_GLOBAL an expansion of the capabilities of the Indian subsidiaries is very obvious. Remarkably, these dynamics were even found in subsidiaries of secondary software suppliers like AUTO_IT and COMM_IT. All subsidiaries were initially established to carry out knowledge-using tasks delegated by their headquarters. Today they are responsible for individual customer relations and products, in the case of BS_GLOBAL even for international markets. Capability building is inherently evolutionary in nature and can be understood as a cumulative path-dependent process shaped by both internal and external factors (Dosi et al., 2008; Eisenhardt and Martin, 2000; Teece et al., 1997; Teece, 2008).

The expansion of the scope of ODIP, which ultimately leads to capability upgrading, depends on technological factors that foster the extent of ODIP and knowledge-related factors that limit it. While standardization and industrialization ease spatially distributed software development processes by separating knowledge-using and knowledge-creating activities, knowledge – the main production factor of software firms – limits ODIP. The process character, context dependence and the social construction of knowledge require different forms of barriers (cognitive, organizational and cultural) to be overcome for effective learning in knowledge interactions.

While the establishment of communication channels or (temporary) spatial proximity appears not to be a considerable problem nowadays, an in-depth, experience-based understanding of the client's business domains, business processes and needs is required, referred to as 'customer domain knowledge'. The codification of the specific customer domain knowledge implies high transaction costs due to its complexity and origin in frequent in-depth interaction. The conceptual set-up and software architecture as steps prior to the detailed definition of requirements are particularly characterized by high demands in customer domain knowledge, causing these value chain stages to be rarely outsourced.

While the cost advantages of non-OECD countries are obvious, the increase in coordination costs due to knowledge-related factors is difficult to account for in firms' strategic decisions as to whether or not the scope of ODIP should be limited or expanded. They face a trade-off between an increase in cost advantage and flexibility on the one hand and a decrease in development speed and efficiency on the other. The implications of ODIP can be very different for software firms due to the idiosyncrasies of their knowledge bases, strategies, products, experiences and organizational structure. Among our cases we found examples of both increases and decreases in costs/speed/flexibility during the decomposition of innovation processes. Yet the technological advancement that enables the spatial organization most certainly does not lead automatically to the offshoring of innovative activities to non-OECD countries. However, the following examples of subsidiaries that were able to upgrade their capabilities show how and why the expansion of ODIP may take place.

The debate about the changing role of subsidiaries originally focused on the global division of labour in manufacturing industries and emphasizes the degree of autonomy attributed to subsidiaries as an important internal determinant. A specificity of the software sector is a generally higher degree of subsidiary autonomy compared to subsidiaries of manufacturing industries, a fact that is grounded in the intangibility and knowledge intensity of the software 'product'. Every development project has a certain degree of novelty and there is more than one way of achieving the final product. Several problem-solving approaches can be chosen and discussed as complementary in software development. To ensure the fitting accuracy of the software product, the responsible teams need context knowledge from their internal or external customers to a varying extent. Even for projects that imply mainly knowledge-using activities, communication processes are still necessary. Compared to their

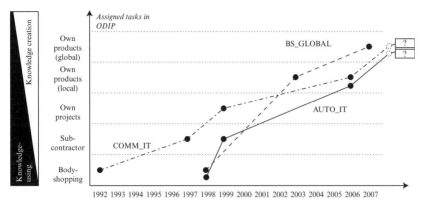

Source: Own figure.

Figure 8.4   Evolution in the autonomy of Indian IT subsidiaries of German software firms

counterparts in manufacturing industries, these sector specificities affect the degree of autonomy and the possibilities for software subsidiaries to learn and to build competence. Since the subsidiaries act in different contexts depending on the customers and the respective projects, they have to acquire knowledge from various domains, thus accumulating a knowledge base that in turn accelerates the upgrading of capabilities on the part of the subsidiary.

The interdependence of capability building and autonomy is visible in the development course of the analysed software subsidiaries. The capabilities and accordingly the degree of autonomy of the subsidiaries evolved along the trajectory given in Figure 8.4. Over time these subsidiaries have been assigned to more and more knowledge-creating tasks such as the development of own products for local and even global markets. With the assignment of subsidiary-led projects and product development the subsidiary gains a certain degree of autonomy.

The analysis of patents also reflects the capability building of subsidiaries, since patents are one of the most important output indicators of the creation of novel technological knowledge. The number of patents may not mirror the quality of the knowledge created or the significance of an invention for the actual products of BS_GLOBAL, but it is definitely useful in analysing the upgrading of capabilities. The number of patents can indicate the scale of knowledge-creating activities carried out in Bangalore over time. To analyse the patents applied by BS_GLOBAL we acquired the relevant data from the USPTO and the EPO and deleted patents that appeared in both patent offices. Patents were counted as being applied for with the participation of BS_GLOBAL Bangalore if the assignee of the patent was BS_GLOBAL and at least one inventor's residence was listed as 'Bangalore' in the patent file. To date (November 2009), BS_GLOBAL Bangalore has participated in the application of 72 patents. Yet despite having been established in 1998, BS_GLOBAL Bangalore was not involved in any patenting activity before 2002. Between 2003 and 2004 the number of patents that Bangalorean employees of BS_GLOBAL accounted for increased rapidly from 8 to 21 patents and remained on a high level until 2006 (17 patents).

Furthermore, the autonomy of BS_GLOBAL Bangalore has increased as well. The share of patents invented solely by employees of BS_GLOBAL Bangalore on all patents applied for by at least one employee of BS_GLOBAL Bangalore may serve as an indicator of knowledge creation activities carried out autonomously by the Bangalore subsidiary in the global division of labour in innovation processes. The level of autonomy of BS_GLOBAL Bangalore increased simultaneously with the rising level of knowledge creation in general. In 2003 the first patents were applied for autonomously, representing 25 per cent of all patents invented at the location. In the following years the share of autonomously applied for patents grew to 33 per cent in 2004 and 53 per cent in 2006.

However, learning at offshore locations is not only limited to technological aspects; Indian software subsidiaries in particular build up vertical domain knowledge as well as capabilities to bridge cultural gaps in knowledge. As our interviews show, some parent firms have meanwhile established internal organizational routines to foster the bridging of cultural gaps. By developing models of organized geographical proximity (Torre and Rallet, 2005) for face-to-face communication and interaction, they support intercultural learning effects aimed at reducing cognitive distance. In the case of AUTO_IT, for example, the Indian subsidiary also has its own marketing unit in Germany to promote its competences and capabilities to customers within the entire corporation. Internal competition between different subsidiaries appears to be another important internal factor that drives subsidiaries to pursue knowledge-creating activities. The stronger orientation of internal performance measurement towards intangibles in governance structures of the parent firms sets additional incentives for the subsidiary management to create inimitable competences. For instance, AUTO_IT measured the performance of its subsidiary in India by the number of patents applied for per year and the target figures have risen in line with the subsidiary's competence building.

Additionally, the empirical analysis in Bangalore underlines the importance of external local factors in capability building. The results underline the fact that the subsidiaries have meanwhile established linkages to external actors, such as public and private KIBS or research institutes, located in the regional context. The empowerment of the subsidiaries that are engaged in knowledge production with a certain degree of autonomy appears to be necessary and in turn fosters the establishment of external networks. Although the subsidiaries are still quite dependent on the headquarters, they build up network linkages to the regional institutions and organizations and embed them in their knowledge-creating activities. These linkages can bring subsidiaries untradable competences or advantages in the sourcing of human resources and knowledge. Even in decomposed innovation processes that spread over national borders, the embeddedness in both low-cost and high-cost locations still matters in the software industry.

8.6 A NEW GEOGRAPHY OF INNOVATION EMERGING?

The chapter focused on the territorial shaping of distributed innovation processes in the software industry. Our findings underline the fact that knowledge dynamics unfolding along such processes have sector-specific characteristics and are often multi-scalar in nature. Software firms do not follow one single mode of ODIP but practise several different forms of decomposition to different extents. In our sample firms of the German software industry, the majority of activities that are spatially decomposed over national borders are knowledge-using ones. Only a few firms are able to perform complex modes of ODIP in which knowledge-creating *and* knowledge-using activities are delegated to intra- and inter-organizational actors. There are several factors preventing or limiting the delegation of knowledge-creating activities to offshore partners. Among those often mutually reinforcing factors are the close connections between knowledge exploration and exploitation, the importance of customer interactions and complex customer domain knowledge. Despite the technological advances in workflow management, business software or communication, the fact that knowledge is an essential production factor and product of software firms limits their ability to outsource some parts of the innovation process. Hence a distinct division of labour of knowledge-creating activities located in OECD countries and knowledge-using activities carried out in non-OECD countries can be noted.

However, ODIP is not static and we doubt that this division of labour is fixed, as we were also able to find cases that underline the upgrading of capabilities in non-OECD countries. There is definitely a qualitative shift in some subsidiaries in non-OECD countries that are able to conduct knowledge-creating activities in innovation processes. Paradoxically this rapid capability upgrading is also caused by the significance of knowledge for the production of software. It implies that subsidiaries of MNCs require a higher degree of autonomy than, for example, those of manufacturing industries to carry out even knowledge-using activities. Their participation in several projects requires and builds up cumulative context-dependent knowledge bases. Subsidiaries are thus able to learn in different customer-dependent contexts and can increase their capabilities for creating knowledge in innovation processes. A qualitative shift in non-OECD countries is visible and may even accelerate, since the upgrading of capabilities opens up new opportunities for subsidiaries to further participate in innovation processes. Additionally, as our findings indicate, software firms in Germany also strategically foster further competence building.

However, there is a qualitative shift not only in non-OECD countries; there is also a qualitative shift in OECD countries that tends to be overseen. Our findings underline the fact that labour division in knowledge production which is required by practising ODIP has distinct qualities due to the process character, the context dependence and the social construction of knowledge. As suppliers and subsidiaries of MNCs in India upgrade their capabilities, mutual learning of German software firms takes place. This establishes organizational capabilities and accumulates procedural knowledge necessary for managing complex modes of organizationally and spatially distributed knowledge production. Without the ability to contextualize, de- and re-contextualize the knowledge created at various locations, software firms are unable to gain advantages from distributed innovation processes. Transferring or replicating such kinds of competences from one economic setting to another in a different geographical context may be rather difficult as they seem to be attributable to local forces. Both the competence building of subsidiaries and suppliers in non-OECD countries as well as the formation of organizational capabilities of software firms in OECD countries that integrate diverse and highly specialized knowledge bases seem to be path-dependent processes. Further research is required on how these processes are shaped by internal and external factors and co-evolve in their multi-scalarity. At the moment only the contours of these territorial knowledge dynamics have so far become apparent.

NOTE

1. The chapter is based on the research project 'The Changing Knowledge Divide in the Global Economy', supported by the Volkswagen Foundation, reference number II/81 311 under the programme: 'Innovation processes in economy and society', which is gratefully acknowledged.

REFERENCES

Altenburg, T., Schmitz, H. and Stamm, A. (2008), 'Breakthrough? China's and India's transition from production to innovation', *World Development*, **36**: 325–44.

Asheim, B.T. and Gertler, M. (2005), 'The geography of innovation: regional innovation systems', in J. Fagerberg, D.C. Mowery and R.R. Nelson (eds), *The Oxford Handbook of Innovation*, Oxford: Oxford University Press, pp. 291–317.

Bettencourt, L.A., Ostrom, A.L., Brown, S., Brown, W. and Roundtree, R.I. (2002), 'Client co-production in knowledge-intensive business services', *California Management Review*, **44**: 100–128.

Boschma, R. (2005), 'Proximity and innovation: a critical assessment', *Regional Studies*, **39**: 61–74.

Bruche, G. (2009), 'A new geography of innovation: China and India rising', *Columbia FDI Perspectives*, No. 4.

Cohendet, P. and Meyer-Krahmer, F. (2001), 'The theoretical and policy implications of knowledge codification', *Research Policy*, **30**: 1563–91.

Cooke, P. (2001), 'Regional innovation systems, clusters and the knowledge economy', *Industrial and Corporate Change*, **10**: 945–74.

Djellal, F., Francoz, D., Gallouj, C., Gallouj, F. and Jacquin, Y. (2003), 'Revising the definition of research and development in the light of the specificities of services', *Science and Public Policy*, **30**: 415–29.

Dosi, G., Faillo, M. and Marengo, L. (2008), 'Organizational capabilities, patterns of knowledge accumulation and governance structures in business firms', *Organizational Studies*, **29**: 1165–85.

Eisenhardt, K.M. and Martin, A.M. (2000), 'Dynamic capabilities: what are they?', *Strategic Management Journal*, **21**: 1105–21.

Friedewald, M., Blind, K. and Edler, J. (2002), 'Die Innovationstätigkeit der deutschen Softwareindustrie', *Wirtschaftsinformatik*, **44**: 151–61.

Frost, T.S., Birkinshaw, J.M. and Ensign, P.C. (2002), 'Centers of excellence in multinational corporations', *Strategic Management Journal*, **23**: 997–1018.

Gallouj, F. (2002), 'Knowledge-intensive business services: processing knowledge and producing innovation', in J. Gadrey and F. Gallouj (eds), *Productivity, Innovation and Knowledge in Services*, Cheltenham, UK and Northampton, MA, USA: Edward Elgar, pp. 256–84.

Gertler, M. (2003), 'Tacit knowledge and the geography of context, or the undefinable tacitness of being (there)', *Journal of Economic Geography*, **3**: 75–99.

Grant, R. (1996), 'Prospering in dynamically competitive environments: organizational capabilities as knowledge integration', *Organizational Science*, **7**: 375–87.

Grimaldi, R. and Torrisi, S. (2001), 'Codified–tacit and general–specific knowledge in the division of labour among firms: a study of the software industry', *Research Policy*, **30**: 1425–42.

Grimshaw, D. and Miozzo, M. (2006), 'Knowledge intensive business services: understanding organizational forms and the role of country institutions', in M. Miozzo and D. Grimshaw (eds), *Knowledge Intensive Business Services: Organizational Forms and National Institutions*, Cheltenham, UK and Northampton, MA, USA: Edward Elgar, pp. 1–25.

Hauknes, J. (2000), 'Dynamic innovation systems: what is the role of services?', in M. Boden and I. Miles (eds), *Services and the Knowledge-based Economy*, London and New York: Routledge, pp. 38–63.

Hipp, C. and Grupp, H. (2005), 'Innovation in the service sector: the demand for service-specific innovation measurement concepts and typologies', *Research Policy*, **34**: 517–35.

Holl, F., Menzel, K., Morcinek, P., Mühlberg, J.T., Schäfer, I. and Schüngel, H. (2006), *Studie zum Innovationsverhalten deutscher Software-Entwicklungsunternehmen*, Berlin: Eigenverlag.

Humphrey, J. (2003), 'Globalisation and supply chain networks: the auto industry in Brazil and India', *Global Networks*, **3**: 121–41.

Jürgens, U. (ed.) (2000), *New Product Development and Production Networks: Global Industrial Experience*, Berlin: Springer.

Jürgens, U. (2001), 'Approaches towards integrating suppliers in simultaneous engineering activities: the case of two German automakers', *Journal of Automotive Technology and Management*, **1**: 61–7.

Lema, R. (2010), 'Adoption of open business models in the West and India's Software Industry', *IDS Research Report*, 62.

Løwendahl, B.R., Revang, Ø. and Fosstenløkken, S.M. (2001), 'Knowledge and value creation in professional service firms: a framework for analysis', *Human Relations*, **54**: 911–31.

Malerba, F. (2002), 'Sectoral systems of innovation and production', *Research Policy*, **31**: 247–64.

Malerba, F. (2005), 'Sectoral systems of innovation: how and why innovation differs across sectors', in J. Fagerberg, D.C. Mowery and R.R. Nelson (eds), *The Oxford Handbook of Innovation*, Oxford: Oxford University Press, pp. 380–406.

Marklund, G. (2000), 'Indicators of innovation activities in services', in M. Boden and I. Miles (eds), *Services and the Knowledge-based Economy*, London and New York: Routledge, pp. 86–108.

Miles, I. and Green, L. (2008), *Hidden Innovation in the Creative Industries*, London: Nesta.

Muller, E. and Doloreux, D. (2007), 'The key dimensions of knowledge-intensive business services (KIBS) analysis: a decade of evolution', Discussion Paper, *Working Papers Firms and Region*, U1, Karlsruhe: Fraunhofer Institute Systems and Innovation Research.

Nooteboom, B., Haverbeke, W.V., Gilsing, V. and van den Oord, A. (2007), 'Optimal cognitive distance and absorptive capacity', *Research Policy*, **36**: 1016–34.

OECD (2008), *Open Innovations in Global Networks*, Paris: OECD.

Pavitt, K. (1984), 'Sectoral patterns of technical change: towards a taxonomy and a theory', *Research Policy*, **13**: 343–73.

Quadros, R. (2009), 'Brazilian innovation in the global automotive value chain: Implications of the organisational decomposition of the innovation process', Universidade Estadual de Campinas.

Royce, W. (1970), 'Managing the development of large software systems', *Proceedings of IEEE WESCON*, **26** (August): 1–9.

Schmitz, H. and Strambach, S. (2009), 'The organisational decomposition of innovation and global distribution of innovation activities: insights and research agenda', *International Journal of Technological Learning, Innovation and Development*, **2**: 231–49.

Segelod, E. and Jordan, G. (2004), 'The use and importance of external sources of knowledge in the software development process', *R&D Management*, **34**: 239–52.

Strambach, S. (2008), 'Knowledge-intensive business services (KIBS) as drivers of multilevel knowledge dynamics', *International Journal of Services Technology and Management*, **10**: 152–74.

Strambach, S. (2010), 'Path dependency and path plasticity: the co-evolution of institutions and innovation – the German customised business software industry', in R. Boschma and R. Martin (eds), *Handbook of Evolutionary Economic Geography*, Cheltenham, UK and Northampton, MA, USA: Edward Elgar, pp. 836–63.

Sundbo, J. (2000), 'Organization and innovation strategy in services', in M. Boden and I. Miles (eds), *Services and the Knowledge-Based Economy*, London: Continuum.

Teece, D.J. (ed.) (2008), *Technological Know-how, Organizational Capabilities, and Strategic Management*, Hackensack, NJ and London: World Scientific Publishing.

Teece, D.J., Pisano, G.P. and Shuen, A. (1997), 'Dynamic capabilities and strategic management', *Strategic Management Journal*, **18**: 509–33.

Tödtling, F., Lehner, P. and Trippl, M. (2006), 'Innovation in knowledge intensive industries: the nature and geography of knowledge links', *European Planning Studies*, **14**: 1035–58.

Torre, A. and Rallet, A. (2005), 'Proximity and localization', *Regional Studies*, **39**: 47–59.

Torre, A. (2008), 'On the role played by temporary geographical proximity in knowledge transmission', *Regional Studies*, **42**: 869–89.

UNCTAD (2005), *World Investment Report 2005: Transnational Corporations and the Internationalization of R&D*, Geneva: United Nations.

Zander, I. (2002), 'The formation of international innovation networks in the multinational corporation: an evolutionary perspective', *Industrial and Corporate Change*, **11**: 327–53.

Zanfei, A. (2000), 'Transnational firms and the changing organisation of innovative activities', *Cambridge Journal of Economics*, **24**: 515–42.

9. The impact of regional institutional characteristics on the location of MNCs – a European perspective*

Knut Koschatzky and Elisabeth Baier

9.1 INTRODUCTION

Multinational companies (MNCs) are often regarded as footloose in the sense that they act independently from their regional environment. With their knowledge-accumulating and knowledge-processing capacities, MNCs can use product, production, distribution and development competences that they have accumulated in their homeland and in all other sociocultural and institutional contexts where branch plants are located. In this respect MNCs combine the advantages of globally coordinated product and production strategies with the advantages of local proximity and specific locational factors (Cantwell and Mudambi, 2000). Nevertheless, through different tangible and intangible interactions with other firms, research institutes and the economic system in general, they are linked to their specific regional environments at least to a certain extent. MNCs can profit from locating in regions that offer advantages of 'local buzz' and regional interconnectedness (Bathelt et al., 2004). The assumption is put forward in this chapter that MNCs are not *per se* footloose (cf. Görg and Strobl, 2003), but are to a certain extent linked to regional environments in the sense of 'being there' (cf. Gertler, 1995; Bunnell and Coe, 2001; Cantwell and Piscitello, 2002). Especially research-oriented MNCs choose locations that provide them with favourable assets for their innovative activities.

With regard to research, development and innovation, the heuristic concepts of national or regional systems of innovation can be used as an analytical framework to identify institutional characteristics that explain the locational pattern of MNCs. According to these concepts, important influential factors are the industrial environment, the public research and higher education environment, the political environment and the market environment. Based on these elements, we compiled a set of indicators for 215 European regions. Using cluster analysis, we shall test empirically whether MNCs are footloose in the sense that their locations can be found everywhere irrespective of the quality of their regional environments or whether these firms show a propensity to locate in regions that reveal certain innovative characteristics.

In section 9.2 we shall discuss arguments provided by the innovation system approach that allow conclusions about the context specificy of innovation and the factors that could positively influence regional linkages of MNCs. In section 9.3 the methodological approach is presented, and results from the cluster analysis will be discussed. Conclusions from the empirical analysis are drawn in section 9.4.

9.2   REGIONAL INSTITUTIONAL SETTINGS AND THE LOCATION OF MNCS

9.2.1   Innovation Systems

The systems of innovation concept is a heuristic approach (or, according to Edquist, 1997: 28–9, a 'conceptual framework') by which 'all important economic, social, political, organizational, institutional, and other factors that influence the development, diffusion, and use of innovation' can be identified and analysed (Edquist, 2005: 182). The first approach towards the understanding of nations as national systems of innovation was made by Freeman (1987, 1988), who analysed technology policy and economic performance in Japan. In the following years Lundvall (1992) made important contributions to the theoretical advancement of the concept while Nelson (1993) enriched it with case studies examples. At the beginning of the 1990s Cooke (1992) developed the concept of regional systems of innovation. Regional systems respond to different rationales, institutional and governance settings that can be found at the sub-national territorial level. 'Region' in this context is understood as 'authentic community of interest', that is, as an economic and political action framework characterized by common normative interests, economic specificity and administrative homogeneity (Ohmae, 1995). It is a distinct feature of the concept that a region does not offer all factors and institutions necessary for innovation but has to cooperate with other regional or national systems in order to merge all necessary resources in the specific territory (Cooke et al., 2004; Asheim and Gertler, 2005). During the mid-1990s Carlsson (1995) also focused on technological systems while Breschi and Malerba (1997) dealt with innovation among a group of firms within a specific sector.

The major focus of the innovation system approach is thus on the institutional set-up that influences the innovative activity of a territory or sector. From an institutional viewpoint, major components are the industrial system, the education and research system, the political system, the system of intermediaries, the infrastructure system, the demand system and other framework conditions and regulations.

9.2.2   MNCs and Regional Links

An important assumption of the innovation system approach is that most innovation processes are context-specific. Depending on their size, sector and the national or regional environments, firms depend differently on external factors and incorporate them into their innovation activities to a varying extent (Porter, 1990; Gertler, 1995; Koschatzky and Zenker, 1999). The spatial context specificy of innovation is a central argument in modern economic geography (Krugman, 1998). Linking this emphasis on geographical aspects with the firm-centred argumentation in the international business economics literature, the question can be raised whether MNCs focus on the exploitation of their global networks in which a single location does not matter or whether the regional factor endowment of the different branch plants is also important for them (Coe et al., 2004). It will be argued here that spatial influences exist by which MNCs exploit and utilize different location-specific and market-related factors (Cantwell and Piscitello, 2002: 70).

This aspect relates to the question of why companies in their geographical diversification strategies opt for inner-organizational forms of control and coordination and not for market-based forms of coordination such as exports or franchising (Dunning, 1988). In a dynamic perspective the major advantages of MNCs are the greater flexibility (Buckley and Casson, 1998) and the cross-border utilization of technological and organizational competences (cf. Howells, 1990; Zander, 1998; Kogut and Zander, 1993: 631; Shimizutani and Todo, 2008; Ito and Wakasugi, 2007). Through internationalization and the exploitation of globally available assets, companies attempt to use their specific competences in several markets and are thus 'footloose' in nature (cf. Chandler, 1992; Zander and Sölvell, 2000; Görg and Strobl, 2003). MNCs can be characterized by a reciprocal exchange between different national subsidiaries. Local, regional and global networks coexist as a result of the interplay of spatial foci in the overall strategy, network capabilities and innovation intensity (Bunnell and Coe, 2001; Geenhuizen, 2007). The relationship between the firm and the region will therefore differ from case to case and thus also the degree of 'footlooseness'. Some companies may indeed make use of globally dispersed knowledge sources, while others are more strongly bound to certain regions (von Zedtwitz and Gassmann, 2002). These strategies depend on the necessity of the firms to gain access to specific localized knowledge skills and technology, on their ability to become a player in the regional innovation system or a cluster and to gain direct access to specific markets (Andersen and Christensen, 2005; Enright, 2000).

In this respect MNCs depend on the quality of the regional environments in which their subsidiaries are located. In parallel, these subsidiaries also use this institutional and inter-organizational context in order to increase their own innovativeness and to improve their position within the MNC (Kristensen and Zeitlin, 2004). This involves, above all, a regional environment that offers strategic advantages for companies, for example through the provision of specific knowledge and competences by regional suppliers and customers (Reger, 1997; Cantwell and Piscitello, 2002; Edler et al., 2003). Nevertheless, these subsidiaries not only rely on their own regional environment but also manage access to other regional environments within or outside the respective national innovation system (Meyer-Krahmer, 2003). However, regional innovation potentials also play a crucial role in the company-wide distribution of responsibilities and resources because the corporate headquarters have to evaluate the comparative advantages of their operating units.

9.2.3   Conceptual Framework and Research Outlook

Regional capabilities are essentially based on the utilization and advancement of context-specific, tacit knowledge in regional, institutionally stabilized communication and cooperation networks. An efficient regional infrastructure and innovative suppliers, buyers, customers and competitors can be a considerable advantage in company-wide exchange processes and in struggles for the company-wide distribution of resources and responsibilities. This might imply that the innovativeness of MNCs also depends on the innovation-supporting conditions at the locations of their subsidiaries, while the capabilities of regional innovation systems depend vice versa on the successful integration of MNCs.

Based on the institutional notion of innovation systems, Figure 9.1 provides a simplified conceptual framework of a company's linkages with its territorial environment and emphasizes the major elements of institutional characteristics at the regional scale. We use the term 'environment' for these institutional set-ups because we cannot automatically assume that they fulfil all characteristics of a system. These environments are expected to influence the decision of a MNC to locate in a certain town or region.

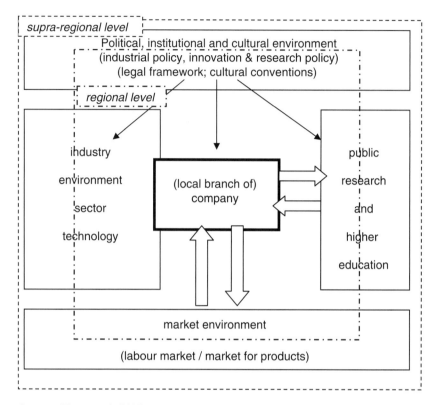

Source: Hemer et al. (2007).

*Figure 9.1   Conceptual framework of a firm's linkages with its regional
            and supra-regional environment*

Taking the possible impacts of the regional factor endowment on innovative activities of MNCs as a starting point, our empirical analysis is
based on two confronting theses that reflect the different positions in the
literature regarding the footlooseness of MNCs:

1.   Due to the need to gain access to strategic relevant knowledge
     resources and to exploit the advantages of innovative locations, the
     number of MNCs is significantly higher in regions that are character-
     ized by a well above average endowment with innovation relevant
     parameters (economic geography rationale).
2.   Due to their global sourcing of knowledge and their independence
     from supportive regional or national environments, MNCs are foot-
     loose in the sense that their locations do not significantly correspond

with the regional endowment of innovation relevant parameters (international business economics rationale).

Regarding the two theses, it can of course be argued that MNCs locate where other MNCs already have their location (signalling favourable location conditions) and a regional concentration of MNCs can therefore be expected. However, on the contrary, not all MNCs must follow the same locational trajectory because they want to minimize disclosure risks and spillover effects, for example through a common labour market, by not being too closely located in the neighbourhood of a competitor (Narula and Santangelo, 2009: 401). MNCs might also differ in their strategic goals and thus in their locational preferences. However, if it can be shown statistically for a broad set of regions that MNCs tend to favour certain types of regions (e.g. agglomerations or metropolitan areas), the conclusion can be drawn that their factor endowment is strongly attractive for MNCs in order to exploit the available skills and competences by closer regional linkages and integration into regional network relationships. This research focus is in accordance with Cantwell and Piscitello (2002: 71), who argue that 'there is still only quite a scant existing empirical research on multinational location at this subnational level'.

9.3   REGIONAL LINKS AND THE PRESENCE AND ABSENCE OF MNCS IN EUROPEAN REGIONS

9.3.1   Methodological Approach

In order to gain an insight into the location pattern of MNCs at the European level and the characteristics of the regions in which these MNCs are located, we pursue a two-step approach. The first step aims to characterize European regions according to the institutional characteristics as depicted in Figure 9.1, while the second step matches the findings of this characterization with the location of MNC headquarters. As a result, regional specificities and MNC locations are commonly considered in order to draw conclusions concerning locational characteristics of regions and their 'attractiveness' for MNCs according to the previously formulated two confronting theses.

For the first step, variables and indicators must be identified that reflect the different environments as displayed in Figure 9.1. It should be pointed out that for a European cross-regional analysis the data availability is limited at the NUTS 2 level.[1] We have to deal mainly with basic indicators because the Eurostat regional statistical database offers full coverage of the NUTS 2 regions only for certain indicators (for similar problems see Aumayr, 2007: 110).[2] Since we apply a cluster analysis for 215 European regions, we need a dataset that is as complete as possible, since data gaps lead to a removal of the respective region from the performed analyses. Our approach therefore cannot go as deep as to identify causes and effects of the location decisions of MNCs. The variables and indicators we used cover the industrial environment, the public research and higher education environment and the market environment. These are shown in Table 9.1. However, Figure 9.1 additionally refers to the political, institutional and cultural environment – aspects that are of high importance in analysing innovation activities and specific (regional) innovation patterns. Unfortunately, a comprehensive database that covers these characteristics with the help of quantitative variables for all European regions does not yet exist. We are therefore unable to integrate these aspects into the following empirical analysis. The rationales behind the selection can be found in the last column of Table 9.1 where we explain the indicators presented by the selected variables. It could be argued that this set of variables implies a strong focus on regional aspects. However, should the analyses show no relationship between regional characteristics and the location of MNCs, then this would be an additional strong support for thesis 2.

For the second step of the analysis we added a variable that represents the existence of MNCs in a region. This central variable is not available in the Eurostat regional database. According to our knowledge, only a few databases or statistics offer research locations of MNCs at the subnational level. We derived the regional location of the headquarters of 700 companies with the highest R&D spending in Europe from an analysis of the 2005 EU Industrial R&D Investment Scoreboard (European Commission, 2005). The headquarters of these research-oriented companies were enumerated and assigned to the respective region by their absolute number. This proxy variable is not an indication for an MNC headquarter *per se* but for the subset of research-oriented MNCs. It could be argued that research-oriented MNCs exhibit a stronger propensity to locate where specific favourable conditions stimulating R&D are available and are thus less footloose in their location pattern. However, we cannot conclude from the Scoreboard data that R&D is carried out at that location. We can only conclude that the location is attractive for a research-oriented MNC and certainly relevant for its R&D activities. We are well aware of the bias in our data, as we are aware of the fact that in the dataset both private and state-owned MNCs are included. The latter could be the subject of non-market-driven location decisions, although also for state-owned MNCs it could be expected that they need to exploit intangible assets provided by only a certain number of regions.

Table 9.1 Indicators and variables for a firm's linkages with different regional environments

Environments	Variable	Indicator for
Industry environment	Location quotient for the manufacturing sector[a]	Regional concentration in manufacturing with respect to the national level
	Employment in knowledge-intensive business services (% of total employment)	Importance of the knowledge-intensive business services sector (**KIBS**) in the regional economy
	Employment in high and medium high-tech manufacturing (% of total employment)	Importance of the medium- and high-tech manufacturing sector in the regional economy
	Number of patent applications at the European Patent Office (EPO) (per million labour force)	Innovativeness of regional economy
Public research and higher education environment	R&D personnel in the government sector (% of total employment)	Potential in public research and higher education
	R&D personnel in the higher education sector (% of total employment)	
	Government expenditures on R&D **GOVERD** (% of GDP)	
	Higher education expenditures on R&D **HERD** (% of GDP)	
Market environment (labour market/ market for products)	Employment rate (%)	Labour market
	People participating in lifelong learning (% of total population)	Labour market/human capital
	Regional GDP in absolute terms (in million euro)	Demand side
	Gross domestic product (GDP) per capita	Market characteristic: Purchasing power
	Average annual growth rate of GDP 1996–2005	Development of regional wealth
	Types of settlement structure[b]	centrality and agglomeration
MNCs	Absolute total number of large firms' headquarters	Presence and decision units of MNCs

Notes:

a. The location quotient has been calculated as regional employment in the manufacturing sectors compared to the respective national value. Location quotients higher than 1 indicate an over-proportional share of regional employment in manufacturing compared to the national level of this region. A location quotient smaller than one indicates an under-proportional share respectively.

b. Categorical variable from 1 = densely populated with large centres to 6 = less densely populated without centres.

Despite these deficiencies, we used this dataset because no other data are available. As a consequence, we have to limit our conclusions to broad trends.

In order to identify regional types across Europe according to regional similarities, we chose the method of cluster analysis (Backhaus et al., 2006: 511ff.). For this purpose we calculated a *k*-means cluster analysis with four clusters with altogether 215 European regions. Second, we performed a discriminant analysis in order to investigate which variables contribute significantly to the discrimination between the clusters. We excluded the MNC variable from these analyses and reintegrated it in the second step, that is, a matching of regional types with the presence of MNC head-quarters in the form of a graphical analysis. With the latter approach the results of the cluster analysis are presented in a map with two attributes: the clusters and the absolute number of MNCs. Finally, we used a Kruskal–Wallis test in order to validate differences in the absolute number of MNCs between the clusters. All statistical calculations were performed with SPSS 11.0.

9.3.2   Clustering European Regions

Table 9.2 shows the results of the *k*-means cluster analysis. It took alto-gether five iterations of the cluster centres to come to the final results. The cluster centroids allow us to characterize the four selected clusters and to derive specificities in these types that distinguish them from the other regional types. The first cluster in which only seven regions are sum-marized has a strong orientation towards knowledge production and its application ('Hubs of knowledge generation and innovation'), whereas the second cluster, which subsumes 94 regions, instead represents regions that are lagging behind in terms of economic development and regional inno-vative capacity ('Lagging regions'). The third cluster includes 30 regions that are oriented towards the production of knowledge services paired with public science activities ('Public science and service-driven innova-tion centres'). Finally, the fourth cluster summarizes 84 regions with an industrial orientation including strengths in high-tech manufacturing ('Industry-driven innovation centres'). Additionally, it seems important to mention that we can find 87 regions in which one or more MNC headquar-ters are present and 128 regions without MNCs. Although regions are not equally distributed between the four clusters, the distribution seems to be plausible given the fact that altogether 128 regions do not host an MNC headquarter at all and that one would expect that leading regions are not as common as others.

Table 9.2   Results of the cluster analysis – as cluster centroids and means

Variables (2005)	Cluster				Means
	1 (N=7)	2 (N=94)	3 (N=30)	4 (N=84)	
Location quotient for the industrial sectors	0.83	0.95	0.81	1.12	1.00
Employment in total knowledge-intensive business services (% of total employment)	5.96	2.07	4.59	3.00	2.99
Employment in high-tech and medium-high-tech manufacturing (% of total employment)	5.39	4.91	6.06	8.10	6.39
Number of patent applications at the EPO (million labour force)	212.65	16.08	140.50	172.99	102.76
R&D personnel in the government sector (% of total employment)	0.28	0.12	0.54	0.09	0.17
R&D personnel in the higher education sector (% of total employment)	1.06	0.53	1.11	0.58	0.65
Government expenditures on R&D as % of GDP	0.30	0.10	0.58	0.12	0.19
Higher education expenditures on R&D as % of GDP	0.57	0.23	0.60	0.39	0.35
Employment rate in %	61.84	48.01	53.58	54.97	51.96
People participating in lifelong learning as % of total population	0.21	0.06	0.11	0.11	0.09
GDP in absolute terms (in mio. Euro)	239 069.07	20 889.66	63 559.60	64 121.24	50 837.60
GDP per capita (in euro)	38 942.86	14 208.51	28 160.00	26 982.14	21 951.16
Average annual growth rate of GDP, 1996–2005 (%)	6.07	6.32	4.56	3.77	5.07
Regional settlement type	2.29	4.60	2.60	3.34	3.76

Source: Own calculations.

9.3.2.1 Hubs of knowledge generation and innovation

Cluster 1 is composed of regions that reveal a very good regional endowment in combination with innovation relevant parameters. With our approach we were able to identify altogether seven regions in Europe for which this holds true. This group includes the following regions: Stockholm, Denmark, the region of Southern Finland, Île de France, London and the East and South-East of the UK.

The industrial environment is characterized by a strong presence of knowledge-intensive business services (KIBS). On average, altogether 5.96 per cent of the workforce is employed in knowledge-intensive business services in these regions (European average: 2.99 per cent). When compared to the cluster centres of the other clusters, this is an exceptionally high percentage. On the other hand, the average location quotient for industry of 0.83 indicates that the manufacturing industry is underrepresented. The average percentage of employment in high- and medium-high-tech manufacturing is below average with 5.39 per cent. Additionally, with 212.65 patent applications filed at the European Patent Office (EPO) per million labour force, the regions in this cluster are extremely productive with regard to innovation output.

The cluster is characterized by a very strong market environment, which comprises indicators of economic wealth as well as labour market indicators and centrality. The regions are on average densely populated and have or are large centres and metropolitan areas. GDP per capita reaches €38 942 and GDP in absolute terms is very high, indicating a high demand. The average annual growth rate of the GDP (in million euros) between 1996 and 2005 is, at 6.07 per cent, well above the European average of 5.07 per cent. Concerning the labour market, our cluster analysis reveals that the employment rate of 61.84 per cent is the highest among the four clusters (European average: 51.96 per cent), as is the percentage of people participating in lifelong learning, a fact that stands for the qualification of the workforce.

The public research and higher education environment is also comparatively strong. Expenditures on public research and higher education are higher than in other clusters. HERD (expenditures in percentage of GDP in the higher education sector) reaches 0.57 per cent and GOVERD (expenditures in percentage of GDP in the government sector) reaches 0.30 per cent respectively. A figure of 1.06 per cent of total employment is accounted for by R&D personnel in the higher education sector, 0.28 per cent by R&D personnel in the government sector. It can be concluded that these regions reveal a high density of higher education institutions (universities) that are also very active in performing R&D. This makes them equally attractive for students but also for companies seeking a highly qualified workforce. It could be expected that the regions that belong to cluster 1 are able to attract many headquarters of research-oriented MNCs due to their favourable regional environment, such as a high presence of KIBS, a high patent activity, economic wealth and a high HERD and GOVERD, which indicates complementary regional assets regarding innovation potential. MNCs have many possibilities to mingle with the amply present regional actors.

9.3.2.2 Lagging regions
Cluster 2 summarizes the characteristics of the regions that are lagging behind regarding the overall regional endowment with factors favouring innovation but also regarding economic aspects. It comprises altogether 94 regions. Among them are many regions from Poland, Hungary, Slovakia, Slovenia, the Czech Republic, Eastern Germany as well as from the Baltic countries. In addition, many regions from south and south-west Europe are found here.

The industrial environment is very weak. The data reveal neither a concentration of industrial sectors (location quotient is smaller than 1) nor a specialization in high-value industries, such as employment in high-tech manufacturing or KIBS. Likewise the market environment is weak. These regions have a very low employment rate of below 50 per cent and only a very small percentage of the population (6 per cent) participates in lifelong learning. GDP per capita is very low with an average of €14 208 (average value €21 951). Since GDP per capita is that low, these regions not surprisingly reveal high annual GDP growth rates of 6.32 per cent, indicating that they are in a catching-up process. Additionally, these regions reveal a settlement structure that can be characterized as less densely populated and even without centres. This makes it very difficult for MNCs to find the respective networks to maintain a leading position.

The public research and higher education environment indicators are characterized by very low percentage shares, none of which reach the European average. A figure of 0.53 per cent of total employment is accounted for by R&D personnel in the higher education sector. Although this value is lower than in the other clusters, education efforts and investment in human capital are important for future attractiveness. A share of 0.12 per cent in R&D personnel can be found in the government sector. Given these characteristics, we conclude that these regions seem to be of lesser interest for research-oriented MNCs to develop territorial links. As a result we would expect the presence of MNCs to be very low.

9.3.2.3 Public- and service-driven innovation centres

The regions in cluster 3 derive their potential from the public science and the service sector. Altogether 30 regions belong to this cluster, including Dresden, Prague, the Midi-Pyrénées, Berlin, Brussels and Rome.

The economic environment can be described by a strong orientation towards knowledge-intensive services. These account for 4.59 per cent of the total employment against a European average of 2.99 per cent. The industrial sector is clearly underrepresented in these regions (location quotient of 0.81 and below average employment in high- and medium high-tech manufacturing).

The market environment of this cluster is slightly above average, especially with regard to the labour market. The employment rate lies at 53.6 per cent and 11 per cent of the total population participate in lifelong learning. GPD per capita builds up to €28 160 per year. The regional growth rate of GDP is, however, slightly below average. In combination, this indicates a slightly less dynamic growth pattern compared to the European average. The regional settlement takes a value of 2.6, indicating that the regions in this type are densely populated and large centres are present.

The public research and higher education environment is characterized by above-average figures, reflecting the public science orientation. HERD reaches a relatively high share of 0.60 per cent and GOVERD 0.58 per cent, the highest value among the four clusters. A figure of 1.11 per cent of total employment is accounted for by R&D personnel in the higher education sector and 0.58 per cent by R&D personnel in the government sector, which is again the highest average value among all clusters. It can be concluded that the regions reveal a high density of higher education institutions and other public research institutes. Government engagement in R&D is very high, which might attract certain types of research-oriented MNCs that depend on a strong public science base and the provision of business services.

9.3.2.4 Industry-driven innovation centres

Cluster 4 summarizes the characteristics of the regions that reveal regional innovation potentials based on a strong industrial base and high-tech manufacturing. Altogether 84 regions belong to this group. Among these regions are Pais Vasco, Swabia, Piedmont, Alsace, Wales and Slovenia, to mention just a few examples.

The economic environment can be described by a strong industrial base, which is indicated by a location quotient of 1.12 and a very high percentage of employment in high- and medium-high-tech manufacturing of 8.10 per cent (average: 6.39 per cent). This corresponds to a relatively high number of patent applications. Altogether 172.99 patent applications are filed per million labour force at the EPO, a number that is well above the European average of 102.76. The presence of KIBS equals the average.

The market environment of this cluster is slightly above average, especially with regard to the labour market. The employment rate lies at 55 per cent and 11 per cent of the total population participate in lifelong learning. GPD per capita builds up to €26 982 per year. The regions reveal a below-average annual growth rate of 3.77 per cent (European average 5.07 per cent). In combination, this indicates a slightly less dynamic growth pattern compared to the European average. The regional settlement type based on population density and centrality is characterized as densely populated and features the presence of large centres with a value of 3.34, which is close to the European average of 3.76.

The public research and higher education environment is characterized by slightly below-average figures. HERD reaches a relatively high 0.39 per cent and GOVERD 0.12 per cent. A figure of 0.58 per cent of the total employment is accounted for by R&D personnel in the higher education sector, which is close to the European average of 0.65 per cent. A total of 0.09 per cent is accounted for by R&D personnel in the government sector, which is the lowest average value in all clusters. From this it can be concluded that the regions reveal a high density of higher education institutions (universities), which are also very active in performing R&D, but government engagement in R&D is very low and is also mirrored by the small R&D employment rate in the government sector.

We conclude from these results that these regions could be attractive for certain research-oriented MNCs, especially those that would like to engage in a strong industrial base or in high-tech manufacturing or see co-location as part of their strategy that requires the respective industrial networks.

9.3.2.5 Discriminant analysis

To avoid misinterpretation, with the help of discriminant analysis we investigated which variables contribute significantly to the discrimination between the clusters. Even with our limited data and indicator approach, we were only able to include 164 European regions (or 76.3 per cent) in our discriminant analysis due to missing data. To obtain information on the relative importance or contribution of each variable towards the discrimination between the clusters, we calculated Wilks's lambda. The Wilks's lambda significance test is used to test the hypothesis that the means of the functions listed are equal across groups, Wilks's lambda being the proportion of the total variance in the discriminant scores not explained by differences among the groups:

$$\Lambda = \frac{1}{1 + \gamma} = \frac{\text{unexplained variance}}{\text{total variance}}$$

A significance value less than 0.05 indicates that the group means differ and therefore the function is a significant discriminator. Additionally, Wilks's lambda is an inverse measure of quality; small values indicate a stronger separating power of the discriminant function.

As we can see from the results in Table 9.3, all variables contribute significantly to the separation between the clusters at the 5 per cent level. Employment in knowledge-intensive services and R&D personnel in the government sector separate best with a Wilks's lambda of 0.39, followed by government expenditures in R&D, with a Wilks's lambda of 0.45, and GDP per capita, which reveals a Wilks's lambda of 0.52. Interestingly, two determinants of knowledge generation and its application dominate the cluster analyses plus the variable on regional wealth. This means that particularly the regional wealth characteristics – in terms of GDP per capita 2005 – but also indicators on knowledge generation are of outstanding importance in building and influencing the types of European regions. Matching this result with the clustering results in Table 9.2, it becomes clear that indeed type 3 regions are strong in these dimensions. On the other hand, GDP growth in type 2 regions exceeds that of the other types, being more than 1.5 times as high as that of the fourth cluster. This inverse relationship points to the fact that leverage effects in regions with a high GDP must be much higher to achieve similar growth rates than regions that are on a lower level.

At the other end of the spectrum, the variables representing the regional settlement structure[3] and employment in high-tech manufacturing prove to be of less importance in determining the clusters of European regions. These findings allow the conclusion that knowledge generation and its application in business settings is a very strong discriminator among European regions, able to reflect their present situation and future development alike.

9.3.3 Matching of the Regional Clusters with the Location of MNCs in Europe

Figure 9.2 shows the result of the second step of our analysis, the matching of the cluster typology with the location of research-oriented MNC headquarters across Europe. The map was produced with ArcGIS 9, choosing

Table 9.3   Wilks's lambda and related significance

Variables (standardized, z-values)	Wilks's lambda	F	df1	df2	Significance
Location quotient for the industrial sectors	0.67	26.67	3	164	0.000
Employment in total knowledge-intensive business services (% of total employment)	0.39	86.46	3	164	0.000
Employment in high-tech and medium-high-tech manufacturing (% of total employment)	0.84	10.28	3	164	0.000
Number of patent applications at the EPO (million labour force)	0.63	31.71	3	164	0.000
R&D personnel in the government sector (% of total employment)	0.39	86.89	3	164	0.000
R&D personnel in the higher education sector (% of total employment)	0.75	18.62	3	164	0.000
Government expenditures on R&D as % of GDP	0.45	66.24	3	164	0.000
Higher education expenditures on R&D as % of GDP	0.76	17.52	3	164	0.000
Employment rate in %	0.73	20.2	3	164	0.000
People participating in lifelong learning as % of total population	0.68	25.94	3	164	0.000
GDP in absolute terms (in mio. euro)	0.69	24.15	3	164	0.000
GDP per capita (in euro)	0.52	51.07	3	164	0.000
Average annual growth rate of GDP, 1996–2005 (%)	0.76	17.27	3	164	0.000
Regional settlement type	0.83	11.6	3	164	0.000

Source: Own calculations, based on the standardized values of the variables.

a central European-centred projection. It presents the regions of the four types and additionally the number of MNCs as circles that differ in size according to the number of MNC locations.

Figure 9.2 reveals a distinct pattern of regional profiles within Europe. In the south and east of the EU, regions of the lagging type (type 2) which include the Baltic States, Poland, the Czech Republic, Hungary, Slovenia, Slovakia, Cyprus, the main part of Greece (except Sterea Ellada), Malta, the south of Italy, Portugal (except Lisbona) and southern Spain can be found. Central and northern Europe are characterized by industrial-driven inno- vation centres (type 4 regions) which comprise the main parts of Finland, Sweden, the UK, Germany, Belgium, the Netherlands, France, northern Spain, northern Italy and Austria. The two Irish regions are made up of types 2 and 3. Type 1 regions are mainly capital or metropolitan regions, as well as Denmark, and they are home to many MNCs. Looking closer at the distribution of MNC headquarters, Figure 9.2 also makes it clear that regions with the highest number of MNCs can be found in central and north- ern Europe. Regions with more than 16 MNCs show a V-shaped distribu- tion within Europe, with the main locations in Finland, Sweden, Denmark, Germany, Austria, the Benelux States, via Paris to the UK and Ireland.

If we take a closer look at both types of analysis, it becomes evident that the majority of research-oriented MNCs are located in regions of types 1 and 3, that is, in the hubs of knowledge generation and innovation, and public- and service-driven innovation centres, whereby hubs of knowledge generation and innovation clearly host the highest average number of MNCs (43.43), followed by public- and service-driven innovation centres with a mean value of 3.8 MNCs. Concerning the lagging regions, only a few of them (Andalucía, Athens, Irish Border and Midlands (http://www. iro.ie/bmw_assembly.html) as well as Wallonia) are a location of MNCs.

As Table 9.4 shows, the four identified clusters display strong differ- ences with respect to the number of research-oriented MNC headquarters located within their territory. Cluster type 1 is the clear 'favourite' region type for MNCs to locate their headquarters: in all regions MNCs have headquarter locations, the number varies between 29 and 65. This leads to the observation that both median and mean values are highest among the regional cluster types; however, the strong difference between these values points to individual regions with high numbers of MNC headquarters.

Type 3 and type 4 regions reveal a similar pattern. Half of these regions (58) do not host any MNC from the sample. This leads to median and mean values between 3.01 and 3.8, strongly below those of the first cluster regions. However, a considerable number of European R&D-oriented large companies seem to appreciate industrial regions as a location for their headquarters. Finally, lagging regions have only eight MNCs

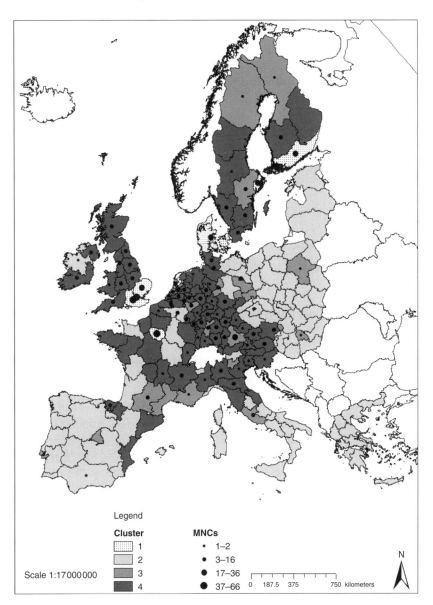

Source: Own illustration based on own calculations.

Figure 9.2   Regional clusters and location of MNC headquarters in Europe

Table 9.4   MNC characteristics of the three cluster types

Cluster	MNC characteristics				
	Minimum	Maximum	Mean value	Median	Sum
1 (hubs of knowledge generation and innovation)	29	65	43.43	36	304
2 (lagging regions)	0	4	0.09	0.04	8
3 (public and service driven innovation centres)	0	21	3.80	2.38	114
4 (industry driven innovation centres)	0	16	3.01	1.68	253

Source: Own calculations.

altogether. As already indicated, the large majority of those regions do not host any MNC headquarters. This produces a median of 0 and a comparatively low mean value of 0.09 MNCs (cf. Table 9.4). Lagging regions must thus be considered as comparatively unattractive locations for research-oriented MNCs.

Differences in the absolute number of MNCs between the four regional types are highly significant, as the mean ranks already indicate. Cluster 1 has by far the highest mean rank, though integrating the smallest number of regions, as opposed to cluster 2 with by far the smallest mean rank but the largest number of regions, as verified by a Kruskal–Wallis test (cf. Table 9.5).[4] As Table 9.5 shows, the test calculates a chi-square of 100.417. The *p*-value (asymptotic significance) is equal to 0.000. There is consequently strong evidence to reject the null hypothesis that the MNC distribution is equal among the four clusters identified. This leads to the following two main conclusions: (i) the four clusters indeed differ in a significant manner concerning the number of MNCs located in their regions, a result that does not seem to be surprising after analysing Table 9.4, but (ii) when keeping in mind that the four cluster types have been built according to regional characteristics with respect to the industrial, market and public research and education environment (as shown in Figure 9.1), it is interesting to see that the MNCs are not equally distributed across the clusters. The four clusters that show distinct regional characteristics also differ with respect to the number of MNCs. The attractiveness of regions as locations for research-oriented MNCs proves to be congruent with a

Table 9.5   Comparison of MNC distribution in clusters: Kruskal–Wallis test

Ranks

Absolute number of MNCs in cluster	N	Mean rank
1 (Knowledge and science hubs)	7	212.00
2 (Lagging regions)	94	68.16
3 (Public- and service-driven innovation centres)	30	140.40
4 (Technology regions)	84	132.35
Total	215	

Kruskal–Wallis test:

Statistics	Absolute number of MNCs
Chi-square	100.417
Asymptotic significance	0.000

Source: Own calculations.

certain extent to regional market, industrial and public research patterns. MNCs seem to be most strongly embedded in regions with a particularly knowledge-related orientation of their industries along with knowledge and qualification orientation of their inhabitants. Those regions consequently offer a larger potential of regional linkages for MNCs.

These results may not be surprising because one would expect that MNCs with an R&D focus might favour locations that offer them sufficient access to an R&D-supporting infrastructure. Nevertheless, we observe a certain distinction among the different types of regions, which, bearing the limitations of our dataset in mind, provide an indication for the fact that MNCs and their subsidiaries fulfil different functions. Some of these functions are related to production and post-production activities (downstream) with a minor focus on development activities, while other focus on pre-production activities (upstream) such as research and head-quarter functions (Defever, 2006: 660). For upstream-oriented MNCs, a high-tech and knowledge orientation of their locations is an important prerequisite.

9.4   SUMMARY AND CONCLUSIONS

Our empirical results can be summarized as follows:

- Regions with an above-average endowment of factors related to knowledge, research and qualification host above-average shares of MNC headquarters in Europe. Research-oriented MNCs are not indifferent towards their regional environments but prefer regions with a high innovation potential, particularly regarding market- and knowledge-related attributes. The regions are characterized by high employment in high- and medium-high-tech sectors as well as a high importance of knowledge-intensive business services. These services are attributed a pertinent role in the generation, diffusion and broker-age of knowledge, all aspects that lead to a strong patent performance as well. The market environment of these regions is also very strong, measured in terms of employment rate, skills and qualifications of the workforce. Finally, public research is also an asset of these regions.

- Additionally, research-oriented MNCs favour regions with a higher population density and with large centres. This corresponds with earlier findings: Sassen (1994) and later Scott (2001) state that so-called global cities are central locations for highly developed serv-ices and telecommunication nodes that are both necessary for the organization and management of global economic activities and in which disproportionally many headquarters of MNCs are present. The observable trend towards the spatial dispersal of economic and innovation activities likewise happens at the metropolitan, national and global level, and large centres seem to provide the necessary infrastructure for MNCs.

- Industrial and technology regions seem to be attractive for (a part of) MNCs. Regions of this type show a strong industrial base with a high and above-average concentration of manufacturing activities and high employment shares in high- and medium-high-tech manu-facturing sectors. This leads to the conclusion that the activities of MNCs located there can be assumed to rely on a strong manufactur-ing base of their environments. Regions of this type also have high numbers of patent applications but do not reach leading regions in terms of inventions filed at the European Patent Office. Both the market environment and public research in these regions are good but not outstanding in comparison to the leading European regions.

Based on two research theses, the objective of this chapter was to analyse whether MNCs need to exploit the advantages of innovative loca-tions and significantly favour certain regions with a well-above-average endowment of innovation-relevant characteristics or whether these firms do not show a propensity to locate in certain locations and are thus footloose in the sense that the quality of their regional environments does not matter. Given the limitations of the data that were available for this analysis, we nevertheless found evidence for our first thesis based on the economic geography argumentation that the number of MNCs is significantly higher in regions characterized by a well-above-average endowment of innovation-relevant parameters. Thesis 2 is less supported. As a first deduction we can conclude that 'geography matters' (Krugman, 1991) also for MNCs.

Although our data do not allow a distinction to be made between different functions that the MNCs fulfil at their respective locations (besides the fact that they are classified as research-oriented), this regional location pattern seems to coincide with results from other studies in the sense that regions displaying a strong industrial base are attractive for downstream activities (production and post-production), while knowledge-oriented regions are favoured by MNCs with upstream functions such as R&D and headquarter activities (Defever, 2006). In this respect our sample is biased in that most of the MNCs classified as R&D-oriented show a high propensity to locate in 'knowledge and science hubs'. This aspect refers to the problem of data availability. Our approach was to link a cluster analysis of European regions with the pattern of the headquarter location of MNCs listed in the EU Industrial R&D Investment Scoreboard (European Commission, 2005). In this European perspective it is possible to derive only a few general conclusions about the location distribution but not about its causes and effects. Limited data availability, both with regard to the mapping of the different regional environments and a better representation of the MNC headquarters and their functions, prevented us from performing a more in-depth analysis. This should be possible for a limited set of regions with more detailed information about the MNCs located there.

The approach we applied was able to show that no even location pattern exists, neither favouring only regional knowledge hubs nor displaying a pattern of footlooseness in locational choices. On the one hand, MNCs favour certain types of regions, but on the other hand they of course have the flexibility to move to other locations that offer similar or even better conditions for their economic activities. The possibility of exploiting advantages of regional interconnectedness, that is, to link and combine different regional advantages through global networks or to shift research and production activities within the MNC to locations that offer specific benefits for specific project needs, is a special characteristic of MNCs (Bunnell and Coe, 2001; Saliola and Zanfei, 2009; Ito and Wakasugi, 2007). We thus finally conclude that MNCs are regionally integrated and disintegrated at the same time, so the question of whether they are footloose or not can be answered in both directions depending on either a regional or a company perspective.

NOTES

*   Major parts of this paper were prepared within the project "Regional Learning in Multinational Companies" financed by the Volkswagen Foundation, whose support is kindly acknowledged.
1.   NUTS = Nomenclature des unités territoriales statistiques, the nomenclature of territorial units for statistics.
2.   We used NUTS 2 whenever possible. In some cases innovation data are not available at the NUTS 2 level. Thus the NUTS 1 level was chosen instead; this is the case for the UK and Belgium. Denmark, Luxembourg, Cyprus, Lithuania, Estonia, Latvia, Slovenia and Malta were analysed on the NUTS 0 (country) level.
3.   This might be an artefact of the ordinal scalation of the variable.
4.   As the normality assumption for performing an analysis of variance is not met, we chose the non-parametric Kruskal–Wallis test, which uses the ranks of the data.

REFERENCES

Andersen, P.H. and Christensen, P.R. (2005), 'From localized to corporate excellence: how do MNCs extract, combine and disseminate sticky knowledge from regional innovation systems?', DRUID Working Paper 05-16, Aalborg, DRUID.

Asheim, B.T. and Gertler, M.S. (2005), 'The geography of innovation: regional innovation systems', in J. Fagerberg, D.C. Mowery and R.R. Nelson (eds), *The Oxford Handbook of Innovation*, New York: Oxford University Press, pp. 291–317.

Aumayr, C.M. (2007), 'European region types in EU-25', *The European Journal of Comparative Economics*, **4**: 109–47.

Backhaus, K., Erichson, B., Plinke, W. and Weiber, R. (2006), *Multivariate Analysemethoden*, 11. Auflage, Berlin: Springer.

Bathelt, H., Malmbergand, A. and Maskell, P. (2004), 'Clusters and knowledge: local buzz, global pipelines and the process of knowledge creation', *Progress in Human Geography*, **28**: 31–56.

Breschi, S. and Malerba, F. (1997), 'Sectoral systems of innovation: technological regimes, Schumpeterian dynamics and spatial boundaries', in C. Edquist (ed.), *Systems of Innovation*, London, Pinter Publishers, pp. 130–56.

Buckley, P.J. and Casson, M.C. (1998), 'Models of the multinational enterprise', *Journal of International Business Studies*, **29**: 21–44.

Bunnell, T.G. and Coe, N.M. (2001), 'Spaces and scales of innovation', *Progress in Human Geography*, **25**: 569–89.

Cantwell, J. and Mudambi, R. (2000), 'The location of MNE R&D activity: the role of investment incentives', *Management International Review*, **40**: 127–48.

Cantwell, J. and Piscitello, L. (2002), 'The location of technological activities of MNCs in European regions: the role of spillovers and local competencies', *Journal of International Management*, **8**: 69–96.

Carlsson, B. (ed.) (1995), *Technological Systems and Economic Performance: The Case of Factory Automation*, Boston, MA: Kluwer Academic Publishers.

Chandler, A.D. (1992), 'Organizational capabilities and the economic history of the industrial enterprise', *Journal of Economic Perspectives*, **6**: 79–100.

Coe, N.M., Hess, M., Yeung, H.W., Dicken, P. and Henderson, J. (2004), '"Globalizing" regional development: a global production networks perspective', *Transactions of the Institute of British Geographers*, **29**: 468–84.

Cooke, P. (1992), 'Regional innovation systems: competitive regulation in the new Europe', *Geoforum*, **23**: 365–82.

Cooke, P., Heidenreich, M. and Braczyk, H.-J. (eds) (2004), *Regional Innovation Systems. The Role of Governance in a Globalized World*, 2nd edn, London and New York: Routledge.

Defever, F. (2006), 'Functional fragmentation and the location of multi-national firms in an enlarged Europe', *Regional Science and Urban Economics*, **34**: 658–77.

Dunning, J.H. (1988), *Multinationals, Technology and Competitiveness*, London: Unwin Hyman.

Edler, J., Döhrn, R. and Rothgang, M. (2003), *Internationalisierung industrieller Forschung und grenzüberschreitendes Wissensmanagement. Eine empirische Analyse aus der Perspektive des Standortes Deutschland*, Heidelberg: Physica-Verlag.

Edquist, C. (2005), 'Systems of innovation. Perspectives and challenges', in J. Fagerberg, D.C. Mowery and R.R. Nelson (eds), *The Oxford Handbook of Innovation*, New York: Oxford University Press, pp. 181–208.

Edquist, C. (ed.) (1997), *Systems of Innovation. Technologies, Institutions and Organizations*, London: Pinter Publishers.

Enright, M.J. (2000), 'Regional clusters and multinational enterprises', *International Studies of Management & Organization*, **30**: 114–38.

European Commission (2005), *Monitoring Industrial Research: The 2005 EU Industrial R&D Investment SCOREBOARD. Volume II: Company Data*, Brussels: European Commission.

Freeman, C. (1987), *Technology Policy and Economic Performance: Lessons from Japan*, London: Pinter Publishers.

Freeman, C. (1988), 'Japan: a new national system of innovation?', in G. Dosi, C. Freeman, R.R. Nelson, G. Silverberg and L. Soete (eds), *Technical Change and Economic Theory*, London, Pinter Publishers, pp. 330–48.

Geenhuizen, M. van (2007), 'Modelling dynamics of knowledge networks and local connectedness: a case study of urban high-tech companies in the Netherlands', *The Annals of Regional Science*, **41**: 813–33.

Gertler, M.S. (1995), '"Being there": proximity, organization, and culture in the development and adoption of advanced manufacturing technologies', *Economic Geography*, **71**: 1–26.

Görg, H. and Strobl, E. (2003), 'Footloose multinationals?', *The Manchester School*, **71**: 1–19.

Hemer, J., Koschatzky, K., Kroll, H. and Zenker, A. (2007), 'Framework conditions for technological change and learning processes in firms and regions', Working Paper, Karlsruhe, Fraunhofer ISI.

Howells, J. (1990), 'The globalisation of research and development: a new era of change?', *Science and Public Policy*, **17**: 273–85.

Ito, B. and Wakasugi, R. (2007), 'What factors determine the mode of overseas R&S by multinationals? Empirical evidence', *Research Policy*, **36**: 1275–87.

Kogut, B. and Zander, U. (1993), 'Knowledge of the firm and the evolutionary theory of the multinational corporation', *Journal of International Business Studies*, **24**: 625–45.

Koschatzky, K. and Zenker, A. (1999), 'The regional embeddedness of small manufacturing and service firms: regional networking as knowledge source for innovation?', Karlsruhe, Fraunhofer ISI (Working Papers Firms and Region R2/1999).

Kristensen, P.H. and Zeitlin, J. (2004), *Local Players in Global Games: The Strategic Constitution of a Multinational Corporation*, Oxford: Oxford University Press.

Krugman, P. (1991), *Geography and Trade*, Leuven, Leuven University Press.

Krugman, P. (1998), 'What's new about the new economic geography?', *Oxford Review of Economic Policy*, **14**: 7–17.

Lundvall, B.-Å. (ed.) (1992), *National Systems of Innovation. Towards a Theory of Innovation and Interactive Learning*, London: Pinter Publishers.

Meyer-Krahmer, F. (2003), 'Lead-Märkte und Innovationsstandorte', in H.-J. Warnecke and H.-J. Bullinger (eds), *Kunststück Innovation. Praxisbeispiele aus der Fraunhofer-Gesellschaft*, Heidelberg, Springer, pp. 23–8.

Narula, R. and Santangelo, G.D. (2009), 'Location, collocation and R&D alliances in the European ICT industry', *Research Policy*, **38**: 393–403.

Nelson, R.R. (ed.) (1993), *National Innovation Systems. A Comparative Analysis*, New York: Oxford University Press.

Ohmae, K. (1995), *The End of the Nation State: The Rise of Regional Economics*, New York: The Free Press.

Porter, M.E. (1990), *The Competitive Advantage of Nations*, New York: The Free Press.

Reger, G. (1997), *Koordination und strategisches Management internationaler Innovationsprozesse*, Heidelberg: Physica-Verlag.

Saliola, F. and Zanfei, A. (2009), 'Multinational firms, global value chains and the organization of knowledge transfer', *Research Policy*, **38**: 369–81.

Sassen, S. (1994), *Cities in a World Economy*, Thousand Oaks, CA: Pine Forge Press.

Scott, A.J. (2001), *Global City-Regions*, Oxford: Oxford University Press.

Shimizutani, S. and Todo, Y. (2008), 'What determines overseas R&D activities? The case of Japanese multinational firms', *Research Policy*, **37**: 530–44.

von Zedtwitz, M. and Gassmann, O. (2002), 'Market versus technology drive in R&D internationalization: four different patterns of managing research and development', *Research Policy*, **31**: 569–88.

Zander, I. (1998), 'The evolution of technological capabilities in the multinational corporation – dispersion, duplication and potential advantages from multinationality', *Research Policy*, **27**: 17–35.

Zander, I. and Sölvell, Ö. (2000), 'Cross-border innovation in the multinational corporation', *International Studies of Management & Organization*, **30**: 44–67.

PART III

The social and political construction of corporate embeddedness

10. Modes of regional embeddedness: companies in seven European regions compared[1]

Dieter Rehfeld

10.1 INTRODUCTION

The region has by no means been rendered obsolete by globalization and a new balance has been established called 'glocalization'. Nevertheless, studies on regional embeddedness or the regional engagement of companies often only focus on regional networks or projects. They do not say much about the meaning of embeddedness or regional engagement in the context of the company's overall strategy. Such a perspective bears the risk of overestimating regional factors (Storper and Venables, 2004; Bathelt et al., 2004). Furthermore, we also have to keep in mind that there are strong varieties in the economic performance of regions, in regional learning and related capacity building, and in the availability of social or symbolic capital.

The CURE project, 'Corporate culture and regional embeddedness', therefore started with the question under which circumstances are regions able to strengthen their position in a global context. In brief, the project is based on the assumption that there are differences between regions, that there is a potential option for regions to make use of the differences by mutual learning and collective actions, and that the external circumstances that support or hinder the realization of a stronger regional position change over time. The CURE project had an interdisciplinary background and in this chapter the focus is placed on regional engagement that leads to regional embeddedness.

To start with, in a very first approximation, we adapt the transaction cost approach of Coase (1988) and state that a company is regionally embedded when the transaction costs of shifting to a new location are higher than the costs of staying. Transaction costs in this context are for example costs to find and evaluate a new location, costs to renew and qualify human capital, costs to adapt to a new business culture, and costs to sustain and renew social capital.

This mode of regional embeddedness is the result of basic social interaction and can be found to a greater or lesser degree in all regions and companies. Making use of the regional labour force and infrastructure, becoming familiar with regional business and work cultures, and being embedded in (personal) regional networks is a process each company undergoes in the course of its existence. Following the categories Coleman (1991) devised for social organization, we can call this 'primordial' or 'spontaneous' regional embeddedness.

This starting point stands in contrast to theoretical assumptions that a company has a day-to-day choice regarding whether to stay or to leave. In reality, however, it seems that transaction costs (and related insecurity), and in many regions path dependences and the advantages of local proximity as well as being an insider in local clusters, are so high that a company is only relocated when the costs to stay become unsustainably high. When this is the case, previous studies show that the new location is in a very dense neighbourhood compared to the original location (Becher and Rehfeld, 1987). Ruigrok and van Tulder (1995: 159) came to a similar conclusion: 'Of the largest one hundred core firms in the world, not one is truly "global", "footloose" or "borderless".'

The question is to what extent this situation has changed in the course of the recent decades of globalization. There are good arguments for the hypothesis that transaction costs for relocation decreased. There have been many locations all over the world attracting foreign investment in the last decades. Therefore companies in search of a new location

- are confronted with several well-established and attractive locations in different sociocultural contexts – often with a high reputation – where companies are already situated so that the uncertainty about the quality of the location is low;
- face a rising quality of human capital on the global level that is committed to global production standards – especially high-qualified technicians and engineers are present on a global level; and
- make use of global communication technologies that substitute face-to-face contacts needed to build social capital (trust etc.) to a certain degree.

With reference to these arguments, the new cultural geography focuses on de-territorialization. Mobility is no longer seen as the exception but as the rule. The 'mobility paradigm' claims that people, resources, social relations and ideas become increasingly volatile, while mobility in the context of global networks becomes the rule (Berndt and Boeckler, 2007: 228f.). This approach takes into account that specific locations are only understandable in the context of global production networks. However, it is a static approach because it ignores the fact that locations have the chance to remain stable and have the possibility to improve in this global context (Coe et al., 2004).

Regions – or locations from the company's point of view – become integrated in a global network and there is no reason to reduce the strategic choice of companies to the dualism of staying or leaving. There is also no reason to assume that regions are passive actors or entities that suffer from global pressure without any chance to influence their own fate. The key question is whether, and if so, to what degree companies are actively involved in strengthening and improving the location in which they are situated and to what degree regions have the capacity to learn and to change. If companies are indeed active in this respect, we assume that the regional embeddedness of companies changes by investing formal and informal resources on the regional level.

The active adaptation of a region in order to become strong in global production networks goes beyond this spontaneous development. The adaption process needs the active and collective more or less strategic engagement of companies. When this engagement is more than a single activity and takes place over time, it leads to a new and stronger mode of embeddedness. We call this mode of embeddedness – again following Coleman – 'constructed' regional embeddedness and study it as a result of the continuous engagement of companies within the region. The notion of regionally constructed embeddedness includes a dynamic perspective and follows Grabher (1993: 5), who writes: 'As in the embeddedness approach, the concept of social context . . . is not one of a once-and-for-all influence but one of an on-going process that is continuously constructed and reconstructed during interaction.' This dynamic perspective is especially relevant in a situation of structural change such as the recent transformation into the knowledge society (cf. Cooke and Leydesdorff's 2006 concept of 'the construction of advantage').

Therefore the following arguments focus on three questions:

- In what thematic fields, to what degree and in what spatial frame are companies regionally engaged (section 10.3)?
- Are there strategies and tools through which companies use regional impulses in a systematic way so that we can identify aspects of 'constructed regional embeddedness' (section 10.4)?
- Under which circumstances do the activities of the single companies work together in a synergetic way, so that competitive regional advantages are constructed (section 10.5)?

The concluding section 10.6 summarizes the arguments.

10.2   THE CURE PROJECT – THE APPROACH

The project 'Corporate culture and regional embeddedness' (CURE) was funded by the 6th European research framework programme. It focused on the relationship between regional and corporate culture studied in seven European regions in a comparative way. It was committed to the question of how companies contribute towards strengthening regions in the European context and towards making the idea of a regionally diverse Europe work. Vice versa, the project discussed the question of what kinds of regions provide a fruitful framework for companies' engagement that results in embeddedness. The project was an explorative one. It focused on new ideas and aimed at a new hypothesis. In this chapter the focus is on the two modes of regional embeddedness and on a hypothesis for forthcoming studies of the mode we call constructed embeddedness.

We assumed that the potential for constructed regional embeddedness is stronger in regions that have not faced strong political and economic shifts. Therefore three regions were selected with a relatively stable development in economy and politics (East Westphalia–Lippe, Basel Area and South Netherlands). Two regions are characterized by deep political and economic shifts (Gyor in Hungary and Brandenburg in Germany). Two further regions are positioned in between, with stronger economic shifts (Styria in Austria and Wales).

Thirty company case studies and seven in-depth studies in firms were performed in each region. The studied firms can be seen as characteristic of the region, that is, regional lead companies, companies from the dominating regional world of production respectively cluster, and a certain spread of different companies in terms of age, size, ownership and market orientation were included.

The case studies focused on the following four fields of activity, assuming that the interest of the regional actors and of the companies in these fields is strongly overlapping: human resources, innovation, sustainability and quality of life.

As far as companies are concerned, there are good reasons why these four fields of activity cover the key aspects of regional embeddedness. Human resources is the key factor in the vast majority of company location decisions, sustainability has top priority in most corporate social responsibility reports, quality of life is related to the company's attractiveness to a qualified labour force and becomes more important in the course of the rising impact of culture (image, reputation) in economic activities, and innovation is strongly connected with the trend towards a knowledge society.

The case studies are based on semi-structured qualitative interviews. Focusing on the four fields of activity, the key aim was to find out how companies (and regional actors) handle dilemmas in balancing global and local activities. The discussion on handling dilemmas is committed to an understanding of companies' cultures and of their non-static or linear, and, in any case, fluent strategies. Nevertheless, the core results of these interviews were interpreted and presented in a standardized manner. These results will be presented in the following section. Later sections are based on the interpretation of the qualitative dimension of these interviews and on the in-depth studies, and focus on the aspect of regional engagement and regional embeddedness.

10.3 PATTERNS OF REGIONAL ENGAGEMENT – COMPANIES AND REGIONS COMPARED

Whereas 'primordial' or 'spontaneous' regional embeddedness results from a continuous and mostly non-reflexive process, constructed embeddedness depends on the intentional and strategic action of companies. Therefore the discussion begins with a debate on companies' regional activities. We start in search of differences between the companies. First of all we assume that some types of companies might be more engaged than others. After this, the interest lies in the companies' field of activities. Special attention is paid to the relationship between activities and the core business of companies, as we assume that in this case the regional commitment and the related embeddedness will be strengthened. Furthermore, we are interested in the time dimension, that is, the change in the types of activities. Finally we are interested in the spatial dimension, especially in differences between the company's view of change and the administrative point of view (for more detailed results see Prud'homme and Dankbaar, 2009).

Table 10.1 shows the differences in the level of engagement between the studied regions.[2] As mentioned above, the hypothesis was that companies in regions with strong economic and political shifts are more engaged than companies in regions that had to face heavy structural shifts. In this sample the two regions suffering from the deepest shifts stand for the regions with the highest share of highly engaged companies. Even when we take into account that there is a bias in Brandenburg South-West because an above-average share of local companies is involved in this sample, we cannot confirm the hypothesis that there is a connection between regional stability and regional engagement of companies. We assume that, especially in regions with structural shifts, there is strong pressure and that there are

Table 10.1   Types of companies and regional engagement: average of all companies per region (%)

Region (number of cases)	Highly engaged	Engaged	Hardly involved	Not engaged
SEN (30 companies)	17	80	3	0
Basel (30 companies)	23	40	27	10
EWL (30 companies)	13	47	30	10
Styria (31 companies)	7	33	43	17
Wales (30 companies)	17	33	40	10
BSW (30 companies)	30	40	23	7
Győr (30 companies)	27	57	16	0

Notes: SEN: South-East Netherlands, EWL: East Westphalia–Lippe, BSW: Brandenburg South-West.

Source: Prud'homme and Dankbaar (2009: 62).

Table 10.2   Types of companies and regional engagement by ownership (%)

Ownership (number of cases)	Highly engaged	Engaged	Hardly involved	Not engaged
Public listed companies (26)	23	42	27	8
Public listed foreign owned (26)	8	61	23	8
Family companies (54)	24	44	23	9
Other non-public (52)	24	42	25	9
Non-public/foreign owned (19)	5	53	37	5
Private equity/venture capital (10)	0	20	60	20
Government involvement (24)	37	54	8	0

political incentives that strengthen the readiness for regional engagement. Before discussing this result, further variables have to be reviewed.

Table 10.2 summarizes the relationship between ownership and regional engagement. In this case the hypothesis was that foreign-owned companies are less engaged than regionally owned companies. This can be confirmed when we look at the share of highly engaged companies: foreign-owned companies score lower regional engagement than regionally based ones. Furthermore, companies owned by private equity and venture capital funds are less engaged in regional activities. When government is involved, companies show the highest share of 'highly involved'. This is not surprising because

Table 10.3   Types of companies and regional engagement by time dimension (%)

Time dimension (number of cases)	Highly engaged	Engaged	Hardly involved	Not engaged
Established companies (93)	30	50	16	4
Medium 10–20 years (70)	13	51	26	10
Young companies/start-ups (48)	12	31	44	13

Table 10.4   Types of companies and regional engagement by roots (%)

Roots (number of cases)	Highly engaged	Engaged	Hardly involved	Not engaged
Founded in region (155)	24	42	24	8
Founded in region/acquired (19)	5	69	21	5
Inward investment (37)	11	49	32	8

most of them focus on the local or regional market and/or are committed to sponsoring by their legal status (e.g. German savings banks). The differences between the other modes of ownership are too small for interpretation.

A clear relationship can be seen when we look at the age of the company: the older the company, the higher the regional engagement (see Table 10.3). On the one hand, this reflects the fact that embeddedness and regional engagement go hand in hand in many companies over time. Nevertheless, this result needs deeper interpretation, as different fields of engagement are involved. For instance, social and cultural sponsoring is typical when companies grow and become more and more regionally rooted. However, social and cultural sponsoring is often driven by phil-anthropic motivation and does not have much in common with the com-pany's core business. On the other hand, this might be a consequence of the fact that young companies have very limited resources and of course have different priorities from established companies.

In this case the hypothesis is that companies with regional roots are more engaged in the region than companies coming from outside the region – we expect some kind of personal commitment from the company founder to the region (see Table 10.4). Indeed, we can see a difference when we look at the share of highly engaged companies, but this differ-ence becomes smaller when we look at the small share of not engaged companies: 60 per cent of the companies coming from outside the region are engaged in regional activities, less than 10 per cent are not engaged.

Table 10.5   Types of companies and regional engagement by size (%)

Size (number of cases)	Highly engaged	Engaged	Hardly involved	Not engaged
Big companies (58)	28	60	12	0
Medium-sized companies (70)	20	48	25	7
Small companies (55)	9	40	35	16
Micro (28)	28	25	36	11

Table 10.6   Types of companies and regional engagement by industry (%)

Industry (number of cases)	Highly engaged	Engaged	Hardly involved	Not engaged
Public services (13)	38	46	15	0
Creative industry/media/artisan (19)	37	37	21	5
Electronics/high-tech (13)	31	61	8	0
Metal/manufacturing/industrial (23)	26	35	26	13
Food/retail/consumer products (21)	24	38	38	0
Life sciences/medical/biotech (36)	22	53	17	8
Automotive (28)	14	68	14	4
Business services (24)	12	37	38	13
Financial (12)	8	37	55	0
ICT (19)	0	32	37	31

Due to the size of the company, we assumed that despite globalization big companies are regionally engaged too. We can say that in our sample those big companies are more engaged in the region than small companies (Table 10.5). Interestingly, micro-companies are above average highly engaged. In this case we assume that micro-companies strongly depend on local and regional markets and that therefore the interest in regional activities is higher than in other companies. Furthermore, we must bear in mind that regional engagement means different ways of thinking, especially when we look at the size of the company. Large companies have the financial resources to support regional activities, while in small companies regional engagement is often driven by the personal engagement of the company's owner.

When we look at the industry to which the companies belong, we also find differences in the level of engagement. In our sample ICT companies show the lowest share of regional engagement (see Table 10.6). This fits with some of the in-depth studies that show that even very small IT companies have an identity as a (potential) global and footloose company.

Table 10.7   Estimation of regional importance by fields of activity (ranked highly important and important, 211 companies)

	Innovation	Human resources	Quality of life	Sustainability
EWL	9	27	20	7
Wales	16	15	17	15
BSW	12	18	28	8
SEN	29	30	27	17
Basel	23	25	21	17
Styria	17	25	10	2
Györ	20	19	20	16
All regions	103	134	102	65

Furthermore, it was surprising that service industries (financial and business services) are engaged below average and that creative industries show an above-average intensity of regional engagement.

The intensity of regional engagement is not an indicator of the companies' field of engagement. The interviews with the companies discussed both their estimation of the importance of the field for the company and their active engagement in this field. The differences between estimation and real activities were very small. Therefore Table 10.7 concentrates on the importance of the four fields from the companies' point of view. We simplified the results by aggregating the notion of 'highly important' and 'important'.

If we look at the companies' estimation of the importance of the region, the picture becomes clearer: human resources is the most important field (and the result is the same when we ask about the company's engagement). Human resources is followed by innovation and quality of life. There are good reasons deduced from our qualitative interview as to why innovation and quality of life are often strongly related to the need to acquire qualified staff. All in all, differences between the estimation of importance of these three fields from the companies' point of view are not very high. Sustainability is ranked lowest in this survey and we assume that activities in sustainability take place in the plant and/or in the context of the value chain.

Furthermore, we have to bear in mind that these results are general estimations and impressions. In some case studies it could be shown that the activities of companies are by no means always without contradiction. If we take the example of sustainability, we see that there is no problem for a company to promote and support regional activities in energy efficiency and waste management while at the same time stressing and bending legal rules for pollution and noise when building a new plant. To provide a further example, many companies are interested in strengthening the regional research base by funding research projects in order to brand the region as an attractive technology region, but at the same time they continue to strengthen their global innovation networks.

We also have to bear in mind that the intensity of companies' regional engagement changes over time. This can be studied when we go behind the aggregated results presented in this section and take a look in the case studies. For instance, an IT company was very engaged in sponsoring culture and sports, in improving infrastructure (fast train, airport) and education and research during the 1960s and 1970s. Regional engagement went down near to zero in the 1990s when the company became integrated in a globally acting group and gained a new dynamic when it was outsourced. Today, the company is one of the key framers of cooperative regional activities for improving the regional brand and regional research activities.

To provide another example, in the 1990s many activities in sustainability were driven by companies (round table, agenda process, certification, waste management). At the time this field was new and inter-company projects and networks helped to reduce insecurity about handling these new challenges. Today sustainability on a certain level is part of day-to-day business and there is no longer any interest in regional cooperation in this field.

Changes in engagement over the course of time often include a change in the spatial dimension. Whereas in the past regional engagement was often in a dense local neighbourhood, it became more and more regional in the 1990s. In the course of the qualitative interviews in one region (East Westphalia–Lippe) we asked the interview partners to draw on a map what the region covers for them (cf. Gärtner and Rehfeld, 2009). Without further prompting, nearly all of them concentrated on the region where their workforce came from. Figure 10.1 shows these mental maps of East Westphalia–Lippe in an aggregated way. We can see that inside the administrative region East Westphalia–Lippe three sub-regions are of importance.

These mental regions combine three aspects. First, cultural roots: one sub-region is a long-standing Catholic one, the second has Protestant roots, the third used to be a separate county and became part of the administrative region after the Second World War. Second, the industrial bases of these regions are different: the first is rooted in textiles and mechanical engineering, the second developed through ICT companies in the last three decades and the third has a strong focus on electronic interfaces. Third, the sub-regions stand for labour force flows, which are partly influenced by the existing traffic infrastructure.

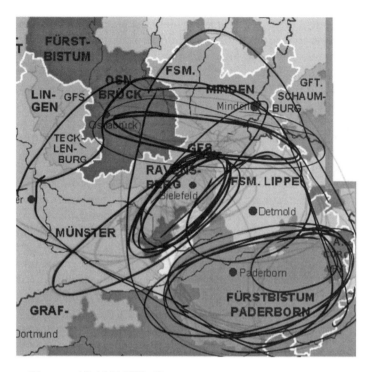

Source: Gärtner and Rehfeld (2009: 41).

Figure 10.1   The regional space from the company's point of view in East Westphalia–Lippe

10.4   CONSTRUCTED REGIONAL EMBEDDEDNESS: MOTIVATIONS, EXPECTATIONS AND STRATEGIES

Regional engagement results in regional embeddedness, and this section thus concentrates on a more detailed discussion of the two initially distinguished modes of regional embeddedness: 'spontaneous' and 'constructed' regional embeddedness. The first question is why companies are engaged and what they expect from their engagement. The initial argument is that donation and sponsorship in culture, social aspects and sports have no or very few links to the core business and that donation and sponsorship are related to spontaneous regional embeddedness. Donation and sponsorship in these fields are driven by philanthropic motivation or social responsibility, and no direct benefit is expected for the core business from this engagement. The response is very indirect and – more importantly – donation and sponsoring in this traditional view are strongly separated from the business activities of the company.

This mode of regional engagement was found in many regions for many decades and related to 'spontaneous regional embeddedness' because it had no direct influence on business activities. In the last decades the situation has changed and new fields of activities have arisen that are strongly related to 'constructed regional embeddedness'. In our case study interviews, four bundles of motivations of engagement could be studied that resulted in constructed embeddedness.

The first motivation is to strengthen a thriving and competent business milieu. Some companies in our case studies say they are driven by the idea of acting in the context of an innovative regional milieu that rises from the competitiveness of the regional economy, hoping that this has effects on the competitive position of their own companies. Nowadays, a thriving and competitive business milieu is often linked with a strong regional knowledge base (Camagni, 1991; Helmstädter, 2003). In our case studies, however, knowledge as regional knowledge was not prominent but it seems to be of growing interest. Sponsoring university chairs that are important for the core business, organizing open innovation activities and participating in innovation networks are activities that are focused on knowledge.

The second motivation is to make use of the local market. This interest in the local market is true first of all for service companies and publicly owned companies, but in historical terms we can see that a specific regional demand helped companies to improve product quality and become successful on an international level (cf. Porter, 1990).

The third motivation is to strengthen regional attractiveness. Indeed, companies are more and more interested in the regional image. Again, the interest in acquiring a qualified labour force is dominant, because especially for companies located in lesser-known regions such as East Westphalia–Lippe it is difficult to explain to their international partners where they are located.

The fourth motivation is to build up social capital. More and more companies are becoming aware of the importance of the social capital that results from regional engagement and networking. There are examples in our case studies that show that large companies include factors such as regional engagement and responsibility by network activities in their criteria when searching for suppliers.

In these bundles of motivation, companies expect at least an indirect return on their engagement and the ties between regional engagement and core business become deeper. A common factor in all these activities is that they strengthen the regional ties of companies and therefore contribute to regional embeddedness.

The strongest link between regional engagement and expectation, in return, exists when companies are engaged in projects that strengthen the links between the university and business, initiating collective projects (often public–private partnership) such as an open innovation campus, research cities and eco-cities. In this case regional activities are aimed at strengthening the companies to show how and what they produce (and again to make the region attractive to a highly qualified labour force). In this case it is important that companies are strongly embedded in the region and not footloose. The assumption is that, in the course of globalization, there is a need to improve the quality of the region in which the company is located. As pointed out above, symbolic capital and the reputation resulting from it (Glückler, 2004) becomes more and more important. Thus there is a strong link between social capital (networks), symbolic capital (reputation) and human resources that is crucial for innovation.

The borders between the two types of regional embeddedness are of course fluid, and activities related to both types can be studied in most companies that are involved in regional activities. Nevertheless, it is helpful to define the differences between the two types in order to study changes in the mode of regional embeddedness.

Constructed regional embeddedness is different from spontaneous regional embeddedness because:

- there is a link between the regional activities and the core business of the company;
- it is often based on collective action (between companies or between companies and public actors) because it cannot be realized by one actor alone;
- it is aimed at strengthening the region because a stronger region (economic environment, knowledge base, attractiveness, regional lead markets) is expected to have a positive influence on the performance of the company;
- the link between the expected results on the regional level and the benefits for the company are not direct but mediated by strengthening the region; the expected impact is important for the core business of the company.

Nevertheless, constructed regional embeddedness is organized by projects and not by long-standing commitments of the companies; even when companies are highly involved in regional activities (projects) they nearly always do so for a specific purpose in a fixed time horizon. Networks are often the social base for organizing such projects, but in contrast to the understanding of Granovetter (1992), networks are only one factor in a broader and more differentiated social organization.

A further limit to deeper constructed embeddedness is that nearly all regional activities analysed in our case study depend on individual actors. In small companies it is the owner who is in charge of regional activities; in medium-sized family companies it is often the junior manager; in large companies it is the head of the research department or the person in charge of human resources (HR) or another department who is a member of regional networks. Active participation in networks is often taken as a strong indicator of the regional embeddedness of companies. But we have to be careful in studying networks. In the region East Westphalia–Lippe we identified three types of networks that are important for companies (cf. Gärtner and Rehfeld, 2009):

- The social network linking the heads of small and medium companies is often ignored in studies. This network is very informal and weak, but especially in regions without global companies is crucial for the collective action of companies and in order to work out the thematic framework from which companies coordinate their regional actions.
- Formal networks are often public–private partnerships and they are the most studied. However, these networks depend on informal networks as mentioned above and on the commitment of political actors (see section 10.5).
- With regard to tacit knowledge, functional networks are supposed to be most important. These networks are grouped around thematic themes such as HR, marketing, environmental standards, energy or logistics and are reported to be decisive for informal exchange.

The members of all these networks are individuals (maybe represented by a specific function), not companies, which is why the feedback of knowledge from those networks depends on individuals. In our case studies we found very few examples of companies that make systematic use of regional networks. One of these examples is the Weidmüller Academy (Figure 10.2), which was established in order to link the region and the company. The academy is in charge of training and education on all levels. It is responsible for contacts between the company and universities, for looking for new technologies and for being present in several regional networks. The academy also has to transfer the results of these activities into the company.

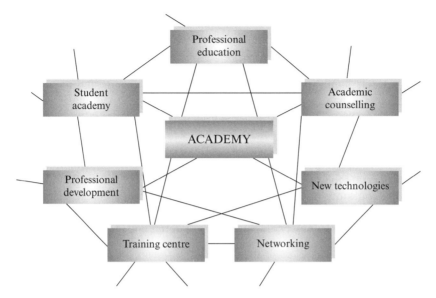

Figure 10.2   The structure of the Weidmüller Academy

Summing up, engagement that is related to constructed regional embeddedness can be found in the regions we studied in our CURE project. These activities do not replace sponsoring and donations that are linked to spontaneous regional embeddedness; they are additional and are based on the vital interest of strengthening the region in the face of the challenges of globalization. The key aspect is that with stronger links between regional activities and core business, a new 'constructed' quality of regional embeddedness arises and this strategy is a strong alternative to moving to a new location.

10.5   CONSTRUCTED REGIONAL EMBEDDEDNESS AND THE CONSTRUCTION OF REGIONAL ADVANTAGES – HYPOTHESIS FOR FURTHER RESEARCH

Constructed embeddedness often depends on the creation of regional advantages; otherwise it can be supposed to be of little interest to the companies. Furthermore, constructed embeddedness cannot be realized by a company alone but needs a third actor who moderates and coordinates the activities, implying a high quality of regional governance (cf. Kleinfeld et al., 2006). Therefore we have to ask under what circumstances and how the activities of different actors work together in a synergetic (and not only additional) way in order to bring out regional advantages. In the context of the CURE project this question was discussed by asking about the preconditions and processes for bringing a virtuous circle into life. A virtuous circle in this sense is based on collective learning and on change competence that strengthens the regional adaption capacity and attractiveness. In sum, four hypotheses can be derived following the results of the CURE project.

1. The company's culture   The active involvement of companies in strengthening the region (and not only the location) needs companies that are not footloose but embedded. However, further aspects are helpful in making a process like this work in a fruitful and dynamic way. Following the CURE results, key characteristic of regional engagement that results in constructed embeddedness are:

- long-term strategies;
- continuity of leadership and labour force;
- responsibility; and
- visibility.

This idea of embedded companies works best in regions where the mentioned characteristics do not simply refer to companies but are furthermore attributes that are strongly embedded in regional culture. The idea of footloose companies is only one aspect of the capitalistic development. Many companies are strongly regionally embedded and relocate their headquarters only if other options fail. This concerns options such as economic reasons (opportunity costs resulting from searching for new locations and a fitting infrastructure, competences etc.) as well as social reasons.

2. Thematic issues are crucial for the competitive position of the companies and provide a common framework   To make companies regionally involved in a long-standing and coordinated way, the following aspects are of importance:

- Topics that are relevant for companies, for example as studied in our project (HR, innovation, quality of life, sustainability)
- The expectation and awareness of further company participation
- The expectation and awareness of political, administrative and intermediate partners taking part in and supporting the process without dominating it

- The ability of relevant partners to develop common aims (to the point of a common vision)
- The acting and steering within functional frames, for which companies feel prepared to assume responsibility
- The decision for a long-term regional commitment, which also depends on the efficiency of the aforementioned factors

The crucial aspect in this respect is not a network or a project but a shared framework concerning the position and the future of the region. Due to this aspect, the difference between regions that have had continuous development and regions that had to face strong structural shifts is decisive. Regions with continuous development have established companies with owners who are known (visible) and strongly embedded in the region, who have a culture of trust, who have learned to manage changes step by step and have a long-standing culture of trust between companies and between companies and politics. If this works, no formal networks are needed. The best example of this is the Basel region, where small and large companies, traditional families and the new class of international managers work together (and from time to time compete) in a dynamic way. Conflicts are needed and productive; this is another result of the case studies. If the region is too homogeneous, it runs the risk of provoking lock-ins.

3. A well-running governance structure that manages a shared framework In some regions a guiding framework, helping to find out where the company stands and where it will be, is under the surface but is strongly embedded in the regional culture. In regions undergoing large changes, a framework of this kind is missing. This has been studied in old industrial regions, in the CURE context in Wales, Styria, Brandenburg and Győr. In these four regions networks exist but a shared framework is missing. In these regions the role of politics has become important in order to work out a discourse that leads to a shared framework.

Therefore, from the regional point of view, well-running regional governance is crucial. Regional actors, in this case first of all political and administrative actors, need to:

- moderate the different interests of the company, as companies have different motivations and interests with regard to strengthening regional links;
- overcome the limits of administrative borders because, as shown in section 10.3, the companies' spatial orientation is different from administrative borders;

- give orientation as a common framework;
- implement the results in a reliable way and improve the governance structure that is needed in order to do so.

4. A dynamic interaction that is open for new challenges and results in regional change management   Interaction between the region and companies is a dynamic process. In order to be able to tap into regional capabilities, companies need to contribute towards 'renewing' the region: a process of 'continuity through renewal'. Today the discussion about innovation and the knowledge economy can work as a driving force for regional embeddedness, as it provides opportunities for overcoming local limits. However, we have to bear in mind that the interests of the companies are much more differentiated and fields of action such as HR or quality of life are often beneath the surface of innovation or knowledge rhetoric.

Successful regional development is primarily about 'change management' and the strengthening of regional distinctiveness (Markusen and Schrock, 2006). Therefore, instead of following the latest global trends that may lead to unintended consequences in the long run, it would be more appropriate to support the region's peculiarities, competences and weaknesses.

Following the CURE approach, 'glocalization' is not a fixed result but a balance that has always to be renewed. It is not a specific cultural feature but the capacity to adapt or change that makes the difference. Furthermore, there is no single solution for working out a balance; it always has to do with facing dilemmas.

- To work out a regional frame, a high level of internal interaction is needed, but if it is too dense, the result is lock-ins.
- To strengthen the innovative milieu within the region, strong company–university relations are needed, but in most sectors academic research is embedded in a strong national and sometimes global division of labour.
- To improve the innovation capacity, open innovation approaches are becoming more and more useful, but innovation as a competitive edge needs property rights and becomes closed the nearer it comes to the market.
- To realize coordinated strategies to strengthen the region, a strong political commitment is needed, but companies act in very different regional spaces and those spaces are often not the same as the political spaces.
- Improving quality of life from the companies' point of view often focuses on global highlights and – even if it is sponsored by

companies – has long-standing follow-up costs that reduce the resources for other activities.
- Especially small and medium-sized companies with limited resources benefit from the improvement of the location, but on the path to realizing this, global players have much more resources and reputation.

Within the CURE regions very different ways of balancing those dilemmas could be studied. Eindhoven, for example, balances regional and global cultures based on a high level of trust and cooperation culture. East Westphalia-Lippe has a strong regional identity but few global links and therefore 'controlled' global cultural impacts. In both regions there are companies that are on the way to strong constructed embeddedness. Basel has no strategic networks but shows a fruitful interplay of strong local culture and global communities. The activities of the key companies are first of all activities to strengthen their own innovative base and their own reputation. However, there are also activities that are aimed at strengthening the regional innovative base and that can strengthen the constructed embeddedness in the long run (Dörhöfer et al., 2009). Styria has networks based on national tradition and on fragmented subcultures with limited links between them; constructed embeddedness is very weak and limited to companies of certain industries. Wales has focused on the global impact for years and is frustrated about the results; it is now on its way to rediscovering the potential of regional culture. Brandenburg has very fragmented subcultures and there is little chance of finding a shared framework between strong links with Berlin on the one hand and the rural periphery on the other. It is not only in a few companies in these regions that constructed embeddedness exists. Győr shows a very interesting interplay of traditional and global cultures, but so far there are no institutions based on trust and it is not yet clear to what extent this interplay results in companies with constructed embeddedness.

10.6 CONCLUSIONS

This chapter summarizes selected results of the CURE project and focuses on embeddedness. The key result is that we need a deeper understanding of embeddedness. Two modes of embeddedness have been distinguished. Understanding the global–local balance cannot be explained with the dualism of embedded companies and footloose companies. By far the most important reason why most companies are not footloose is transaction costs. The options of either leaving or learning (Schoenberger, 1995) increasingly tend towards the direction of learning, and learning means collective learning. As companies tend to stay within the region in which they are located while the global division of labour and, increasingly importantly, of knowledge is changing, the key question is how companies are involved in strengthening the region into a strong node within global production networks.

The results show that there are strong examples indicating that the mode of embeddedness is changing and that, under the circumstances discussed in the hypothesis in section 10.5, embeddedness is becoming more and more constructed. As pointed out in section 10.4, constructed embeddedness is different from spontaneous embeddedness because it is based on collective action; it is aimed at strengthening the region because a stronger region is expected to have a positive influence on the performance of the company and has strong links to the company's core business.

The results and examples presented in sections 10.3 and 10.4 show that there are huge differences in the way companies are involved. However, constructed embeddedness is a result of the strategic decision of a company not to leave the location and to engage in improving the location and making better use of the benefits offered by the location. As shown in sections 10.4 and 10.5, there are two key obstacles to the realization of constructed embeddedness. First, constructed embeddedness is aimed at regional advantages, and regional advantages provide benefits for all companies. This runs the risk of producing a free-rider situation for those companies not engaged in constructed embeddedness. Therefore a high-quality regional governance capacity is needed to motivate and coordinate the activities of the individual companies. Second, despite links to the core business, most companies avoid long-standing commitments and prefer clearly defined project-driven activities. Again, regional governance becomes crucial for integrating these short-term project-driven activities in a long-term strategy.

NOTES

1. This chapter benefits from a great deal of discussion, criticism and ideas. It summarizes the results of interdisciplinary research in the CURE project. The project partners and the papers are available at www.cure-project.eu. Furthermore, I have benefited considerably from criticism and input from Martin Heidenreich and Örjan Sölvell. All my colleagues from the Innovation, Space and Culture department contributed towards a very lively and helpful discussion and, moreover, Saskia Dankwart provided competent support.
2. When we started the empirical research we distinguished four types of regional engagement along a continuum. The estimation of the intensity of regional engagement results from the discussion within the research teams and is based on the results of the case

studies and the reported activities in the four fields mentioned in section 10.2. Roughly speaking, it can be said that high engagement of companies leads to constructed embeddedness.

REFERENCES

Bathelt, H. et al. (2004), 'Clusters and knowledge: local buzz, global pipelines and the process of knowledge creation', *Progress in Human Geography*, **28**: 35–56.
Becher, G. and Rehfeld, D. (1987), *Forschungsbericht zum Stand der Regionalforschung*, Braunschweig: Edition Braunschweig.
Berndt, C. and Boeckler, M. (2007), 'Kulturelle Geographien der Ökonomie: Zur Performativität von Märkten', in C. Berndt and R. Pütz (eds), *Kulturelle Geographien. Zur Beschäftigung mit Raum und Ort nach dem Cultural Turn*, Bielefeld: Transcript Verlag, pp. 213–58.
Camagni, R. (ed.) (1991), *Innovation Networks: Spatial Perspectives*, London: Belhaven Press.
Coase, R.H. (1988), *The Firm, the Market, and the Law*, Chicago and London: University of Chicago Press.
Coe, N.M. et al. (2004), '"Globalizing" regional development: a global production networks perspective', *Transactions of the Institute of British Geographers*, **29**: 468–84.
Coleman, J.F. (1991), 'Prologue: constructed social organisation', in P. Bourdieu and J.F. Coleman (eds), *Social Theory for a Changing Society*, New York: Westview Press, pp. 1–14.
Cooke, P. and Leydesdorff, L. (2006), 'Regional development and the knowledge-based economy: the construction of advantage', *The Journal of Technology Transfer*, **31**: 5–15.
Dörhöfer, S., Minnig, C. and Pekruhl, U. (2009), *Regional Report Basel-Area*, Olten: www.cure-project.eu.
Gärtner, S. and Rehfeld, D. (2009), *Regional Report East Westphalia Lippe*, Gelsenkirchen: www.cure-project.eu.
Glückler, J. (2004), *Reputationsnetze. Zur Internationalisierung von Unternehmensberatern. Eine relationale Theorie*, Bielefeld: Transcript Verlag.
Grabher, G. (1993), 'Rediscovering the social in the economics of interfirm relations', in G. Grabher (ed.), *The Embedded Firm. On the Socioeconomics of Industrial Networks*, London and New York: Routledge, pp. 1–32.
Granovetter, M. (1992), 'Problems of explanation in economic sociology', in R. Eccles and N. Nohria (eds), *Networks and Organizations*, Boston, MA: Harvard Business School Press, pp. 25–56.
Helmstädter, E. (2003), *The Economics of Knowledge Sharing. A New Institutional Approach*, Cheltenham, UK and Northampton, MA, USA: Edward Elgar.
Kleinfeld, R. et al., (eds) (2006), *Regional Governance*, Osnabrück and Göttingen: V&R Verlag.
Markusen, A. and Schrock, G. (2006), '"The distinctive city": urban occupational specialization and implications for development policy', in R. Sonnabend and R. Stein (eds), *The Other Cities. Vol 4: Urban Distinctiveness*, Dessau: Edition Bauhaus, pp. 51–9.
Porter, M. (1990), *The Competitive Advantage of Nations*, London: The Free Press.

Prud'homme van Reine, P. and Dankbaar, B. (2009), 'Empirical results. Fact sheet. Empirical *results from 210 case studies and 21 in-depth studies in seven European regions*', Nijmegen: www.cure-project.eu.

Ruigrok, W. and van Tulder, R. (1995), *The Logic of International Restructuring*, London and New York: Routledge.

Schoenberger, E. (1995), 'Leaving or learning?', in F. Lehner et al. (eds), *Regiovision. Neue Strategien für alte Industrieregionen*, München and Mering: Hampp Verlag, pp. 146–54.

Storper, M. and Venables, A.J. (2004), 'Buzz: face-to-face contact and the urban economy', *Journal of Economic Geography*, **4**: 351–70.

11. The *pôles de compétitivité*: regional innovation clusters with a French touch

Christoph Barmeyer and Katharina Krüth

11.1 INTRODUCTION

In the context of increasing global competition and rapidly developing information and communication technologies, knowledge is considered to be a key economic resource for gaining and maintaining competitive advantages (Rammert, 2004). Accordingly, the dynamics of R&D activities have been identified as a crucial factor for global industrial competitiveness. Strategies of firms are increasingly oriented towards the creation and diffusion of new or newly combined knowledge and thus the development of innovations. Innovations can be defined as the successful transfer of knowledge into marketable products, processes or services (Edquist, 1997).

Furthermore, innovation can be understood as an interactive learning process that takes place in social networks due to the circulation and transfer of knowledge and the combination and implementation of new competences (Fagerberg, 2004; Lundvall, 1992, 1999). According to Fagerberg (2004: 3), 'innovation is by its very nature a systemic phenomenon, since it results from continuing interaction between different actors and organizations'. Social interaction and the combination of heterogeneous competences are thus considered to be substantial factors for generating innovations. In this context multinational companies (MNCs) are crucial actors due to their high investments in R&D (European Commission, 2007), their ability to disperse R&D activities internationally and to use transnational and thus heterogeneous competences (Narula and Zanfei, 2004; Dunning, 2000; Bartlett and Ghoshal, 1998).

Nevertheless, the competitiveness of MNCs not only depends on the use of cross-border capabilities and the internationalization of R&D activities. MNCs also need to rely on competences and resources that are allocated in the regional surroundings of their subsidiaries (Heidenreich, 2006).

Since close interaction, trust-based relationships and tacit knowledge represent important preconditions for generating innovations, various studies in the field of economic geography have acknowledged the importance of regions and regional networks for learning and innovation processes (Cooke, 2004; Bathelt et al., 2004; Asheim and Isaksen, 2002; Koschatzky, 2001). Accordingly, an efficient regional environment may be essential for innovative capacities of MNCs. The strategy of being integrated in international and regional networks at the same time thus represents a further means for MNCs to maintain and broaden their innovative competitiveness.

This trend has also reached policy makers. Within the EU the focus of innovation policy is increasingly shifting towards the promotion of regional network initiatives and in particular towards cluster policies (Sölvell et al., 2003; OECD, 1999). In this context, the French government launched the programme of regional competitiveness clusters, the *pôles de compétitivité* (in the following also referred to as competitiveness clusters) in 2005. These clusters aim to bring together MNCs, small and medium-sized companies (SMEs), research centres and educational institutions in close geographic proximity for the purposes of conducting cooperative innovation projects. Hence this concept provides additional opportunities for the cluster members to create new networks or to widen and institutionalize already existing partnerships. A side effect of this cluster policy consists in strengthening the institutional embeddedness of MNCs within a given region.

The aim of our chapter is to examine the specific network structures, the functioning and the country-specific characteristics of the competitiveness clusters. We analyse to what extent a change in the institutionally and culturally deep-rooted French innovation system has been initialized due to the creation of the *pôles de compétitivité* and which roles are designated to the different cluster members, with a specific focus on MNCs. In our analysis we also consider cultural aspects and patterns which reflect the 'Frenchness' of this cluster policy. However, we do not conduct an evaluation of the French cluster policy and thus do not focus on discussing the success or failure of the *pôles de compétitivité*.[1]

We expect that the creation of the competitiveness clusters affects the structures of the French innovation system and leads to a shift from

1. centralized and top-down mechanisms of political coordination by the state towards decentralized structures in terms of innovation policy;
2. personalized and homogeneous social networks as the basis of cooperative innovation activities towards multiple and heterogeneous cooperation structures.

In order to test our theses we additionally use interviews conducted with cooperation partners within three competitiveness clusters and examine how the cluster members perceive the *pôles de compétitivité*.[2]

In the following section we introduce the French context and discuss culturally specific characteristics of French institutions and companies. In the third section we concentrate on the policy evolution of the French innovation system and present the idea, goal and main principles of the policy of the *pôles de compétitivité*. Finally, we analyse the ways in which a French touch is inherent in the *pôles de compétitivité* and which role is assigned to MNCs within the clusters.

11.2 THE 'FRENCHNESS' OF INSTITUTIONS AND COMPANIES IN FRANCE

11.2.1 The Institutionalist and the Cultural Approach: a Conceptual Framework

Innovation takes place in specific contexts, mainly in countries that, due to historical and political structures, develop specific institutions as norms, values and structures (Hofstede, 1980; Inglehart and Welzel, 2005; North, 1990) that constitute a social system by attaining a certain degree of homogeneity (d'Iribarne, 1989, 2009; Whitley, 2002). Therefore knowledge and experience in combination with rules and values have led to certain characteristics and successful patterns in organizing and developing a social system (Hall and Soskice, 2001; Porter, 1990). As a result, the national context thus influences innovation policies (Lundvall, 1992, 1999; Roure, 2001; Waarts and van Everdingen, 2005; Heidenreich et al., 2010).

A socioeconomic system and its innovation policies can be analysed from an institutionalist and a cultural perspective. The institutionalist approach is based on the assumption that an economic system is shaped and controlled by dominant national institutions, even if it is divided into different regions (Whitley, 2002: 44). These include the legal system, the state, interest groups such as employer and employee associations, and the financial and education systems (Hancké, 2009; Hall and Soskice, 2001; Maurice et al., 1982; Maurice, 1991). The cultural approach rests on the assumption that cultural norms and values are a learned system for orientation and reference that have developed and taken root as a result of a particular type of socialization and communication (Davel et al., 2008; Elias, 1979; Hofstede, 1980; Parsons, 1952). Since they have a relatively similar value system, it is particularly common for groups and societies to develop specific types of solutions that distinguish them from other groups and societies.

In this chapter we rely on a combination of both approaches, as developed in neo-institutionalism (Berger and Luckmann, 1966; DiMaggio and Powell, 1983; North, 1990). By explaining how institutions shape the behaviour of individuals, neo-institutionalism considers both the institutional and cultural approaches of social systems in order to gain a better understanding of social systems.

Due to a certain configuration of institutions, over the centuries France has developed a specific socioeconomic system that is often called 'Le modèle français' (Albert, 1991; Barmeyer et al., 2007; Gauchon, 2008; Lesourne, 1998). What are the main characteristics of the French system in comparison with other industrialized countries? The next section centres on this precise question.

11.2.2   Characteristics of the French Socioeconomic System

11.2.2.1   The state's strategy, centralism and hierarchy

France is known as a country in which hierarchy and authority play a more important role compared to other western countries (Hofstede, 1980; Mendel, 2002). Due to France's *républicain* state model a certain degree of mistrust exists concerning individual interests, uncontrolled market liberalism and globalization (d'Iribarne, 2006). Therefore the central state fulfils the role of a strategic actor, a steering motivator, a guarantor of social responsibility and a coordinator of industrial and social relations (Albert, 1991; Ammon, 1989; Barmeyer et al., 2007; Hancké, 2002). As a result political matters are considered to be more important than economic matters within the French economic system and take precedence over purely market aspects:

> Economic thinking is mainly politico-strategic thinking. It is less concerned with economic criteria, such as supply and demand, market potentials, market niches and sales opportunities, but is concerned with economic strength in sectors/branches which are considered as strategically important. (Ammon, 1990: 123, our translation)

To achieve this strategic orientation, *le modèle français* is characterized by a strong hierarchy and centralized coordination style that function in a 'top-down' manner. Until now, and especially after the Second World War, the French economic and innovation systems have been steered by the state or close state actors (Hancké, 2002). Vertical coordination and corporation structures were established by the state or with the state as an important stakeholder in MNCs, such as Alstom, EDF or Renault (Barmeyer et al., 2007). This has led to the non-implication and exclusion of intermediate actors such as SMEs, research centres and other actors that are not based in the Parisian region. Hancké (2001: 309) gives nuances to this thesis by underlining the fact that SMEs became 'much stronger technologically and organizationally' between 1980 and 1990.

The importance of hierarchy can also be observed between and within organizations (Maurice et al., 1982). The attitude towards hierarchy is therefore expressed in vertical relations between business partners and between employers and employees. Decision processes lean towards a top-down structure: vertical relations are therefore more important than horizontal ones. Hierarchical authority is the most important steering principle (Hofstede and Hofstede, 2005: 252). As a consequence, French organizations display relatively low levels of delegation and decisions must be considered at different hierarchical levels, thus taking a long time to be determined.

In the past, this top-down and vertical coordination made it difficult to initiate highly innovative and successful clusters without Parisian influence.

11.2.2.2 The logic of honour and rank

To understand the importance of hierarchy, its genesis and its crucial impact on modern France, the works of Philippe d'Iribarne provide a cultural explanation (d'Iribarne, 1989, 2006): a specific French and historically steady value orientation is *honneur* (honour) because it determines the French social relations in general as well as the working relations. *Honneur* assigns to every individual a social standing, a rank with certain privileges and duties. According to d'Iribarne, today's social relations are based on the pre-revolutionary society of the *ancien régime*: nobility, clergy, bourgeoisie and farmer. As a consequence, France remains a court society for Elias (1969).

> France remains the fatherland of honour, rank, the opposition of noble and vulgar, of orders and of the states, which are characterized as much by their duties as by their privileges. Nobody is willing to yield to the common law but everyone will have the heart to meet the responsibilities which are determined by the tradition of its rank. And the sense of honour prohibits those who claim to defend their interests in the petty way which belongs to the vulgar. (d'Iribarne, 1989: 258, our translation)

This characteristic is opposed to the horizontal working relationships to be found in an Anglo-Saxon or even Germanic logic of goals, functions and processes, where mutual contracts between 'equal' partners organize the duties and rights of every actor (d'Iribarne, 1989, 2008; Hampden-Turner and Trompenaars, 1993; Hofstede and Hofstede, 2005).

The consequences of the French logic of honour are expressed in strong hierarchical relationships and especially in the critical mutual judgement of actors. Paris is more 'noble' than the region, the client is always considered as more 'noble' than the supplier and MNCs are more 'noble' than SMEs. This is a cultural explanation of why SMEs have traditionally never played an important role in the French economy or its innovation system (Barmeyer et al., 2007; Colletis and Uterwedde, 2005). In comparison to Germany, French SMEs are much less internationalized, have few financial resources, invest respectively small sums in research activities and do not attract the brilliant and ambitious graduates from the *grandes Ecoles* who prefer the mighty MNCs as their employers, as discussed in the next section.

11.2.2.3 Trust and segmentation in social networks

Trust as a potential force for reducing social complexity and shaping the future is considered as a significant factor in the growth and success of economies and organizations (Whitley, 2002). Trust is established and maintained through social interaction and networks.

The French word for network is *réseau*. But where are important strategic networks built in France? Particularly influential are the elitist *Grandes Ecoles*, which exist in addition to the regular public universities. Whereas public universities do not have a high reputation, *Grandes Ecoles* are considered to be the 'talent hotbed' (*pepinières*) of the future elite in the fields of administration, management and engineering (Hancké, 2001; Hartmann, 2007; Joly, 2005). The *Grandes Ecoles* are not known for intense research activities but rather for their strong links to influential political institutions and companies. In general, graduates from the *Grandes Ecoles* easily secure a relatively high position of employment in public administration or companies without having undergone any process of professional in-house socialization.

In particular, graduates from the most prestigious and Parisian-based public *Grandes Ecoles* will start their careers in a French administration or ministry in Paris. After a few years of service, they have the possibility of entering an MNC such as Renault, Thales or EDF, but still remaining civil servants at the same time. They are thus able to return to the public service at any time. This French phenomenon is called *pantouflage*, which literally means that the actors can regain their 'slippers' that they left in the administration. The centralized education and training of the elite in Paris fosters the formation of influential networks, described as 'state nobility' by Bourdieu (1989). It must be stressed that most of the time this connection between state and MNCs is not formal or official but an informal, *officieux* connection that contributes to a growing 'osmosis of the elites' (Barmeyer et al., 2007). These actors are closely linked by an *esprit de corps* that leads to strong, stable and lifelong interconnections between politics, administration and private finance. In this sense the coordination of economic actors is not predominantly fulfilled by the market but by 'elites in the state apparatus, large firms, and high finance, which assured that large firms were able to construct a novel institutional environment' (Hancké, 2001: 333).

It is important to mention that traditionally neither SMEs nor France's most important institution for basic research, the National Centre for Scientific Research (CNRS), are part of this influential social network: they are not considered as 'noble' and will therefore not attract the brilliant graduates from the prestigious *Grandes Ecoles*. As a result, knowledge transfer and competence combination is limited to central actors belonging to specific social networks.

To conclude, in this section three institutionalist and cultural characteristics of French institutions and organizations have been presented that firstly contribute to a strong vertical top-down coordination (of a centralized state) and second to a strong segregation between actors of Paris and the regions, MNCs and SMEs. On the other hand, close relations exist between the state and French MNCs due to the specific social networks of the *Grandes Ecoles*. These long-lasting characteristics not only constitute and stabilize the 'Frenchness' of France's economic system, often discussed in the literature (Ammon, 1990; Barmeyer et al., 2007; Hampden-Turner and Trompenaars, 1993) and shown as differing from the Anglo-Saxon or Germanic economic systems (Albert, 1991; Hall and Soskice, 2001; Lesourne, 1998), but also have an important effect regarding the creation and evolution of innovation policy and regional clusters (cf. sections 11.3 and 11.4).

Following this institutionalist and culturally orientated introduction to the French context, we shall now focus on the French innovation system and its evolution in the following section.

11.3 FROM DIRIGIST TO REGULATORY: RESEARCH AND INNOVATION POLICY IN FRANCE

11.3.1 The French Colbertist Model and its Gradual Disappearance – a Shift in Paradigm?

The policy structures that were created in the course of the economic reconstruction of France after 1945 shaped the French innovation system with a lasting effect. The years between 1945 and 1973 are called 'The Glorious Thirty' and were marked by continually growing prosperity

(Fourastié, 1979). During these years the state acted as a modernization agency in order to reconstruct and modernize the country. France created 'capitalisme à la française' with the principle of state dirigisme as a central element (Schild and Uterwedde, 2006).

This Colbertist philosophy also significantly influenced the French innovation and research system. The state developed, promoted and coordinated technologically promising branches by implementing 'grand projects' and 'large programmes' that became predominant in the 1960s (Cohen, 2007; Mustar and Larédo, 2002; Chesnais, 1993). The applied research was organized through mission-oriented public research institutes linked to the various ministries (Chesnais, 1993). Furthermore, the state cooperated intensively with a few selected big companies, known as 'national champions', which were responsible for the development and commercialization of high-tech innovations (Barmeyer et al., 2007). Again, the close link between MNCs and the state becomes obvious here (cf. 11.2.2).

During the 1980s and the 1990s, the influence of national political institutions decreased due to advancing globalization, Europeanization and regionalization (Cohen, 2007; Hancké, 2001). France began to move away from its vertically integrated industrial policies and the importance of the 'grand projects' gradually diminished (Mustar and Larédo, 2002). Schild and Uterwedde (2006) observe a paradigm shift concerning French industrial policy since 1983, moving away from state dirigisme towards a liberal economy that is increasingly regulated by the market. Nevertheless, the gradual adjustments merely represent the beginning of a policy shift. The basic economic structures, institutional setting and innovation-promoting policies did not undergo major changes during that period. Accordingly, France's competitiveness gap increased during the 1990s. During this period scepticism regarding French industrial and innovation policy increased among the scientific community and particularly among authors, who tended to assume more liberalist positions (Hancké, 2002; Levy, 1999).[3] An often-cited example of a French industrial policy that is not considered to have succeeded in the long run is the *Technopôles*. This initiative started slowly in the 1970s but became more prominent in subsequent years until the 1990s. The idea of these centres consisted in co-locating research centres and innovation-intensive firms in science and technology parks (Cooke, 2001; Benko, 2000). However, synergies did not emerge to the expected extent.

11.3.2 Recent Reforms and the Changing Role of the State

At the end of the 1990s the political elite became more active in terms of political reforms and adopted a large number of propositions in the middle of the first decade of the 2000s (Cohen, 2007). The reforms concerned institutional structures as well as policy measures, were preceded by several strategic innovation plans and often came along with adopted new laws. These reforms initiated the ongoing transformation of political structures in France and can no longer be attributed to the Colbertist philosophy.

The first decisive reforms were introduced in 1999 with the Innovation Act, referred to as the *Loi Allègre*, followed by the Innovation Plan in 2003 and the Pact for Research in 2005. These reforms were aimed at benchmarking the French innovation and research system in the international context, supporting cooperation between public and private research and promoting enterprises' research efforts and scientific careers (Beatson et al., 2007).

A whole package of reforms came along with the Pact for Research and the associated law. Different institutions for scientific and technological advice and monitoring have been created, for example the agencies ANR and Oseo. While Oseo offers support for innovative SMEs in the form of public funding and consultancy, the National Agency for Research (ANR) promotes and finances the development of basic and applied research as well as technological transfer. Today Oseo and ANR represent two of the most important national agencies. Both of them act at the regional level as well through regional departments.

Altogether, the substantial reforms led to a clear policy shift from vertically integrated and mission-oriented policies towards the promotion of network-oriented and bottom-up initiatives. Furthermore, the role of the state now tends to be more regulatory than dirigiste (Barmeyer et al., 2007; Muller et al., 2009; Cohen, 2007).

One policy measure that is a prominent example of the evolution described above is the cluster programme of the *pôles de compétitivité*. This governmental measure is particularly aimed at MNCs and is considered to be a crucial instrument of the new innovation policy in France (Muller et al., 2009). In the following section we shall give a more detailed presentation of the competitiveness cluster policy and take a closer look at the way in which the clusters function.

11.3.3 Filling the Gap between Local and Global Knowledge: the *Pôles de Compétitivité*

The policy of the *pôles de compétitivité* can be interpreted as the advancement of the policy of the productive local systems (SPL), which were initiated in 1997 by the French government and inspired by the concept of the 'Italian districts' (Barthet and Thoin, 2009; Weil and Fen Chong, 2008; Jacquet and Darmon, 2005). Whereas productive local systems are clusters of production, the *pôles de compétitivité* are R&D-intensive clusters (Weil and Fen Chong, 2008). Currently 71 clusters exist in France (Barthet and Thoin, 2009).[4]

The policy of the *pôles de compétitivité* follows the idea of a triangular network structure: MNCs, SMEs and research institutes are addressed at the same time. The intention is that they should cooperate on an equal footing and in spatial proximity (Retour, 2009). This approach is aimed at stimulating and strengthening partnerships and at effecting technological transfer between the heterogeneous actors who conduct cooperative innovation projects. These joint innovative activities are expected to foster the specialization of regions in certain key branches and to raise their international visibility. Due to the participation of MNCs, global knowledge is to be integrated in regional contexts. A side effect of this cluster structure is thus a stronger institutional embeddedness of MNCs within a given region.

The concept of the *pôles de compétitivité* is based on three principles:

1. Cooperation between MNCs, SMEs and public or private research institutes.
2. Cooperation should be based on a common development strategy and target a specific technology but assemble experts from different fields. The aim is to combine knowledge from different fields in common innovation projects.
3. Geographic proximity of the members of the *pôles*.

These conceptual considerations correspond to the core aspects of the recently introduced reforms regarding French innovation policy. On this basis a competitiveness cluster has been defined as 'an association of companies, research centres and educational institutions in a given local area, working in partnership (under a common development strategy) in order to generate synergies in the execution of innovative projects in the interest of one or more given markets'.[5]

All actors of the cluster have to coordinate their action under a framework contract; the concept of cluster aims for a global approach: every step, from R&D through to a common commercialization strategy and the sharing of material and immaterial resources, should be integrated in an overall strategic frame. The way of handling this policy with calls for projects and a national competition is aimed at strengthening local bottom-up initiatives to build clusters (Jacquet and Darmon, 2005).

Figure 11.1 presents the structure of a competitiveness cluster and illustrates which inputs are provided by the different partners.

While the MNCs are required to define a general thematic orientation,

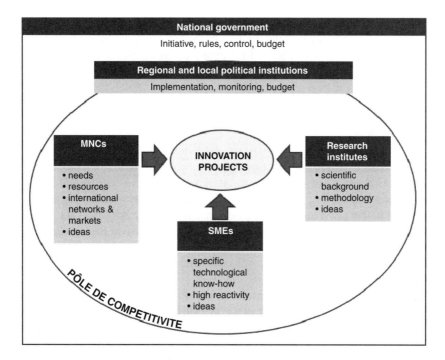

Source: Own presentation.

Figure 11.1 *Concept of a* pôle de compétitivité

the research institutes develop scientific methods and approaches and the SMEs (or 'technology providers') provide technological know-how in specific fields. However, the coordination of these constellations and the decision making within the clusters also result in governance difficulties (Bocquet and Mothe, 2009).

11.3.4 Administrative Framework and First Effects of the Competitiveness Clusters

The competitiveness clusters are a form of public–private partnership but the idea is that the private sector should take the main responsibility and initiative for the partnership (European Commission, 2009; Jacquet and Darmon, 2005). The different public administrative institutions at the regional level accompany the respective cluster initiatives in their regions but do not guide them in a centralist way (Jacquet and Darmon, 2005; cf. Figure 11.1).

The first period of this programme lasted from 2005 until the end of 2008. The overall budget for this period was €1.5 billion. Local and regional administrative institutions provided some supplementary financial support, which differed from cluster to cluster. In 2008, after an evaluation of the first period of the *pôles de compétitivité*, the French government launched a second phase from 2009 to 2011, called 'poles 2.0'. In 2010 this phase was prolonged until 2012. As in the first period, the budget is €1.5 billion.

Overall, the policy of the *pôles de compétitivité* has been designed to overcome several weaknesses that have been repeatedly identified in the French innovation system. It is important to mention the way in which the policy of the competitiveness clusters differs from the policy of the productive local systems and the *Technopôles*. As in the case of the SPL and the *Technopôles*, the competitiveness clusters are in fact characterized and pushed by a strong political will (Defélix et al., 2008; Retour, 2009). In contrast to the SPL, however, the *pôles de compétitivité* concentrate on R&D and not on productive capacities. In comparison with the initiative of the *Technopôles*, the competitiveness cluster approach promotes networking, which corresponds to the current understanding of innovation as an interactive process and which emphasizes systemic factors (Cooke, 2001). The integration and the prominent role that is assigned to MNCs constitute a further novelty (cf. 11.4.4).

To sum up, the intentions of the cluster policy are the following. First, it aims to foster bottom-up initiatives and to actively involve local and regional authorities in innovation policy making. Furthermore, local, regional and national agencies are obliged to coordinate their actions. Thus the cluster programme contributes to the decentralization process of innovation policies in France and serves as an example of the rise of systemic, network-oriented policy instruments. Second, the policy links together different actors from public and private research in order to support technological transfer and overcome the duality of the French research system. Third, the aim is get MNCs and SMEs to cooperate. This approach is aimed at reinforcing the prosperity of SMEs and integrating MNCs in their regional surroundings at the same time. Consequently, conditions are expected to improve in terms of the creation of synergy and spillover effects within regional and the national innovation systems.

In the next section we shall pick up on these aspects and examine them in greater detail in order to explain the specific 'Frenchness' about them.

11.4   THE FRENCH TOUCH OF THE *PÔLES DE COMPÉTITIVITÉ*

11.4.1   Three Case Studies

In order to examine the structures and the functioning of the French competitiveness clusters, we additionally use empirical material as a data source. This empirical material consists of 60 expert interviews conducted with members of three *pôles de compétitivité*. For each of the three cases, in 2007 and 2008 we interviewed between 15 and 25 employees of MNCs, SMEs and research institutes who were working together in joint innovation projects. In order to obtain a complementary perspective on the cooperation structures within each cluster, we also conducted interviews with representatives of the political institutions that were monitoring the activities within the *pôles de compétitivité*. All interviews rely on a non-standardized interview guideline, which left enough scope for open conversation and narrative digressions of the interviewees (Lamnek, 2005; Patton, 1987). The interviews took between one and two hours and were conducted in the context of a research project about the regional learning of MNCs (cf. introduction).

The three cases encompass key sectors of innovative activities: the automotive sector, the transport sector and the chemical industry. With the help of the interviews we were able to gain an inside and in-depth perspective of the functioning of the *pôles de compétitivité* and thus to reconstruct a more comprehensive picture of this new political programme.

11.4.2   National Coordination versus Regional Initiatives

Although the idea of the *pôles de compétitivité* is aimed at regional bottom-up initiatives and stronger involvement of political actors at the regional level, this policy was initiated by the national government and started with a nationwide call for projects. The national government is also responsible for the coordination of the programme, which includes the budgeting, the nomination, the categorizing and the evaluation of all *pôles*. The regional and local political institutions are required to implement the policy, that is, to accompany and to monitor the activities in the *pôles* within the geographic region of their responsibility. Moreover, they are required to provide additional funding. Regions and communities thus act as agents of the national policy.

On the one hand, this constitutes an evolution of the former structures and assigns a more active role to the regional and the local political level. Furthermore, the idea of the competitiveness clusters as tools for economic and scientific development has been created with the aim of creating self-energizing dynamics of already existing structures (Muller et al., 2009). In order to become labelled as a *pôle de compétitivité*, the members have to be highly proactive. This procedure represents a typical bottom-up element. In two of our cases, regional business agencies supported the initiatives during this phase of candidature and were also involved in launching the conceptual plan for the respective *pôle*.

> When I was involved in the cluster, in my role I was asked to initiate a file on the intention to create a cluster on the regions of l'Île-de-France and Normandy. It was like implementing a political will . . . Once I finished writing the first document, my job was to push for projects and structure the constellations of cluster members of the industrial world . . . So really this job entailed defining the strategic axes for the actors' federation and structuring. (Regional business development, Île-de-France, 1)

On the other hand, the competences of the French regions are still limited and of minor influence despite several regionalization reforms. This particularly concerns the budgeting (European Commission, 2008; Muller et al., 2009). As the initiating and coordinating institution, the national government still has administrative sovereignty over the clusters and constitutes the highest board of decisions. The strong political will behind the policy of the *pôles de compétitivité* serves as an example of the central role of the state. Instead of several smaller actions in the field of cluster policies, the French government focused on one extensive programme with the competitiveness clusters. Accordingly, the principle of authority and centralization becomes apparent: the state is designated as a strategic actor and central coordinator (cf. 11.2.2.1).

To conclude, this policy combines bottom-up and top-down tendencies as well as central and decentralized principles at the same time. Whereas the important role of the national state as the central coordinator and promoter represents traditional country-specific patterns, the bottom-up principle and the decentralized elements break with the former conventions of French policy making.

11.4.3   Cooperation of Multiple and Heterogeneous Partners

The concept of the competitiveness clusters follows the idea of a triangular network structure: MNCs, SMEs and research institutes are encouraged to ally for the purposes of joint innovative activities. This kind of cooperation structure represents a novelty within the French innovation system. Cooperation between MNCs and SMEs has not been particularly significant so far, at least in the form of an equal partnership.

We often come from two very different worlds despite connections sometimes between suppliers and clients. I think the cooperation is good but it is very, very weak. Cooperation is notoriously insufficient between the MNCs and the SMEs in France, despite the fact that each year we try to launch programmes or activities to develop such cooperation. (Regional business association, Rhône-Alpes, 4)

Cooperation between MNCs and SMEs has happened fairly coincidentally and always followed a buyer–supplier logic. However, the policy of the competitiveness clusters allowed and fostered the building of stronger links between MNCs and SMEs, providing knowledge in specific technological fields. MNCs especially appreciate these newly built partnerships.

Yes, partner relations [with SMEs] at the intellectual property level, which are no longer referred to as such, did not previously exist. Yes, since we got the seal of approval as a cluster, we will now share knowledge and developments . . . it was not part of the culture, which is to say that we plainly kept with the totally classic buyer–supplier relations. Whereas now we are opening up with partnerships in research. (R&D 1, Transport-F, 8)

In contrast, cooperation between MNCs and research institutes has been more common. It represents a considerable change in the French innovation system that MNCs and SMEs cooperate as quasi-equal partners and establish institutionalized linkages.

This is new to everyone because, while we have done cooperative projects in the past, they were industry-academic, industry-laboratory projects. What's new is that we now keep the SMEs in the loop, which we never used to do . . . We never used to see them! There was nothing there. So it was only by fluke that the SMEs would have some tool which could be useful to us. A fluke! It used to be the result of a coincidence, but now we make it happen . . . (Head of R&D 1, cluster board member, Auto-F, 15)

In general, the *pôles de compétitivité* facilitated the building of more institutionalized links between all partners, including also research institutes. Initial and rather informal business meetings within the framework of the *pôles de compétitivité* have been a useful platform for the cluster members to get in touch with potential partners. These kick-off meetings served as a basis for the building of new and more heterogeneous social networks and trust-based partnerships. For successful joint innovation projects, the cluster members perceive trust as a key factor.

If they don't know each other, they don't work together. By offering them an agora-like setting, in which they get to know one another, and in which they share and discuss their needs, they will make plans to meet up again later. . . .

this is how trust is built. . . . So when you have people who have trust in each other, it builds the foundation supporting each project. There is a very important interpersonal aspect here. (Project leader R&D 1, Auto-F, 10)

It's enormous; we discovered a whole world of market stimulation. People from different places came to the first meetings saying 'Sure, I came. But I'm an SME, I'm going to get devoured by the MNCs. It's not going to work well'. And then people would leave the meetings saying 'we were able to express ourselves, it was brilliant'. (External relations and business valuation, cluster board member, Chemistry-F, 11)

Besides the newly established links between cluster members, many partners within the *pôles de compétitivité* have already cooperated in the past. They know each other and already have a trust base.

And perhaps people with whom you have already worked? – Of course! That's where there is even less spontaneity . . . We know who we work with. We are accustomed to working with our tier 1 equipment suppliers, so that relationship is already in place. And in the same way, equipment suppliers are used to working with certain labs, as we are used to working with certain SMEs, this automatically happens. (Head of R&D 1, Cluster board member, Auto-F, 8)

This example demonstrates the importance of social networks, which are often built within the *Grandes Ecoles* in France and which lead to a certain social segregation of employees. This segregation can be interpreted as one reason for the weak cooperative structures between MNCs and SMEs. Indeed, they are partly rooted in the different cultures of organization, which especially prevail in MNCs and SMEs in France, but also in different cultural attributions. As already mentioned in section 11.2.2.2, MNCs are perceived as being more 'noble' than SMEs, which goes back to the logic of honour and rank (d'Iribarne, 1989, 2009).

Finally, the policy of the competitiveness clusters potentially represents a means of overcoming this weakness of the French innovation system, even if personal contacts and networks that existed before the creation of clusters remain an important factor. Nevertheless, the *pôles de compétitivité* also enable and promote newly built contacts and partnerships.

11.4.4   MNCs as Motors within the Clusters

Another phenomenon of the *pôles de compétitivité* is also related to the logic of rank and honour, and thus to the particularly powerful position of MNCs in France: the particular role MNCs play within the clusters. In fact, they have to perform a balancing act. On the one hand, projects and partnerships within the clusters are supposed to be cooperative at eye level. On the other hand, MNCs are assigned a special responsibility because they are supposed to act as stimulators and boosters within the cooperative innovation projects. It is up to the MNCs to formulate their needs in terms of technological innovations. Thus they mostly have the final say about proceedings within the projects, but at the same time the MNCs need to integrate the expertise of their partners. As a result, MNCs mostly have the strongest weight within the clusters, even if all members are supposed to cooperate as equal partners.

> But we absolutely do not want [Transport-F] to head this, even if we are the ones piloting the whole project, we grease the wheels. Overall we want it to be a win–win situation . . . On decision-making, we listen to them and we take as much into account as possible. Most often, however, the final decision is ours . . . (Project leader R&D, Transport-F, III.3)

Thus MNCs play a predominant role within the competitiveness clusters. However, due to their size and their limited resources, SMEs have more difficulties in engaging and investing in large common innovation projects and thus in participating in a *pôle de compétitivité*. This fact leads to a weakened role of SMEs within the clusters.

> Our only reservation, and we are not alone in feeling this way, is the participation by SMEs . . . since their participation is still fairly low. The MNCs are who mainly define the research programmes . . . SMEs have the least amount of power [within the competitiveness clusters]. (Chamber of Commerce, Île-de-France, 9)

A further reason for the central role of MNCs within the clusters is undeniably a certain commercial logic that stands behind the concept of the clusters. Finally, MNCs are often the distributors and thus the final users of the innovations. Furthermore, they simply have a considerable amount of resources at their disposal that they are able to provide for innovation projects.

> In fact, there is no hierarchy between partners. In the end it's more of a sphere of influence and commercial logic. In other words, as a manufacturer, [Auto-F] is finally at the end of the production line. They are the ones who sell the final product, so, inevitably, they have a lot of influence. They are very unifying. (R&D 1, Auto-F, 17)

Even though MNCs are expected to be stimulators and boosters of the competitiveness clusters and thus mostly receive a leading role, their importance also depends on the sector. In some sectors, for example the video game industry, SMEs are more likely to be innovative and thus function as the driving actors. Therefore the roles of the cluster members differ from cluster to cluster.

To conclude, the strong position of the MNCs within the competitiveness clusters can be partly traced back to a certain commercial logic but also to the traditionally extra-powerful role of MNCs in France. Accordingly, a tendency towards a vertical organization of members within the *pôles de compétitivité* is observable, contradicting the original idea of the policy and representing a dilemma between the idea and the structurally given circumstances within the clusters.

11.5   CONCLUSION AND OUTLOOK

Combining institutional and cultural perspectives, we discussed whether the French competitiveness clusters contributed to a transformation of political and innovative cooperation structures in France and to what extent cultural patterns play a role in this evolution.

Initially, we presented crucial country-specific structures within the French economic, societal and innovation system, concluding that aspects of hierarchy and social networks within the political and economic elite play central roles in France. Moreover, the cultural attribution of MNCs and SMEs differs significantly, as shown by comparing the principle of 'noble' and 'vil'. This fact constitutes an important aspect for a deeper understanding of the *pôles de compétitivité*. In order to understand the novelty of these clusters, we presented an outline of the evolution of French innovation policy, demonstrating that a policy shift has taken place in France. There is a clear tendency to shift away from vertically integrated and mission-oriented policy making towards the promotion of network-oriented initiatives, involving elements of decentralization. With the help of interviews with members of three *pôles de compétitivité*, we provided an in-depth insight into the structures and the functioning of the competitiveness clusters.

The first important purpose of the cluster policy is the stronger involvement of regional and local political actors. They act as agents of the national state and are assigned with an active role regarding the implementation of the policy. However, the national government still has a strong influence in terms of thematic orientation, budgeting and controlling the *pôles de compétitivité*. So, even if it is aimed at bottom-up initiatives, the policy has been initiated and controlled in a clearly top-down manner.

Second, *pôles de compétitivité* are expected to enable and strengthen links between heterogeneous actors such as MNCs, SMEs and research institutes. Within the framework of the clusters they combine their diverse resources and competences and generate joint innovation projects. The *pôles de compétitivité* seem to provide a platform for stabilizing already-existing contacts as well as for building new partnerships, especially between MNCs and SMEs. This provides a basis for the successful combination of local and global knowledge and competences.

Third, French MNCs remain the crucial innovative players within innovation systems and especially within the competitiveness clusters. Within the French innovation system they have a particularly powerful position, which is also due to cultural attributions and the lack of a net of SMEs in France. Accordingly, MNCs are intended to function as motors within the *pôles de compétitivité* in most cases. This causes a dilemma situation and difficult governance structures because they often have to take final decisions, even though partnerships within the clusters should be equal. Thus MNCs are requested to display diplomatic and federate competences in order to successfully integrate all partners. In a few years it must be reviewed whether MNCs are the cluster members benefiting the most from the cooperation and whether the policy of the competitiveness clusters could be interpreted as a modern means of coddling MNCs with public funds in the old French way.

To conclude, all of these analysed phenomena reveal a certain 'French touch' within this specific type of cluster policies. Even if these aspects may seem to be typical effects of cluster policies in general and emerge in other countries as well, they emerge in a particularly distinct form in France due to country-specific structures and cultural patterns. First, even if the influence of the powerful nation-state has been diminished by the implementation of the cluster policy, the national government still fulfils a strong strategic function that clearly outshines regional competences. Second, new cooperative structures have originated within the *pôles de compétitivité* but old networks remain important for successful innovation projects. Third, innovation projects are supposed to be conducted in equal partnerships but MNCs still often seem to have slightly more power in terms of informal authority than other partners, which corresponds to the dominant role that MNCs traditionally assume within the French economic system.

However, the *pôles de compétitivité* constitute a new initiative for overcoming some of the typical 'weaknesses' of the French innovation system. Regarding our two theses in the introduction, on the basis of our three cases studies we observed clear tendencies that confirm the expected shift towards decentralized structures in terms of innovation policy as well as towards heterogeneous and less socially segregated cooperation structures. In this sense the *pôles de compétitivité* have created new opportunities and new forms of cooperation.

The question remains whether the discussed evolution of the French innovation system will continue and further consolidate. Furthermore, the next few years will show whether the policy of the *pôles de compétitivité* will have consequences for the structures and processes of the French economic system in the long term and whether this policy will also affect deep-rooted and country-specific cultural patterns.

NOTES

1. A first evaluation has been carried out by two consulting agencies in 2008 (Boston Consulting Group and ICM International, 2008). However, this evaluation mainly contains advice regarding the administrative structures of the clusters.
2. The interviews were conducted in the context of the research project 'Regional Learning in Multinational Companies' (Heidenreich et al., 2010). The project was financed by the Volkswagen Foundation.
3. Levy (1999) argued in his analysis that the transfer of economic responsibilities from the central state to regional actors and to 'civil society', in the form of associations, largely failed. This results in an obligation of the French state to re-intervene. In this sense the title of the book *Tocqueville's Revenge* refers to France's enduring pattern of a strong state versus a weak society, identified two centuries ago by Tocqueville and which continues to hamper economic transitions.
4. A complete list of the current 71 *pôles de compétitivité* is available at http://competitivite. gouv.fr (12 January 2011).
5. Cf.http://competitivite.gouv.fr/politique-des-poles/quest-ce-quun-pole-de-competitivite-472.html (18 November 2010).

REFERENCES

Albert, M. (1991), *Capitalisme contre capitalisme*, Paris: Seuil.
Ammon, G. (1989), *Der französische Wirtschaftsstil*, München: Eberhard Verlag.
Ammon, G. (1990), 'Wirtschaftsstil und Identität', in Deutsch-Französisches Institut (ed.), *Frankreich Jahrbuch 1990*, Opladen, pp. 117–30.
Asheim, B. and Isaksen, A. (2002), 'Regional innovation systems: the integration of local 'sticky' and global "ubiquitous" knowledge', *Journal of Technology Transfer*, **27**: 77–86.
Barmeyer, C., Schlierer, H.-J. and Seidel, F. (2007), *Wirtschaftsmodell Frankreich. Märkte. Unternehmen, Manager*, Frankfurt and New York: Campus.
Barthet, M.-F. and Thoin, M. (2009), *Les pôles de compétitivité*, Paris, La documentation française.
Bartlett, C.A. and Ghoshal, S. (1998), *Managing across Borders – The Transnational Solution*, Boston, MA: Harvard Business School Press.
Bathelt, H., Malmberg, A. and Maskell, P. (2004), 'Clusters and knowledge: local buzz, global pipelines and the process of knowledge creation', *Progress in Human Geography*, **28**: 31–56.
Beatson, M., Edlund, S.-G., Riera, C.M., Pristovsek, P. and Pukl, B. (2007), 'CREST 3% OMC Third Cycle Policy Mix Peer Review Country Report

France', available at: http://ec. europa.eu/invest-in-research/pdf/download_en/ omc_fr_review_report.pdf (9 July 2009).

Benko, G. (2000), 'Technopoles, high-tech industries and regional development: a critical review', *GeoJournal*, **51**: 157–67.

Berger, P.L. and Luckmann, T. (1966), *The Social Construction of Reality*, New York: Doubleday.

Bocquet, R. and Mothe, C. (2009), 'Gouvernance et performance des pôles de PME', *Revue Française de Gestion*, **190**: 101–22.

Boston Consulting Group and ICM International (2008), 'Evaluation des pôles de compétitivité: Synthèse du rapport d'évaluation', available at: http://www. competitivite.gouv.fr/IMG/pdf/synthese_BCG-CMI_evaluation_des_poles_de_ competitivite.pdf (22 June 2009).

Bourdieu, P. (1989), *La Noblesse d'Etat. Grandes Ecoles et esprit de corps*, Paris: Les Editions de Minuit.

Chesnais, F. (1993), 'The French national system of innovation', in R.R. Nelson (ed.), *National Systems of Innovation*, Oxford: Oxford University Press, pp. 192–229.

Cohen, E. (2007), 'Industrial policies in France: the old and the new', *Journal of Industry, Competition and Trade*, **3–4**: 213–27.

Colletis, G. and Uterwedde, H. (2005), 'Zwischen Wettbewerbsfähigkeit und Attraktivität. Frankreichs Wirtschaft in der Globalisierung', in A. Kimmel and H. Uterwedde (eds), *Länderbericht Frankreich*, Wiesbaden: VS Verlag, pp. 209–27.

Cooke, P. (2001), 'From technopoles to regional innovation systems: the evolution of localised technology development policy', *Canadian Journal of Regional Science/Revue canadienne des sciences régionales*, **24**: 21–40.

Cooke, P. (2004), 'Regional innovation systems: an evolutionary approach', in P. Cooke, M. Heidenreich and H.-J. Braczyk (eds), *Regional Innovation Systems. The Role of Governances in a Globalized World*, London: UCL Press, pp. 1–18.

Davel, E., Dupuis, J.-P. and Chanlat, J.-F. (eds) (2008), *Gestion en contexte interculturel: approches, problématiques, pratiques et plongées*, Québec: Presse de l'Université Laval et TÉLUQ/UQAM.

Defélix, C., Retour, D. and Valette, A. (2008), 'Travailler au sein d'un pôle de compétitivité. Un défi pour la gestion des ressources humaines', in R. Beaujolin-Bellet, P. Louart and M. Parlier (eds), *Le travail. Un défi de la GRH*, Paris: Anact, pp. 174–91.

d'Iribarne, P. (1989), *La logique de l'honneur. Gestion des entreprises et traditions nationales*, Paris: Seuil.

d'Iribarne, P. (2006), *L'étrangéte française*, Paris: Seuil.

d'Iribarne, P. (2008), 'Culture et gestion en France', in E. Davel, J.-P. Dupuis and J.-F. Chanlat (eds), *Gestion en contexte interculturel: approches, problématiques, pratiques et plongées*, Québec: Presse de l'Université Laval et TÉLUQ/UQAM, Ch. V.2 (CD).

d'Iribarne, P. (2009), 'National cultures and organisations in search of a theory: an interpretative approach', *International Journal of Cross Cultural Management*, **9** (3): 309–21.

DiMaggio, P.J. and Powell, W.W. (1983), 'The iron cage revisited: institutional isomorphism and collective rationality in organizational fields', *American Sociological Review*, **48**: 147–60.

Dunning, J.H. (2000), 'Regions, globalization, and the knowledge economy: the issue stated', in J.H. Dunning (ed.), *Regions, Globalization and the Knowledge-Based Economy*, Oxford: Oxford University Press, pp. 7–41.

Edquist, C. (1997), 'Systems of innovation approaches. Their emergence and characteristics', in C. Edquist (ed.), *Systems of Innovation. Technologies, Institutions and Organizations*, London, Pinter, pp. 1–35.

Elias, N. (1983 [1969]), *Die höfische Gesellschaft*, Frankfurt am Main: Suhrkamp.

Elias, N. (1979), *Über den Prozess der Zivilisation. Soziogenetische und psycho-genetische Untersuchungen. Zweiter Band: Wandlungen der Gesellschaft. Entwurf zu einer Theorie der Zivilisation*, Frankfurt am Main: Suhrkamp.

European Commission (2007), *The 2006 EU Industrial R&D Investment Scoreboard*, Luxembourg: European Commission.

European Commission (2009), 'ERAWATCH Country Report 2008 France: An assessment of research system and policies', available at: http://www.eurosfaire. prd.fr/7pc/doc/1240907467_jrc_erawatch_france.pdf (09 February 2010).

European Commission, Enterprise Directorate-General (2008), 'INNO-Policy TrendChart – Policy Trends and Appraisal Report France 2008', available at http://www.proinno-europe.eu/extranet/upload/countryreports/Country_ Report_France_2008.pdf (30 June 2009).

Fagerberg, J. (2004), 'Innovation: a guide to the literature', in J. Fagerberg, D. Mowery and R. Nelson (eds), *Handbook of Innovation*, Oxford: Oxford University Press, pp. 1–26.

Fourastié, J. (1979), *Les trente glorieuses*, Paris: Fayard.

Gauchon, P. (2008), *Le modèle français depuis 1945. Capituler, résister, s'adapter?* Paris: PUF.

Hall, P.A. and Soskice, D. (eds) (2001), *Varieties of Capitalism: The Institutional Foundations of Comparative Advantage*, Oxford: Oxford University Press.

Hampden-Turner, C. and Trompenaars, A. (1993), *The Seven Cultures of Capitalism*, New York: Currency and Doubleday.

Hancké, B. (2001), 'Revisiting the French model: coordination and restructuring in French Industry', in P.A. Hall and D. Soskice (eds), *Varieties of Capitalism: The Institutional Foundations of Comparative Advantage*, Oxford: Oxford University Press, pp. 307–34.

Hancké, B. (2002), *Large Firms and Institutional Change: Industrial Renewal and Economic Restructuring in France*, Oxford: Oxford University Press.

Hancké, B. (ed.) (2009), *Debating Varieties of Capitalism*, Oxford: Oxford University Press.

Hartmann, M. (2007), *Eliten und Macht in Europa. Ein internationaler Vergleich*, Frankfurt: Campus.

Heidenreich, M. (2006), 'Die Organisationen der Wissensgesellschaft. Zwischen regionalem und grenzüberschreitendem Lernen', in Heinrich-Böll-Stiftung (ed.), *Die Verfasstheit der Wissensgesellschaft*, Münster: Westfälisches Dampfboot, pp. 43–56.

Heidenreich, M., Barmeyer, C. and Koschatzky, K. (2010), 'Product development in multinational companies', in P. Ahrweiler (ed.), *Innovation in Complex Social Systems*, New York: Routledge, pp. 137–49.

Hofstede, G. (1980), *Culture's Consequences. International Differences in Work-Related Values,* London: Sage Publications.

Hofstede, G. and Hofstede, G.J. (2005), *Cultures and Organizations*, New York: McGraw-Hill.

Inglehart, R. and Welzel, C. (2005), *Modernization, Cultural Change, and Democracy: the Human Development Sequence*, Cambridge: Cambridge University Press.
Jacquet, N. and Darmon, D. (2005), *Les pôles de compétitivité – le modèle français*, Paris: La documentation française.
Joly, H. (2005), *Formation des élites en France et en Allemagne*, Paris: Cirac.
Koschatzky, K. (2001), *Räumliche Aspekte im Innovationsprozess. Ein Beitrag zur neuen Wirtschaftsgeographie aus Sicht der regionalen Innovationsforschung*, Münster: LIT Verlag, Reihe Wirtschaftsgeographie.
Lamnek, S. (2005), *Qualitative Sozialforschung*, 4th edn, Weinheim and Basel: Beltz Verlags Union.
Lesourne, J. (1998), *Le modèle français. Grandeur et décadence*, Paris: Odile Jacob.
Levy, J. (1999), *Tocqueville's Revenge. State, Society, and Economy in Contemporary France*, Cambridge, MA: Harvard University Press.
Lundvall, B.-Å. (ed.) (1992), *National Systems of Innovation: Towards a Theory of Innovation and Interactive Learning*, London: Pinter Publishers.
Lundvall, B.-Å. (1999), 'National business systems and national systems of innovation', *International Studies of Management and Organization*, **29**: 60–77.
Maurice, M. (1991), 'Methodologische Aspekte internationaler Vergleiche: Zum Ansatz des gesellschaftlichen Effekts', in M. Heidenreich and G. Schmidt (eds), *International vergleichende Organisationsforschung*, Opladen: Westdeutscher Verlag, pp. 82–90.
Maurice, M., Selier, F. and Silvestre, J.-J. (1982), *Politique d'éducation et organisation industrielle en France et en Allemagne*, Paris: Presses Universitaires de France.
Mendel, G. (2002), *Une histoire de l'autorité. Permanences et variations*, Paris: La Découverte.
Muller, E., Zenker, A. and Héraud, J.-A. (2009), 'France: innovation system and innovation policy', Karlsruhe, Fraunhofer ISI, Discussion Papers 'Innovation Systems and Policy Analysis', 18.
Mustar, P. and Larédo, P. (2002), 'Innovation and research policy in France (1980–2000) or the disappearance of the Colbertist state', *Research Policy*, **21**: 55–72.
Narula, R. and Zanfei, A. (2004), 'Globalization of innovation: the role of multinational enterprises', in J. Fagerberg, D. Mowery and R. Nelson (eds), *Handbook of Innovation*, Oxford: Oxford University Press, pp. 318–48.
North, D. (1990), *Institutions, Institutional Change and Economic Performance*, Cambridge: Cambridge University Press.
OECD (1999), *Managing National Innovation Systems*, Paris: OECD.
Parsons, T. (1952), *The Social System*, New York: Free Press.
Patton, M.Q. (1987), *How to Use Qualitative Methods in Evaluation*, Newbury Park, CA: Sage Publications.
Porter, M.E. (1990), *The Competitive Advantage of Nations*, London and Basingstoke: Macmillan.
Rammert, W. (2004), 'The rising relevance of non-explicit knowledge under a new regime of knowledge production', in N. Stehr (ed.), *The Governance of Knowledge*, New Brunswick, NJ and London: Transaction Publishers, pp. 85–102.
Retour, D. (2009), 'Pôles de compétitivité, propos d'étape', *Revue Française de Gestion*, **190**: 93–9.

Roure, L. (2001), 'Product champion characteristics in France and Germany', *Human Relations*, **55**: 663–82.

Schild, J. and Uterwedde, H. (2006), *Frankreich: Politik, Wirtschaft, Gesellschaft*, Wiesbaden: VS Verlag.

Sölvell, Ö., Lindquist, G. and Ketels, C. (2003), *The Cluster Initiative Greenbook*, Stockholm: Ivory Tower.

Waarts, E. and van Everdingen, Y. (2005), 'The influence of national culture on the adoption status of innovations: an empirical study of firms across Europe', *European Management Journal*, **23**: 601–10.

Weil, T. and Fen Chong, S. (2008), 'Les pôles de compétitivité français', *Futuribles*, **342**: 5–27.

Whitley, R. (ed.) (2002), *Competing Capitalisms: Institutions and Economics*, Cheltenham, UK and Northampton, MA, USA: Edward Elgar.

12. Multinational companies and the production of collective goods in Central and Eastern Europe[1]

Bob Hancké

The comparative study of capitalism has, since the publication of the *Varieties of Capitalism* volume (Hall and Soskice, 2001), directed attention to market and strategic coordination as the critical variables that differentiate (as ideal types) liberal and coordinated market economies (LMEs and CMEs) – and beyond. Business coordination can help us to understand how France adjusted (Hancké, 2002) after failing to reinvent itself along CME lines (Culpepper, 2001). It is a useful perspective to make sense of the development of Latin American political economies (Ross-Schneider and Soskice, 2009) and of the economic organization of Mediterranean countries (Molina and Rhodes, 2007). In its 'negative' version, lamenting the absence of domestic business coordination – or at least some of its proto-institutional forms such as high trust or social capital (Stiglitz, 2000; Levy, 1999) – as a condition for economic upgrading, business coordination is an equally crucial variable in understanding divergent outcomes. All these views share the underlying idea that business coordination is exogenously given, usually handed down through history, or – conversely – destroyed under particular historical conditions. Hall and Soskice (2001) are relatively silent on the origins of coordination, and Hancké et al. (2007) explore these to some extent, but ultimately conclude in favour of the historical hypothesis. Whilst the argument in Feldmann (2007) is more dynamic – transition policies in Estonia had a network-destroying and in Slovenia a network-preserving effect, two pathways that he causally relates to the absence or presence of business coordination in these countries – his analysis also underscores the importance of historical junctures and irreversibilities.

Whilst business coordinating capacity certainly is a relatively scarce semi-institutional good, such a historically deterministic perspective has unfortunate implications: in the limiting instance, business coordination becomes, for those who think of it as a worthwhile asset, a bit like a rich uncle: nice to have, but there is not much you can do about it if you do not (cf. Levy, 1999). If a political economy missed the *rendez-vous* with business coordination at a critical juncture or destroyed existing or incipient forms of business coordination for whatever political reason, it seems to have lost this chance for ever. As a result of these obstacles to building business coordinating capacity endogenously, nations are likely to drift from low and medium levels of strategic coordination into a position approximating pure market coordination. Since deregulating an institutional framework that supports business coordination is considerably easier than building it, political–economic adjustment will follow a neoliberal path by default when faced with inconsistent and often underperforming institutions (Hall and Gingerich, 2009) – true in continental Western Europe, but possibly even more so in Central Europe, where nominally neoliberal policies forced these new capitalist nations on to a path of rapid market making without the concomitant (welfare-)state making (Innes, 2010).

This chapter addresses this problem of what I call 'endogenous coordination' through an analysis of industrial upgrading in Central Europe. The theoretical ambition of this chapter is modest, but its implications might be wide-ranging. If building business coordination capacity is as difficult as it appears, then demonstrating the empirical possibility of endogenous coordination, and identifying conditions under which it emerged, shifts the debate from pessimistic necessitarianism to a more optimistic world of possibility – particularly in early 2000s Central Europe, not necessarily a very fertile breeding ground for such complex institutional arrangements. My empirical focus is on the complex engineering sector in Central Europe – the regional economy that encompasses most of the Czech Republic, south-west Poland, western Slovakia and north-western Hungary, an area dominated by large foreign multinational companies (MNCs). The rapid and massive re-industrialization of these highly FDI-dependent, neo-capitalist political economies offers a laboratory to study the emergence of potentially different forms of capitalism and market organization (see also Nölke and Vliegenthart, 2009). It thus also allows us to compare different forms of emergent market and strategic coordination. The chapter identifies instances of inter-firm coordination of the type that Hall and Soskice (2001) address as 'strategic' (i.e. non-market) and analytically examines the conditions under which they emerged. Since these forms of strategic coordination came into existence in institutional environments that had historically been 'thin' and in regions and countries where states and private associations were weak but foreign MNCs very strong, I call the emergent form of coordination 'endogenous' – not primarily given by history or imposed from the outside, but following from the way MNCs rationally pursue their interests in the region. The main purpose of this chapter is to retrace and analyse the conditions under which such endog-enous forms of business coordination can occur.

The first part of this chapter examines the profiles of re-industrialization in different CEE economies since the mid-1990s and distills two broad economic development patterns, each with very different strategic impli-cations for firms in those economies. Second, since these patterns of 'complex' versus 'basic' industrialization result in different levels of asset specificity and therefore of fixed costs, they present both labour, and espe-cially capital, with very different time horizons. When faced with bottle-necks in the production of collective goods such as skills and regional technological capacity, firms therefore run into classic collective action problems. These problems – the third step in the argument – are resolved through non-firm actors that provide forums for deliberation and strategic coordination. In the concluding section I shall discuss these conditions for endogenous coordination in a more analytical form.

12.1 LEADING SECTORS AND COMPARATIVE INSTITUTIONAL ADVANTAGE

The post-1989 re-industrialization of Central Europe is in essence a story of the crucial role of foreign direct investment (FDI). Foreign capital, as the history of recent industrializations in other parts of the world such as Latin America and Southern Europe suggests, can produce very dif-ferent outcomes, ranging from relatively benign developmental effects to uncontrollable extra-governmental powers that locate in newly industrial-izing areas in order to exploit significant (wage) cost advantages. Central Europe initially was no exception. Even though before the late 1980s some market-seeking logic may have been at the basis of activity of MNCs in Central Europe, there is little doubt that the post-1989 investments were primarily guided by the low wage, tax and other cost advantages of the region relative to Western Europe. However, since productivity levels were low and basic infrastructural networks weak in the early and mid-1990s, many medium-sized Western firms in search of cheap labour quickly retreated to the home base after discovering that context conditions were considerably less beneficial than initially thought.

Large companies faced a different set of constraints when locating abroad in this under-industrialized region: their weight relative to the local and national economies where they settled allowed them to negotiate from a position of strength with local and national authorities, their financial autonomy allowed them to internalize costs as well as benefits and their long-term links with other firms allowed them to build a state-of-the-art

---

BOX 12.1 LEADING SECTORS

'Complex' sectors

- **Light–complex**: only human capital intensive: e.g. pharmaceuticals, office and data processing machines, electrical machinery, scientific equipment, optical goods, clocks
- **Heavy–complex**: intensive in both physical and human capital intensive: e.g. chemicals, machinery and equipment, road vehicles and transport equipment

'Basic' sectors

- **Light–basic**: intensive neither in physical nor human capital, but unskilled labour: e.g. cork and wood, textile, rubber, furniture manufacturing, clothing and accessories and footwear
- **Heavy–basic**: intensive only in physical capital: e.g. food, live animals, beverages and tobacco, fuels, vegetable oils, iron and steel, pulp and paper, non-ferrous metals

Source: Greskovits (2005).

---

supplier network by bringing other firms along. MNCs, furthermore, can cross-subsidize a few years of losses in new operations if they assume that strategic gains lie further down the road.

A careful comparison of foreign investment in and export profiles of different CEE member states, based on the asset-specificity typology that Greskovits (2005) has constructed, suggests quite convincingly that broadly speaking two very different production profiles, related to different leading sectors, have emerged in the region over the last 10–15 years. The typology is based on the degree to which industries are labour or capital intensive, and, dichotomizing the positions for both factors of production, leads to four types, which are summarized in Box 12.1: intensive (a) only in physical capital; (b) in both physical and human capital; (c) only in human capital; and (d) in neither physical nor human capital but unskilled labour. In the following these factor combinations are referred to as (a) heavy–basic; (b) heavy–complex; (c) light–complex; and (d) light–basic profiles (Greskovits, 2005; Bohle and Greskovits, 2007). Two very

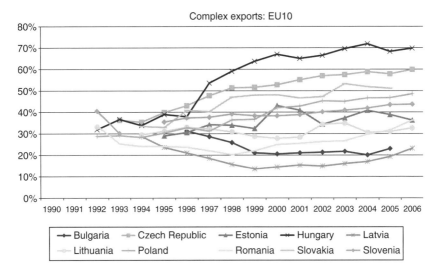

Source: UN COMTRADE (2007). Own calculations.

Figure 12.1 The evolution of leading sectors in Central Europe

different production profiles thus emerged: the 'complex' sectors relying on relatively complex technologies and sophisticated skills, while 'basic' sectors do considerably less so.

Using this typology as a perspective to look at re-industrialization and investment, Central Europe in particular shows a remarkable differentiation across the region. As Figure 12.1 demonstrates, Slovenia and the Visegrád 4 (Czech Republic, Poland, Hungary and Slovakia) have increasingly specialized in complex export industries, while in the others (the Baltic states and south-eastern Europe) heavy–basic and light–basic profiles dominate. In the V4 and Slovenia at least 40 per cent of their exports – and usually considerably more – over the last ten years consisted of complex goods; 40 per cent appears to have become the ceiling for complex product exports in the remaining countries. In addition, the trajectories of the V4 and Slovenia contrast sharply with the Baltics and south-eastern Europe (SEE). In the first group, the share of complex products in exports rises almost immediately after the transition recession of the early 1990s, while that share first fell in the other group and began to rise only toward the end of the decade, and then only slowly. While it may be too early to treat these different outcomes as stable, there are reasons to believe that it is very difficult for the Baltics and SEE to catch up with the V4 in terms of the importance of complex manufacturing. The initial wave of investment in CEE seems to have produced significant network externalities: complex manufacturing is likely to locate where other companies with a similar profile are already located because they can draw on existing collective competition goods. The western parts of Central Europe are now the new industrial heartland for medium-tech complex goods, such as cars and light engineering. The region produces more cars per capita than anywhere else in Europe and possibly the world, and a sophisticated supplier network has emerged, particularly in the centrally located Czech Republic.

12.2 FROM LOW-WAGE LOCATION TO HIGH-VALUE-ADDED MANUFACTURING

Most (possibly all) multinationals settled in the region in search of low labour costs – in the early 1990s, wages in Central Europe were considerably below wage levels in the West, and even controlling for productivity, which was lower in CEE, wage costs remained significantly below Western levels. Moreover, many companies were aware of the relatively high skill levels prevailing in CEE: even though the pre-1989 production and productivity statistics turned out to be deeply misleading, and Central Europe was not quite the industrial powerhouse that many Westerners had thought for several decades, training systems in many Central European countries often were adopted during the Habsburg period and therefore resembled the (west) German skill formation system. In addition, many governments made an effort, in an attempt to rapidly re-industrialize, to attract foreign capital through privatizations and especially tax holidays and subsidies (often supported by the EU's PHARE programme). Add to this the high unemployment rates, which made recruitment of skilled labour a relatively easy task and produced a relatively docile workforce happy to have a job at all in the rapidly unraveling Central European labour market, and there is little doubt that the multinationals' motivations may have been severely skewed towards low costs. This location strategy of MNCs was reflected in the initial low relative unit values (RUV) of the products they produced.[2] Taking the case of the automotive sector, CEE started at an RUV level that was less than one-fifth of the EU average in the early 1990s, and in the car industry specifically only about a quarter of the unit value relative to production in Spain and Portugal (Scepanovic, 2008).

By the year 2000, however, a break with this underlying model occurred, both in the automotive sector and beyond. This break has been true for industrial production of export goods in general, going beyond the automotive sector. Between 1992 and 1994, the export profiles of the different countries in CEE, as expressed in the proportion of complex products in total exports, were and remained remarkably similar (cf. Figure 12.1). Even as late as 1996, in practically none of the V4 did complex products account for more than 40 per cent of total exports, and the differences between the high-value-added and the low-value-added exporters remained relatively narrow for another few years. By 1998 the different profiles had become established and for several years these differences became more pronounced (before a slow upward move among the low-complexity exporters beginning after 2003).

The upgraded export profile is sustained by an upward technological shift in product (and process) profiles. Many of the multinationals, especially in the motor vehicle and related industries, shifted their production profile away from the relatively low-end, low-value-added cars that they had been making to the high to mid-end first, and high-end cars and car parts afterwards. Volkswagen (VW) was the front-runner: by 2000, production in Škoda moved up from the low-tech Favorit to the sophisticated Octavia and Fabia, with more R&D autonomy for the years to come. Similarly, the VW factory in Bratislava shifted production from the entry-level VW Polo to the high-end sport utility vehicles (SUV) variably known as Audi Q7, VW Touareg or Porsche Cayenne; and Audi engine production in the Hungarian Györ has become one of the world's leading engine producers (Janovskaia, 2007). At about the same time, sophisticated multinational complex systems suppliers such as Bosch, Valeo, VDO and Delphi entered the region: by 2007, the Czech Republic was home to around 200 of them. Several of these – such as Siemens, VDO and TRW – set up R&D centres in the country (Janovskaia, 2007). Overall, as Scepanovic (2008) suggests, the RUV of the car industry in CEE converged on and by 2002 slightly surpassed that of the Iberian peninsula (Figure 12.2).[3]

Whatever was at the basis of this slow but unmistakable upgrading process in the car industry specifically and in complex industries in general in the V4, the effects have been important. Upgrading has several components that have to move in tandem in order for them to have the desired effect: skills need to be redefined and their acquisition organized, technology upgraded, supplier networks need to move and infrastructure needs to be upgraded. While some of these processes are well within the control of the upgrading companies (especially capital investment), supplier links and infrastructure are less so. But the most interesting area is possibly in skills: the collapse of the firm-based training systems, the lack of public investment in education for a decade after 1989, the temporary emigration of a large section of the relevant young cohort and the massive entry of foreign companies have turned a region that originally had an abundance of skilled labour into a region where significant skills shortages exist. The rapid and large-scale process of upgrading produced strategic bottlenecks

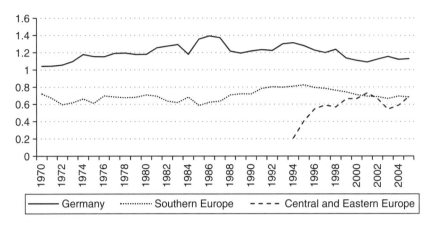

Source: UN COMTRADE; Scepanovic (2008).

Figure 12.2   Evolution of the relative unit value of exports of motor vehicles

that could not easily be resolved through a combination of public policies and deep (private and public) pockets. These bottlenecks and the interesting and surprising solutions they produce are the topic of the next section.

12.3   EMERGING FORMS OF INTERFIRM COORDINATION

MNCs in the V4 are therefore on the whole very different from their counterparts in the other Central European states. Foreign direct investment in the region had a high degree of asset specificity, and much of the investment in complex production led to high fixed costs. A plant in the automotive, chemical or steel industries is highly capital-intensive, and often requires a relatively long (>10–15 year) period for the investment to be written off. Precisely because such investments can only be realized over the medium to long run, these companies are unlikely to rapidly relocate in new lower-cost jurisdictions, since that would mean foregoing the gains from the initial investment. In sum, the V4 and to some extent Slovenia thus seem to have attracted long-term, 'rooted' FDI that brings better jobs and pushes economies upwards, while the others appear to have attracted companies with a much more footloose capital structure and relatively short-term amortization periods, which allow them to relocate rapidly without incurring tremendous costs as a result of non-realized investment.

Companies may initially have decided to invest in Central Europe because of low labour costs, but around the turn of the century they started to discover the problems associated with that strategy. The most important one was that, as the Central European economies became more integrated in the EU economy, wages slowly started to rise alongside productivity. Trade unions appear careful (or too weak) not to negotiate inflationary wage settlements, and in fact still negotiate below-productivity wage increases in most V4 countries, but real wages in the export sector in the V4 have none the less increased substantially over the last decade. Another, related, issue was that companies began to face skill bottlenecks as the result of two mutually reinforcing processes. As more foreign companies took advantage of the beneficial labour market conditions in CEE, and an often large part of the relevant age groups sought employment outside their country of origin, the number of available workers fell rapidly. Second, companies lacked adequately qualified labour due to the complete (Poland) or partial (Slovakia, Czech Republic) dismantling of vocational and technical training systems that had been established before 1989. Finally, the remnants of vocational and technical training have been simply inadequate for the industrialization trajectory that the V4 have adopted, since they are organized along the traditional Soviet-era industrial lines emphasizing the skills for *heavy–basic* instead of *complex* industries.

The effect of these different pressures has been that the level of specific skills in younger age cohorts, and particularly those of the type that such fast-growing high-value-added export sectors require, has fallen rapidly. A similar development took place in the relations with suppliers: a large multinational firm in an assembly-based industry such as automobiles and consumer goods is ultimately only as good as its suppliers – of which there were few indigenous ones left after 1989. For a while firms avoided these types of bottlenecks by importing the necessary parts from the West, but transportation costs made such a strategy at best a temporary stop-gap. Thus large firms were forced to negotiate with their suppliers how they would settle in CEE or arrange for domestic firms to upgrade their operations and become suppliers.

The solutions to these bottlenecks – resolving the skills shortage and technical upgrading of suppliers – led to well-known collective action problems. The problem takes its paradigmatic form in the area of skills: if company A sets up an in-house training programme to alleviate the skill shortages it experiences, then company B has a strong incentive *not* to do the same and instead poach the workers trained by A – which leaves A, in an open labour market (i.e. assuming that skills are to a large degree transferable and workers free to change jobs), with only two options: either abandon training (lest the company subsidizes training among its competitors); or cooperate with B. The first option, which leads to a low-skill equilibrium, is far from optimal (though not unheard of, as Finegold and Soskice, 1988 analyse for the UK); the result is that A abandons the training system and thus gradually ceases production as skills dry up. But the medium- to long-term investment horizon of the newly established companies in CEE makes that a very unfavourable move: unless A is willing to divest after only a few years and thus incur significantly negative returns on its investment, A is forced to stay in the market. The alternative option – cooperation – is therefore a considerably more attractive one, but this one runs into the standard problem that in the absence of binding sanctions neither A nor B will contribute to the public good that skills have *de facto* become. The stalemate that ensues as a result of this failure to provide public goods is, other things being equal, impossible to overcome without a third party enforcing cooperation, a role usually played by the state or private associations in most OECD countries. Yet governments have been reluctant to play such a *dirigiste* role in the labour market of most CEE economies, and the few attempts to build non-state associational governance mechanisms to handle these types of collective action problems (by making membership of industry chambers compulsory, for example) were abandoned quickly in most of the places where they were tried.

The growth in production volume in the region implied that (even when correcting for productivity growth) labour force growth was significantly below the needs of the many MNCs locating in the central region of the V4. Being large operations, car plants often rapidly depleted the available skilled workforce (*a fortiori* when they located in the same area with a relatively tight labour market to begin with) and they faced the skills bottleneck earlier than companies in other industries would. The solution to this hard constraint has been that car assembly plants, especially VW, which was one of the earliest Western investors in the region, have started recruiting workers from a slightly wider area and train them themselves. But other companies have also increasingly located in the region, usually as a result of the positive network externalities associated with being a second mover: they benefit from the policies and institutions that the first mover and local governments have put in place without having to invest in them. In Slovakia, for example, VW has been recruiting and training workers from 50–60 km away and bussing them into the Bratislava area. When Peugeot (PSA) opened a car plant in the area of Trnava a few years later, most of the workers quite reasonably preferred to work close to home over the daily trip to Bratislava. VW thus not only implicitly trained workers for PSA but also failed to resolve the key problem at the basis of the reinstatement of firm-level training, since it lost its trained workers to PSA. The solution was found in the construction of a complex network of non-market private actors that offered VW a chance to negotiate cooperation directly with PSA. VW used its strong relations with the local German chamber of commerce to open conversations with the French chamber first – thus opening indirect communication with PSA – and other chambers, especially the Slovak and the American chambers, afterwards. Once agreement on cooperation had been reached between the main companies, these chambers then set out to organize a *de facto* industry-wide training system with them – and acted as enforcers, less by stick than by carrot – using their economic clout to induce the local and national governments to fill in the institutional and policy holes (such as the provision of basic general industry skills and skill certification).

As the circumstances have forced major multinational firms to react to the issue, the process has seen an evolution from worker poaching in the case of PSA Trnava and VW Bratislava to different forms of coordination. Companies did not turn to existing institutions and organizations (which were largely absent anyway) but started building voluntarist forms of private network arrangements. These networks take different forms, but they usually seem to involve local chambers of commerce of the FDI-sending and of the FDI-receiving countries, local and regional authorities, and sometimes central support from, for example, the Ministries of Labour, Education or Economic Affairs. The role of the chambers of commerce is perhaps the most surprising: since many of the companies were large firms (often of German origin), which were privileged partners of the local (German) chamber, they used this institutional vehicle to build links with other companies, not directly but through the different chambers, asking them to provide a cooperative framework that increased and secured contributions by individual companies to the collective good. These proto-institutional frameworks built around the chambers and the large foreign investors became the building blocks for local forms of coordinated problem solving in which collective goods – club goods, in fact, but often with spillovers into the rest of the local economies – were produced and access to them was regulated through these governance networks.

Coordination can therefore be constructed *de novo*, but this process mirrors the collective action dynamics associated with industrial upgrading in other CMEs such as Germany and Japan. Inter-firm coordination emerges when a third party has the ability to enforce (at least in the limiting case) compliance with the arrangement that produces the public good.

To a large extent international chambers of commerce (ICCs) can rely on carrots for this soft form of enforcement: since the MNCs depend on them for many important but often intangible services and local representation, they will also look favourably upon requests by ICCs to resolve a bottleneck problem. But there appears to be more to this than simple goodwill. ICCs actually play a crucial role in informal dispute settlement through mediation between MNCs and local suppliers: contract enforcement through courts may take several years, is unpredictable and therefore something MNCs would, *ceteris paribus*, prefer to avoid. ICCs offer mediation services that allow the problem to be resolved quickly – as a result the vast majority of disputes (some informal estimates suggest up to 98 per cent!) pass through the ICCs rather than through local courts. This club good is the sanctioning capacity that supports the carrot when ICCs try to negotiate a collective solution to training bottlenecks.

12.4　CONCLUSION

By the middle of the first decade of the 2000s embryonic forms of strategic coordination between MNCs were emerging in CEE, one of the places where such informal collective arrangements would *ex ante* seem highly unlikely. MNCs located there for very egoistic, possibly even relatively short-sighted cost-related reasons, governments and non-market actors appeared too weak to push for such forms of business coordination and inter-firm cooperation, and constructing this type of coordination is, in general terms, considerably more difficult – possibly impossible – than destroying it. This outcome was, somewhat ironically, linked to the nature of FDI in the region itself. Greskovits (2005) has drawn our attention to what he calls 'thorough versus shallow' paths of industrialization. The crucial operational difference between these two models of industrialization can, in more analytical language, be captured in the time horizons that foreign investors face. In the case of 'shallow' industrialization, the part of investment made up by fixed costs is small, and capital is, as a result, highly mobile; in the case of 'thorough' restructuring, the part of fixed costs is high, capital is therefore considerably less mobile, and the structural asymmetry *vis-à-vis* labour and suppliers is substantially mitigated: problems that occur simply have to be resolved, and that often includes negotiations with workers and their representatives in industries such as the automotive industry, and with suppliers and regional authorities. In short, high set-up costs limit exit options of firms; as a result they cannot simply leave when faced with bottlenecks, but have to weigh the costs of divesting against the costs associated with resolving the problems that the bottlenecks produce. When production profiles become more asset-specific, as they seem to have done in the last decade in the region and especially in the industry examined above, both the costs incurred as a result of problems associated with bottlenecks and the relative costs of divesting rise steeply.

This particular arrangement, which ties capital locally after an initial investment, is at the basis of the emerging modes of inter-firm coordination in Central Europe that are documented in this chapter. If the relative advantages of problem solving outweigh other considerations, companies are, all other things being equal (which they can be taken to be in this particular case), prone to engage in problem solving. However, in the absence of existing local or national policies and institutions that provide a blueprint or at least a policy matrix that companies can draw on, they are forced to solve problems on their own. The issue then is that the solution to a problem that one company is trying to resolve is likely to produce positive externalities for other companies – in effect, the solution has the key characteristics of a collective good: it is non-rival and excludability is low. Under those conditions, as we know since Olson, the good is not produced or consumption of the good is subject to selective incentive mechanisms. Due to the small number of actors, the second is highly possible – but hard to build in the absence of external institutions. This is where coordination across firms comes in (see Hall and Soskice, 2001 for the general argument). If a small number of firms can be persuaded that cooperation to produce a good is both in the individual and the collective interest, they are likely to contribute. However, for that to happen, some deliberative mechanism has to be in place that allows them to agree on a joint initiative (remember that the state is too weak to offer this on its own). This mechanism is provided by the ICCs, whose reputation allows them to nudge MNCs into cooperation and whose exclusive provision of a club good that is crucial for the MNCs gives that nudge some bite.

What, then, does this analysis suggest regarding the conditions for such forms of endogenous coordination? Two conditions appear crucial – and combined they point toward a third mechanism. The first is a high level of asset specificity in both capital and labour. High asset specificity implies that capital, usually the more mobile factor of production, has high fixed costs, and that both therefore face a more or less equally long-term time horizon to realize their investment. The second is that local bottlenecks have to emerge that threaten this investment – in the form of skill bottlenecks in the example in this chapter or underdeveloped supplier links. The ensuing coordination problems are resolved through the involvement of a third party that wields influence and sanctioning power. The outcome is that, as MNCs rationally pursue their self-interest, they are forced to produce islands of non-market coordination. Both these conditions appear necessary for endogenous coordination to emerge. In cases of low asset specificity, as in France in the 1980s (Hancké, 2002), coordination did not increase; instead, large firms unilaterally imposed modernization paths. And if the bottlenecks disappear, as they seem to have done in the depressed economic climate of the 2008–09 crisis when unemployment rose sharply, levels of inter-firm coordination dropped dramatically in response.

Endogenous strategic coordination between large firms is therefore, and somewhat surprisingly, possible without a battery of historical conditions present, even in circumstances where it is highly unlikely to emerge, as in Central Europe in the middle of the first decade of the 2000s. However, the historical hypothesis correctly suggests that strategic coordination can be a highly asymmetric process. While building coordination requires a complex set of conditions, destroying it can be relatively simple, with small changes in the environment jeopardizing this fragile process, and thus undermining its sustainability. Having identified some of the necessary conditions for strategic coordination to emerge without a supporting history, that begs the question how such benign processes can be sustained in the absence of historical frameworks conducive to sustainability.

NOTES

1. This chapter is based on material in Bob Hancké and Lucia Kurekova, 'Varieties of capitalism and economic governance in Central Europe'. Final report for Project CIT1-CT-2004-506392 (NewGov STACEE), September 2008 (www.eu-newgov.org/database/DELIV/D20D09_Final_Report_STACEE.pdf). Comments from participants in the workshop that led to this volume, in the EGOS colloquium in Amsterdam July 2008, and at a PERG seminar at the Central European University in October 2007, as well as from Bela Greskovits, Lucia Kurekova, Gunnar Trumbull and Michel Goyer are gratefully acknowledged.
2. The formula to calculate the RUV is: (Total value of exports in sector A for region X/total volume in units of exports in sector A for region X) / (Total value of EU exports in sector A/total volume in units of EU exports in sector A). RUV is a proxy to measure the degree of sophistication and value of the exported products, correcting for the endogenous developments within and cyclicality of the industry as a whole.
3. It is too early to tell exactly why the V4 appear able to avoid the low-value-added path in which Southern Europe seems to be caught. One of the difficulties is that the key elements were very similar in both regions: low wages, a rapid transition, attraction of FDI through targeted government policies and relatively weak labour unions. In fact, from a slightly broader political–economic perspective, conditions for an upward product market shift were possibly better in the Iberian peninsula: some recent acquaintance with capitalism (as opposed to a planned economy), a rapid expansion of government into the economy after 1975 and a more active stance with regard to supply-side policies afterwards (Boix, 1998; Smith, 1998), and trade unions that had been associated with opposition to the dictatorships instead of (with the exception of Poland) the transmission belts that unions often were in CEE.

REFERENCES

Bohle, D. and Greskovits, B. (2007), 'Neoliberalism, embedded neoliberalism and neocorporatism: towards transnational capitalism in Central and Eastern Europe', *West European Politics*, **30**: 433–66.

Boix, C. (1998), *Political Parties, Growth and Equality: Conservative and Social Democratic Economic Strategies in the World Economy*, Cambridge: Cambridge University Press.

Culpepper, P. (2001), 'Employers, public policy and the politics of decentralised cooperation in Germany and France', in P. Hall and D. Soskice (eds), *Varieties of Capitalism: The Institutional Foundations of Comparative Advantage*, Oxford: Oxford University Press, pp. 275–306.

Feldmann, M. (2007), 'The origins of varieties of capitalism: lessons from post-socialist transition in Estonia and Slovenia', in B. Hancké, M. Rhodes and M. Thatcher (eds), *Beyond Varieties of Capitalism: Conflict, Contradictions and Complementarities in the European Economy*, Oxford: Oxford University Press, pp. 328–50.

Finegold, D. and Soskice, D.W. (1988), 'The failure of training in Britain: analysis and prescription', *Oxford Review of Economic Policy*, **4**: 21–53.

Greskovits, B. (2005), 'Leading sectors and the varieties of capitalism in Eastern Europe', *Actes de Gerpisa*, **39**: 113–28.

Hall, P. and Gingerich, D. (2009), 'Varieties of capitalism and institutional complementarities in the political economy: an empirical analysis', *British Journal of Political Science*, **39**: 449–82.

Hall, P. and Soskice, D. (2001) (eds), *Varieties of Capitalism: The Institutional Foundations of Comparative Advantage*, Oxford: Oxford University Press.

Hancké, B. (2002), *Large Firms and Institutional Change: Industrial Renewal and Economic Restructuring in France*, Oxford: Oxford University Press.

Hancké, B., Rhodes, M. and Thatcher, M. (eds) (2007), *Beyond Varieties of Capitalism: Conflict, Contradictions and Complementarities in the European Economy*, Oxford: Oxford University Press.

Innes, A. (2010), 'Are democratic welfare states compatible with emerging markets? Evidence from Central Europe', manuscript, London School of Economics.

Janovskaia, A. (2007), 'Industrial upgrading in the automotive MNC subsidiaries in Central Europe: the case of the VW Group', manuscript, London School of Economics.

Levy, J. (1999), *Toqueville's Revenge. Dilemmas of institutional reform in post-dirigiste France*, Cambridge, MA: Harvard University Press.

Molina, O. and Rhodes, M. (2007), 'The political economy of adjustment in mixed market economies: a study of Spain and Italy', in B. Hancké, M. Rhodes and M. Thatcher (eds), *Beyond Varieties of Capitalism: Conflict, Contradictions and Complementarities in the European Economy*, Oxford: Oxford University Press, pp. 223–52.

Nölke, A. and Vliegenthart, A. (2009), 'Enlarging the varieties of capitalism: the emergence of dependent market economies in East Central Europe', *World Politics*, **61**: 670–702.

Ross-Schneider, B. and Soskice, D. (2009), 'Inequality in developed countries and Latin America: coordinated, liberal and hierarchical systems', *Economy and Society*, **38**: 17–52.

Scepanovic, V. (2008), 'Varieties of foreign-led industrialisation: comparison of automobile industry development in East Central and Southern Europe', Department of Political Science, Central European University, PhD Dissertation Prospectus.

Smith, W.R. (1998), *The Left's Dirty Job: The Politics of Industrial Restructuring in France and Spain*, Pittsburgh, PA: University of Pittsburgh Press.

Stiglitz, J. (2000), 'Whither reform? Ten years of the transition', Keynote Address, Annual World Bank Conference on Development.

UN Comtrade (2007), United Nations Commodity Trade Statistics Database (http://comtrade.un.org/db).

13. The role of multinational corporations in the national innovation systems of the EU new member states

Rajneesh Narula and José Guimón

13.1 INTRODUCTION

In analyses of the role of multinational corporations (MNCs) in national innovation systems, much of the literature focuses on the subject of foreign direct investment (FDI) and on knowledge flows taking place through equity relationships, be it between the parent and the subsidiary or among the partners of a transnational joint venture. For the purposes of this chapter we take a broader perspective – that of the MNC and the linkages it creates. Indeed, MNCs develop a variety of other informal and non-equity agreements to engage in knowledge exchange, including trade of products and services, technology licensing, strategic partnerships, technological collaboration and so on. Moreover, FDI should be interpreted not as a discrete, single-period flow, but as a multi-period building up of FDI stock through deepening and spreading of value-adding activities, not all of which occur as a consequence of new flows of foreign capital (Narula and Dunning, 2010). Thus, rather than FDI flows, the subsequent evolution of MNC subsidiaries should be the focus of attention. This is especially true when the objective is to attract the R&D investments of MNCs, since generally firms engage in R&D abroad either sequentially or through the acquisition of an existing foreign entity, but rarely through greenfield FDI (Costa and Filippov, 2008; Guimón, 2009).

The pervasive role of MNCs in a globalizing world and their ability to utilize technological resources located elsewhere makes the use of purely national systems of innovation approach rather limiting (Narula and Zanfei, 2005). National innovation systems are becoming more integrated in global innovation networks and more dependent on foreign sources of knowledge. Indeed, MNCs undertake the bulk of global R&D

expenditure and their R&D activity is gradually evolving from a centralized and hierarchical function towards one that builds upon a network of geographically dispersed R&D centres (Jaruzelski and Dehoff, 2008). R&D-intensive FDI was initially closely connected to the internationalization of manufacturing operations and driven primarily by the adaptation of products and processes to overseas markets (Mansfield et al., 1979), but in recent years tapping into foreign sources of knowledge and specialized clusters has become a more important motivation behind the expansion of global innovation networks (Carlsson, 2006). Another recent trend is the higher involvement of emerging economies – especially China and India – in the global innovation networks of MNCs, which in the past were more constrained to developed countries (Bruche, 2009; Puga and Trefler, 2010).

The impact of MNCs in national innovation systems unfolds through a variety of direct and indirect effects that often lead to net benefits, but also entail some risks (Cantwell and Piscitello, 2000; Carlsson, 2006; Görg and Strobl, 2001; Narula and Dunning, 2010). The direct benefits are associated with increased R&D activity and employment, while the indirect benefits generally arise through linkages and knowledge spillovers, and can be characterized as a process of 'learning-through-interacting' with MNC subsidiaries.

However, the constituents of national innovation systems need a certain level of absorptive capacity to be able to benefit from the indirect effects associated with the R&D activity of MNCs (Cohen and Levinthal, 1989). Indeed, from a growth and learning perspective, externalities matter only if they can be captured by other economic actors in the host economy. For externalities to be optimally utilized there needs to be an appropriate match between the nature of potential externalities and the absorptive capacities of domestic actors.

Moreover, the potential impact on the national innovation system depends on the entry mode of FDI. In particular, when FDI in R&D occurs through the acquisition of an R&D-intensive national firm by a foreign entity, the only short-term effect for the host country is a change of ownership, while in the medium to long run there is a trade-off between the potential for expansion and indirect benefits on the one hand, and the risk that the foreign acquirer ends up downgrading the subsidiary's R&D mandate to avoid duplication with other existing units on the other hand. Therefore the mode of entry is an important factor to consider in impact evaluation and policy formulation. While most governments are eager to attract greenfield FDI in R&D, many are often reluctant towards FDI in R&D through international acquisitions and may opt for technonationalistic policies oriented to the protection of national champions

(Archibugi and Iammarino, 1999; Cantwell et al., 2004; Ostry and Nelson, 1995).

An additional concern is the perceived loss of control over domestic innovative capacity, leading to a higher dependence and vulnerability of the national innovation system. In some instances the R&D of MNCs may come at the expense of a 'crowding-out' effect whereby innovative domestic firms are displaced by foreign-owned MNC subsidiaries. This is not only the case in the product market but also in the factor market: foreign presence might damage the technological competitiveness of local firms through intensified competition for scarce assets, including financial and human capital (Girma et al., 2001; Meyer-Krahmer and Reger, 1999). In other cases complementarity between domestic and MNC activity may produce a 'crowding-in' – rather than a crowding-out – effect. For example, if the national innovation system is specialized in basic research, the entry of MNCs that conduct applied research may activate the system's latent capabilities and increase the commercial orientation of innovative efforts (Manea and Pearce, 2001).

In sum, it cannot be affirmed that MNCs consistently contribute to the upgrading of domestic clusters rather than to reducing their long-run potential (Rugman and Verbeke, 2008). The benefits for national innovation systems will be larger when MNCs engage in projects that contribute to enhancing domestic technological strengths and location-specific assets (Pearce, 2004). Thus the role of MNCs in national innovation systems should be interpreted in relation to the current structure and developmental aspirations of host countries. It is also essential to analyse impacts from a dynamic perspective. For example, Barrios et al. (2005) found that in Ireland a negative competition effect initially prevailed, leading to the exit of domestic competitors, but over time this was gradually outweighed by other positive externalities deriving from linkages and spillovers. This means that crowding-out was eventually followed by crowding-in. However, this virtuous circle depends upon the ability of countries to match FDI with domestic capacity building.

It is against this background that we analyse the case of the ten new member states (NMS) from Central and Eastern Europe that joined the European Union (EU) in 2004 (Czech Republic, Estonia, Hungary, Latvia, Lithuania, Poland, Slovakia and Slovenia) and 2007 (Bulgaria and Romania).[1] These countries share certain key features that can realistically constitute the basis for some common impact evaluation and policy recommendations. We contrast this group with the 'core' and 'cohesion' countries of the EU. The core countries (Austria, Belgium, Denmark, Finland, France, Germany, Italy, Luxembourg, Netherlands, Sweden and the UK) are the most important markets and the most advanced technologically, and thus presumably the most likely to benefit from the internationalization of corporate R&D. Cohesion countries joined the EU in the 1970s and 1980s and consist of Greece, Ireland, Portugal and Spain. These countries have benefited from large amounts of EU funds and have been engaged in a process of convergence with the core countries in the last two decades, with different degrees of success. They are also somehow peripheral within the EU, although arguably to a lesser extent than the NMS.

The rest of this chapter further explores the role of MNCs in the national innovation systems of the NMS, contrasting the current situation with the past and with the situation in other EU countries. Section 13.2 analyses the transformations in the national innovation systems of the NMS that occurred as a result of the transition from a socialist to a market system and of the subsequent integration into the EU. Section 13.3 focuses on the role of MNCs and the challenges that lie ahead in the post-EU-accession era with regard to enhancing their developmental impact. Finally, section 13.4 summarizes some conclusions and policy implications emerging from our analysis.

13.2   TRANSITION AND NATIONAL INNOVATION SYSTEMS

In order to understand innovation systems we need to consider the complex interactions between a firm and its environment. These consist, first, of interactions between firms, especially between a firm and its network of customers and suppliers. Second, it involves interactions between firms and the non-firm sector (universities and R&D centres). In addition to the firm and non-firm sectors – which account for the majority of innovative activities – knowledge creation, dissemination, acquisition and utilization are also shaped by the actions (or inactions) of governments. The environment also involves broader factors influencing the behaviour of firms, including the social and cultural context, the institutional and organizational framework, infrastructures and other processes of generation and diffusion of scientific knowledge. The linkages and interactions between the different actors of innovation systems may take many different forms, which evolve with time. In addition, national innovation systems link with foreign sources of knowledge through international scientific collaborations, technological alliances, technology trade, foreign direct investment, mobility of students and researchers, and so on. As discussed in section 13.1, the interaction between national innovation systems and MNCs is of critical importance and represents the main focus of this chapter.

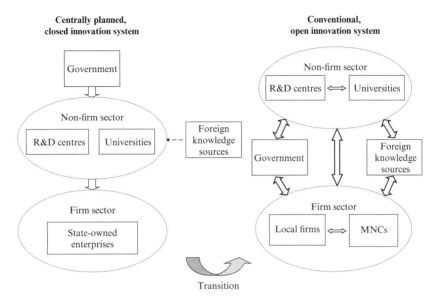

Source: Adapted from Narula and Jormanainen (2008).

Figure 13.1 The transition from centrally planned to conventional innovation systems

National innovation systems in centrally planned economies, as were prevalent in the NMS until the 1990s, differ largely from conventional, open innovation systems that exist in developed market economies, including the core and cohesion EU countries (Figure 13.1). Pre-transition economies had largely closed innovation systems where knowledge sources were determined primarily by domestic elements (Radošević, 1999, 2003). The technological development trajectory was planned centrally in response to state-defined priorities. National governments formulated domestic industrial policy, which in turn determined domestic industrial structure. National non-firm actors also defined the kinds of skills that the local labour force might possess; the kinds of technologies in which these actors had appropriate expertise; the kinds of technologies in which basic and applied research was conducted, and thereby, the industrial specialization and competitive advantages of the firm sector. Technology planners in socialist systems were influenced by the linear model of innovation, which viewed technological progress as following a discrete path from basic and applied research to technological development and eventually to innovation. This scenario led to rigid and hierarchical interactions between the different actors in the system, where user–producer and university–industry linkages were weak and the pressures for commercialization of R&D results were low. With regard to foreign sources of knowledge, FDI was almost non-existent before the transition era and any linkages to international sources were sporadic and state controlled. Furthermore, these weak foreign linkages were characterized by a gap between the technology used and the knowledge frontier, as well as by a tendency to reproduce foreign research in an autarkic economic environment (Inzelt, 1999).

During the 1990s the transition from a socialist to a market system brought radical changes to the socioeconomic structure of the NMS through rapid economic liberalization and the adoption of Washington Consensus type policies. In just a few years many state-controlled industries were transferred to foreign ownership through privatizations. This was exacerbated by national budget constraints, pressures from supranational institutions (including EU, IMF, WTO) and, in some instances, the inability of domestic capitalists to compete effectively with foreign firms. FDI, through both privatizations and new investments, grew drastically and as a result the share of foreign ownership in total capital stock today is much higher than in the older EU member states, although with considerable variation across countries and sectors (Narula and Bellak, 2009).

The subsequent process of accession into the EU was also an important driver for the transformation of the national innovation systems of the NMS. The required supranational institution building impinged greatly on the restructuring of national institutions in post-communist states (Bruzst and McDermott, 2008). One of the primary conditions for EU membership was that the economic systems of candidate countries needed to demonstrate a convergence towards the EU norm, which meant that EU-wide regulatory and competition policy, social and economic treaties and the like became binding and overrode national law. This provides certain location advantages relative to non-member states but it also constrains policy options available to member states. For example, as we discuss later, import substitution policies became almost infeasible.

In addition to the growing influence of MNCs, the significance of other sources of foreign knowledge also increased with EU accession. The framework programmes of the European Commission played an important role in facilitating cross-border collaboration between economic actors within the EU (Narula, 2003) and this extends further to collaborations between public research organizations and firms (Arundel and Geuna, 2004; Fontana et al., 2006). Universities and research centres – both as organizations and as individual research groups – increased their collaboration with other universities and research institutes in other countries as well as with MNCs.

However, the NMS still demonstrate significant features of the pre-transition era in their innovation systems. Of course, this varies considerably by country as a result of path dependences, which reflect different sociopolitical and economic histories. Largely speaking, the advanced NMS (including the Czech Republic, Estonia, Hungary, Poland, Slovakia and Slovenia) have made more progress in the institutional transformation involved in redesigning their innovation systems around the conventional model, while the rest of NMS are at an earlier stage of transition. The ability of different economies to make such a transition reflects the strength of existing institutions and the political will to implement reforms (Newman, 2000) as well as their stage of economic development and the associated absorptive capacity of domestic actors (Chobanova, 2009). In order to properly understand the transition process it is important to realize that modifying and developing informal institutions is a complex and slow process, particularly since they cannot be created simply by government fiat. It takes considerable time and effort to create informal networks of government agencies, suppliers, politicians and researchers, which, once created, have a low marginal cost of maintenance.

13.3 THE ROLE OF MULTINATIONAL CORPORATIONS

It seems evident that inward FDI and the subsequent operations of MNCs contributed to institutional change and technological upgrading in the NMS (Lavigne, 2000; Radošević, 2006). Initially, the main drivers of FDI were cost advantages (low labour costs and low taxes), but with time many MNCs upgraded their operations. According to Chobanova (2009), the preservation and effective restructuring of existing socialist supplier networks enabled the formation of transnational linkages between local firms and MNCs, which contributed to industrial upgrading. Djankov and Murrell (2002) show how foreign-led upgrading is evidenced by the fact that MNC subsidiaries performed significantly better than local firms. Günther et al. (2009) claim that many of the MNC subsidiaries in Central and Eastern European countries are to some extent technologically active in terms of conducting their own R&D and generating product and process innovations, and they argue that this stimulates technological transfer and upgrading. MNCs brought benefits to the national innovation systems of the NMS through different mechanisms, among others by increasing the commercial orientation of innovative efforts and by providing opportunities for interaction-based learning and for integrating into global innovation networks.

Table 13.1   R&D expenditure of MNC subsidiaries as a percentage of total business expenditure in R&D (1994–2006)

	1994[1]	2000[2]	2006[3]
Belgium	:	:	56.8
Finland	13.9	13.4	17.0
France	14.2	21.5	20.8
Germany	13.0	22.1	38.3
Italy	:	33.0	26.6
Netherlands	20.4	26.1	27.5
Sweden	19.3	40.7	42.3
UK	29.1	31.3	38.4
Average core	**18.3**	**22.9**	**28.5**
Spain	30.0	33.6	35.6
Portugal	:	30.9	47.4
Ireland	66.8	64.2	75.9
Average cohesion	**10.3**	**13.1**	**21.7**
Poland	48.4	42.9	53.0
Hungary	22.6	68.4	57.8
Czech Republic	20.9	36.9	58.6
Slovakia	4.1	15.2	64.1
Average NMS	**14.5**	**33.4**	**50.6**

Notes:
1. 1995 for Czech Republic, Finland, Germany, Ireland, Spain and Sweden, 1997 for Poland and Netherlands. Manufacturing sector only for Germany, Ireland, Portugal, Slovakia and Spain, across all years.
2. 2001 for France, Germany, Italy, Portugal, Spain and Sweden.
3. 2005 for Belgium, Germany, Hungary, Ireland, Portugal, Slovakia, Spain and Sweden, 2004 for Netherlands.
Average values for the country groups correspond to unweighted mean.
: = not available.

Sources: OECD (2009) and UNCTAD (2005).

Quantifying the role of MNC subsidiaries in national innovation systems at the aggregate level is not an easy task, given the limitations of existing statistical sources and the intangible nature of many of the potential impacts. A typical way of measuring the role of MNCs in national innovation systems is to look at the R&D expenditure of MNC subsidiaries relative to total business expenditure in R&D.[2] Table 13.1 shows how this indicator grew much faster in the NMS than in the core and cohesion countries: from 14.5 per cent in 1994 (well below the average for core and cohesion countries) to 50.6 per cent in 2006 (significantly above the average for core and cohesion countries). Thus, in 2006 the R&D expenditure of foreign MNC subsidiaries in the NMS exceeded that of firms of national ownership. Compared to other EU countries, in 2006 only Ireland showed a higher ratio than Slovakia, the Czech Republic or Hungary; but Ireland is an outlier in the EU in terms of its high degree of openness and its MNC-driven technological development strategy. There are, however, large differences among the four NMS in the sample, ranging from 64.1 per cent in Slovakia to 21.7 per cent in Poland.

The data show clearly that since 1994 the weight of MNC subsidiaries in total business expenditure in R&D has increased sharply and at a significantly higher rate in the NMS than in the core and cohesion countries. But the interpretation is not straightforward: is this overreliance on FDI good or bad for the upgrading of national innovation systems? A high level of foreign contribution may be the result of a dynamic system that is successful in attracting the R&D of MNCs or, alternatively, it may be a reflection of the crowding-out of national innovative efforts. A possible way to further clarify this is by comparing the R&D intensity of foreign subsidiaries and local firms. Table 13.2 shows that the relative R&D intensity of MNC subsidiaries in the NMS is similar to that in the core and cohesion countries, that is, a bit higher on average than the R&D intensity of local firms. In absolute terms, however, the NMS clearly lag behind the core and cohesion countries in terms of business R&D intensity, irrespective of ownership. The results for the different NMS are mixed. Out of the four NMS in the sample, only in the Czech Republic is the R&D intensity of MNC subsidiaries higher than that of local firms. In Slovakia and Poland it is equivalent, while in Hungary it is lower.[3]

Furthermore, in order to evaluate the impact of MNCs in the NMS one must consider that much of the R&D activity of MNCs was inherited through privatization-driven acquisitions. This implies that the direct effects in terms of new R&D activity or employment generation were small, while the indirect benefits were constrained by the continuous rationalization and restructuring of the EU operations of MNCs. In addition, the developmental impact of FDI was often limited by the inability of domestic actors to build the kind of linkages with foreign MNCs that enhance the indigenous innovation system, either because they lacked sufficient absorptive capacity, because they operated largely in different sectors or because they evolved separately. Moreover, in some instances local actors were reluctant to integrate MNCs into the system (Damijan et al., 2003; Sinani and Meyer, 2004; Javorcik and Spatareanu, 2008). Very often the activities conducted by domestic firms as a result of their interaction with MNCs were low-value-adding tasks characterized by

Table 13.2   R&D intensity of foreign subsidiaries and local firms (2006)

	R&D intensity of local firms	R&D intensity of foreign subsidiaries
Belgium	0.4	0.9
UK	0.5	0.7
Finland	1.2	1.1
France	0.5	0.6
Germany	2.1	2.1
Sweden	1.2	1.7
Italy	0.2	0.5
Average core	**0.9**	**1.1**
Ireland	1.1	0.8
Portugal	0.2	0.5
Spain	0.5	0.9
Average cohesion	**0.6**	**0.7**
Hungary	0.4	0.3
Slovakia	0.1	0.1
Poland	0.1	0.1
Czech Republic	0.2	0.5
Average NMS	**0.2**	**0.3**

Note: R&D intensity is defined as R&D expenditure as a percentage of turnover.
2005 for Belgium, Germany, Hungary, Ireland, Portugal, Slovakia, Spain and Sweden.
Manufacturing sector only for Germany, Ireland, Portugal, Slovakia and Spain.

Source: OECD (2009).

a somewhat hierarchical relationship with the MNC. Cases of deeply embedded MNCs are often attributable to the replacement of previous state-owned firms by MNCs in the industrial milieu of the host country through foreign acquisitions. In some cases the domestic linkages of the acquired firms were maintained, but in other cases they were replaced with those of the parent MNCs global network of affiliates and partners.

Therefore a key challenge for governments of the NMS was to try to ensure that privatized firms continued to operate, create employment, perform R&D and source locally. During the first years of transition from a socialist to a capitalist system, the standard approach was to encourage MNC embeddedness through protectionist policy measures such as high tariffs and customs duties, rules of origin, local content requirements, joint venture requirements and so on. However, EU accession meant that former import substitution type policies needed to be replaced by openness and non-discrimination. Upon accession, many MNCs relocated activities as market distortions introduced by protectionist regulations disappeared. In the absence of large markets or sufficiently well-developed innovation systems and industrial clusters, many MNCs preferred to see economies of scale and scope in their existing activities within the core EU countries despite the low-cost advantages the NMS offered (Chobanova, 2009).

To date, the R&D of MNC subsidiaries in the NMS has been primarily demand-driven, that is related to the adaptation of products, services or processes to overseas markets (Chobanova, 2009; Günther et al., 2009; Hancké and Kurekova, 2008; Radošević, 2006). Demand-driven R&D is either market-seeking or efficiency-seeking, and generally linked to manufacturing operations (process rather than product innovations) or to minor product adaptations to meet the specificities of local demand. In contrast, supply-driven motivations (i.e. tapping into localized knowledge and technology) seem to be less relevant, suggesting that the NMS have not developed their science and technology infrastructure to the level that they possess an absolute advantage in basic research for which MNCs will, in rare circumstances, seek to locate a stand-alone, specialized R&D facility. Supply-driven R&D activities tend to be more autonomous and knowledge-intensive than demand-driven R&D, implying a considerably greater dependence on domestic knowledge sources and infrastructure. Demand-driven R&D activities tend to be more 'footloose' and vulnerable to global corporate strategies and competition from other emerging economies.

As EU integration proceeds, MNCs are continuously restructuring their EU-wide supply chains to better rationalize their operations by responding to the heterogeneity of location-bound advantages across the different member states (Dimitropoulou et al., 2008; Dunning, 2008; Hancké and Kurekova, 2008; Majcen et al., 2009; Narula and Bellak, 2009). According to Majcen et al. (2009), EU countries that are furthest away from convergence with the EU norm and with poorly defined innovation systems are often host to single-activity subsidiaries, primarily in sales and marketing or labour-intensive manufacturing and assembly, as well as in natural resource extraction. In contrast, the most advanced economies with domestic technological capacity, such as the core EU countries, host the least truncated subsidiaries – often with R&D departments and (regional) headquarter functions. We provide additional empirical support to these arguments through an analysis of a sample of 22 503 announcements of inward FDI projects in EU countries from the European Investment Monitor database of Ernst and Young.[4] This database is one of the few sources available to study empirically the functional structure of FDI within the EU.

As shown in Table 13.3, the share of R&D projects in total FDI projects

Table 13.3   *Functional structure of inward FDI announcements (% share*
of each function in total FDI announcements during the period
1997–2006)

	1	2	3	4	5	6	N
Austria	12.5	6.6	33.3	29.4	13.8	4.3	513
Belgium	5.0	6.5	37.5	26.0	18.0	7.1	1190
Denmark	11.1	26.8	10.4	42.9	6.1	2.8	396
Finland	14.4	3.4	26.0	49.3	4.1	2.7	146
France	6.7	5.4	45.4	26.1	10.5	5.8	3867
Germany	8.3	6.3	30.1	39.4	8.4	7.5	1818
Italy	11.0	4.5	24.3	48.0	5.0	7.2	444
Luxembourg	5.7	13.2	22.6	43.4	7.5	7.5	53
Netherlands	5.5	13.7	25.0	31.8	15.1	8.8	780
Sweden	12.6	8.5	14.7	51.0	4.7	8.5	681
UK	8.6	16.3	28.8	31.6	5.4	9.2	5539
Average core	**9.2**	**10.1**	**27.1**	**38.1**	**9.0**	**6.5**	**15427**
Greece	7.0	5.3	29.8	43.9	7.0	7.0	57
Ireland	18.3	7.2	32.9	20.9	2.7	17.9	884
Portugal	4.3	1.1	57.4	18.4	9.4	9.4	277
Spain	10.0	5.4	46.0	23.5	8.2	6.8	1315
Average cohesion	**9.9**	**4.7**	**41.5**	**26.7**	**6.8**	**10.3**	**2533**
Czech Republic	6.4	0.9	69.8	12.4	4.9	5.5	849
Estonia	0.6	0.0	58.4	21.3	11.2	8.4	178
Hungary	4.2	1.4	67.1	12.5	8.4	6.5	1026
Poland	3.1	0.7	67.2	15.2	8.7	5.2	1046
Slovakia	2.1	0.3	73.8	13.9	6.6	3.3	332
Slovenia	6.3	0.0	56.3	29.2	8.3	0.0	48
Bulgaria	3.1	0.3	60.8	29.9	5.2	0.7	291
Latvia	1.6	0.0	42.3	37.4	13.0	5.7	123
Lithuania	1.3	0.7	48.3	40.4	7.9	1.3	151
Romania	4.0	1.2	64.9	20.6	5.2	4.0	499
Average NMS	**3.3**	**0.5**	**60.9**	**23.3**	**8.0**	**4.1**	**4543**

Notes: 1 = R&D; 2 = Headquarter functions (including regional headquarters); 3 =
Manufacturing; 4 = Sales and marketing; 5 = Logistics; 6 = Others (including contact
centres, shared services centres, testing and servicing, and others); N = sample size; average
values for the country groups correspond to unweighted mean.

Source: Authors' calculations based on European Investment Monitor database, Ernst
and Young.

is much larger in the core and cohesion countries than in the NMS.[5] The share of investment in headquarter functions is also lower in the NMS, while the share of manufacturing projects is much higher. This shows that FDI influences the functional specialization patterns in the EU, with the NMS becoming more specialized in manufacturing operations and the core and cohesion countries retaining the most strategic R&D and headquarter functions. As in the case of the R&D expenditure indicator, our analysis reveals significant differences across the NMS, with the Czech Republic, Slovenia and Hungary exhibiting the highest capacity to attract FDI in R&D. At the other extreme, Estonia, Lithuania and Latvia attract the lowest share of R&D projects.

13.4   CONCLUSIONS AND POLICY IMPLICATIONS

Inward FDI played a very important role in the transition process and is often regarded as one of the main positive effects deriving from EU integration. However, this overdependence on FDI to drive industrial upgrading has its risks, which are becoming more evident in the post-EU-accession era. FDI-assisted development strategies require institutional change and rapidly rising capabilities as wages rise and skill demands change (Dunning, 2008; Lall, 2004). After most liberalization, privatization and institutional reforms have been accomplished, the focus of industrial policies in the post-EU-accession is shifting towards selective interventions to support the embeddedness and upward evolution of existing MNC operations.

This implies that governments of NMS are now focusing their efforts on promoting sequential investments that pull the MNCs' activities such that they become simultaneously deeply integrated with the MNC global structure and deeply embedded within the domestic innovation system. The underlying goals are to enhance the benefits for the domestic innovation system and to increase the strategic importance of the subsidiary to the MNC headquarters, such that sequential investments become increasingly knowledge intensive. Along these lines, governments should evaluate the existing stock of foreign subsidiaries in order to identify specific opportunities for upgrading, which would be followed by enhanced dialogue and collaboration with subsidiary managers and by the offering of customized aftercare services and incentives.

In this context, a key role of policies is to stimulate clusters around MNCs by facilitating linkages between the MNC subsidiary and local organizations. For example, fiscal and financial incentives to MNCs should be designed so as to increase the propensity of MNCs to collaborate with other domestic agents in innovative, high-value-added activities. This means that incentives should be linked to aftercare services and MNC-embedding policies. A typical approach in many EU countries is to offer 'research hosting' services to foreign firms through technology parks, which may include subsidized office space, access to research equipment, recruitment services, administrative support and so on. However, incentives should always be offered cautiously after carefully considering what the potential spillovers and linkages will be and how these can be converted to actual benefits.

It is our understanding that the key challenge in creating clusters around MNCs is associated with matching the industrial structure and comparative advantage of the region with the kinds of FDI that are being attracted. Indeed, it becomes necessary for policy makers to place the endowments of the innovation system in a global context, identifying spaces for coupling domestic innovatory capacities with the dynamics of global value chains.

An additional challenge is that, as MNCs increasingly seek to rationalize their activities through global sourcing strategies, decisions about local linkages are not always made at the subsidiary level but rather at the headquarters level by comparing the various options available to the MNC globally. Governments of the NMS therefore need to create incentives for the MNC to consider local partners and not expect these to happen naturally. A typical constraint for many of the NMS is that there are existing firms that, while in the appropriate industry, do not currently meet the quality and reliability requirements of the MNC. Thus policies to upgrade reliability and quality in local firms are of critical importance.

Besides stimulating linkages and clusters, another critical role of governments is to provide public goods by contributing to the development of the kind of R&D infrastructure and human capital that enable the attraction and embeddedness of MNC subsidiaries. The focus of policies here should be to foster demand-oriented upgrading of technological capabilities in response to MNC current activities, aimed at creating the conditions that enable existing subsidiaries to embrace R&D mandates, rather than radical (and expensive) actions to specialize in new R&D areas with the hope that this will be followed by greenfield FDI in higher-value-adding activities. This is especially true given that the R&D activity of MNC subsidiaries in the NMS is primarily demand-driven rather than supply-driven.

The proper role for governments of the NMS to enhance the impact of MNCs on their national innovation system is a subject worth more debate, and this extends further to other peripheral economies around the world. We have recommended a systemic approach focused on subsidiary development and linkage facilitation, implying a closer connection between

FDI, industrial and innovation policies. We have also supported the case for a selective approach to FDI policies, where limited resources are given to efforts to support the kind of investment projects that provide the greatest opportunity for linkages between foreign firms and domestic actors.

Finally, it is important to acknowledge that it is still too early to assess the full impact of transition, EU accession and inward FDI on the upgrading of national innovation systems in the NMS, since those transformations are still recent in history and would need to be analysed from a dynamic, longer-term perspective. It is also important to stress that despite our attempts to generalize, each individual NMS would require a different mix of policies depending on its technological and institutional profile.

NOTES

1. Malta and Cyprus, which also joined the EU in 2004, are excluded from our analysis given their small size and the fact that they are significantly different from the rest of NMS (both are Mediterranean islands without a socialist past).
2. This indicator is available from the AFA database of the OECD, but only for a limited set of countries and generally starting in 1994. In particular, it only provides data for four out of the ten NMS. This can be contrasted with a sample of three (out of four) cohesion countries and eight (out of eleven) core member states.
3. These results need to be interpreted with care, as a proper analysis of R&D intensities would require controlling by industry and firm size (Molero and Álvarez, 2003). In addition, transfer pricing strategies of MNCs may distort the measurement of R&D intensity (Barry, 2005), resulting in an artificially lower R&D intensity of MNC subsidiaries in countries with lower corporate tax rates, such as most of the NMS and Ireland.
4. The European Investment Monitor database includes investments made by European and non-European firms in all the EU member states starting in 1997. It includes greenfield investments and expansions but excludes mergers and acquisitions (M&As). It also excludes real-estate investments; retail, leisure and hotel facilities; fixed infrastructure investments; and extraction activities. The information in the database is compiled through global, national and regional media; financial information providers (such as Reuters); corporate websites; and government websites (such as the websites of investment promotion agencies).
5. It is striking to see that the share of R&D announcements in cohesion countries is higher than in core countries, although this difference is explained by the special case of Ireland: if we exclude this country, the share of R&D projects for the cohesion group would decrease to 7.1 per cent, below the level in core countries (9.2 per cent).

REFERENCES

Archibugi, D. and Iammarino, S. (1999), 'The policy implications of the globalisation of innovation', *Research Policy*, **28**: 317–36.
Arundel, A. and Geuna, A. (2004), 'Proximity and the use of public science by innovative European firms', *Economics of Innovation and New Technology*, **13**: 559–80.

Barrios, S., Görg, H. and Strobl, E. (2005), 'Foreign direct investment, competition and industrial development in the host country', *European Economic Review*, **49**: 1761–84.

Barry, F. (2005), 'FDI, transfer pricing and the measurement of R&D-intensity', *Research Policy*, **34**: 673–81.

Bruche, G. (2009), 'The emergence of China and India as new competitors in MNCs innovation networks', *Competition & Change*, **13**: 267–88.

Bruzst, L. and McDermott, G.A. (2008), 'Transnational integration regimes as development programs', Program on Central & Eastern Europe Working Paper Series, 67.

Cantwell, J., Dunning, J.H. and Janne, O. (2004), 'Towards a technology-seeking explanation of U.S. direct investment in the United Kingdom', *Journal of International Management*, **10**: 5–20.

Cantwell, J. and Piscitello, L. (2000), 'Accumulating technological competence: its changing impact on corporate diversification and internationalization', *Industrial and Corporate Change*, **9**: 21–51.

Carlsson, B. (2006), 'Internationalization of innovation systems: a survey of the literature', *Research Policy*, **35**: 56–67.

Chobanova, Y. (2009), *Strategies of Multinationals in Central and Eastern Europe*, Basingstoke: Palgrave Macmillan.

Cohen, W. and Levinthal, D. (1989), 'Innovation and learning: the two faces of R&D', *Economic Journal*, **99**: 569–96.

Costa, I. and Filippov, S. (2008), 'Foreign-owned subsidiaries: a neglected nexus between foreign direct investment, industrial and innovation policies', *Science and Public Policy*, **35**: 379–90.

Damijan, J., Knell, M., Majcen, B. and Rojec, M. (2003), 'The role of FDI, R&D accumulation and trade in transferring technology to transition countries: evidence from firm panel data for eight transition countries', *Economic Systems*, **27**: 189–204.

Dimitropoulou, D., Pearce, R. and Papanastassiou, M. (2008), 'The locational determinants of foreign direct investment in European Union core and periphery: the influence of multinational strategy', in J.H. Dunning and P. Gugler (eds), *Foreign Direct Investment, Location and Competitiveness*, Oxford: Elsevier, pp. 51–79.

Djankov, S. and Murrell, P. (2002), 'Enterprise restructuring in transition: a quantitative survey', *Journal of Economic Literature*, **40**: 739–92.

Dunning, J.H. (2008), 'Institutional reform, FDI and the location competitiveness of European transition economies', in J.H. Dunning and P. Gugler (eds), *Foreign Direct Investment, Location and Competitiveness*, Oxford: Elsevier, pp. 175–201.

Fontana, R., Geuna, A. and Matt, M. (2006), 'Factors affecting university–industry R&D collaboration: the importance of screening and signalling', *Research Policy*, **35**: 309–23.

Girma, S., Greenaway, D. and Wakelin, K. (2001), 'Who benefits from foreign direct investment in the UK?', *Scottish Journal of Political Economy*, **48**: 119–33.

Görg, H. and Strobl, E. (2001), 'Multinational companies and productivity spillovers: a meta-analysis', *The Economic Journal*, **111**: 723–39.

Guimón, J. (2009), 'Government strategies to attract R&D-intensive FDI', *Journal of Technology Transfer*, **34**: 364–79.

Günther, J., Jindra, B. and Stephan, J. (2009), 'FDI and the national innovation system – evidence from emerging economies in Central and Eastern Europe', Globelics 2009 Conference, Dakar.

Hancké, B. and Kurekova, L. (2008), *Varieties of Capitalism and Economic Governance in Central Europe*, Report for NewGov/STACEE.

Inzelt, A. (1999), 'The transformation role of FDI in R&D: analysis based on material from a databank', in D.A. Dyker and S. Radošević (eds), *Innovation and Structural Change in Post-socialist Countries: A Quantitative Approach*, Dordrecht: Kluwer Academic Publishers, pp. 185–201.

Jaruzelski, B. and Dehoff, K. (2008), 'Beyond borders: the global innovation 1000', *Strategy+Business*, **53**: 1–17.

Javorcik, B. and Spatareanu, M. (2008), 'To share or not to share: does local participation matter for spillovers from foreign direct investment?', *Journal of Development Economics*, **85**: 194–217.

Lall, S. (2004), 'Reinventing industrial strategy: the role of government policy in building industrial competitiveness', G-24 Discussion Paper Series, *28*.

Lall, S. and Narula, R. (2004), 'Foreign direct investment and its role in economic development: do we need a new agenda?', *European Journal of Development Research,* **16** (3): 447–64.

Lavigne, M. (2000), 'Ten years of transition: a review article', *Communist and Post-Communist Studies*, **33**: 475–83.

Majcen, B., Radošević, S. and Rojec, M. (2009), 'Nature and determinants of productivity growth of foreign subsidiaries in Central and East European countries', *Economic Systems*, **33**: 168–84.

Manea, J. and Pearce, R. (2001), 'Multinational strategies and sustainable industrial transformation in CEE transition economies: the role of technology', in J.H. Taggart, M. Berry and M. McDermott (eds), *Multinationals in a New Era*, Basingstoke: Palgrave, pp. 118–40.

Mansfield, E., Teece, D. and Romeo, A. (1979), 'Overseas research and development by US-based firms', *Economica*, **46**: 187–96.

Meyer-Krahmer, F. and Reger, G. (1999), 'New perspectives on the innovation strategies of multinational enterprises: lessons for technology policy in Europe', *Research Policy*, **28**: 751–76.

Molero, J. and Álvarez, I. (2003), 'The technological strategies of multinational enterprises: their implications for national systems of innovation', in J. Cantwell and J. Molero (eds), *Multinational Enterprises, Innovative Strategies and Systems of Innovation*, Cheltenham, UK and Northampton, MA, USA: Edward Elgar, pp. 177–204.

Narula, R. (2003), *Globalization and Technology*, Cambridge: Polity Press.

Narula, R. and Bellak, C. (2009), 'EU enlargement and consequences for FDI assisted industrial development', *Transnational Corporations*, **18**: 69–90.

Narula, R. and Dunning, J.H. (2010), 'Multinational enterprises, development and globalisation: some clarifications and a research agenda', *Oxford Development Studies*, **38**: 263–87.

Narula, R. and Jormanainen, I. (2008), 'When a good science base is not enough to create competitive industries: lock-in and inertia in Russian systems of innovation', MERIT–UNU Working Papers, 59.

Narula, R. and Zanfei, A. (2005), 'Globalization of innovation: the role of multinational enterprises', in J. Fagerberg, D.C. Mowery and R.R. Nelson (eds), *The Oxford Handbook of Innovation*, Oxford and New York: Oxford University Press, pp. 318–45.

Newman, K. (2000), 'Organizational transformation during institutional upheaval', *Academy of Management Review*, **25**: 602–19.

OECD (2009), *Science, Technology and Industry Scoreboard 2009*, Paris: OECD.

Ostry, S. and Nelson, R.R. (1995), *Techno-nationalism and Techno-globalism: Conflict and Cooperation*, Washington, DC: The Brookings Institution.

Pearce, R. (2004), 'National systems of innovation and the international technology strategy of multinationals', University of Reading Discussion Paper, 6.

Puga, D. and Trefler, D. (2010), 'Wake up and smell the ginseng: international trade and the rise of incremental innovation in low-wage countries', *Journal of Development Economics*, **91**: 64–76.

Radošević, S. (1999), 'Transformation of science and technology systems into systems of innovation in Central and Eastern Europe: the emerging patterns and determinants', *Structural Change and Economic Dynamics*, **10**: 277–320.

Radošević, S. (2003), 'Patterns of preservation, restructuring and survival: science and technology policy in Russia in the post-Soviet era', *Research Policy*, **32**: 1105–24.

Radošević, S. (2006), 'Central and Eastern Europe between domestic and foreign led modernization', Working Paper, School of Slavonic and East European Studies, University College London.

Rugman, A.M. and Verbeke, A. (2008), 'Location, competitiveness and the multinational enterprise', in A. Rugman and T.L. Brewer (eds), *The Oxford Handbook of International Business*, Oxford and New York: Oxford University Press, pp. 151–69.

Sinani, E. and Meyer, K.E. (2004), 'Spillovers from technology transfer: the case of Estonia', *Journal of Comparative Economics*, **32**: 445–66.

UNCTAD (2005), *World Investment Report 2005: Transnational Corporations and the internationalization of R&D*, New York and Geneva: UNCTAD.

14. Conclusion: corporate embeddedness as a strategic and dynamic process of skilled actors

Jannika Mattes and Martin Heidenreich

The chapters of this book have illustrated multiple aspects of corporate embeddedness. We have focused on how the relationship between MNCs and their regional and national surroundings can be shaped in order to increase corporate capabilities for generating and absorbing knowledge as well as strengthening the contribution of the regional and national context towards higher corporate innovativeness. On the basis of existing studies on national and regional innovation, business systems and various forms of corporate embeddedness, we outlined a concept of corporate embeddedness based on selected results of these debates: (a) institutions, cultures and policies as well as inter-organizational networks shape the regional and national environment of MNCs and their subsidiaries, and thus the opportunities and resources on which companies rely in order to solve the manifold coordination problems linked to the uncertainties of innovation processes; (b) these institutions are often based on a common logic and the different dimensions of the corporate environment reinforce themselves ('institutional complementarities'); (c) MNCs in particular can choose where, in what dimensions and to what extent they want to rely on the multiple institutional, political, cultural and inter-organizational contexts of the countries and regions in which they are present. They can actively, strategically and selectively use different opportunities of 'multiple embeddedness'; (d) given the risks of embeddedness (especially lock-in effects) and the advantages of not being embedded (e.g. the opportunity of using the most advanced knowledge resources in a global context), companies are faced with the dilemma between embeddedness and disembeddedness; (e) corporate embeddedness, however, is not only the result of active or emergent, strategic and selective choices of MNCs, but it also reflects the interests, opportunity structures and path-dependent evolution of the respective regions and countries. From a process-oriented perspective, embeddedness should thus be conceived as the result of the dynamic co-evolution of institutions and organizations, shaped by the heterogeneous, that is, economic, political, scientific, educational and technical logics of different actors.

On the basis of the chapters in this volume, we shall now draw together some of the ideas presented in order to illustrate more clearly the complexity of corporate embeddedness. While far from being an automatic or even clearly advantageous phenomenon, it remains subject to multiple dilemmas (1); it is dependent upon external knowledge structures (2); and it is facilitated via strategic actions of policy makers and corporate actors (3). Even in cases where it exists, corporate embeddedness is a selective and dynamic phenomenon that forms an essential basis for corporate innovativeness and competitiveness (4).

14.1 THE DILEMMAS OF CORPORATE EMBEDDEDNESS

A basic feature of innovation processes is their dilemmatic nature, as innovation represents both the basis for new technological and economic opportunities and a temporary monopoly rent, while at the same time being a process of 'creative destruction' (Schumpeter) that destroys existing business models and devalues previous investments and knowledge. The definition of innovations as 'new creations of economic significance of either a material or an intangible kind [which] may be brand new but are more often new combinations of existing elements' (Edquist, 2001: 219) shows that innovation always entails a change of routines, a move away from common structures and a rupture in reference to the past. Learning in stable structures, be it organizations or regions, is thus an inherent contradiction (or an oxymoron, as Weick and Westley, 1996 put it). In the case of MNCs this general challenge re-emerges as the well-known dilemma of globalization and localization (Ghoshal and Bartlett, 1990), which goes hand in hand with the dilemma of disembeddedness and embeddedness.[1]

This shows that innovations in MNCs are risky endeavours involving high costs and an extreme level of uncertainty. Furthermore, successful innovation simultaneously devalues previously used methods and qualifications. These inherent risks and costs of innovations justify a certain degree of resistance to change (Heidenreich, 2004; Crouch and Farrell, 2004). Organizational innovation theory has dealt with these dilemmas from different viewpoints (cf. for example Zaltman et al., 1973; Hage and Hollingsworth, 2000). Similarly, the debate on regional learning analyses regionally embedded networks as a central prerequisite for innovations, even though this can also entail locking into existing structures to a degree that completely inhibits further renewal (cf. Grabher, 1993; Fritsch, 2001; cf. also Rehfeld, Chapter

10 in this volume). Regional processes of closure are accompanied by global linkages in order to be able to take advantage of new opportunities (Amin and Thrift, 1995; Bathelt et al., 2004). This book draws on both organizational and regional perspectives, highlighting various aspects regarding what the dilemma of embeddedness consists of, how it occurs and how it can be dealt with (cf. also Mattes, 2010; Heidenreich et al., 2012).

Embeddedness is a combination of various dimensions, namely the advantages of regional proximity, regionally available institutions, local collective competition goods and access to allocated service providers (cf. Heidenreich and Mattes, Chapter 2 in this volume). Whilst MNCs want to draw on these advantages, they are also reluctant to embed themselves as they fear a loss of control and do not want to disclose their proprietary knowledge. At the same time embeddedness involves a trade-off between global and local orientations (Bartlett and Ghoshal, 1989; cf. also Sölvell, Chapter 3 in this volume). While embeddedness may be a primarily local phenomenon, it necessarily has global implications, as a local focus may come at the expense of stronger connectedness to global networks. The chosen strategy of embedding is closely interrelated with internal knowledge structures, or in other words, the corporate set-up influences its external orientation. This becomes evident when looking at synthetic and analytical knowledge bases of MNCs (Asheim et al., Chapter 4 in this volume; cf. also Asheim et al., 2007): synthetic knowledge bases favour regional embeddedness due to the importance of co-location and geographical proximity in these constellations. On the other hand, analytical knowledge can be exchanged more easily across greater distances, and hence industries with these knowledge bases are more globally oriented. Other forms of proximity then substitute geographical factors (Mattes, 2011). The consequence of these findings is that embeddedness cannot be defined and established at will, but it is constructed via the internal set-up.

Moreover, embeddedness is not only an inner-organizational strategy but results from the interaction of regional and corporate efforts. This dimension mirrors the constellation of activities in regard to the surrounding region and shows the extent to which external (regional) partners play a role (Grabher, 1993). The dilemma between embeddedness and disembeddedness hence involves a complicated internal decision. At the same time, this internal decision is also connected to the external surroundings. Depending on their institutionalized solutions to the outlined dilemma, MNCs assume different roles in their interaction with SMEs (cf. Cooke, Chapter 5 in this volume). The externalization strategy depends upon the type of embeddedness into a region, that is, whether the available skills are 'Jacobian' or 'Porterian'. Based on the increasing user and design orientation, these external arrangements render embeddedness set-ups more and more complicated. As has been shown (Heidenreich and Mattes, Chapter 2 in this volume), the resulting embeddedness can assume various weaker or stronger forms that result from the followed strategies of exploitative embeddedness, augmentative embeddedness, broad industrial policies and tailored industrial policies.

Moreover, MNCs are also internally complex as they represent heterarchical corporate constellations that combine hierarchical aspects with network forms of organization (Hedlund, 2005). In contrast to small firms with a single site, MNCs have the possibility of distributing an innovation project among various subsidiaries and drawing on their specific competences. The strategic company orientation (ethnocentrism or polycentrism) decides whether projects take place in a concentrated or dispersed setting (Ghoshal and Bartlett, 1990; Mattes, 2010). This turns the decision about (multiple) embeddedness into one that also affects the corporate strategy as a whole, and any solution to the outlined dilemma – if one can be found at all – involves a dynamic adaptation process to changing conditions and strategic aims. In this sense local embeddedness is both an internal and an external topic of 'insiderization' and 'outsiderization' (cf. Sölvell, Chapter 3 in this volume; cf. also Zander and Sölvell, 2004; Morgan, 2001). The MNC's orientation towards its regional surroundings will affect its strategic position in the corporate network (cf. Strambach and Klement, Chapter 8 in this volume; cf. also Holm and Pedersen, 2000; Holm et al., 1995), implying that embeddedness becomes a crucial strategic question for internationally active organizations.

In order to cope with the outlined dilemma of corporate embeddedness, MNCs try to combine the contradicting orientations – an endeavour that is not easily achieved at all (cf. e.g. Lindqvist et al., 2000). They thus arrange selected embedding strategies differentiated between social, scientific, political and educational sub-systems. In this way our analysis illustrates that embeddedness is a complicated phenomenon that can take place in a very selective and cautious fashion, and is in no way automatic. On the contrary, we have shown that a strategy of mutual non-interference can also be a strategic choice, and avoiding strong embeddedness is in many cases rational. Embeddedness is an ambivalent phenomenon, and in consequence the result of a risky strategy.

14.2   THE EXTERNAL CONSTRUCTION OF EMBEDDEDNESS

The dilemmatic perspective from which this book starts shows that embedding involves a multitude of strategic and organizational questions for MNCs. We have already shown that neither the dilemma nor the embedding strategies are exclusively corporate questions, but instead take place at the interface of organizational actors and their institutional surroundings. Knowledge infrastructures act as embedding devices, rendering knowledge creation in organizations and regions interdependent (cf. Iammarino et al., Chapter 7 in this volume).

In this way MNCs tap into their external surroundings and establish an additional layer of knowledge and activities that complements their internal networks (Escribano et al., 2009; Narula and Santangelo, 2009; cf. also Ahrweiler et al., Chapter 6 in this volume). The knowledge that they obtain externally backs up their internal activities and contributes to their competitiveness (von Tunzelmann, 2009). It can even enhance a subsidiary's strategic position within its corporate group (cf. Strambach and Klement, Chapter 8 in this volume). Based on these considerations, it is essential to look at the whole picture and to simultaneously analyse internal and external structures of MNCs (Westney and Zaheer, 2008).

The case of Ireland illustrates how external infrastructure can stimulate the embeddedness of MNCs and result in intensified interaction relations between the company and other actors in the relevant national innovation system (cf. Ahrweiler et al., Chapter 6 in this volume). Embeddedness is hence not only of interest (be it for integration or for detachment) for the MNC itself, but also an aspect that is highly relevant to the surroundings at both the regional and the national level: clusters that commonly emerge around MNCs are hubs of economic activity (cf. Koschatzky and Baier, Chapter 9 in this volume; cf. also Malmberg et al., 1996; Markusen, 1996), and regional capability building takes place in a dynamic exchange process with allocated MNCs (cf. Iammarino et al., Chapter 7 and Koschatzky and Baier, Chapter 9 in this volume). Complicated learning processes between the involved actors can evolve, some of which Ahrweiler et al. (Chapter 6 in this volume) describe in an agent-based modelling approach. Changes in the corporate strategy then go hand in hand with shifts in the external environment, resulting in a 'fit' between the involved activities (Dicken et al., 2001). The interface between MNCs and their institutional surroundings can thus be analysed as a process of mutual influence and learning that also triggers a complementary arrangement of competences in the region, especially between MNCs and scientific or higher education institutes. The external and the internal arrangements remain interdependent, with corporate decentralization and knowledge management affecting if and how regional embedding occurs (cf. Iammarino et al., Chapter 7 in this volume).

Embeddedness mirrors the fact that MNCs are not 'footloose' companies but instead remain bound to geography (cf. Koschatzky and Baier, Chapter 9 in this volume). At the same time, the innovation process takes place in a decomposed fashion, and the analysed example in the software industry shows that parts of the activities can be decontextualized from their original environment (cf. Strambach and Klement, Chapter 8 in this volume). This goes along with increasing internationalization (Bartlett and Ghoshal, 2000), a process that also reflects the fact that strong embeddedness is not absolutely necessary in order to draw upon local collective competition goods (Le Galès and Voelzkow, 2001). Instead, MNCs may limit their connectedness with allocated partners to arm's-length relationships, referring to the strength of weak ties (Granovetter, 1973). Furthermore, not only geographical but also cognitive, social and organizational proximity are important (Boschma, 2005), and the various proximity forms complement and substitute each other (Mattes, 2011). Based on these complementation effects between proximities, innovation processes become multi-scalar and MNCs may be embedded not only in one regional or national context but also in multiple contexts simultaneously (cf. Strambach and Klement, Chapter 8 in this volume). Such multiple embeddedness leverages the outlined innovation dilemma: a simultaneous focus on several relevant spheres of interest helps to avoid at least some of the pitfalls of embeddedness. In this sense internationalization and the existence of several relevant orientation frames do not necessarily result in disembedding but can also entail a multi-territorial orientation.

No matter which form of embeddedness emerges, the involved external networks and business structures of customers, suppliers and political authorities can significantly contribute to creating and using knowledge (cf. Strambach and Klement, Chapter 8 in this volume). It is therefore not surprising that particularly R&D-intensive MNCs are extremely clustered in Europe (cf. Koschatzky and Baier, Chapter 9 in this volume). Their allocation does not seem to be random but is interdependent with the available regional characteristics, and knowledge-intensive regions with a good endowment of infrastructure coincide with a high presence of research-oriented MNCs. The resulting self-reinforcing dynamics even intensify concentration tendencies: MNCs tend to allocate in strong regions, and their activities in turn back up the regional evolvement, favour the allocation of other companies and thus strengthen the region even further (cf. also Enright, 2000).

Innovation in MNCs, in conclusion, remains context-specific and is strongly reliant upon the provided infrastructure, as embeddedness in institutionally stabilized regional orders provides additional input and back-up for inner-organizational innovation processes (cf. also Malmberg et al., 1996). A close interrelation can be observed between inner-corporate innovation processes and their embeddedness in external knowledge infrastructures.

14.3 THE SOCIAL AND POLITICAL CONSTRUCTION OF CORPORATE EMBEDDEDNESS

Corporate embeddedness is frequently conceived as a taken-for-granted by-product of the location of a company or subsidiary in its home region or host country. These 'primordial' or 'spontaneous' forms of embeddedness (cf. Rehfeld, Chapter 10 in this volume) have been described for traditional, often craft-based industrial districts in England, Central Italy, France, Denmark or Southern Germany (Piore and Sabel, 1984; Pyke and Sengenberger, 1992). However, the empirical evidence on creative and high-tech industries shows that political support is crucial for the development and competiveness, for example of film, publishing, advertising, financial, information technology, green technology or biotechnology clusters, as these industries strongly depend on public subsidies, regulations and orders, on knowledge spillovers and qualified employees (Scott, 2005; cf. Cooke, Chapter 5 in this volume).

In the case of MNCs, the institutional and political environment is even more important because these companies are at least in principle able to choose the most attractive sites for each part of their global value chain – or to combine the advantages of being embedded in different regional and national environments. Even though the actual mobility of MNCs, and especially their headquarters, should not be overestimated, these companies are able to select and exploit the institutional, political and fiscal advantages of their locations. Especially regions and countries that strongly rely on external MNCs and their investments (Wales, Ireland, Slovenia, Singapore, Ontario, Tohoku; cf. the case studies in Cooke et al., 2004) have to take into account the interests and requirements of MNCs. The economic development of Ireland and the Central and Eastern European countries is largely dependent upon subsidiaries of foreign MNCs, as shown by indicators such as the employment in affiliates under foreign control and high FDI (cf. OECD, 2009; and Ahrweiler et al., Chapter 6, and Narula and Guimón, Chapter 13 in this volume). These countries usually develop cluster, network, R&D, technology transfer and educational policies in order to strengthen the embeddedness of the foreign companies in the industrial networks and domestic institutions. Hancké (Chapter 12 in this volume) points out that regional embeddedness is also the result of corporate strategies. MNCs thus not only select the most adequate institutional and entrepreneurial environment for their subsidiaries but also contribute in a more or less active way to the construction of their institutional and business environment. Embeddedness can thus be conceived as the result of a recursive process in which socially embedded administrative, political, scientific, educational, associational and corporate actors actively and often strategically interact with each other. Garud et al. (2007: 961) analyse this as the 'embedded agency' of skilled social actors: '[A]ctors are embedded in an institutional field and subject to regulative, normative and cognitive processes that structure their cognitions, define their interests and produce their identities.'

Rehfeld (Chapter 10 in this volume) designates this 'active and collective more or less strategic engagement of companies' and regions as 'constructed regional embeddedness' and describes embeddedness as a dynamic relationship between regional and organizational actors: '[T]he concept of social context . . . is not one of a once-and-for-all influence but one of an on-going process that is continuously constructed and reconstructed during interaction' (Grabher, 1993: 5). Rehfeld points out that (constructed) embeddedness has to take into account both regional capabilities of linking 'social capital (networks), symbolic capital (reputation) and human resources' and corporate interests (e.g. by providing skilled employees, innovative capabilities and pleasant regional living conditions).

These active strategies of constructing embeddedness can take place in different settings. Barmeyer and Krüth (Chapter 11 in this volume) highlight the role of political interventions and illustrate this with the example of 'competitiveness poles' in France. They ask if and to what extent political interventions are able to change and transform culturally deeply rooted patterns of centralized governance and of non-cooperation between companies, observing a 'shift away from vertically integrated and mission-oriented policy making towards the promotion of network-oriented initiatives, involving elements of decentralization'. Political action is thus able to create and transform patterns of regional embeddedness – but only within the limits of national governance and business systems.

Complementary to the role of political initiatives, Hancké (Chapter 12 in this volume) shows that corporations are also able to act as institutional entrepreneurs (DiMaggio, 1988). In the investigated cases in Eastern Europe, he observes that foreign subsidiaries in cooperation with international chambers of commerce took the lead role in the creation of collective competition goods, for example by resolving skills shortages. In pursuing their own interests MNCs are able 'to produce islands of non-market coordination'. A precondition for this unlikely outcome is the reduced mobility of foreign capital (due to high set-up costs), which limits the exit options of companies. Lock-in effects in one dimension may thus create opportunities in other dimensions, a phenomenon that Garud et al. (2007: 691) analyse as the 'paradox of embedded agency': '[E]mbedding structures do not simply generate constraints on agency but, instead, provide a platform for the unfolding of entrepreneurial activities.' Skilled social actors are thus able to develop forms of institutionally embedded coordination in order to deal with skill bottlenecks – a result that suggests that 'embedded agency' may be crucial for the dynamic co-evolution of the initially mentioned institutions and organizations.

For Narula and Guimón (Chapter 13 in this volume), industrial policies should strengthen the regional embeddedness of subsidiaries by 'facilitating linkages between the MNC subsidiary and local organizations' and by providing public goods 'that enable existing subsidiaries to embrace R&D mandates'. Such a policy, 'focused on subsidiary development and linkage facilitation', conceives embeddedness as the outcome of strategic public action. It simultaneously highlights the fact that the 'embedded agency' of political, administrative and corporate actors has to take into account the structural limitations of the existing institutional and economic environment. Institutional embeddedness is therefore often the outcome of incremental transformations by which institutional complementarities are created between various dimensions of regional and national innovation systems.

14.4 CORPORATE EMBEDDEDNESS AS A STRATEGIC, DYNAMIC AND DILEMMATIC PROCESS OF SKILLED SOCIAL ACTORS

The contributions in this volume thus show that corporate embeddedness is a strategic and dynamic process driven by skilled social actors in MNCs and in regional and national institutions. These actors have to deal with the corresponding dilemmas, as embeddedness facilitates not only mutual learning, strong social ties and the provision of collective competition goods, but also various lock-in effects. Strongly embedded actors might, for example, miss new economic or technological opportunities and may overlook new markets and competitors. In addition, corporate and institutional actors have to deal with existing institutional routines, business structures, organized capabilities and incorporated competences and sedimented competences that shape and limit the opportunities for the creation of new knowledge. The three dimensions of corporate embeddedness around which this book is organized (the dilemmatic nature of embeddedness, the shaping power of knowledge infrastructures and the crucial role of skilled social actors) will now be shortly summarized and integrated into a conceptual framework that will, we hope, be useful for further research in the field.

In the first section of this volume (Chapters 2–5) the contributors looked at the multiple dilemmas of corporate embeddedness. One outcome is that the basic tension between embeddedness and disembeddedness cannot be definitely resolved. While embeddedness offers the chance of learning and of drawing upon locally available resources and knowledge, it also bears the danger of losing proprietary knowledge and of foregoing a more open or international orientation through a predominantly local embedding perspective. Dilemmas of embeddedness hence involve complicated strategic decisions and inner-corporate bargaining processes. Depending on their own position in the corporate network, on the properties of their knowledge bases and on the type of locally available skills, subsidiaries institutionalize different forms and degrees of embeddedness. At the same time, embeddedness is not the only rational strategy, and it remains a selective phenomenon. In some cases, sectors and countries, and often also in later phases of the innovation process, disembeddedness carries advantages that outweigh local embedding strategies.

A MNC's decision about embedding its activities is closely interrelated with the available knowledge infrastructures. The external institutional frameworks described especially in Chapters 6–9 vary greatly in their attractiveness for MNCs. In this manner, regional and national characteristics not only influence the allocation of these companies but also their involvement in regional or national processes of knowledge creation. Despite all internationalization tendencies, the embeddedness into stable business structures or institutional settings provides innovation processes with additional knowledge, inputs and – maybe most importantly – means of reducing uncertainty. Even if the connections between MNCs and the available infrastructure often remain weak and selective, particularly knowledge-related capabilities are frequently drawn upon in corporate innovation projects. This is also mirrored in the emergence of interconnected clusters and regional innovation systems in which MNCs act as central hubs.

The contributions in Chapters 10–13 focus especially on the role of corporate and political actors in embedding organizations because embeddedness is generally not a natural or automatic phenomenon that can be taken for granted. On the contrary, it is often the result of consciously devised links and complementarities between regional and national companies, networks, rules and resources (or opportunities). At least two categories of skilled social actors are actively involved in such a systematic coupling of institutional and organizational structures and strategies. As well as being the result of active and selective strategies of MNCs that try to enhance their innovative capabilities by acceding to

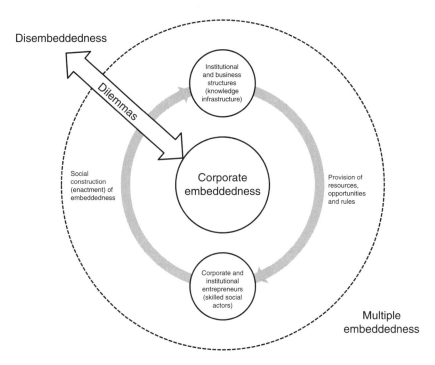

Figure 14.1 Corporate embeddedness and the dilemma between embedded agency, knowledge infrastructures and disembeddedness

external resources and competences, embeddedness is also the result of political strategies by which domestic actors try to strengthen the links between companies and their regional and national context, contributing to reducing the structural asymmetry between highly mobile corporations and territorially bound institutions and actors. Both types of actors are shaped by existing rules, taken-for-granted accounts, complementarities and experiences. Embedded agency is therefore at the core of the dynamic, yet generally incremental and path-dependent co-evolution of institutions and organizations.

These three dimensions of corporate embeddedness (dilemmas, knowledge infrastructures and embedded agency; cf. Figure 14.1) should be taken into account by further research on the societal context of MNCs.

Corporate embeddedness is hence not an easy, automatic or straightforward phenomenon. Instead, it is a selective, constructed and dynamic process, as we have shown in this book and summarized in this chapter. It is *selective* in that companies have various strategic options as to how to design and organize their innovation activities, embeddedness being just one of them. They institutionalize different constellations for different subsidiaries, projects, knowledge bases and countries. Second, embeddedness is *constructed* because it results not only from path-dependent and emergent processes but can be established at least partly through strategic corporate and political intervention. The externally available knowledge infrastructures and business systems play an important role here, and external as well as internal factors contribute to the degree and type of embeddedness which is formed. Socially skilled actors hence 'build' embeddedness in a complicated process of mutual interaction. However, this is not a reciprocal constellation: MNCs tend to have the final word, and even if the institutional and business context of MNCs is designed to perfectly meet the corporate needs, embeddedness remains dependent upon the corporate disposition to make use of this framework. Finally, corporate embeddedness is a *dynamic* phenomenon, and it does not take place just once and for all, but is subject to a constant process of embedding, disembedding and re-embedding. A relationship that exists between a company and its surroundings today can thus always change again, either due to a new strategic set-up of the company itself or also because of external changes in the embedding infrastructure.

We can conclude that embeddedness is not always the aspired-to strategy, and indeed it cannot be. Cautious and selective forms of interaction between MNCs and their institutional reference frames prevail, and even if such relationships become institutionalized, they will always be questioned again. Corporate embeddedness is hence a process, not a fixed state – and it involves disembedding and re-embedding just as much as embedding processes. Simple answers and one-size-fits-all policy suggestions are very unlikely to be found for such a complicated phenomenon, which is why this book has raised at least as many questions as it has provided answers. Given this multifaceted nature of embeddedness, however, the relationship between MNCs and their knowledge infrastructures remains an exciting topic for further research.

NOTE

1. With reference to welfare policies and the decommodification of labour, Ebner (2011: 19) terms this the 'Polanyi problem' of reconciling 'the globalisation of the market system as a dis-embedding process . . . with reembedding moves'. He proposes solving this problem by pointing to the mutually reinforcing dynamics of market creation and regulation, paralleled in our field by the mutually reinforcing dynamics of cross-border production and innovation strategies of MNCs and the local sourcing of embedded competences and resources. However, we are afraid that such a 'prestabilized harmony' does not exist in our field.

REFERENCES

Amin, A. and Thrift, N. (1995), 'Territoriality in the global political economy', *Nordisk Samhällsgeografisk Tidskrift*, **20**: 3–16.

Asheim, B., Coenen, L. and Vang, J. (2007), 'Face-to-face, buzz, and knowledge bases: sociospatial implications for learning, innovation, and innovation policy', *Environment and Planning C*, **25** (5): 655–70.

Bartlett, C.A. and Ghoshal, S. (1989), *Managing across Borders: The Transnational Solution*, Boston, MA: Harvard Business School Press.

Bartlett, C.A. and Ghoshal, S. (2000), 'Going global. Lessons from late movers', *Harvard Business Review*, **78** (2): 132–42.

Bathelt, H., Malmberg, A. and Maskell, P. (2004), 'Clusters and knowledge: local buzz, global pipelines and the process of knowledge creation', *Progress in Human Geography*, **28** (1): 31–56.

Boschma, R.A. (2005), 'Proximity and innovation: a critical assessment', *Regional Studies*, **39** (1): 61–74.

Cooke, P., Heidenreich, M. and Braczyk, H.-J. (eds) (2004), *Regional Innovation Systems*, 2nd edn, London and New York: Routledge.

Crouch, C. and Farrell, H. (2004), 'Breaking the path of institutional development? Alternatives to the new determinism', *Rationality and Society*, **16** (1): 5–43.

Dicken, P., Forsgren, M. and Malmberg, A. (2001), 'The local embeddedness of transnational corporations', in A. Amin and N. Thrift (eds), *Globalization, Institutions and Regional Development in Europe*, Oxford: Oxford University Press, pp. 23–45.

DiMaggio, P. (1988), 'Interest and agency in institutional theory', in L. Zucker (ed.), *Institutional Patterns and Organizations: Culture and Environment*, Cambridge, MA: Ballinger Publishing Company, pp. 3–22.

Ebner, A. (2011), 'Transnational markets and the Polanyi problem', in C. Joerges and J. Falke (eds), *Karl Polanyi, Globalisation and the Potential of Law in Transnational Markets*, Oxford: Hart Publishing, pp. 19–41.

Edquist, C. (2001), 'Innovation policy: a systemic approach', in D. Archibugi and B.-Å. Lundvall (eds), *The Globalizing Learning Economy*, Oxford: Oxford University Press, pp. 219–37.

Enright, M.J. (2000), 'Regional clusters and multinational enterprises: independence, dependence or interdependence?', *International Studies of Management & Organization*, **30** (2): 114–38.

Escribano, A., Fosfuri, A. and Tribó, J.A. (2009), 'Managing external knowledge flows: the moderating role of absorptive capacity', *Research Policy*, **38** (1): 96–105.

Fritsch, M. (2001), 'Kooperation in regionalen Innovationssystemen: ein interregionaler-internationaler Vergleich', in R. Grotz and L. Schätzl (eds), *Regionale Innovationsnetzwerke im internationalen Vergleich*, Münster: Lit, pp. 2–18.

Garud, R., Hardy, C. and Maguire, S. (2007), 'Institutional entrepreneurship as embedded agency', *Organization Studies*, **28** (07): 957–69.

Ghoshal, S. and Bartlett, C.A. (1990), 'The multinational corporation as an interorganizational network', *Academy of Management Review*, **15** (4): 603–25.

Grabher, G. (1993), 'Rediscovering the social in the economics of interfirm relations', in G. Grabher (ed.), *The Embedded Firm. On the Socioeconomics of Industrial Networks*, London and New York: Routledge, pp. 1–31.

Granovetter, M.S. (1973), 'The strength of weak ties', *American Journal of Sociology*, **78** (6): 1360–80.

Hage, J. and Hollingsworth, R. (2000), 'A strategy for analysis of idea innovation networks and institutions', *Organization Studies*, **21** (5): 971–1004.

Hedlund, G. (2005), 'Assumptions of hierarchy and heterarchy, with applications to the management of the multinational corporation', in S. Ghoshal and E.D. Westney (eds), *Organization Theory and the Multinational Corporation*, Basingstoke: Palgrave Macmillan, pp. 198–221.

Heidenreich, M. (2004), 'Conclusion: the dilemmas or regional innovation systems', in P. Cooke, M. Heidenreich and H.-J. Braczyk (eds), *Regional Innovation Systems: The Role of Governances in a Globalized World*, London: Routledge, pp. 363–89.

Heidenreich, M., Barmeyer, C., Koschatzky, K., Mattes, J., Beyer, E. and Krüth, K. (2012), *Multinational Enterprises and Innovation: Regional Learning in Networks*, London and New York: Routledge.

Holm, U. and Pedersen, T. (eds) (2000), *The Emergence and Impact of MNC Centres of Excellence: A Subsidiary Perspective*, Basingstoke: Macmillan.

Holm, U., Johanson, J. and Thilenius, P. (1995), 'Headquarters' knowledge of subsidiary network contexts in the multinational corporation', *International Studies of Management & Organization*, **25** (1/2): 97–119.

Le Galès, P. and Voelzkow, H. (2001), 'Introduction: the governance of local economies', in C. Crouch (ed.), *Local Production Systems in Europe: Rise or Demise?*, Oxford: Oxford University Press, pp. 1–24.

Lindqvist, M., Sölvell, Ö. and Zander, I. (2000), 'Technological advantage in the international firm: local and global perspectives on the innovation process', *Management International Review, Special Issue* (1): 95–126.

Malmberg, A., Sölvell, Ö. and Zander, I. (1996), 'Spatial clustering, local accumulation of knowledge and firm competitiveness', *Geografiska Annaler B*, **78** (2): 85–97.

Markusen, A. (1996), 'Sticky places in slippery space: a typology of industrial districts', *Economic Geography*, **72** (3): 293–313.

Mattes, J. (2010), *Innovation in Multinational Companies: Organisational, International and Regional Dilemmas*, Frankfurt and London: Peter Lang.

Mattes, J. (2011), 'Dimensions of proximity and knowledge bases: Innovation between spatial and non-spatial factors', *Regional Studies*: First.

Morgan, G. (2001), 'The multinational firm: organizing across institutional and national divides', in G. Morgan, P.H. Kristensen and R. Whitley (eds), *The Multinational Firm: Organizing across Institutional and National Divides*, Oxford: Oxford University Press, pp. 1–24.

Narula, R. and Santangelo, G.D. (2009), 'Location, collocation and R&D alliances in the European ICT industry', *Research Policy*, **38** (2): 393–403.

OECD (2009), *OECD Science, Technology and Industry Scoreboard 2009*, Paris: OECD.

Piore, M.J., and Sabel, C.F. (1984), *The Second Industrial Divide. Possibilities for Prosperity*, New York: Basic Books.

Pyke, F. and Sengenberger, W. (eds) (1992), *Industrial Districts and Local Economic Regeneration*, Geneva: International Institute for Labour Studies.

Scott, A.J. (2005), *On Hollywood: The Place, the Industry*, Princeton, NJ: Princeton University Press.

von Tunzelmann, N. (2009), 'Regional capabilities and industrial regeneration', in P. McCann, M. Farshchi and O. Janne (eds), *Technological Change and Mature Industrial Regions: Firms, Knowledge and Policy*, Cheltenham, UK and Northampton, MA, USA: Edward Elgar, pp. 11–28.

Weick, K.E. and Westley, F. (1996), 'Organizational learning: affirming an oxymoron', in S. Clegg, C. Hardy and W. Nord (eds), *The Sage Handbook of Organization Studies*, London: SAGE, pp. 440–58.

Westney, D.E. and Zaheer, S. (2008), 'The multinational enterprise as an organization', in A.M. Rugman (ed.), *The Oxford Handbook of International Business*, Oxford: Oxford University Press, pp. 341–66.

Zaltman, G., Duncan, R. and Holbek, J. (1973), *Innovations and Organizations*, New York et al.: John Wiley & Sons.

Zander, I. and Sölvell, Ö. (2004), 'Cross-border innovation in the modern multinational: three dilemmas', in M.G. Serapio and T. Hayashi (eds), *Internationalization of Research and Development and the Emergence of Global R&D Networks*, Amsterdam: Elsevier, pp. 13–40.

Index